T0136739

Holographic Reduced
Representation

CSLI Lecture Notes
Number 150

Holographic Reduced Representation

Distributed Representation for Cognitive Structures

Tony A. Plate

CSLI
PUBLICATIONS

Center for the Study of
Language and Information
Stanford, California

Copyright © 2003
CSLI Publications
Center for the Study of Language and Information
Leland Stanford Junior University
Printed in the United States
07 06 05 04 03   5 4 3 2 1

Library of Congress Cataloging-in-Publication Data

Plate, Tony A., 1962–
Holographic reduced representation: distributed representation for
cognitive structures /
Tony A. Plate.
p.   cm. – (CSLI lecture notes ; no. 150)
Includes bibliographical references and index.

ISBN 1-57586-430-4 (paper : alk. paper)
ISBN 1-57586-429-0 (cloth : alk. paper)

1. Knowledge representation (Information theory).
2. Connectionism.
I. Title. II. Series.
Q387.P73   2003
006.3'32–dc21   2003043513

∞ The acid-free paper used in this book meets the minimum requirements
of the American National Standard for Information Sciences—Permanence
of Paper for Printed Library Materials, ANSI Z39.48-1984.

CSLI was founded in 1983 by researchers from Stanford University, SRI
International, and Xerox PARC to further the research and development of
integrated theories of language, information, and computation. CSLI headquarters
and CSLI Publications are located on the campus of Stanford University.

CSLI Publications reports new developments in the study of language,
information, and computation. In addition to lecture notes, our publications
include monographs, working papers, revised dissertations, and conference
proceedings. Our aim is to make new results, ideas, and approaches available as
quickly as possible. Please visit our web site at
http://cslipublications.stanford.edu/
for comments on this and other titles, as well as for changes and corrections by the
author and publisher.

Contents

Preface

This book is a based on my PhD thesis, completed in 1994 at the University of Toronto under the supervision of Professor Geoff Hinton. It has been significantly rewritten and updated for publishing as a book. The major changes include: relevant new work in the background chapter; a new section surveying techniques for learning in distributed representations; and complete rewriting of the chapter on analogy processing, including redesigned experiments and a discussion of the relationship between HRRs and kernel methods for computing similarity. Many references to new work have been added.

Many thanks are due to Pentti Kanerva, without whose generous assistance this book would not have been published. Thanks are also due to Whitney Tabor, Dan Fass, Dieter Plate, and Ross Gayler for careful readings of the manuscript and valuable suggestions for improvements. Any remaining errors are of course mine.

1

Introduction

Since the early 1980's there has been considerable interest in connectionist models for higher-level cognitive activities such as language processing and reasoning. Many models have been proposed and built. The success of these models has been mixed – most appear to have severe limitations.

In connectionist models, even more than in other types of cognitive or Artificial Intelligence (AI) models, the representations chosen for the data determine what the system can do, since the processing is generally simple. Consequently, if we want to understand the difficulties and possibilities of applying connectionist models to higher-level tasks, it is appropriate to focus on the types of representations that are and can be used in models of such tasks.

Much of the interest in connectionist models for higher-level processing stemmed from dissatisfaction with the limitations of symbolic rule-based systems. These include brittleness, inflexibility, difficulty of learning from experience, poor generalization, domain specificity, and sloth of serial search in large systems. Initial results with connectionist models seemed to suggest potential for overcoming these limitations. Various connectionist models have tantalized researchers with many attractive properties: pattern completion, approximate matching, good generalization, graceful degradation, robustness, fast processing, avoidance of sequential search, parallel satisfaction of soft constraints, context sensitivity, learning from experience, and excellent scaling to larger systems. These models have possible applications both in cognitive modeling, where the goal is to model human performance, and in the engineering of AI systems, where the goal is to achieve a high level of performance.[1]

---

[1] Since human performance often defines high performance for higher-level cognitive tasks, there is often much synergy between building cognitive models and

However, no single connectionist model has had all these properties and researchers have found it very difficult to perform higher-level reasoning tasks in connectionist models. The difficulties can in part be traced to two characteristics of higher-level reasoning tasks. The first is that the temporary data structures required for higher-level reasoning are often complex, and cannot be represented in common connectionist representation schemes. The second is that many higher-level reasoning problems appear to at least sometimes require sequential processing, and connectionist models lack the procedural controls necessary to control sequential processing.

In this book I focus on how some of the structures that are required for higher-level reasoning can be represented in a distributed fashion. In this introduction I first discuss issues of representation. Next I summarize the advantages and disadvantages of localist and distributed representations. Finally, I review Hinton's (1987, 1990) influential notion of a *reduced description*, which provides ideas and desiderata about the representation of hierarchical structure in connectionist models.

I assume that the reader is familiar with the basic principles of connectionist models. For a tutorial introduction, I refer the reader to Rumelhart et al. (1986b).

1.1 Representations, descriptions, and implementations

In this book I am more concerned with how complex data structures[2] can be implemented elegantly in distributed representations than with the choices involved in devising a good knowledge representation for a particular task, though I do approach the latter in Chapter 6.

In contrast to Fodor and Pylyshyn (1988), but in common with Hinton et al. (1986), I do see implementation issues as interesting and important because implementation choices often determine which operations are fast and easy to compute and which are slow and difficult. Chalmers (1990) and Niklasson and van Gelder (1994) note that connectionist representations for compositional data structures are especially interesting because they raise the possibility of content-sensitive manipulation without decomposition, also called *holistic processing*, which appears to have no analogue in conventional symbol-based rep-

---

engineering AI systems. Indeed, an apparent deficiency in an AI model that happens to coincide with a known human deficit is sometimes taken as a sign that there is something right about the AI model.

[2]An object with *compositional structure* is composed of other objects. An object with *hierarchical structure* has multiple levels of composition. *Complex structure* means either or both compositional structure and hierarchical structure.

resentations.[3]

Some authors use the word *representation* to refer to a scheme for representing a class of entities, and *description* to refer to the way a particular entity is described. I use *representation* to refer to both representation schemes and descriptions of particular entities – the context should make the intended meaning clear.

1.2 Connectionist models

A connectionist model is typically a fixed network of simple processing units. The units are connected by weighted links and communicate only via these links. The messages sent along the links are typically scalar values, which are modulated by the weight on the link. Units compute some simple function of the input they receive, such as the sigmoid of a weighted sum. The value of the function is the state or activation of the unit, and this is the message passed on to other units. In nearly all connectionist models, units can (in theory) compute their values in parallel, and the overall computation time is short – on the order of 100 steps or less.

There are two distinct locations for representing knowledge (or more neutrally, data) in connectionist models. The first is in the activation values of the units. These are typically used for representing short-term data; the particular instance of the task, intermediate states in the computation, and the result. The second location for representing knowledge is the weights on the connections among units. These comprise the long-term memory of the model and are typically used for representing knowledge about the domain. They can also be used to store particular episodes – the weights can be set so that they can later reinstantiate a particular activity pattern over the units.

There are two main ways in which links can be used to encode domain knowledge. One is as constraints on solutions to a task, the other is as transformations between input and output patterns. Constraints are often used with those localist models that compute by settling to a stable or low-energy state. These states are (or are hoped to be) those in which most constraints are satisfied. In the network the constraints represented by a link are very simple: either the connected units should be active together (an excitatory link), or if one is active, the other should inactive (an inhibitory link). Constraints are generally soft, in that they can be overridden – the importance of a constraint is indicated by the weight on the link. Pattern transformations are generally

---

[3]The techniques in mainstream computing most closely related to holistic processing are probably those based on hashing.

used in feedforward and recurrent networks, and are usually learned from examples. Some networks, such the Hopfield (1982) network (an error-correcting associative memory) can be interpreted in both ways.

In contrast, there is a great diversity of representation schemes for temporary data structures. The components of the task can be sentences, words, letters, phonemes, features, concepts, visual or auditory signals, measurements, etc. These components must be represented in temporary data structures as activations over the units of the network. To a large extent, the representation chosen for the task constrains how the knowledge is encoded in the links and determines what the network can compute.

1.3 Representational issues

Representations are of critical importance in connectionist models. To a large extent, the representation scheme used determines what the system can compute. Representations are the source of both strengths and weaknesses of connectionist models. Carefully constructed connectionist representations can endow systems with useful properties such as robustness, ability to learn, automatic generalization, graceful degradation, etc. These properties tend to be more associated with distributed representations than with localist representations (though localist representations are not without uses). However, there are serious problems with the adequacy of distributed representations for storing the type of information necessary to perform complex reasoning.

In this section I give an overview of issues that arise with connectionist representations. The issues concerning representational adequacy, computational properties, scaling, and suitability for learning are central to the work in this book. There are other important but less pressing issues that I mention here but do not return to.

1.3.1 Representational adequacy

A system will not be able to perform complex reasoning tasks if it cannot even represent the objects involved in the tasks. For many complex tasks it seems necessary to be able to represent complex structures, such as hierarchical predicates. This is an issue especially for models using distributed representations. When distributed representations first began to catch people's interest there was no satisfactory way of representing complex structure with them and, although several methods have been proposed since, all have had serious drawbacks. The difficulty with representing complex structure was highlighted by Fodor and Pylyshyn (1988) in their strong and influential criticisms of connectionist models.

The main categories of structures that complex reasoning seems to require are: variable bindings, sequences of arbitrary length, predicate structures, and hierarchical predicate structures. Some sort of variable binding is required anywhere that general rules are used. Systems that deal with sequential input, such as written or spoken language, must have some way of storing relevant aspects of the input, since the appropriate output may depend upon input encountered some time previously. For example, in speech understanding, the appropriate interpretation of vowel sound can depend on the preceding sounds. Often, the amount of input that must be stored is unknown. The ability to represent predicate (relational) structures is necessary in systems that deal with input in which relationships among the entities are important. In tasks like language understanding, the relationships can be hierarchical, leading to the need to represent hierarchical predicates. For example, the object of a predicate such as *think*, *see*, or *want* can be another predicate.

Connectionist representations are often very different from conventional data structures, such as variables, records, lists, and trees. Sometimes the representations are nearly unintelligible and appear to have little or no relationship to conventional data structures. However, if a model can be shown to work correctly, it must be representing the information required for the task in some fashion. Often, this can be analyzed in terms of conventional data structures. Furthermore, when designing a connectionist model to perform some task, one must consider what sort of structures the model is going to represent and how it will manipulate them. When designing or analyzing connectionist representations for complex structures, a number of questions concerning several aspects of representation and processing arise:

- Composition, decomposition, and manipulation: How are components composed to form a structure, and how are components extracted from a structure? Can the structures be manipulated using connectionist techniques?
- Productivity: A few simple rules for composing components can give rise to a huge variety of possible structures. Should a system be able to represent structures unlike any it has previously encountered, if they are composed of the same components and relations?
- Immediate accessibility: What aspects of components and structures does the representation make explicit and accessible without pointer-following?
- Systematicity: Does the representation allow processes to be sensitive to the structure of the objects? To what degree are the processes

independent of the identity of components of structured objects? (The term *systematicity* comes from Fodor and Pylyshyn (1988).)

There have been three broad classes of reactions to the problem of representing complex structure. The first is exemplified by the argument of Rumelhart and McClelland (1986b) that the importance of the ability to compose and decompose complex structure is overrated. The second is exemplified by the work of Smolensky (1990) on designing connectionist representations for complex structure. The third is exemplified by the work of Pollack (1990) and Elman (1990) on connectionist networks that learn representations for complex structure. In this work, I take the same approach as Smolensky, because I believe compositional structure is important, and because the properties of designed representations are easier to analyze and understand than those of learned representations.

1.3.2 Computational properties

The computational properties of a representation relate to what can be computed using the representation, the simplicity and speed of the computation, and the resources required. Connectionist networks usually have very simple processing, so if a representation does not make something simple to compute, it most likely cannot be computed by the network at all.

Computational properties commonly possessed by connectionist representations, and often cited as reasons for interest in connectionist models, include the following:

- Immediate accessibility (explicitness): information can be extracted with simple processing and without further access to memory.
- Analogical representation: similar objects have similar representations.[4]
- Representational efficiency: representational resources are used in an information-efficient manner.
- Affordance of generalization: the representation supports generalization of knowledge.
- Robustness and graceful degradation: the information in the representation is still usable when parts are corrupted or missing.

---

[4]In connectionist systems, the vector dot product (inner product) is often used as a measure of the similarity of two representations. In an *analogical representation*, similarity of representations (i.e., a high dot product) signals conceptual similarity of the objects being represented. Note that *analogical representation* is a type of representation. It should not be confused with representations that can be used in processing analogies, which are discussed extensively later in this book.

- Affordance of error correction and pattern completion: the representation contains redundant information that makes this possible.
- Affordance of easy associative access: the representation make associative access simple.

This list is not, and cannot be, complete, because it is always possible to invent new representations with novel computational properties. The properties in this list are interrelated, and some can be considered as superclasses or prerequisites of others.

The most important of these properties is immediate accessibility. Information in a representation is immediately accessible if it can be extracted with little computation and without further access to memory (as would be entailed by pointers). Accessibility, or explicitness, is really a matter of degree: information that requires only a little computation to extract is somewhat explicit, but information that requires extensive computation to extract is non-explicit. Almost all connectionist representations are explicit – by necessity, since the processing they use is so simple.

One type of explicitness that is ubiquitous (and very useful) in distributed representations is explicit representation of similarity. Similarity is explicit when it is based on immediately accessible information. This type of explicitness is one of Marr (1982) desiderata for representations of 3-D objects, which specifies that representations should be analogical. By this he means that representations should in some sense be analogues of the objects they represent, and should reflect their similarity. Another of Marr's desiderata, which complements that of having analogical representations, is that representations should make differences between similar objects explicit. This property has been discussed little in connectionist work to date, but will probably become important as connectionist models grow more sophisticated.

I will have more to say on the other computational properties in the next section, where I discuss localist and distributed representations.

1.3.3 Scaling

Connectionist models are often demonstrated on toy problems that involve only a small fraction of the entities and relationships found in real-world problems. Hence, the way in which the resource requirements of a representation scale with increasing numbers of entities and relationships is important. The way in which increasing size of representation affects the rest of the system must also be considered. For example, if the number of components in a representation scales linearly with the number of different objects, and the system involves interactions among all pairs of components of the representation, then the scaling of the entire system is quadratic.

1.3.4 Learning representations for new concepts

One of the main attractions of connectionist models is their ability to learn. This is related to scaling: while it is possible to fashion by hand representations for toy problems, it would be very time consuming and difficult to fashion representations for real-world problems. Consequently, the suitability of a representation for use with learning algorithms is important.

1.3.5 Other representational issues

There are a number of philosophical issues that arise in symbolic-AI research, and that are also relevant to connectionist research. However, connectionist models have not, for the most part, reached the level of sophistication where these issues become crucial. Hence, I mention these issues here, but do not present any detailed discussion of them. There are also other technical issues concerning meta-level reasoning and procedural control, which I mention here but not elsewhere for similar reasons.

Sophistication of knowledge representations

Most connectionist models have extremely simple knowledge representation schemes that do not make strong distinctions between ontological categories such as concepts, roles, classes, and individuals. Whether or not the lack of these distinctions is a problem remains to be seen. Some connectionist representations do support abilities such as property inheritance, without marking entities as concepts, subconcepts, or individuals. Generally, these abilities arise from analogical properties of the representations.

The Knowledge Representation Hypothesis

The Knowledge Representation Hypothesis (Brachman, 1985b) is an explicit statement of an idea that has guided much work in symbolic AI. It states that intelligence is best served by representing knowledge explicitly and propositionally. Connectionist researchers would, for the most part, appear not to believe in this hypothesis. In some connectionist models knowledge about the domain is represented propositionally, e.g., in Shastri's (1988) and Derthick's (1990) models, but this knowledge is compiled into the links of the network and the processing does not access the propositional representations. Most connectionist researchers appear to take the view that if the relevant aspects of the particular task are represented suitably, then fast processing can be accomplished with knowledge represented implicitly in the links of the network.

Logical soundness and completeness vs. computational tractability

Connectionist models do not escape the tradeoff between computational tractability and logical soundness and completeness (Levesque and Brachman, 1985). However, computational speed has always been important to connectionist researchers, and most models are built to provide fast answers, but with no guarantee of correctness. Shastri's (1988) is one exception; he has investigated what types of limited reasoning can be performed both soundly and correctly.

Meta-level reasoning

Almost all connectionist models make a strong distinction between long-term knowledge about how to perform the task, which is stored in the weights on the connections, and the short-term knowledge about a particular instance of the task, which is stored in the unit activations. It would seem impossible to reason about the rules, because they are represented in the weights and cannot be (at least directly) transferred into the activations. However, some other types of meta-level reasoning, e.g., monitoring the progress of a long chain of processing, are possibly very useful. A way to do this might be to have one network monitor the activity of another.

Procedural control

Connectionist models that perform higher-level reasoning such as following chains of inferences will undoubtably require some form of procedural control, possibly involving subroutines. Ideally, the behavior of the control mechanism should be error-tolerant and generalize to novel situations. Very little work has been done on this problem.

1.4 Connectionist representations

There are two distinct styles of representation used for short-term data in connectionist models: localist and distributed representations. They appear to have quite different properties but are best regarded as endpoints of a continuum. I am most interested in distributed representations, but, as there is considerable insight to be gained from considering localist representations, I will discuss both in this introduction and in the review chapter. The main topic of this book is how complex structure can be embodied in distributed representations in a way that preserves the attractive properties of distributed representations.

1.4.1 Localist representations

In a localist representation concepts (objects, features, relationships, etc) are represented by particular units. For example, the *celestial body* sense of *star* is represented by a single unit in Waltz and Pollack's (1985) model of word-sense disambiguation. Activity on this unit represents the *celestial body* meaning of the word *star*, as opposed to the *movie star* sense. Localist representations are commonly used in constraint-satisfaction and in spreading-activation networks. Waltz and Pollack (1985) describe an interesting example of such networks, which is described further in Section 2.1.1.

Advantages of localist representations

The advantages of localist representations mostly relate to explicitness and ease of use. Some prominent advantages are the following:

- Explicit representation of the components of a task is simple.
- The interface for the experimenter is convenient.
- It is easy to represent a probability distribution over different possibilities.
- It is relatively easy to design representational schemes for structured objects.

The principal virtue of localist representations is that they make all the possible components of a solution explicit. A unit represents a component, and activity on the unit represents the presence of that component in the solution. Global constraints on solutions are transformed into a set of simple local constraints, each involving two of the possible components of the solution. These simple constraints can be reinforcing or inhibiting; the presence of one component encourages or discourages the presence of another component in the solution. Each simple constraint on how components interact is implemented by an excitatory or inhibitory link. The constraints are usually symmetric: if A and B are linked, then A excites or inhibits B to the same degree that B excites or inhibits A. Converting constraints to simple local constraints can require the creation of more units. For example, if the existence of a relationship between two entities depends on the existence of another relationship between two other entities, then units must be assigned to these relationships. This can lead to large numbers of units for even simple problems. Once all the interacting components are explicitly denoted by units, and constraints embodied in links, reasonably good solutions can be found using simple computation. If links are symmetric, the computation can be viewed in terms of energy minimization, as in Boltzmann machines (Ackley et al., 1985) and Hopfield networks (Hopfield, 1982).

Localist representations are convenient to use for input and output to a network because they are simple and unambiguous and can be easily compared against desired results.

Presenting output as a probability distribution over possibilities is very useful for tasks that involve prediction or classification. This requires using activation values between zero and one and constraining the activations of a set of units to sum to one. The units must represent a complete set of mutually exclusive possibilities.

Problems with localist representations

The main problems with localist representations concern inefficiency and learnability:

- Inefficiency of localist representations for large sets of objects.
- Proliferation of units in networks that represent complex structure.
- Inefficient and highly redundant use of connections.
- Questions about the learnability of elaborate representations for complex structure.

There are several ways in which localist representations are inefficient. The most obvious way is that it is inefficient to use n units to represent n different objects. While it might be practical to use a hundred units to represent one hundred different objects, it is seldom practical to use a million units to represent one million different objects. Another type of inefficiency occurs with some localist representations for complex structure. When problems involve complex structure, the number of possible components of a solution tends to increase very quickly with the size of the problem. Representations that devote units to all possible components of a solution tend to require very large numbers of units for large problems. The third way in which localist representations can be inefficient has to do with the use of connections. If A and B are units representing similar things, then A and B will have similar interactions to other units. However, in a localist network, these similar interactions must be represented by independent duplicate sets of links. This can result in duplication and inefficient use of links. All of these inefficiencies lead to poor scaling properties.

The localist networks that researchers design to perform complex reasoning tasks can be quite elaborate. Although various learning algorithms can be used with localist networks, none of these algorithms would be able to derive localist networks such as those I review in Chapter 2. Furthermore, the representations derived by connectionist learning algorithms that do build internal concepts, such as multilayer feedforward (backpropagation) networks, tend to be distributed rather than localist.

1.4.2 Distributed representations

Hinton et al. (1986) define a distributed representation as one in which each concept is represented over a number of units, and in which each unit participates in the representation of a number of concepts. The size of distributed representations is usually fixed, so that the representation can be instantiated over a fixed set of units. The units can have either binary or continuous-valued activations.

Hinton et al. (1986) give a good general introduction to distributed representations. Anderson (1973) proposes and analyzes a psychological model for memorizing lists, which uses superimposed continuous distributed representations. Rosenfeld and Touretzky (1987) discuss binary distributed representations and analyze how many patterns can be superimposed before the individual patterns become unrecognizable. van Gelder (1990) analyzes distributed representations from a more philosophical viewpoint and develops an alternative definition to that of Hinton et al. (1986).

In some distributed representations the individual units stand for particular features, like *is-red*, and in others it is only the overall patterns of activity that have meaning. Hinton et al. (1986) use the term *microfeatures* to describe individual units that can be given an unambiguous meaning. To the extent that this can be done, these parts of the representations are like localist representations.

Distributed representations are in many ways analogous to grayscale images or photographs. Distributed representations are vectors (one-dimensional arrays) with many elements (units). Concepts are represented by patterns in this continuous, high-dimensional space. Grayscale images are two-dimensional arrays with many elements (pixels). (The two-dimensional nature of images is irrelevant to this analogy, what matters is that elements of a grayscale image take a scalar value, and have a fixed position.) Physical objects are represented by patterns in this fine grained, high-dimensional space. In both, the information content is distributed and redundant, which makes them robust and suitable for error correction. Many pixels in an image can be changed without making the image unrecognizable. Similarly, in a distributed representation some noise can be added to the activation levels of units without making the representation of an object unusable.

When viewing superimposed images (like multiple-exposure photographs) it is easy to tell apart the individual images if they are distinct and coherent. Similarly, distributed representations of several items can also be superimposed by adding the vectors together. It is easy to identify the various items in the resulting vector, provided that they are not too similar and the representation has sufficient capacity.

Advantages of distributed representations

The attractiveness of distributed representations is largely due to the ease of endowing them with the following computational properties:

- Explicit representation of relevant aspects of objects.
- Analogical representation, i.e., similar representations for similar objects (explicit similarity).
- Redundant storage of information.
- Efficient use of representational resources.
- Continuity, i.e., representation in a continuous vector space.

Explicitness is possible with distributed representations because they are wide and flat, which provides much opportunity for representing relevant aspects of objects. Explicit representation makes fast processing possible, because it is not necessary to chase pointers or perform deductions to get at the information in a representation.

A ubiquitous type of explicitness is that which makes similarity explicit – similar concepts have similar representations. The similarity of distributed representations can be defined as the Euclidean or Hamming distance between two representations, which can be computed quickly. Thus, the similarity of objects represented by distributed representations can be quickly computed.

Explicit similarity, the ability to represent similar objects by similar representations, is probably the most useful property of distributed representations. It can assist in the fast retrieval of similar instances from memory, and in matching against prototypes and rules. In Chapter 6, I investigate how far this idea can be taken – I look at whether distributed representations can support judgments of the structural similarity of structured objects.

Automatic generalization is another useful benefit of explicit similarity. The nature of processing in connectionist models, which involves units computing weighted sums of their inputs, results in systems that usually respond similarly to similar representations. A novel input that is similar to a familiar input will likely result in an output similar to that for the familiar input, which will often be an appropriate output for the novel input.

Information in a distributed representation is generally stored in a redundant fashion – we only need to see some part of the representation to know what the whole is. Because of this, distributed representations are robust in the presence of noise and degrade gracefully as noise is added. Redundancy makes pattern completion and error correction possible.

The ability to superimpose the representations of multiple items in the same set of units is another benefit of redundancy. Individual items can still be recognized, depending on the degree of redundancy and the number of representations superimposed. There is a soft limit to number of items that can be superimposed – representations degrade as items are added.

Distributed representations usually require far fewer units to represent a set of objects than do localist representations. This is because the number of possible patterns of activation over a set of units is much greater than the number of units. At one extreme, a binary-number style representation is maximally efficient – there are 256 different patterns of ones and zeros over eight units. At the other extreme, a localist representation is minimally efficient – eight units can represent only eight different objects.

The efficiency of a representation has consequences for the rest of the system. An inefficient representation can lead to duplication of computational machinery. For example, in a localist representation, two units representing concepts that interact with other concepts in the same or a similar way will have many similar connections, which could likely be avoided through the use of a more efficient representation.

To some extent, efficiency is in opposition to redundancy (though inefficiency does not necessarily result in redundancy). However, in practice, a moderate number of units provides so many possible patterns that it is easy to make distributed representations sufficiently efficient and redundant.

If units have continuous activation values, then concepts are represented in a continuous vector space. One benefit of continuity is that it makes for natural representations of inherently continuous concepts, such as color, the degree of danger presented by a wild animal, or the meaning of an utterance. This gives a system the potential for coping with such things as nuances of meaning and slight variations in context.

Another important benefit is that having a continuous representation space allows us to make small changes to representations. This means that continuous distributed representations can be used in neural networks that learn by gradient descent techniques. An appropriately constructed system can learn good distributed representations for the objects in its domain.

Problems with distributed representations

Some of the major problems that arise when trying to use distributed representations in networks that perform cognitive tasks are as follows, and are expanded upon below:

- Difficulties with representing arbitrary associations and variable bindings.
- Difficulties with representing sequences of arbitrary length.
- Difficulties with representing predicates and hierarchical structure.
- Questions about the origin of patterns that represent particular objects.
- Difficulties with using distributed representations for inputs to and outputs from the network.

Many of the difficulties with using distributed representations concern representational adequacy. Work on models for complex tasks has been held back by difficulties with representing complex structure.

In many types of distributed representations, patterns can be superimposed to indicate the presence of several different objects. However, this does not represent associations between the objects. Furthermore, crosstalk and illusory conjunctions can occur. For example, if we store *red circle* and *blue square*, by superimposing the representations of *red*, *circle*, *blue*, and *square*, it will appear as though *red square* was also stored (among other possibilities, such as *blue circle*, *square circle*, *blue red*, etc., depending on how the simultaneous presence of features is interpreted.) Similar problems can arise with variable binding.

Storing variable-length sequences in distributed representations is difficult, because both the identity and the order of inputs can be important and must be remembered. One of the most common techniques for dealing with time varying input is to turn time into space, which is done by having a set of buffer units for storing the input for some fixed number of time steps in the past. As each new input is received, previous inputs are shifted back in the buffer. This is somewhat inelegant and is limited in that the network only remembers inputs for however many time-slices there are in the buffer – input which is pushed out of the end of the of the buffer is irretrievably lost. A different approach is to use recurrent networks (Section 2.3.2) to try to learn what and how much input must be remembered.

A distributed representation of a predicate such as `bite(spot,jane)` (for "Spot bit Jane") must be carefully designed to preserve the information about which entity is associated with which role. An obvious way to avoid ambiguity about who is the agent ('Spot') and who is the object (or patient, 'Jane') is to divide the representation into several blocks, and devote a block to each role. However, this method is unsuitable for representing recursively nested predicates such as "Spot bit Jane, causing Jane to flee from Spot": `cause(bite(spot,jane),flee(jane,spot))`, because the representation of a predicate is larger than the representation of an object, and cannot be squeezed into the same set of units. The difficulty is not so much with representing the objects involved (we could simply superimpose them) as it is with representing the relationships among the objects in an unambiguous and explicit fashion.

Another concern with distributed representations is how the patterns are obtained. Researchers have generally used one or a combination of the following three methods: hand-design, random generation, or learning. In many of the early connectionist systems, the representations were designed by hand, using units to code for features of objects. This made it easy to introduce and control explicit similarity among representations, which often underlie the interesting properties of these systems. However, hand-design tends to be unsatisfactory for several reasons: it is very laborious to construct representations for each entity a system deals with, sometimes the relevant features of the objects are not known, distributed representations are often so wide that there are many more units than features, and finally, an intelligent system should be able to develop its own representations.

Another method for obtaining patterns is to use random patterns. This is done in many psychological models, e.g., those of Anderson (1973) and Murdock (1982). In Chapter 3, I describe how this method can be combined with feature-based methods in order to introduce explicit similarity among representations.

The most promising and interesting method for obtaining patterns is to have the system learn appropriate representations for the given task. Hinton (1989) showed that this could be done in a feedforward network trained using backpropagation. I describe this and related methods in Sections 2.2.2 and 2.5.

Distributed representations are usually not suitable for input and output to a network, because they do not provide a single value that indicates to what degree some object is present in the representation. This is not a big problem, but it is usually necessary to translate between distributed and localist representations for input and output. This can require significant amounts of computation, especially for translating from distributed to localist representations.

1.4.3 Relationships between localist and distributed representations

The definitions of localist and distributed representations are matters of degree. Representations in which many units are active are fully distributed, those with just a few units active are somewhat localist and are sometimes called sparse distributed representations, and those with just one unit active are fully localist. Furthermore, whether or not we consider a representation to be localist or distributed depends on the level at which we examine it. The representation of the lowest-level concepts or features in a model may be clearly localist while the representation of concepts composed of those features may have the characteristics of a distributed representation. One such system is Derthick's (1990) μKLONE (Section 2.1.2).

Smolensky (1986) discusses transformations between localist and distributed representations, and the conditions under which operations on both are equivalent. Transforming representations of a set of objects from a localist representation to a distributed one is simple. It usually just involves superimposing the distributed representations of the objects present in the localist representation. If the superposition operation is linear (as opposed to a nonlinear threshold operation), then this transformation from localist to distributed representations is linear. A system that performs linear operations on the distributed representation is equivalent to one that performs linear operations on the localist representations. If the distributed representations for all objects are linearly independent, then there is a linear transformation from the distributed to the localist representation. However, requiring linear independence of patterns is inefficient, as there are only n linearly independent patterns over n units.

Some representations like the binary system for numbers satisfy the generally accepted definition of a distributed representation, but there is a common sentiment that they are not distributed representations (van Gelder, 1990, e.g.,). I take the pragmatic position that they are distributed representations, but without most of the useful properties that distributed representations make possible. The aspect of numbers that binary representations make explicit is a somewhat odd one – the power-of-two components of the number. This is useful for logic circuits that add and multiply numbers, but it is not very useful for anything else. In particular, the similarity structure this induces on numbers has little relationship to any human judgments of similarities of numbers.

There is no single representation that is the best for all tasks – the choice of representation depends on the demands of the task at hand. Page (2000) provides many good arguments that localist representations are often more appropriate in psychological models than distributed ones.

1.5 Reduced Descriptions

Hinton (1987, 1990) introduced the idea of a *reduced description* as a method for encoding complex conceptual structure in distributed representations. Reduced descriptions make it possible to use connectionist hardware in a versatile and efficient manner. According to Hinton, there should be two ways of representing a compositional concept (i.e., a structured object whose parts are other, possibly compositional, objects). One way is used when the concept is the focus of attention. In this case all the parts are represented in full, which means the representation of the concept could be several times as large as that of one of its parts. The other way of representing the concept is a reduced description, which is used when the concept is not the focus of attention, but is a part in another concept. In this case the representation of the concept must be the same size as that of other parts. Concepts are taken to be simple frame-like structures, with a number of roles or slots. Relations (i.e., propositions) can be represented by allowing one role to be the relation name and the other roles to be the arguments of the relation. The two different ways a concept can be represented in the system are shown in Figure 1. The concept D, which has E, F, and G filling its roles, can either be the focus of the system, or can be a filler in the representation of the concept A. A reduced description is like a label or pointer for a concept, to be used when we want to refer to the concept, but not focus on it. Since reduced descriptions provide a pointer-like facility, they allow us to represent concepts linked in an arbitrary tree or graph structure.

Figure 2 shows the steps involved in accessing a full representation from a reduced description. To begin with, the full concept A is instantiated in the network. The reduced description of concept D is the filler of its third role. To access the full representation of D we first transfer D into the focus position, and then expand the reduced description of D to get its full representation.

This scheme for mapping structures to hardware is versatile and efficient because it allows many different concepts to be represented on the same hardware. An alternative is to have hardware dedicated to each different type of concept, but this can require excessive amounts of hardware and cannot easily represent nested structures.

Hinton's description of reduced descriptions involve four desiderata,

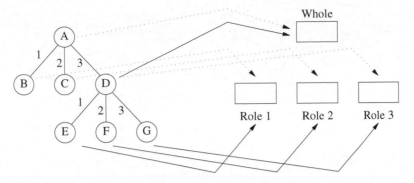

FIGURE 1 Two ways of mapping parts of a conceptual structure (the tree on the left) to the units in a connectionist system. In the first way (the solid arrows) the concept D is the focus of attention, and the fillers of its roles are mapped to the appropriate sets of units. In the second way (the dashed arrows) A is the focus of attention and just the reduced description for D is mapped to a set of units. The rectangles labeled *Whole*, *Role 1*, etc, are sets of units over which a distributed representation can be instantiated. (Adapted from Hinton (1990).)

all of which seem to be essential for any useful distributed representation of structure:

- Representational adequacy: it should be possible to reconstruct the full representation from the reduced description.
- Reduction: the reduced description should be represented over fewer units than the full representation.
- Systematicity: the reduced description should be related in a systematic way to the full representations.
- Informativeness: the reduced description should tell us something about the concept that it refers to, without it being necessary to reconstruct the full representation.

The necessity of the representational adequacy desideratum is self-evident – if the reduced description does not provide enough information to reconstruct the full representation, then it is not an adequate representation. The reduction desideratum comes from practical considerations of working with a fixed-size set of computational units. Furthermore, the precision with which activation values must be represented should not be greater for the reduced description than for the full description – it is possible, but not realistic, to store an infinite amount of information in an infinite precision number. This means that the reduced description must have less information about components

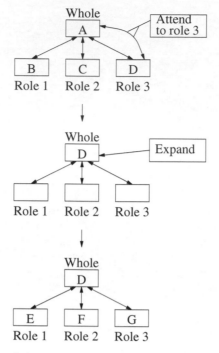

FIGURE 2 A network focusing on a reduced description (D) in another concept (A) and expanding it to a full representation (E F G). The concepts A, B, C, D, etc. are possible fillers of the roles *Role 1*, *Role 2*, etc. (Adapted from Hinton (1990).)

than the full description – some information must be thrown away in constructing the reduced description. This ties in with Miller's (1956) notion of a chunk and his claim that people can store "seven plus or minus two" chunks in short-term memory. The idea of *recoding* a set of items (which are themselves chunks) into one chunk is central to Miller's explanations of how human short-term memory works. A reduced description is equivalent to a chunk, and a full representation is equivalent to the contents of the chunk.

The systematicity and informativeness desiderata are for something more than that supplied by conventional pointer-based ways of representing hierarchical structure. Pointers are generally arbitrarily related to the contents of the structure they point to. Having a systematic relationship between label and structure makes it easier to find one given the other. The desire for informativeness is for a form of representational explicitness – the reduced representation should make explicit some information about the concept it refers to.

Pointers in conventional random-access memory serve the same structural function as reduced descriptions. A record corresponds to a concept, and fields in a record are the roles. The contents of the fields are the fillers. The entire record is the full representation of a concept, and the pointer to the record is the reduced description. Hierarchical structure is represented by allowing fields to be pointers to other records. If we have a pointer, we can reconstruct the full concept by following the pointer (i.e., by accessing the memory). However, without the use of some sort of indexing, it is difficult to find the pointer to a structure given its contents.

The difference between pointers and reduced descriptions is that the relationship between a pointer and what it points to is arbitrary. Pointers tell us nothing about what they point to – the only way we can find anything out about the record pointed to, or its fillers, is to follow the pointer.[5] Hash indexing is a technique from conventional data-structure theory that is close in spirit to reduced representations. It provides a way of deriving the *label* of a full representation given its contents. However, the hash value alone seldom provides any information about the contents – memory lookup is usually necessary to discover anything about the contents.

The chief potential advantage of reduced descriptions over pointers is that they could provide more explicit labels for concepts. This could make it possible to process concepts more efficiently, since it would not always be necessary to follow pointers to discover information about subconcepts.

It is also illuminating to consider the role of reduced descriptions in content-addressable memory. By definition, an item stored in content-addressable memory can be accessed by an abbreviated,[6] or noisy, version of the content of that item, instead of by the arbitrary address of the item as in conventional random-access memory. A particular item in content-addressable memory can be accessed by querying with any one of a probably extremely large number of possible abbreviations or noisy versions of the item (though not all possible abbreviations can be guaranteed to resolve back to the same item). In these terms, a reduced description for items is a systematic way of abbreviating items,

---

[5]Except in *tagged* memory hardware, such as was used in some LISP machines. In these systems, several address bits were used to indicate the type of the object at that address, e.g., an atom or cons cell. This helped to increase the speed of LISP programs.

[6]*Abbreviation* is used here in a broad sense that includes any way of encoding the item so that it can be communicated using less information.

with the property that abbreviations are unambiguous. Any particular reduced description for a particular item is just one of many possible abbreviations of that item.

A reduced description can be seen as a (lossily) compressed version of a full concept. The compression must be invertible, since we need to be able to reconstruct the full concept from the compressed version.[7] Hinton (1990) suggested that the encoding of reduced representations could be performed by a linear operation:

$$\mathbf{W}_R = R_1\mathbf{f_1} + R_2\mathbf{f_1} + R_3\mathbf{f_3},$$

where $\mathbf{W}_R$ (a vector) is a reduced representation of the whole, $\mathbf{f_1}$, $\mathbf{f_1}$, and $\mathbf{f_3}$ are fillers, and R_1, R_2, and R_3 are random square matrices *representing* roles 1, 2 and 3. This operation is easily computed in a neural network. Hinton suggested that decoding could also be performed using linear operations. In this framework, Pollack (1990) used backpropagation to simultaneously learn reduced descriptions for tree structures (Section 2.4.2), along with the encoding and decoding matrices for different roles. Holographic Reduced Representations (Chapter 3) are closely related to Hinton's linear technique for reduced representation, but use vectors rather than matrices to represent roles.

1.6 Book outline

The computational properties that can be built into distributed representations make them worth considering as a representation for higher-level cognitive tasks. In Chapter 2, I review various connectionist models that are relevant to the representation and processing of complex structure, paying particular attention to representation schemes. I also review methods for learning distributed representations.

In Chapter 3, I present and discuss a representational scheme for hierarchical structure, called *Holographic Reduced Representations* (HRRs), which I believe overcomes some of the flaws of other representations. HRRs use a simple scheme for building up representations of structures from representations of components, and are amenable to analysis. HRRs support the useful properties of distributed representations that were identified in Section 1.4.2: explicitness, redundancy, continuity, and efficiency. In Chapter 4, I describe how HRRs can be

---

[7]MacLennan (1991) claims this is impossible to do with continuous representations, due to a theorem of Brouwer's which states that Euclidean spaces of different (but finite) dimensions are not homeomorphic. This means that it is not possible to have a continuous function $f : E^n \times E^n \to E^n$ with a continuous inverse $f^{-1} : E^n \to E^n \times E^n$. However, this does not preclude the existence of systems that work most or nearly all of the time.

implemented with distributed representations based on complex-valued numbers. This makes some of the operations faster to compute, and makes it possible to perform an advantageous type of normalization.

In Chapter 5, I describe how the convolution operation, the basic association mechanism for HRRs, can be incorporated into recurrent networks. This allows representations for items and arbitrary length sequences to be learned using gradient descent procedures. I claim that for the purposes of storing sequences in a *context* layer (à la Elman (1990), described in Section 2.3.2) this type of network is superior to a standard recurrent network.

In Chapter 6, I investigate the extent to which the explicit similarity of HRRs is related to useful forms of similarity. It is obvious from first principles that HRRs will induce some sort of similarity structure on structured objects, since convolution is a similarity-preserving operation. The question is whether the induced similarity structure is useful or related to any other commonly used measures of similarity. I discuss Falkenhainer et al.'s (1989) and Holyoak and Thagard's (1989) notions of the analogical similarity of structured objects. Using a set of simple examples, I show how the similarity structure induced by HRRs captures some aspects of analogical similarity, and how including other types of associations in addition to role-filler associations can help to capture more aspects of analogical similarity.

In Chapter 7, I discuss various issues: how HRRs can be transformed without decomposition, differences between HRRs and some psychological notions of chunks, how other vector-space multiplication operations could be used instead of convolution, how a disordered variant of convolution might be implemented in neural tissue, and weaknesses of HRRs.

2

Review of connectionist and distributed memory models

In this chapter, I review various connectionist models and distributed memory models that are relevant to performing higher-level tasks. I begin with some localist models for higher-level reasoning, and then describe some distributed models that deal with simple structures. Following that I discuss some models that have dealt with problems of representing hierarchical structure in implicit ways, by trying to get relatively simple recurrent networks to learn to process language. Finally, I discuss some models and representation schemes that are explicitly designed to represent hierarchical structure. The selection of models for this review was made on the basis of how interesting, novel, or influential the representation scheme is. The primary goal of this review is to discuss the advantages and disadvantages of various connectionist representation schemes, so I tend to ignore aspects of these models that do not have much to do with representational issues. The secondary goal is to familiarize the reader with the range of connectionist approaches to higher-level cognitive tasks, and the limitations that many of these approaches share, the most prominent of which are difficulties with scaling up to larger than toy problems. The reader who is only interested in models closely related to HRRs should just read Section 2.2.3 and from Section 2.4.2 onwards.

2.1 Localist connectionist models

Localist networks that compute by spreading activation and local inhibition were among the first connectionist models of higher-level tasks. A unit in one of these networks generally represents a proposition, and the activation of the unit represents the degree of truth or likelihood of the proposition. Links represent interactions between propositions;

propositions can either activate or inhibit each other. The networks are run by allowing them to settle to a stable state. Some of the more formal work with localist networks treats links as constraints between propositions, and analyzes the settling of the network as a search for an energy minimum.

One of the main attractions of this type of model is its style of computation, in which multiple and diverse constraints are satisfied in parallel. This contrasts with the generally sequential style of computation in rule-based models. In rule-based models much time can be wasted searching entire classes of answers that will be rejected en masse by constraints applied later in processing.

The representations are generally localist in the sense that units represent propositions in a one-to-one fashion. However, as pointed out in the discussion of the localist versus distributed issue (Section 1.4.3), sometimes localist representations can be considered to be distributed at a higher level, where the units are the features of objects. Derthick (1990) emphasizes this point, and his model is sensitive to similarities induced by sharing representational units.

In all of these networks, relevant propositions are made explicit by devoting units to represent them. It is this enumeration of propositions that makes possible the simple style of computation. Everything that needs to be considered, including all possible interactions, is laid out explicitly. Connections usually encode pairwise interactions between atomic entities, so interactions among more than two units must be expressed as several pairwise interactions, which requires more units. The downside of this simple and explicit style of representation is that networks can become very large when there are many possible propositions. Holyoak and Thagard's (1989) *Analog Constraint Mapping Engine* (ACME), which performs analogical matching, is an example of this; the propositions are hypotheses about matches between structure elements, and there are many possible matches when the structures contain many elements.

In most of the networks described here the representations and the interactions are constructed by hand or by a computer program from a priori knowledge, rather than being learned from examples. Shastri's system is an exception to this – its connection strengths are derived from frequency observations. There are other localist systems that learn connection strengths, e.g., Neal's (1992) and Pearl's (1988) belief networks. Furthermore, general schemes such as the Boltzmann machine learning algorithm (Ackley et al., 1985) can be used to learn connection strengths in a localist network.

I review six models here: three for parsing natural language, two for doing simple inference, and one for mapping analogies. Natural language processing is a popular task because it requires complex temporary data structures, and more processing power than provided by a finite state machine. Explicit representation is a common theme in these models – and it results in large networks when many combinatorial interactions must each be represented with separate nodes.

2.1.1 Interpreting and parsing language by constraint satisfaction

Waltz and Pollack: *Massively Parallel Parsing*

Waltz and Pollack (1985) devise a *Massively Parallel Parsing* model of natural language interpretation, which integrates constraints from diverse sources into a homogeneous model. The constraints range from syntactic, i.e., word order, phrase structure, etc., through semantic, e.g., selectional restrictions on case-roles of verbs, and contextual, to pragmatic, e.g., typical situations. Figure 3 shows a network that integrates all the constraints for parsing and interpreting the sentence "John shot some bucks." One goal of their research is to demonstrate a system that could apply all of these constraints in parallel during the computation. They consider this style of processing more efficient and more psychologically plausible than rule-based systems that perform syntactic processing first, followed by semantic analysis, etc.

Their model uses different units to represent different syntactic interpretations of words or phrases and different senses of words. Links among the units are either inhibitory, for mutually exclusive interpretations, or excitatory, for consistent interpretations. When run, the network settled to a stable interpretations after fifty or so cycles.

The system constructs a new network for each sentence presented to it. It uses a chart parser to find all possible syntactic parses, and translates these into a network form. Units standing for propositions corresponding to different parses are connected by inhibitory links, and units standing for propositions corresponding to the same parse are connected by excitatory links. The example shown has only one full parse, but nodes are constructed for the alternative parts-of-speech of the words. The system adds further nodes and links to the network to represent the semantic and pragmatic interpretations and constraints.

One serious limitation of this model as a technique for language understanding is that a conventional symbolic computer program must construct a network that embodies all possible syntactic and semantic interpretations of the sentence. It seems that most of the work of parsing and interpreting is being done by this program – the connectionist network is only choosing among pre-computed alternatives. Another

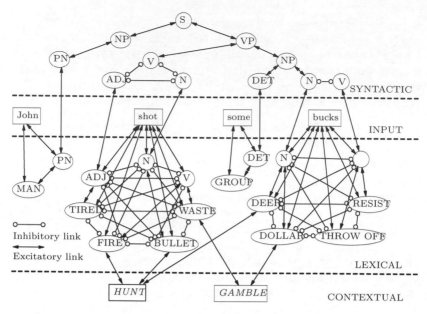

FIGURE 3   Waltz and Pollack's network for parsing and interpreting the sentence "John shot some bucks". (Adapted from Waltz and Pollack (1985).)

limitation is that all possible units and links must be supplied to the system in advance. Waltz and Pollack discuss this issue and speculate that distributed representations with microfeatures might somehow be used to overcome this problem.

Cottrell and Small's (1983) model of word-sense disambiguation has many similarities to Waltz and Pollack's model. It differs in that a single network is used to deal with all stimuli, but the part of the model that analyzes syntax is undeveloped. They acknowledge that as the network gets larger, i.e., as more words, senses, or syntactical alternatives are added, it gets difficult to control – the network can settle into states that do not represent any sensible interpretation of the input.

Selman and Hirst: parallel parsing network

Selman and Hirst (1985) show how a context-free grammar can be encoded in a connectionist network, so that parsing is accomplished by letting the network settle to an energy minimum. Unlike Waltz and Pollack's network, their network can parse any sentence (up to some prespecified maximum length). However, it does not incorporate any semantic or pragmatic constraints. The advantage of their system over traditional parsers is that rules are applied in parallel, and that top-

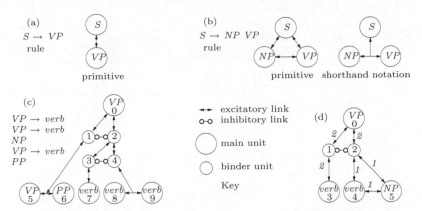

FIGURE 4 Components of Selman and Hirst's network for parsing sentences from a simple grammar. (a) and (b): two examples of grammar rules and the connectionist primitives that implement them. (c): How binder units (units 1, 2, 3, and 4) are used to implement three rules for *VP*. (d) The weights on excitatory links in part of a typical parsing network. (Adapted from Selman and Hirst (1985).)

down and bottom-up processing is integrated. They show how to derive the weights and thresholds from the rules in a principled manner, which guarantees that the system will find the correct parse when run as a Boltzmann machine to thermal equilibrium.

Each grammar rule is translated into a small network, and networks for rules are combined with *binder* units (Figure 4a). Alternative productions (i.e., the right-hand sides or bodies of rules) are linked by inhibitory connections and the head of a rule is linked with excitatory connections to the nodes in the body of the rule. The weights are set according to a simple scheme. The system does not learn from experience, though it is conceivable that the weights on the links could be learned using the Boltzmann machine learning algorithm. Constituents can be shared using binder units, rather than duplicated, which can save many units and links. Figure 5 shows the grammar rules and a network for parsing sentences of up to five words.

To parse a sentence, the lexical types of the words are instantiated in the bottom row of the network. The first word goes in input group 1, the second in input group 2, etc. If a word has more than one possible lexical type, then more than one unit in the group can be turned on. The network is annealed,[8] and when it reaches thermal equilibrium the

---

[8] *Annealing* refers to *simulated annealing*, which is a technique for finding a set of activations that minimizes the *energy* of a network. Informally, low-energy activation

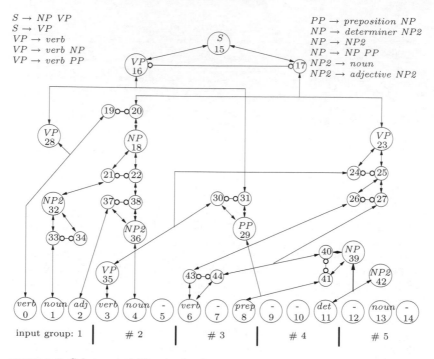

$S \rightarrow NP\ VP$
$S \rightarrow VP$
$VP \rightarrow verb$
$VP \rightarrow verb\ NP$
$VP \rightarrow verb\ PP$

$PP \rightarrow preposition\ NP$
$NP \rightarrow determiner\ NP2$
$NP \rightarrow NP2$
$NP \rightarrow NP\ PP$
$NP2 \rightarrow noun$
$NP2 \rightarrow adjective\ NP2$

FIGURE 5 Selman and Hirst's simple grammar and the network for parsing sentences generated by it. The network can handle sentences with up to five words. (Adapted from Selman and Hirst (1985).)

correct parse can be extracted from the average activations of the units.

Again, this network can use very simple computation because it has a very explicit representation. The nodes in the network can be seen as an enumeration of the ways in which a sentence can be parsed. There is a node for every non-terminal in every position it can appear in the parse tree. For example, Node 32 is the *NP2* that can begin at the first word, Node 36 is the *NP2* that can begin at the second word, and Node 42 is the *NP2* that can begin at the fifth word.

One problem with this system is that there is a hard maximum on the length of sentences that it can parse. Another is that the number of units grows rapidly with the maximum length of sentence to be parsed (n^2), and the time to reach thermal equilibrium grows with the number of units. For unfrustrated systems, the time to reach thermal

_____

states of a network have the same activations on the units at both ends of an excitatory link, and do not have high activity on the units at both ends of an inhibitory link. See Ackley et al. (1985) for details.

equilibrium can scale well. However, if there are high energy barriers, Boltzmann machines take a very long time to reach thermal equilibrium.[9] In practice, the system can only be run for a finite time, which means that the parse found is not guaranteed to be the best one.

Charniak and Santos: parsing network

Charniak and Santos (1987) attempt to overcome the fixed length limitation of systems such as Selman and Hirst's by having a window of processing units past which the inputs are slid. The title of their paper gives some hint as to how they view this attempt: "A Connectionist Context-free Parser which is not Context-free but then it is not really Connectionist either".

The network consists of a rectangular array of cells, the bottom row of which contains units for each terminal symbol of the language (the lexical types of words – noun, verb, determiner, etc). Each of the cells in the rows above the bottom row contains a unit for each non-terminal in the language (sentence, noun phrase, etc). A sentence is presented to the network by activating the appropriate units in the bottom row of the rectangle – one word per column. After the network settles the parse tree of the input is represented in the activations of units. Each column of units represents a path from a leaf to the root. Links to units above and below and in adjacent columns constrain the system to represent valid parse trees. Other binding units indicate when units in adjacent cells represent the same non-terminal. If the sentence has more words than there are spaces in the rectangle, the input is shifted by one column and the network allowed to resettle. This continues until the whole sentence has been processed. As words slide out of the back of the network, their interpretation (i.e., their path to the root) is presumed stable and is recorded. The total parse is considered to be what is in the system and what has slid out of the back. The system is limited in the height of parse trees it can represent, but the parts of the parse tree that get pushed out of the top can be treated in the same way as the parts that slide out of the back.

As with Selman and Hirst's connectionist parser, the connection strengths in Charniak and Santos's network are not learned, but are derived from the context-free grammar rules. The interesting thing about this network is that it overcomes, to some extent, the fixed sentence length restriction of other connectionist parsers. The memory limita-

---

[9]Geman and Geman (1984) show that approach to thermal equilibrium is guaranteed if the temperature at time k, $T(k)$, satisfies $T(k) \geq \frac{c}{\log(1+k)}$, where c is proportional to the maximum height of energy barriers. Since we are interested in the distribution at low temperatures, the settling times required can be very long.

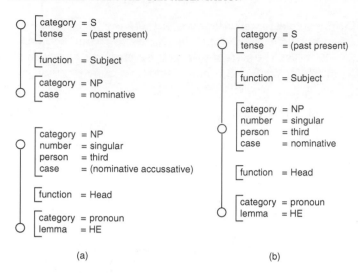

(a)   (b)

FIGURE 6   Parse-tree segments in Kempen and Vosse's simulated annealing approach. The two segments shown in (a) have compatible features and
can be joined to form the larger parse-tree fragment in (b). (Adapted from
Kempen and Vosse (1989).)

tions of the network result in it being able to cope with some types
of long sentences better than others. It can correctly parse sentences
with right-branching parse trees, because the parse of later segments of
the sentence does not depend upon the exact parse of earlier segments.
However, it is unable to find the correct parse for center-embedded sentences because relevant parts of the parse tree slide out of the back of
the network and are no longer available when they are needed. It is not
clear if there is any deep relationship between these limitations and the
relative difficulties people have with these classes of sentences.

Kempen and Vosse: parsing by simulated annealing

Kempen and Vosse (1989) describe an approach to parsing that, although it is not connectionist, has enough in common with the spirit of
connectionist approaches to be mentioned here. Kempen and Vosse in-
tend their scheme to be a cognitive model of how people form syntactic
trees when understanding linguistic utterances. In common with many
connectionist approaches, their approach is interactive in that both top-
down and bottom-up influences act on the choices made while forming
a syntactic tree.

In Kempen and Vosse's approach, a parse tree is a assembled out
of parse-tree *segments* using simulated annealing. A segment is a link

from a parse tree, and includes the nodes from each end of the link. The top and bottom nodes of a segment also have a set of attribute-value pairs (features). A segment also corresponds to left-hand-side and one of the children from the right-hand-side of a syntactic production rule. Two example segments are shown in Figure 6(a). Two segments can be joined together as part of a parse tree if the features on the nodes to joined are compatible, that is if there are no attributes that have different values in the two nodes. The two segments in Figure 6(a) are compatible, and can be joined to form the larger parse-tree fragment in Figure 6(b). The formation of a syntactic tree proceeds by joining together (or breaking apart) parse-tree fragments, under the control of a simulated annealing algorithm. The algorithm evaluates potential parse-trees and fragments based on various semantic, pragmatic, and syntactic factors, e.g., how well the fragment reproduces the word order of the original utterance. Kempen and Vosse's approach is similar to other connectionist approaches in that it attempts to find a solution that satisfies a multitude of constraints, and does so in a parallel manner.

Sampson et al. (1989) describe another approach to parsing that is based on a simulated annealing.

2.1.2 Simple reasoning

Shastri: semantic networks

Shastri (1988) describes a connectionist network that can efficiently compute a useful but limited class of formal reasoning. The network can perform property inheritance, which is finding the appropriate properties of a concept from superordinate concepts, and recognition, which is finding the concept that best matches a set of properties. Shastri uses *evidential reasoning* to deal with exceptions, multiple inheritance, and conflicting information in a principled manner. In contrast to other connectionist networks, there are proofs that this network computes the correct answer in a strictly limited time. This comes at the cost of expressiveness and power – Shastri has picked an extreme point in the tractability-expressiveness tradeoff identified by Levesque and Brachman (1985).

In Shastri's network, nodes represent concepts, properties, and individuals, and links represent relations between them. There is no learning involved – the architecture of the network is derived from statements written in the formal *knowledge level* language of the system. The processing is a form of spreading activation and inference is completed in time proportional to the depth of the conceptual hierarchy. The network can only reason about the properties of a single object at any one time.

Shastri's formulation of the inheritance and recognition problems permits them to be solved in time linear in the depth of the hierarchy (on parallel hardware). Previous formulations of inheritance, e.g., Touretzky's (1986b) inheritance networks or Etherington and Reiter's (1983) inheritance hierarchies with exceptions allowed problems that could take exponential time to solve (on serial hardware).

Ajjanagadde and Shastri (1991) describe an enhancement of Shastri's network that allows simple rule following. They use temporal synchrony in the phase of unit activations to bind variables from rules with values – a network cycle has a number of phases during which units can be active.

Derthick: μKLONE

Derthick's (1990) μKLONE system for *Mundane reasoning*, like Shastri's, is another implementation of a formal logic in a parallel constraint system. The language implemented is a subset of Brachman's (1985a) KL-ONE: all constructs except number restrictions, role chains, inverse roles, and structural descriptions are provided.

The type of reasoning the system did is quite limited – hence the name *mundane reasoning*. The system finds the most likely set of properties and role fillers for an individual in a particular situation. Although it is based on a logical language, it performs *foolhardy* reasoning as the assignment of truth values is based on one model of one logical extension of the rules of the system. This sacrifice of logical soundness is made so that the system can find an answer in a reasonable time, in the belief that some answer, even if sometimes wrong, is better than none at all. The system can deal with inconsistent facts or rules and still find a plausible interpretation.

The system is derived from a specification of frames and relations written in a simplified version of the KL-ONE. To process a query about an individual the system builds a network with the individual, its properties, its roles, its role fillers and properties of role fillers. Inheritance is performed by the compiler. The resulting network has a unit representing the conjunction of each role and each filler (even anomalous roles and filler), a unit representing the conjunction of each property and each filler, and units representing the properties of the individual concerned. The links between units are constraints derived from the propositions and rules concerning the concepts in the network. Simulated annealing is used to search for the model with the lowest energy (which has most constraints satisfied).

The representation in μKLONE can be seen as both localist and distributed. Simple concepts are represented by single units, but higher-level concepts are represented by patterns of the simple concepts. In one example *sailing* is originally the filler of the *job* role for *Ted*. However, when the system is told that Ted is a millionaire playboy, and thus does not perform manual labor for a living, it shifts the role that sailing fills to Ted's hobby. This is possible because the job role and the hobby role are similar, both being instances of the *has-interest* role.

Like Shastri's system, μKLONE does not learn – the network is derived from rules written in a formal language. μKLONE also reasons about just one entity, but can represent temporary associations with other roles and fillers. μKLONE is unable to represent complex hierarchical structure because it only represents immediate relationships to other entities and has no way of representing a chain of relationships.

2.1.3 Connectionist models of analogical mapping

Holyoak and Thagard: analogical mapping by constraint satisfaction

Holyoak and Thagard (1989) describe a localist connectionist model that finds a good analogical mapping between two structured descriptions. The descriptions are in the form of sets of predicates, with nesting allowed. A good mapping is defined by three constraints: isomorphism, semantic similarity, and pragmatic centrality. A mapping defines a one-to-one pairing of the elements from each structure. The isomorphism of a mapping is high when mapped elements are in the same relationships in each structure. The mapping can be incomplete, but more complete mappings are preferred. The semantic similarity of a mapping depends on the similarity of the mapped predicates, and the pragmatic centrality depends on whether the mapping involves predicates that are believed a priori to be important.

The model is embodied in a computer program called ACME (Analogical Constraint Mapping Engine). ACME constructs a connectionist network in which nodes represent competing and cooperating hypothesis about mappings between the elements of the structures. Nodes representing competing mapping hypothesis are connected by inhibitory links, and nodes representing complementary hypothesis are connected by excitatory links. The network is run and allowed to settle to a stable state, and the active nodes represent the mapping found by the network.

Consider the two structures $\{F : f(a,b), G : g(b,a)\}$ and $\{P : p(x,y)\}$. F, G, and P are particular instances of predicates, f, g, and p are predicate names, and a, b, c, d, x, and y are atomic objects. Figure 7 shows the network ACME would build to find an analogical

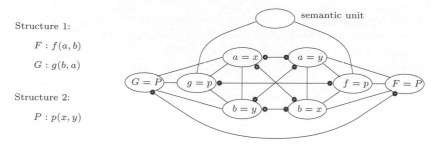

Structure 1:

$F : f(a, b)$

$G : g(b, a)$

Structure 2:

$P : p(x, y)$

FIGURE 7 The network ACME would construct to find an analogical mapping between the two sets of propositions $\{F : f(a, b), G : g(b, a)\}$ and $\{P : p(x, y)\}$.

mapping between these two structures. It has a node for each possible pairing of elements from the structures, where elements are atomic objects, predicate names and whole predicates. There are inhibitory connections between pairs of nodes that represent inconsistent mappings, e.g., $a = x$ and $a = y$. These connections all have the same weight and serve to constrain the mapping to be one-to-one. There are excitatory connections between nodes that represent mappings of elements of the same predicate, e.g., between $F = P$, $f = p$, $a = y$ and $b = x$. These connections all have the same weight and support isomorphic mappings. ACME builds a *semantic unit* and connects it to predicate name mapping units with an excitatory link whose strength is related to the degree of similarity between the names. If g were similar to p, then the connection between the $g = p$ and the semantic unit would be strong. There is also a *pragmatic unit*, which has excitatory links to predicate name mapping units that involve a predicate deemed important (the pragmatic unit is not shown in this figure). This network has two stable states; in one the nodes on the left are active, in the other the nodes on the right are active. These stable states represent P mapping to G, and P mapping to F. Mappings such as $\{G = P, g = p, a = y, b = x\}$ are not isomorphic and will not be stable states of this network. Note that ACME does not build an explicit representation of either structure – it only builds an explicit representation of the mapping between the structures, and the constraints on the mapping.

There is no guarantee that the state ACME settles in will be the best mapping or even a one-to-one mapping, but it appears to almost always find good solutions. ACME works because every possible correspondence between the two structures is represented explicitly by a node, and the compatibility of the correspondences is represented by connections between the nodes. The networks that ACME builds can be large – if the size of the structures is n, the size of the ACME mapping network is $O(n^2)$.

2.2 Distributed connectionist models for simple structure

One of the big problems with localist representations is their inefficient use of resources, which can lead to a proliferation of units. Distributed representations offer the potential for more efficient use of resources. In this section I review some models that represent objects and relationships among them in a distributed manner.

2.2.1 Learning associations between objects

To represent relations in a neural network, we must have representations for both objects and the associations among them. Early work in this area typically uses pre-coded distributed representations for objects. Associations among pairs or triples of these objects are represented in the connection weights, which are found by some sort of learning procedure.

Hinton: implementation of semantic networks

Hinton (1981) describes a distributed connectionist network that implements a content-addressable memory for relations. This is one of the first attempts to represent relational data in a distributed fashion. Instead of representing atomic concepts by single units, Hinton represents concepts by patterns of activity over groups of units, and represents the relations between them by interactions among the groups of units.

The network stores two-place predicates, which are triples consisting of a relation name and two roles. A typical set of triples is:

> (John has-father Len)
> (Mary has-father Len)
> (John has-sister Mary)
> (Kate has-father John)

The principal task the network performs is associative retrieval (pattern completion). Given any two concepts in a triple, the network finds the matching stored triple. Given the query (John has-sister ?) the system should fill in the blank with *Mary*, and given the query (Kate ? John) the system should fill in the blank with *has-father*.

The model has a separate group of units for each element of a triple. A concept, such as 'John' or *has-father*, is represented by a pattern of activity over the appropriate group of units. The patterns of activity are pre-coded and are chosen so that similar concepts have similar patterns of activity.

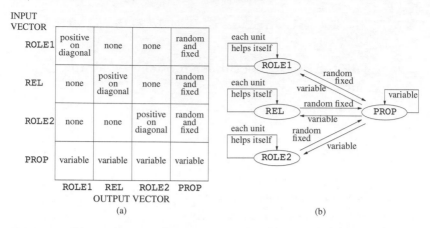

INPUT
VECTOR

	ROLE1	REL	ROLE2	PROP
ROLE1	positive on diagonal	none	none	random and fixed
REL	none	positive on diagonal	none	random and fixed
ROLE2	none	none	positive on diagonal	random and fixed
PROP	variable	variable	variable	variable

ROLE1   REL   ROLE2 PROP
OUTPUT VECTOR
(a)

(b)

FIGURE 8 Two schematic representations of the connections in Hinton's triple memory. (a) shows the matrix of weights, which connect the units, in block form. Many of the submatrices are null, e.g., the weights from the ROLE1 units to the REL units. (b) shows the groups of units, each arrow represents a submatrix of weights connecting the groups. The matrix of weights from a group to itself (except for the PROP group) is the identity matrix, it is intended to cause the group to retain whatever pattern it is initialized with. Adapted from Hinton (1981).

The network architecture is shown in Figure 8. In addition to the three groups of units for each element of the triple – the relation name and the two roles – there is a fourth group of units labeled PROP (for *proposition*). The PROP units help to implement interactions among the different groups, and are necessary because direct connections between groups are too limited in the types of interactions that they can implement. A triple is retrieved by instantiating two of the groups with the known pattern and then allowing the network to settle to a stable state. A triple is stored in the network by instantiating its concept patterns on the three groups of units and then adjusting the variable weights so that the pattern is stable.

Hinton discusses how this type of model can also implement a form of property inheritance. As mentioned before, similar concepts (or individuals) are represented by similar patterns. Hinton suggests that the representation of a super-type concept should be the set of features that all its subconcepts have in common. Relations that depend on the type of the individual can be implemented by interactions among the microfeatures that are common to individuals of that type. Exceptions can be implemented by interactions among the microfeature patterns that are specific to the exceptional individuals. This is illustrated in Figure 9 for

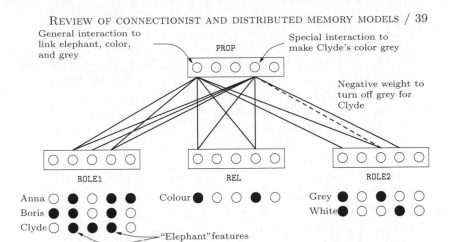

FIGURE 9 Implementation of inheritance and exceptions in Hinton's (1981) triple memory. The solid links indicate positive weights, the dashed link indicates a negative weight, and weights in opposite directions have the same sign. The first unit in the PROP group comes on when an elephant and *color* are instantiated in the ROLE1 and REL groups, it causes 'grey' to be instantiated in the ROLE2 group. The fourth unit in the PROP group detects the special case of Clyde's color being asked for, suppresses the *grey* pattern, and excites the *white* pattern. In an actual trained network the interactions in the PROP group would probably be implemented by many units.

three elephants. There are two microfeatures common to all elephants, these code for the *elephant* type, and the corresponding units in ROLE1 interact with the color pattern in REL to support the grey pattern in ROLE2. Most elephants, e.g., Boris and Anna, will be thought by the system to be colored grey. However, Clyde is an exceptional elephant, and the microfeature pattern unique to Clyde interacts with the color pattern to suppress the grey pattern and support the white pattern, overriding the default inference that Clyde is grey.

There are two types of conceptual structure in this model. The pattern of microfeatures that represents a concept constitutes the *direct content* of the concept. The links to other concepts constitute the *associative content* of the concept. Hinton suggests these two types of conceptual structure correspond to two separate components of human memory sometimes called *integrative* and *elaborative* structure. The first has to do with internal coherence, and the second to do with external relations. The interesting thing about this model is that direct content of the concepts causes the associative content. Furthermore, small changes in the direct content (pattern) will usually lead to small changes in the associative content, which results in the system having some automatic inheritance and generalization abilities.

One limitation of this model is that it can only represent one relation at a time, not can it represent multiple relations, let alone a structure among a set of relations. Another limitation is that there are a fixed number of roles in the system. Adding more groups of units for more roles is not a good solution because it is wasteful for relations that do not use all the roles, and because it makes it difficult to represent similarity among roles. Hinton suggests that roles could also be given distributed representations and role-filler bindings represented by coarse conjunctive codings. I discuss this approach in Section 2.2.3.

Anderson, Spoehr, and Bennet: Arithmetic

Anderson et al. (1991) describe a model of learning multiplication tables that uses analogical distributed representations. Their representation of a number has two components: an analogical component in which numbers of similar magnitude have similar representations (using a *sliding bar* method), and a random component. The representation is very wide – 422 units for each number. The random component is necessary to make the representations sufficiently different, but the interesting properties of the model arise from the analogical component of the representation. The model is trained to remember triples of two operands and one result, using a *Brain-state in a box* network (Anderson et al., 1977) (a type of auto-associative memory).

As the title indicates ("A Study in Numerical Perversity: Teaching Arithmetic to a Neural Network"), this model is not intended to be a good way of having a machine remember multiplication tables. Rather, it is a demonstration of how a simple connectionist model that uses analogical distributed representations can model human performance. The overall error patterns and the relative response times for false products (people are quicker to identify $5 * 3 = 42$ as incorrect than $8 * 7 = 63$) are similar to people's performance on the task of learning multiplication tables. These performance characteristics are a direct consequence of the analogical structure of the representations of the numbers.

Rumelhart and McClelland: learning past tenses of verbs

Rumelhart and McClelland (1986a) describe a distributed connectionist model that learns to produce the past-tense forms of regular and irregular verbs. They represent words as phonemic strings in a distributed fashion over about 500 units. Each word is represented by a set of phonemic triples, which in turn are represented by sets of finer-grained conjunctions called *Wickelfeatures*. The set of Wickelfeatures for a word is stored in the distributed memory. For example, the word 'sit' would be represented by three triples: '#si', 'sit', and 'it#', where '#' is the start and end symbol. This representation makes local order explicit, but leaves global order implicit – it is a puzzle to see how the triples of a long word could fit together. It is possible that different words could have the same representation, but this problem does not arise with the words used in the model. The network takes the representation for the root form of a verb (e.g., 'sit') as its input and is meant to produce the representation for the past-tense form (e.g., 'sat') on its output. Rumelhart and McClelland trained a noisy perceptron-style map to do the mapping from input to output.

Although the network eventually learns to produce the correct past-tense forms for both regular and irregular verbs, the interesting thing about it is the pattern of errors it makes during learning. Early on in the learning process it produces the correct past-tense forms for irregular verbs (e.g., 'sat' for 'sit'), but as it learns the regular verbs it begins to produce incorrect overgeneralized past-tense forms for irregular verbs (e.g., 'sitted'). In the final stage, it learns the correct forms for both regular and irregular verbs. The fully trained network is also able to generalize; it can produce the correct past-tense form for some words that were not in the training set. Although this model has received extensive criticism as a psychological model of acquisition of verb tense (e.g., from Pinker and Prince (1988), who point out that the stratified training set might have something to do with the time-course of errors), it is still interesting as a demonstration of how rules and exceptions can be learned using a single homogeneous network.

2.2.2 Learning distributed representations for objects

The models we have seen so far have used hand-coded feature-based distributed representations. For reasons mentioned in Section 1.4.2, it is better if a system can develop its own distributed codes. Hinton (1989) shows how this can be done in a feedforward network by using localist input layers and extra intermediate layers. The method involves connecting each localist input layer to its own distributed coding layer, as shown in Figure 10. Only one unit in the input layer is ever active, so its weights determine the activations on the coding layer. These weights can be trained along with the other weights in the network. This scheme does not significantly increase the amount of computation, because only the weights from the active unit to the coding layer need to be considered in both the forward and backward computations.

Usually, the distributed coding layer has far fewer units than the localist input layer, hence this layer is often called a *bottleneck* layer. The bottleneck layer has two purposes. The first being to keep the number

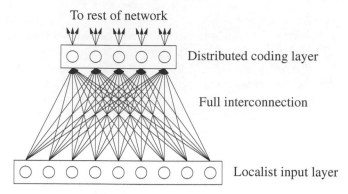

To rest of network

Distributed coding layer

Full interconnection

Localist input layer

FIGURE 10 An extra intermediate layer in a feedforward network can convert from localist to distributed representations. Only one unit in the input layer is active at any time. The links from the active input unit determine the activations on the units in the distributed coding layer.

of parameters down, so that not too many examples are required to train the network. The second reason is to force the network to develop useful distributed codes. If the code layer has fewer units than the input layer, then the network must develop some sort of distributed representation on the coding layer, just to be able to represent inputs with different codes. The hope is that these distributed codes will be based on commonalities the network discovers while learning to perform the task. Indeed, this is what appears to happen in the networks that use this technique. Zemel and Hinton (1994) have shown that it is possible to use a wide distributed coding layer and still learn useful codes, by imposing various constraints on the codes.

This technique can also be used for output representations. However, doing this can significantly increase the amount of computation, because it is not possible to ignore any of the connections from the distributed output code to the localist output code, except by making some risky approximations.

Hinton: Family trees network

Hinton (1989) demonstrates that a backpropagation network can learn good distributed representations in the course of learning to perform a task. The network he describes learns the relations embodied in the two isomorphic family trees shown in Figure 11. The form of the relations is (Person1 Relation Person2), e.g.:

Sophia	has-aunt	Angela
Charlotte	has-aunt	Jennifer
Charlotte	has-father	James

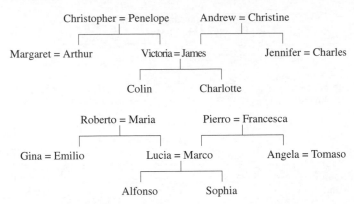

FIGURE 11 The family trees stored in Hinton's (1989) *family trees network* network. The two trees, for English (top) and Italian (bottom) people are isomorphic.

The network is a feedforward architecture which, given a person X and a relationship R, completes the relation by outputting the person who is in relation R to person X. The architecture of the network is shown in Figure 12. The network uses bottleneck local-to-distributed mappings on the inputs and outputs. There are 24 individuals, and six units in the encoding units, so the network must learn a relatively efficient distributed encoding.

Hinton trained the network using the backpropagation with weight decay on 100 of the 104 instances of relations in the two family trees. The trained network successfully processes the remaining four relations, indicating that the learned representations and mappings can support generalization. Presumably, the isomorphism of the two trees makes the knowledge about mappings transferable across nationalities. Upon examination, some of the units in the input encodings for people were found to stand for identifiable features of the individuals, e.g., nationality and generation. Sex is not encoded in any unit – it is actually not useful in determining the correct output. The network does not "know" that nationality and generation are meaningful features, it is only told things like "when unit 19 in input block 1 and unit 3 in input block 2 are on, turn on unit 13 in the output block". It gives some objects similar representations merely because this helps to solve the mapping problem. It turns out that these similar representations can be interpreted in terms of common features.

Although this network stores relations, it is not an auto-associative memory like Hinton's triple memory (Section 2.2.1). This network can only produce Person 2 given Person 1 and the relationship – it cannot

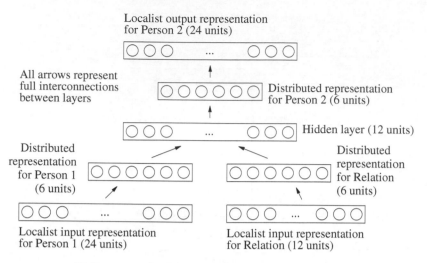

FIGURE 12 Architecture of Hinton's (1989) network for storing family trees as a set of relationships. Each of the arrows between groups of units indicate full feedforward interconnections.

produce Person 1 or the relationship given the other two elements of the relation. The reason for this limitation is the difficulty of incorporating local-to-distributed mappings in recurrent auto-associative memories.

Other networks that learn distributed representations

Harris (1989) uses this same technique in a system that learns to categorize the meanings, according to the theory of Cognitive Linguistics, of the preposition *over* in sentences. The network learns distributed representations for words that code for properties relevant to how 'over' should be interpreted. The learned representations also exhibit some of the properties of the *radial categories* of Cognitive Linguistics.

When a network has a number of input blocks, weight sharing can be used to force all distributed input groups to use the same distributed representation. This has several advantages: objects have the same distributed representation no matter where they appear in the input; the distributed representations combine information from many sources; and the network has fewer parameters. Le Cun et al. (1990) implement a spatial version of this technique to learn translation-invariant spatial features in their model of handwritten digit recognition.

Miikkulainen and Dyer (1989) extend this local-to-distributed mapping technique to force the distributed output representation to be the same as the distributed input representation. In Hinton's *Family trees* network *Charlotte* can have different representations on the distributed output units and the distributed input units. Miikkulainen and Dyer dispense with the localist output layer, and instead give the network a target pattern on the distributed output layer. This target pattern is the distributed input representation of the target object currently used by the network. They use this technique in a network that processes sentences, and the network learns representations for many varied objects. The resulting representations have many analogical properties. The advantage of using the same representation on input and outputs is that all the information in the training set is used to construct a single representation for each object. However, the targets change as the distributed input representations change, which can make learning slower (a *moving targets* problem). A potentially serious problem with this technique is that the network can give all objects the same representation, which results in zero error. This points to a deficiency in the error function – it lacks a discriminative term. Miikkulainen (1993) reports that networks rarely give all objects the same representation,[10] and suggests that this problem could be avoided entirely by clamping at least two of the representations to different values.

2.2.3 Conjunctive coding

Conjunctive coding is a way of binding together the representations of two objects. A conjunctive code has a unit for every possible conjunction of the units used for representing the objects. If the representation for one object has N units, and the representation for another has M units, then the conjunctive code will have $N \times M$ units. Conjunctive coding can be used whenever it is necessary to bind several representations together: for binding roles and fillers, for binding variables and values, for binding the positions and identities of objects, and for binding multiple features of objects together.

   Suppose we want to bind colors with shapes, and are using the following four-bit distributed representations: *red* ($\mathbf{r} = [0011]^\mathrm{T}$), *blue* ($\mathbf{b} = [1001]^\mathrm{T}$), *square* ($\mathbf{s} = [1010]^\mathrm{T}$), and *circle* ($\mathbf{c} = [0110]^\mathrm{T}$). The conjunctive code for this will have sixteen units. Figure 13 shows a network implementation of a conjunctive code – a conjunctive unit is active if both the units it is connected to are active. The conjunctive codes for *red square* and *blue circle* are shown in Figure 14 (the network is not shown). Conjunctive codes can be superimposed without the appearance of illusory conjunctions such as *blue square*, provided that not too many bindings are superimposed. In the terms of linear

---

[10]This is probably because Miikkulainen does not use the correct derivatives for training the network – he omits the term that would provide a strong push for all the representations to take on the same value.

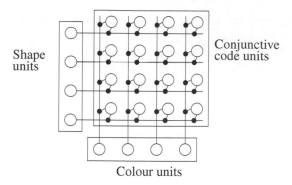

Shape units

Conjunctive code units

Colour units

FIGURE 13 A network that implements a conjunctive code for color and shape. A unit in the conjunctive code is active if both of the shape and color units it is connected to are active.

algebra, a conjunctive code is a (thresholded) superposition of vector outer products:

$$B = f(\mathbf{r}^{\mathrm{T}}\mathbf{s} + \mathbf{b}^{\mathrm{T}}\mathbf{c}),$$

where f is the superposition threshold-function.

To find out what shape is bound to a certain color, we treat the color units as input units and the shape units as output units. If a conjunctive unit is active, and the color it is connected to is active, then it sends activation to its shape unit. The shape units sum the activation they receive, and output 0 or 1 according to whether their total activation is below or above a suitable threshold.[11] In the terms of linear algebra, this is equivalent to multiplying the color vector by the binding matrix, and thresholding the result:

$$f(B\mathbf{r}) = \mathbf{s} \quad \text{and} \quad f(B\mathbf{b}) = \mathbf{c},$$

where f is the decoding threshold-function. This decoding process works in the presence of noise, and with superimposed codes. It can also be inverted to find the color given the shape. Figure 15 shows the decoding of the superimposed bindings: the procedure correctly discovers that *red* was bound to *square* and *blue* to *circle*, despite the overlap in the representations.

Hinton (1981) discusses how distributed conjunctive coding for role-filler bindings can solve two potential problems with systems that use blocks of units to represent the fillers of different roles, such as the memory for triples (Section 2.2.1). One problem is the number of role blocks required. A system that could represent a variety of predicates

---

[11] With zero-one representations of objects, the appropriate value for the threshold depends on the number of ones in the representations.

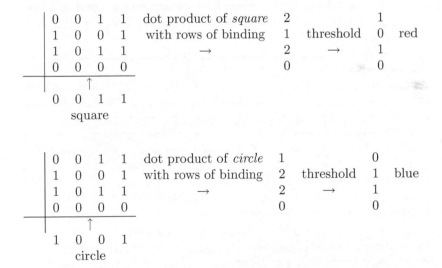

		red square						blue circle			
	1	0	0	1	1		0	0	0	0	0
red	0	0	0	0	0	*blue*	1	1	0	0	1
	1	0	0	1	1		1	1	0	0	1
	0	0	0	0	0		0	0	0	0	0
		0	0	1	1			1	0	0	1
		square						*circle*			

```
| 0  0  1  1
| 1  0  0  1     Superimposed bindings of
| 1  0  1  1     red square and blue circle
| 0  0  0  0
|
```

FIGURE 14 The conjunctive codes for the *red square* and *blue circle* bindings are the outer products of the representations of *red* and *square*, and *blue* and *circle*. These bindings can be superimposed without confusing which color is bound with which shape.

```
| 0  0  1  1    dot product of square    2                  1
| 1  0  0  1    with rows of binding     1    threshold     0    red
| 1  0  1  1              →              2        →         1
| 0  0  0  0                             0                  0
|       ↑
| 0  0  1  1
    square
```

```
| 0  0  1  1    dot product of circle    1                  0
| 1  0  0  1    with rows of binding     2    threshold     1    blue
| 1  0  1  1              →              2        →         1
| 0  0  0  0                             0                  0
|       ↑
| 1  0  0  1
    circle
```

FIGURE 15 Decoding the superimposed bindings of *red square* and *blue circle*, to discover which color is bound to *square* and which color is bound to *circle*. The first operation is the dot product of the shape representation with each row of the superimposed bindings, the second is comparison with a threshold.

with role blocks would need a large number of them for all the different roles, and could become unmanageably large.[12] Additionally, such a system would be representationally inefficient, as only a small fraction of the blocks would be in use at any one time. Conjunctive coding with distributed representations of roles can make better use of representational resources – one conjunctive code block can represent the binding of a filler with one of many roles. The other problem is that having different blocks for different roles makes it difficult to represent similarity between roles. Using distributed representations for roles allows the similarity structure of roles to be reflected by their representations. These similarity relationships are preserved by conjunctive coding – the bindings of a filler with similar roles are similar.

Conjunctive codes work with both distributed and localist representations, but can grow very large, especially when higher-order conjunctions are used. This is more of a problem for localist representations than for distributed representations, because localist representations require a larger number of units to represent a given number of objects. Conjunctive codes also work with continuous-valued distributed representations: the activation of a unit in the conjunctive code is the product of the activations of the units it is connected to. The use of conjunctive codes generally imposes some constraints on the distributed representations for objects, e.g., that they should have approximately uniform density.

Outer product conjunctive codes are equivalent to matrix-style heteroassociative memories, such as the Willshaw net (Willshaw, 1989b), and like them are able to exploit redundancy in the conjunctive code to compensate for noisy or incomplete input patterns. The encoding and decoding operations of matrix memories can be implemented in several different ways, giving rise to a variety of ways of using conjunctive codes. For example, instead of superimposing bindings in a binary-OR fashion (as in Figure 14), we can superimpose bindings by ordinary summation. The best choice of operations for a conjunctive code depends upon the properties of the distributed representation of objects (such things as its density, and whether it is binary or continuous).

Outer product codes are the most straightforward conjunctive codes for distributed representations. More complex conjunctive codes can be constructed by involving more than one unit from the object representations in the conjunctions, as Touretzky and Geva (1987) do in their

---

[12]Actually, a system that uses different blocks of units for different roles can be regarded as using a conjunctive code with an inefficient localist representation for roles. The active unit in the role representation indicates which row (or column) of the binding matrix should be used to store the filler.

DUCS system (described in the next section). This makes it possible to increase redundancy in the conjunctive code, since more than $N \times M$ higher-order conjunctions are available. Increased redundancy gives the system greater ability to correct errors and complete patterns.

Conjunctive coding can also be extended to bind more than two objects together. Smolensky (1990) describes a framework for this, based on tensor-product algebra. A tensor product can be viewed as an outer product operation generalized to any number of vectors. I review tensor products in Section 2.4.3. Tensor products provide a general framework for understanding conjunctive codes – all conjunctive codes, including the complex code Touretzky and Geva use in DUCS, can be viewed as tensor products or subsets of tensor products.

Touretzky and Geva: DUCS

Touretzky and Geva (1987) use conjunctive coding to store simple frame-like structures in a distributed memory. Their system, called DUCS, is able to retrieve a role-filler pair given an approximation of the role, which can be interpreted as generalization or error correction. This ability is a consequence of the use of distributed representations and redundant conjunctive coding.

A frame consists of a number of role-filler pairs. For example, the frame describing *Fred the cockatoo* is:

NAME:	FRED
BODY-COLOR:	PALE-PINK
BEAK:	GREY-HOOKED-THING
CREST:	ORANGE-FEATHERED-THING
HABITAT:	JUNGLE
DIET:	SEEDS-AND-FRUIT

DUCS can store several role-filler pairs in a frame, and several frames in its memory. DUCS is pattern-completing and error-correcting at the role level and at the frame level. It can retrieve a frame given a partial or corrupted version of the frame, and can retrieve a role-filler pair from a frame given a corrupted or similar version of a role in the frame.

The architecture of DUCS is shown in Figure 16. Roles and fillers have binary distributed representations 20 units wide. The binding of roles and fillers is a highly redundant (and rather complex) set of 1280 conjunctions of role and filler units. Each conjunction can involve the activation of a unit, or its logical complement, and the set of conjunctions is designed so that exactly 40 of the 1280 units are active. A *selector* block holds a single role-filler binding and has extra internal units that exploit the redundancy of the conjunctive code to error correct roles and fillers during frame decoding. A frame is a superposi-

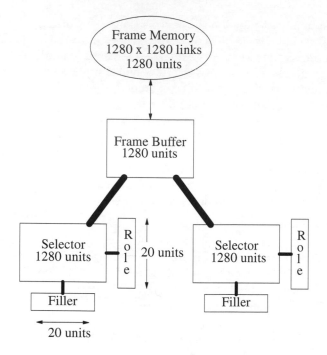

FIGURE 16 DUCS architecture. (Adapted from Touretzky and Geva (1987).)

tion of role-filler bindings, and is stored in the frame buffer over 1280 units. The number of active units in the frame buffer will be approximately the number of roles in the frame times 40. The frame memory is an auto-associative Willshaw net (Willshaw, 1989b), which is a pattern-completing and error-correcting memory. It can store a number of frames, and can retrieve one given a partial or corrupted version. The frame memory has 1, 638, 400 links.

The representations on the role and filler units are chosen to reflect the similarity of the concepts they represent. This allows the system to retrieve a filler from a binding given an approximation of the name of the role. For example, suppose the representation for *nose* is similar to that for *beak*. If we request the filler of the *nose* of Fred role then the system will change the requested role to *beak* and say the filler is a *grey hooked thing*.

Touretzky and Geva discuss how hierarchical structure (in which a frame can be a filler in another frame) could be represented in DUCS. This is difficult because the representation of a frame is 1280 units, whereas the representation of a filler is 20 units. They suggest that the first 20 units of the 1280 could serve as a reduced description for the frame, and could be used as a filler in other frames. However, this is unlikely to be an adequate reduced description. The code for a frame is sparse, so in any 20 units of a frame there will only be a few active units. If there are a reasonably large number of frames, the chances are that some will have the same reduced description.

2.3 Connectionist models that learn to process language

The prospect of processing natural language has been a prime motivation for the interest among connectionists in the representation of hierarchical structure. Language processing tasks of practical interest occur at all levels of language understanding, e.g., predicting the next symbol in a string, assigning case-roles to words in a string (i.e., deciding which is the subject, object, etc), pronunciation, deciding whether a string is grammatical, and translation from one language to another. On top of the problems with representing and manipulating complex temporary structures in neural nets, several related characteristics of language add to the difficulty. The input consists of a variable number of objects, typically in sequential form. Furthermore, the appropriate output at any particular time can depend upon input received an arbitrary number of time steps in the past. A network that can only deal with sequences up to some fixed length will be of limited use, and any learning it does is unlikely to reveal much of interest about how language can be processed. To process language in a satisfactory manner, it is necessary to use some sort of network that is capable of sequential processing, can retain complex state information, and has context-dependent control over what state information is retained.

Inspired by the ability of feedforward networks to develop useful representations in the course of learning to perform a task, some researchers tried this approach with recurrent networks on language processing tasks. Recurrent networks are a modification of feedforward networks in which the activations of some units are considered to be the state of the machine and are recycled as inputs to the network at the next time step. Such a network can process a sequence of inputs and maintain an internal state. However, before I discuss recurrent networks I want to review NETtalk, which is a feedforward network that learns to pronounce English text. NETtalk serves to show that neural networks can learn some regularities and exceptions in a language task (English pronunciation), and clarifies the limitations of non-recurrent networks.

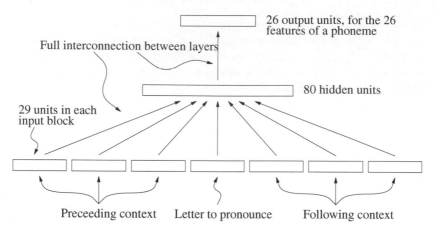

FIGURE 17 Architecture of Sejnowski and Rosenberg's (1986) NETtalk system.

2.3.1 Non-recurrent networks

Sejnowski and Rosenberg: NETtalk

Sejnowski and Rosenberg's (1986) NETtalk system, which learns to pronounce English text, is a feedforward network that looks at a seven-character window of text. Its task is to output the phoneme corresponding to the central character in the input window. The architecture of the NETtalk system is illustrated in Figure 17. Each input buffer represents one letter (or punctuation mark) in a localist fashion, and the output is the set of features for the phoneme for the central letter. For cases where more than one letter generates a single phoneme, the output phoneme can be 'null' for all but one of the letters.

The most obvious limitation of this windowing technique is that the *memory* it provides is strictly limited to inputs that occurred within a fixed number of time steps. This is due to the network having no internal state. Once an input passes out of the window it can have no effect on the output. While having access to the three previous input symbols might be adequate, in most cases, for pronunciation, it is inadequate for more complex language processing tasks. Merely increasing the window size would be inelegant, inefficient, and impractical – the window would need to be quite large to be large enough most of the time, there would be an impractically large number of parameters, and there would always be otherwise reasonable inputs that were too large.

Another limitation of this windowing technique is that it is difficult to design the system so that it can recognize and exploit invariances in the input. For example, words often mean the same thing independent of which buffer window they appear in, and it is wasteful to duplicate the machinery that recognizes words. A possible solution is to share the weights for localist to distributed maps on input buffers. However, the problem is more difficult to solve at higher levels, e.g., in the interpretation of the meanings of short sequences of words.

2.3.2 Recurrent networks

Rumelhart et al. (1986a) describe how recurrent networks can be trained using a modification of backpropagation algorithm for feedforward networks. In a recurrent network activations on certain units are fed back into the network at the next time step. Figure 18 shows the architecture of one such network. A complete forward propagation, from the input to the output units is one time step. The backward connections copy activations to special *holding* units, which preserve the activation (i.e., the internal state of the network) for use at the next time step.[13] In the first time step all the holding unit activations are set to some fixed value. In subsequent time steps they assume the activations at the previous time step of units they are connected to. The activations of any unit in the network can be recycled into the net at the next time step by including a holding unit for it. The network can have different input values and output targets at each time step, and inputs and targets can be left undefined at some time steps. Rumelhart et al. describe how to calculate error gradients for such networks, using an *unfolding in time* procedure. This involves running the network backwards for the same number of time steps as it was run forwards.

Rumelhart, Hinton, and Williams trained a network like the one in Figure 18 to complete sequences. They used 25 different sequences six symbols long, e.g., *AB1223*, and *DE2113*. The sequences have the regularity that the third and fourth symbol are determined by the first, and the fifth and sixth by the second. The first two symbols are presented to the network as input at the first two time steps. The remaining four symbols, which are completely determined by the first two, are the output targets at the subsequent four time steps. After training on 20 of the sequences the network could correctly generate those and could generate completions for the sequences it had not seen. In one training run the network generated completely correct completions for the unseen sequences, and in another it made just one mistake. This generalization ability indicates that the network is able to extract the regularity in the training set.

---

[13]Rumelhart et al. (1986a) use different classes of links rather than holding units, but the results are the same.

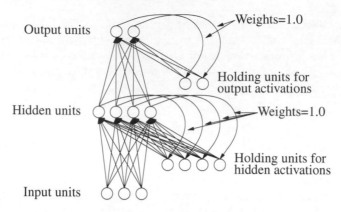

FIGURE 18 A recurrent network, as described by Rumelhart et al. (1986a). The curved backward connections serve to copy the activations to holding units, for use at the next time step.

Elman: Learning to remember

Elman (1988, 1990, 1991) performed several experiments with recurrent networks, in order to investigate how well they can process language. The results show that simple recurrent connectionist networks can build representations that stored relevant information from previous input, that these representations seem to possess internal structure, and that this structure can be used by the network to account for structure in the input. However, these results need some qualification: the learning is slow, the domains tested on are simple and small, the representations are difficult to interpret, and the scaling and generalization properties are uncertain.

Elman uses recurrent networks in which the activations of the hidden layer are recycled to the next time step.[14] Figure 19a shows a typical network. He calls the holding units the *context* units, because these units hold the memory of previous inputs – they provide the context for the net to work in. The task of the network at the tth time step is to predict the $(t + 1)$-th symbol in the sequence, given the tth symbol as input and the context computed so far by the network. In the course of making this prediction new activations are computed on the hidden units. These are used as the context for the following time step, when the actual $(t + 1)$-th symbol is presented on the inputs and the network has to predict the $(t + 2)$-th symbol. There are nearly always

---

[14] Jordan (1986) used recurrent networks in which output activations are recycled. However, this type of network is not very suitable for processing language strings because language tasks usually require the retention of state information that is independent of the outputs.

several symbols that can occur at a given point in the sequence. The network can minimize its error by predicting all possible items, but with lower values (*confidences*). In order to make optimal predictions (and thus minimize the error) the network must discover all the constraints, syntactic and otherwise, on the language it is presented with. It must also learn to preserve relevant information about previous inputs in its context layer, and learn to ignore or discard irrelevant information.

Elman does not compute exact error gradients in the networks. Rather than running the net backwards through the training sequence to correctly compute errors, Elman truncates the backpropagation of error signals at the context layer. Figure 19b shows an unfolded network and the forward and backward propagation paths. Truncating the error signals makes the gradient computation much simpler, as it is no longer necessary to store a history of activations at each unit and run backwards through the sequence. The backpropagation of errors can be performed at each time step, resulting in an algorithm that is local in time. However, the gradients are not correct, since there is no back-propagation of error signals from an output to an input that occurred on preceding time steps. This means that if an input is only important several time steps in the future, the network will not adjust its weights to preserve information about that input. If by chance the information is preserved, the network can use it, but the calculated gradients only force the network to transfer information about the input into the hidden layer if that information is useful for the current output.[15]

Elman's simplest experiment (Elman, 1990) is with a recurrent network that learned the sequential XOR task. In this task a string of bits is presented to the network, and the network must predict the next bit. Every third bit is the XOR of the previous two random bits, and the network should learn to predict its value. For example, in the string "011110101..." the underlined numbers are predictable. For unpredictable bits, the total error over the training set is minimized when the network predicts both with lower confidence. The network learned this task after a moderately long training period: a string of approximately 3000 bits. This experiment demonstrates that this type of network can learn to remember.

Another experiment involves learning to predict the next word in two- and three-word sentences generated by a simple template grammar with a vocabulary of 29 words. The grammar incorporates some semantic constraints, e.g., that the subject of *eat* must be an animate

---

[15]Williams and Zipser (1989) describe an algorithm for correctly computing error gradients that does not require going backwards through the sequence. However, the algorithm is non-local, and expensive both in time and space.

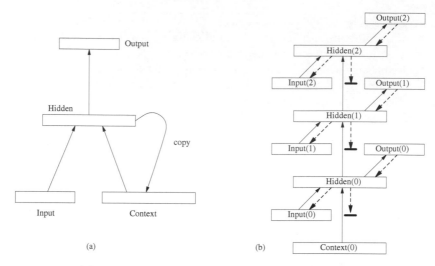

FIGURE 19   (a) The type of recurrent net used by Elman (1990). (b) The unfolded network showing the patterns of forward and backward propagations. The numbers in parentheses are the time steps. The learning rule does not use the full gradient information in that error signals are not backpropagated from the hidden units at time $t + 1$ to the hidden units at time t.

noun. Elman generated $10,000$ sentences from the grammar and concatenated them with no begin or end markers to form a continuous sequence of $27,354$ words. The words are represented in a localist fashion on the input and output units. The network has one hidden layer with 150 units. It learned to make good predictions in six passes over the data. Elman attempted to analyze the representations by computing the average hidden-unit representation in response to a particular word in all contexts. He performed a hierarchical cluster analysis on these average representations and found that they cluster, in a hierarchical fashion into verbs, nouns, animates, inanimates, animals, humans, etc. Elman interprets this as showing that the network, as a result of learning to predict, had discovered the semantic structure of the vocabulary. However, as Elman acknowledges, the observed clusters may be an artifact of the averaging and not due to the learning. The network, whether trained or not, constructs contexts for individual word occurrences. The averaging procedure then constructs average contexts for each word. These would be expected to cluster in ways that Elman observed, even without any learning, since similar words have similar contexts. Elman (private communication) reports that this is in fact what happens, although the clusters extracted from an untrained

S → NP VP "."
NP → PropN | N | N RC
VP → V (NP)
RC → *who* NP VP | *who* VP (NP)
N → *boy* | *girl* | *cat* | *dog* | *boys* | *girls* | *cats* | *dogs*
PropN → *John* | *Mary*
V → *chase* | *feed* | *see* | *hear* | *walk* | *live* | *chases* |
     feeds | *sees* | *hears* | *walks* | *lives*

Additional restrictions:

• number agreement between N and V within clause, and (where appropriate) between head N and subordinate V
• verb arguments:

chase, feed → require a direct object
see, hear → optionally allow a direct object
walk, live → preclude a direct object
(observed also for head/verb relations in relative clauses)

FIGURE 20 Elman's grammar that allows embedded clauses. (Adapted from Elman (1991).)

network were less clean than those from the trained network. To test what the network has learned, it would be more appropriate to do a cluster analysis on the outgoing weights from the input layer, as these form a local-to-distributed mapping, and any systematic similarities in these weights must be a result of the learning.

Elman's (1991) most complex experiment uses sentences generated from a grammar that allows embedded phrases in the form of relative clauses, e.g. "Dog who chases cat sees girl." This experiment shows that a recurrent network can learn to represent several levels of hierarchical structure. The grammar, shown in Figure 20, has 23 words and one end-of-sentence marker. This grammar has a number of properties in common with natural language: number agreement, verb argument structure, interactions with relative clauses (the agent or subject in a relative clause is omitted), center-embedding, and viable sentences (there are positions in which the end of sentence marker cannot occur).

The network architecture is shown in Figure 21. Localist representations are used on the inputs and outputs, with two units reserved for unspecified purposes. The hidden layer consists of 70 units, which are recycled to the next time step via the context units. Local-to-distributed maps, with 10 units in the distributed representations, are used for

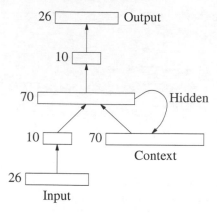

FIGURE 21 Elman's recurrent network for predicting words. (Adapted from Elman (1991))

both input and output. The training regime involves four sets of 10, 000 sentences. The first set of sentences have no relative clauses and each subsequent set has a higher proportion of more complex sentences, with the fourth set having 75% complex sentences. Each set is presented to the network five times. This gradated training regime beginning with simple sentences is necessary for the network to learn the task. At the end of the training (a total of 200, 000 sentence presentations) the network learned all of the above properties, i.e., it predicted verbs that agreed in number with the noun, etc. Elman tested the trained network on a new set of test sentences generated in the same way as the fourth training set, and claimed the network gave reasonably good predictions. However, it is difficult for the reader to evaluate how good these predictions were because although Elman does report the average error on the testing set, he does not report the average error on the training set, so there is nothing to compare it to. Also, Elman does not say how many of the sentences in the testing set were not actually in the training set. There are only 440 different sentences with two or three words, so it is unlikely that many of the shorter sentences in the testing set are not in the training set.

Another reason for questioning whether the network does more than rote learning is that the size of the vocabulary gives a misleading impression of the complexity of the input. There are actually only 11 different classes of vocabulary symbols (including the period) which must be distinguished in order to make optimal predictions. For example, *boy*, *girl*, *cat*, and *dog* can all be treated as the same for the purposes of prediction. Thus, although there are 400 sentences of three words, there are

Length	# of patterns	# of sentences	Length	# of patterns
2	6	40	10	1024
3	18	400	11	12288
4	8	128	12	36864
5	96	5120	13	10240
6	288	51200	14	122880
7	96	12288	15	368640
8	1152		16	98304
9	3456			

TABLE 1 Numbers of different sentences and sentence patterns generated by Elman's grammar. The length does not include the period.

only 18 different sentence patterns of this length, e.g., "singular-noun singular-transitive-verb plural-noun". When this is taken into account, the number of distinct sentence patterns is small compared to the size of the training sets, for sentences with up to 2 or 3 relative clauses. Table 1 lists the numbers of sentence patterns for sentences of various lengths. The network could be learning the classes of vocabulary symbols on the first training corpus, and then rote learning sentence patterns on the later training corpora.

Elman attempted to analyze what the network was doing by looking at the trajectories of the hidden units through time. In order to visualize these trajectories, he extracted the principal components of the hidden-unit space (70 dimensions) and plotted the projection of the trajectories onto the principal components. Three example trajectory projections are shown in Figure 22a. The three verbs have different argument structure and after receiving the verb the hidden units are in a different region of state space. *Chases* requires a direct object, *sees* takes an optional object, and *walks* precludes an object. One presumes that *feeds*, *hears*, and *lives* behave similarly, but this is not reported. When a sentence can legally end, the trajectories are within a small region (at least on these two components).

Observing trajectories for sentences with center-embedded clauses gives an opportunity for gaining some insight into how the network is representing structured state information. Figure 22b shows the trajectories of the hidden units while processing two similar sentences with embedded clauses: "Boys who boys chase chase boy" and "Boy who boys chase chases boy" (these sentences were not in the training corpus.) To correctly process these sentences the network must remember the number (plural or singular) of the main clause noun (the first word) while processing the intervening relative clause "who boys chase". Also,

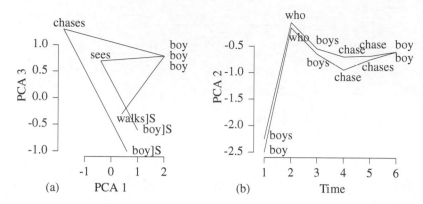

FIGURE 22 Trajectories of hidden units during processing of various sentences, projected onto principal components. In (a) the final word in each sentence is marked with "]S". (Adapted from Elman (1991).)

the network must ignore the number of main clause noun when processing the verb of this relative clause. To do this in general requires a stack, since an intervening clause can have more relative clauses embedded within it. Figure 22b does show that differences in the trajectories are maintained while the number information is relevant, but it does not explain how the network is implementing the operations of a stack. Elman states that representations seemed to degrade after about three levels of embedding, so it is possible the network did not learn to push and pop number information but merely learned the patterns for sentences with low degrees of center-embedding.

Elman's experiments do not provide conclusive evidence that recurrent networks can learn to represent complex structure in an interesting way. His networks definitely do learn some structure, but it is unclear whether they rote learn many sentence patterns or actually learn computational primitives for encoding and decoding hierarchical structures.

St. John and McClelland: sentence comprehension

St. John and McClelland (1990) apply recurrent networks to processing sentences. Their model concurrently learns to represent a *gestalt* meaning of the whole sentence while learning to answer questions about the sentence, based on the information in the gestalt. The model is shown in Figure 23. It consists of two networks, one a recurrent network that builds up a gestalt of the sentence meaning as it receives the syntactic constituents of the sentence, and the other a feedforward network that decodes the gestalt into role-filler pairs. All inputs and outputs are represented in a localist fashion. Sentence constituents (simple noun

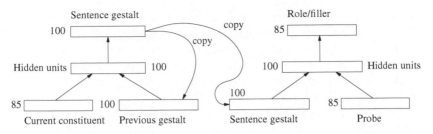

FIGURE 23 St. John and McClelland's (1990) sentence processing network.

phrases, prepositional phrases, and verbs) are fed to the network in sequence, and the sentence gestalt develops recursively. After the presentation of each constituent, the gestalt is probed for all role-filler pairs in the meaning of the sentence, including ones that depend upon constituents not yet presented. This forces the network to anticipate upcoming constituents and discover regularities in sentences that allow it to make good guesses about the entire meaning based on just part of the sentence. The network performs well, although training times are long, and the training corpus is small, which raises questions about how the network might scale to cope with larger corpora.

One of the motivations for this model is to see whether good representations for sentence meanings (a collection of role-filler pairs, in this case) can be learned by backpropagation. St. John and McClelland report that the conjunctive coding representation used by McClelland and Kawamoto (1986) proved unworkable, and they wanted to see if a backpropagation network could develop a more usable representation. It does seem as though the network did develop good representations for the task, but unfortunately, St. John and McClelland do not investigate the nature of this representation. Neither do they address the difficult and important problem of how hierarchical structure could be represented – the model only deals with sentences without embedded clauses

Sopena: parsing sentences with embedded clauses

Sopena (1991) describes a recurrent network that can process embedded sentences. He finesses the problem of representing the hierarchical structure of embedded sentences by using a sequence of simple clause frames as targets. As the network processes each word in a sentence, it outputs known information about the current clause, such as the predicate, agent, object, location, and instrument. For example, the sentence "The man that the boy was looking at was smoking" contains two simple clauses: "The man was smoking" and "The boy was looking at the man." When processing the words "the man", the first clause is the current one. Next, the second clause becomes the current one, and finally the first clause again becomes the current one.

Sopena's network is considerably more complicated than the networks used by Elman. It has two modules with context-hidden recurrences, one is for storing information about the current clause, and the other is for storing information about previous clauses. Sopena found that it was necessary to delete most of the recurrent connections (leaving less than 5% connectivity between context and hidden layers) in order for the network to be able learn to retain information over several time steps. The output for the network is organized as a set of case-roles. As each word is read, it must be assigned to the appropriate case-role, and output on the appropriate set of units.

The performance of the network seems quite good. Sopena trained it on 3000 sentences for 50 epochs. He reports that the network generalized well to new sentences with both familiar and novel templates. The network only had difficulties when sentences had three or more levels of center-embedded clauses.

Case-role assignment seems to be a better task than prediction for training a recurrent net. It requires that the network remembers more information during processing, and also results in more informative error signals being fed back to the network. However, the task does not require the network to represent the entire meaning of the sentence at once – it only has to maintain a stack of incomplete clauses. The hidden layers in the network are so large (five times the width of a clause) that the network could be learning to implement a shift-register style stack. It is unclear whether the task allows for clauses to be forgotten once they are complete. The network can perform anaphora resolution, but Sopena does not give enough details to determine whether a referent lies outside of the current and incomplete clauses.

Servan-Schreiber *et al*: Graded State Machines

Servan-Schreiber et al. (1991) conduct a deeper investigation into the grammar learning abilities of recurrent networks like those used by Elman. They trained a network to learn a regular grammar from examples, and showed that the fully trained network has learned to be a perfect recognizer for the language. Their analysis of the acquisition of the internal representations shows that the network progressively encodes more and more temporal context during training.

Figure 24 shows the grammar that generates the strings, and the network used to learn the grammar. Servan-Schreiber et al. use the same truncated error backpropagation scheme as Elman.

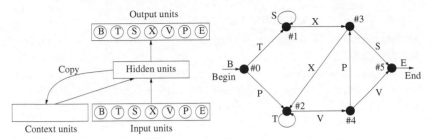

FIGURE 24   Servan-Schreiber *et al*'s grammar and recurrent network. (Adapted from Servan-Schreiber et al. (1991).)

Servan-Schreiber et al. investigate how well the network can carry information about distant correlations across intervening elements. They use two copies of the above finite state machine (FSM) embedded in a larger finite state machine to produce strings that will test this capability. This finite state machine produces strings of the form "$T < S > T$" and "$P < S > P$", where "$< S >$" is a string generated by the above FSM. To successfully predict the last letter of the string, the network must remember the first. Servan-Schreiber et al. report that the network is unable to perform the task if the two embedded strings have the same characteristics. However, if they have different statistical properties (from different transition probabilities on the arcs) the network is able to learn the task. This shows the network has a tendency to forget inputs unless they are relevant to predicting the following item. This inability to learn long-range dependencies is probably due to a large extent to the truncation of the error propagation path. The network only backpropagates errors one time step, thus there is no path for the error feedback to influence what was remembered about input presented more than one time step before. This does not mean that the network cannot remember information if it is not needed on the next time step; rather it means that there is no pressure for it to do so. As it happens, both Elman's and Servan-Schreiber *et al*'s networks often do retain information across several time steps – it is difficult to quickly wipe out all traces of previous input in a machine with a continuous high-dimensional state. Moreover, when input is slightly relevant to the processing of intervening input, the network can learn to preserve information about it for a large number of time steps. Servan-Schreiber et al. suggest that natural language might have the property that the information needed to correctly process long-range dependencies is also useful for processing intervening elements, and thus could be learned by this simple type of network. However, they do not present any particularly compelling evidence to support this suggestion.

Other recurrent nets for learning regular and context-free languages

A number of researchers have continued the investigation of how well recurrent networks can learn languages from examples (Watrous and Kuhn, 1992, Giles et al., 1992, Das and Mozer, 1994). This work shows that recurrent networks, similar to those used by Elman and Servan-Schreiber et al., can reliably learn small regular grammars. Some of this work uses higher-order recurrent networks, in which connections are from pairs of units to another unit. In most cases, the training procedures use correct gradients rather than those given by Elman's truncated error propagation scheme. However, there have not been any reported successes with getting simple recurrent networks to learn context-free languages. Giles et al. (1990) and Das et al. (1992) show that a higher-order recurrent network with an external stack can learn simple deterministic context-free grammars (e.g., parenthesis matching, $a^n b^n$, $a^n b^n c b^n a^n$). While it is interesting that a neural network can learn to use the stack, this avoids the problem of how more complex state information can be represented in a distributed representation in the hidden layer of a recurrent net.

For further information on various more recent approaches to training recurrent neural networks to remember sequences and recognize languages, see also Pearlmutter (1995), Casey (1996), Rodriguez et al. (1999), Tabor (2000), Rodriguez (2001), and Tabor (2002).

2.4 Distributed connectionist models for explicit representation of structure

Researchers who have attempted to train networks to develop representations for complex structure have labored under the burden of not knowing how a network can represent and manipulate structure. This creates a number of problems. It makes it difficult to analyze or explain the properties of any representations the network does develop, or to make definitive pronouncements about how well the network will generalize to novel data or scale to larger tasks. It also forces the use of very general network architectures, which means that the learning procedure must conduct a long, slow search through a large function space in order to find suitable composition, manipulation, and decomposition functions.

In this section I review some distributed connectionist models that deal explicitly with the problem of how compositional structure can be represented and manipulated. Only one of these models (Pollack's

D	O	C
C	G	K
F	L	R
A	H	O
E	Q	E
P	Y	P

TABLE 2 A example receptive field table for a unit in the memory of DCPS. A unit having this table would respond to (D G R), but not (G D R).

RAAMs) satisfies to some degree all four desiderata for Hinton's reduced descriptions: adequacy, reduction, systematicity, informativeness. The designers of these models accept the claim that connectionist models must have primitives for composing and manipulating structure if the models are to be adequate for higher-level cognitive tasks. This is in contrast to many connectionist researchers who deny this claim. For example, MacLennan (1991) comments colorfully that decomposing and recomposing symbolic structures in neural networks is "just putting a fresh coat of paint on old, rotting [symbolic] theories."

2.4.1 Touretzky and Hinton: DCPS

Touretzky and Hinton (1985, 1988) constructed a *Distributed Connectionist Production System* (DCPS) to demonstrate that connectionist networks are powerful enough to do symbolic reasoning. In later papers, Touretzky (1986a,c, 1990) describes how the distributed memory of DCPS can represent variable-size tree structures.

The coarse-coded distributed memory in DCPS stores a set of triples. Each element of a triple is one of the 25 symbols, A B ... Y, so there are 15, 625 possible triples. The memory has 2000 units. Each unit has a *receptive field* of 216 triples, i.e., a particular unit is turned on when one of the 216 triples it responds to is stored in the memory. The receptive fields are constructed in a factorial fashion. Each unit has a receptive field table containing six symbols for each position in the triple. Table 2 shows an example receptive field. A unit responds to a triple if each symbol in the triple appears in the unit's table in the correct position.

A triple is stored in the memory by turning on the units that respond to it. On average, 28 of the 2000 units will respond to a given triple.[16] A triple is deleted from memory by turning off the units that respond to it.

---

[16]The system does not work well if many more or less than 28 units respond to some triples, as is the case with random receptive fields. Touretzky and Hinton (1988) describe how the receptive field tables were carefully chosen so as keep this number close to 28.

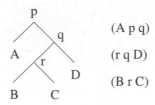

FIGURE 25 A binary tree and the triples that can be used to represent it.

To test whether a triple is stored in memory we check how many of the units responding to it are active. If the triple is present in memory and no other triples have been deleted from memory, then all of the units responding to that triple will be active. However, if other triples have been deleted from memory, some of the units may have been turned off. Touretzky (1990) suggests that a threshold of 75% of units should be used to decide whether a triple is present in memory. DCPS can reliably store around 6 or 7 distinct triples. The probability of error on retrieval increases with the number of triples stored, and with similarity among the stored triples.

This triple memory is used as the working memory in DCPS. DCPS has four other groups of units that serve to represent rules, extract clauses, and bind variables. The rules DCPS works with are all in the following form:

Rule 2: (=x A B) (=x C D) → +(=x E F) +(P D Q) −(=x S T)

Rules can have one variable (here "=x"), which, when it appears in a triple, must appear in the first position. This rule says that if there are triples matching (=x A B) and (=x C D) (which would match (F A B) and (F C D), but not (F A B) and (G C D)), then two triples should be added to the working memory, and one deleted, with the appropriate variable substitutions.

Touretzky (1986a,c, 1990) later designed BoltzCONS, a system that manipulates LISP-like structures (i.e., binary trees). This system uses the same triple memory to represent the structures, and has much additional machinery to interpret rules and modify memory contents. The tree representation is straightforward – each internal node in the structure is represented by a triple: left-contents, label, and right-contents. The left and right contents can be another label or an atomic symbol. Node labels function like pointers or addresses. Figure 25 shows a example tree and the set of triples that represent it.

The label of a triple is equivalent to the address of, or pointer to, a CONS cell in LISP memory. One advantage of this representation over a conventional pointer-based one is that the memory for triples is associative, so one can retrieve triples given any of the elements, not just the label. This allows traversal of binary trees without additional memory (a stack is usually required to traverse a binary tree).

This representation for structure has two of the four desiderata for reduced descriptions. The label is an adequate representation, in that one can recover the structure given the label, and it is also a reduced representation. However, the label is not systematically related to the contents or structure of the tree it refers to, and gives no information about the same. It is not an explicit representation of either the contents or structure of binary trees. To find out anything about a subtree one must chase labels instead of pointers.

2.4.2 Pollack: RAAMs

Pollack (1990) uses backpropagation to learn reduced descriptions for trees. He sets up an autoencoder net to learn to compress the fields of a node to a label, and uncompress the label to the fields. Pollack calls this type of network a *Recursive Auto-Associative Memory* (RAAM).

Figure 26 shows the architecture of the network for binary trees, and Figure 27 shows the three auto-associations the network must learn to encode a simple tree. The codes for terminal nodes (A, B, C, and D) are supplied to the network, but the network must learn suitable codes for the internal nodes (p, q, and r). The training is a moving target problem, because when the weights are adjusted for one example (e.g., for (B C) → r → (B C)), this changes the representation for r, which changes the target for another example. This can cause instability in the training, so the learning rate must be kept small, which results in long training times.

A RAAM can be viewed as being composed of two networks – an encoding net (the bottom half), and a decoding net (the top half). The encoding net converts a full representation to a reduced representation, and the decoding net performs the inverse function. The reduced representation for the tree (B C) is r, the reduced representation for ((B C) D) is q, and so on. The network learns the decoding and encoding functions simultaneously during training. Both encoding and decoding are recursive operations. The encoding procedure knows, from the structure of the tree, how many times it must recursively compress representations. However, the decoding procedure must decide during decoding whether or not a decoded field represents a terminal node or an internal node that should be further decoded. Pollack solves this problem by using binary codes for terminals (i.e., each value in the code is 0 or 1). The reduced descriptions (i.e., codes for internal nodes)

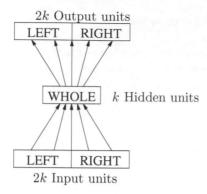

FIGURE 26 A Recursive Auto-Associative Memory (RAAM) for binary trees. The *WHOLE* is the code for an internal node in a tree, and *LEFT* and *RIGHT* can be codes for either internal or external nodes. (Adapted from Pollack (1990).)

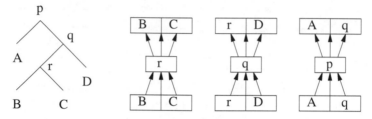

FIGURE 27 A simple tree and the auto-associations that encode it in a RAAM.

developed by the network tend to have values between 0 and 1, but not close to 0 or 1. If a decoded field has all its values sufficiently close to 0 or 1, then it is judged to be a terminal node and is not decoded further.

RAAMs are not limited to binary trees – a RAAM with M input fields (each of K units) can encode trees in which each node has up to M children. Nodes with less than M children can be encoded with special nil labels taking the place of the "missing" children. Each child must appear in a particular place – the left subtree is distinct from the right subtree. The locations of subtrees correspond to roles in simple frames, so RAAMs can be seen as having a fixed set of roles.

Pollack trained a RAAM with three roles to encode compositional propositions such as (thought pat (knew john (loved mary john))) ("Pat thought that John knew that Mary loved John"). The network has 48 input units, 16 hidden units, and 48 output units. The network learned to store the training set of 13 complex propositions. It is also able to encode and decode some, but not all, of the novel propositions presented to it. Pollack performed a cluster analysis on the codes for trees, which shows that similar trees tended to have similar codes. For examples, the codes for the trees (LOVED JOHN PAT), (LOVED MARY JOHN), (LOVED JOHN MARY), and (LOVED PAT MARY) are all more similar to each other than any of the codes for other trees.

The similarity structure in the codes (reduced descriptions) indicates that they do provide some explicit information about subtrees (full representations). Pollack probed the nature of this representation by testing whether it is possible to manipulate representations without decoding them. He trained another network to transform reduced descriptions of propositions like (LOVED X Y) to (LOVED Y X), where X and Y can take on four different values. This network has 16 input units, 8 hidden units and 16 output units. Pollack trained the network on 12 of the 16 propositions, and the network correctly generalizes to the other four. Chalmers (1990) explores this type of *holistic processing* further with a network with a RAAM that stores syntactic structures and another network that transforms reduced representations for passive structures to reduced representations for active structures, without decoding.

The requirement that RAAMs be trained is both good and bad. The benefit is that RAAMs have the potential to learn to use their resources to represent, efficiently and reliably, the types of structures and terminals that are commonly encountered. The drawback is that a RAAM may be unable to represent some unfamiliar structures and terminals.

RAAMs do satisfy, to some extent, all four desiderata of reduced descriptions – they are adequate (in some cases), systematic (all have the same compression and expansion mapping), reduced, and informative. However, as a representation for complex structure, RAAMs have a number of problems. One problem is with the types of structures RAAMs can represent. RAAMs have a fixed number of fixed roles and there is no way of representing similarity between roles. Another problem is the lengthy training RAAMs require. Yet another problem is with the amount of information stored in a reduced description – as trees get deeper, more information must be stored in a fixed-size set of units, whose activations are presumably of limited precision. Some method of chunking subtrees is needed. The most serious problem is that the generalization and scaling properties are largely unknown but do not appear to be terribly good. The uncertainty about them is partly due to not knowing the method by which the network compresses a full representation into a reduced one.

2.4.3 Smolensky: Tensor products

Smolensky (1990) describes how tensor-product algebra provides a framework for the distributed representation of hierarchical structure. Tensor products are a way of binding multiple vectors together. A tensor product can be seen as a generalized outer product[17] or conjunctive codes (Section 2.2.3). Given two n-dimensional column-vectors $\mathbf{x}$ and $\mathbf{y}$, the second-order tensor product $T = \mathbf{x} \otimes \mathbf{y}$ is equivalent to the outer product $\mathbf{x}\mathbf{y}^\mathsf{T}$. T has n^2 elements, and $T_{ij} = x_i y_j$. Both lower-order and higher-order tensors exist: a first-order tensor is just a vector, and a zero'th-order tensor is a scalar. A third-order tensor is the tensor product of three vectors: $T = \mathbf{x} \otimes \mathbf{y} \otimes \mathbf{z}$, where $T_{ijk} = x_i y_j z_k$ and T has n^3 elements. Higher-order tensor products are constructed in a similar fashion – a k'th-order tensor is the product of k n-dimensional vectors and has n^k elements. The *rank* of a tensor is another name for its order. Tensor products can be built up iteratively – multiplying a third-order tensor and a second-order tensor gives a fifth-order tensor. Tensor products can be decoded by taking inner products,[18] e.g., if $T = \mathbf{x} \otimes \mathbf{y} \otimes \mathbf{z}$, then $T \cdot (\mathbf{x} \otimes \mathbf{y}) = \mathbf{z}$ (under appropriate normalization conditions on the vectors). The inner product can be taken along any combination of dimensions. For example, given a third-order tensor $\mathbf{x} \otimes \mathbf{y} \otimes \mathbf{z}$, we can take the inner product with a second-order tensor in three different ways: along the first and second dimensions to extract $\mathbf{z}$, along the first and third dimensions to extract $\mathbf{y}$, or along the second and third dimensions to extract $\mathbf{x}$. Care must be taken to use the appropriate inner product.

Dolan and Smolensky: reimplementing DCPS with tensor products

Dolan and Smolensky (1989) use third-order tensors to reimplement Touretzky and Hinton's (1985) *Distributed Connectionist Production System* (DCPS). They first show how Touretzky and Hinton's triple memory can be interpreted as a rather complex, sparse, third-order tensor-product representation. Next they show how a system based on

---

[17]A conventional outer product is a operation on two vectors that returns the matrix whose elements are all the pairwise products of the elements of the vectors. The outer product operation typically increases dimensionality.

[18]The inner product of two vectors is also known as the dot product. It is the sum of the products of matching elements of the two vectors. Inner products are also defined for matrices and higher-order arrays (i.e., tensors). For example, the inner product of an n by m matrix and a m-element vector is the standard matrix-vector product and results in an n-element vector. The inner product operation typically decreases dimensionality (i.e., *order*).

straightforward tensor products is simpler and more principled. This system performs the same task as DCPS; they call it the *Tensor Product Production System* (TPPS). It has two main advantages over DCPS. One is that it is easier to analyze. The other is that the representations are designed at the level of atomic symbols, combined with a general-purpose scheme for representing structured collections of these symbols. This is in contrast to the approach taken with DCPS, which was to design the representation at the level of structures. The DCPS representation is both difficult to fine-tune and limited to specific structures (binary trees).

Role-filler tensor representations for predicates

The ability to bind multiple vectors provides a number of ways of representing predicates. The simplest is the role-filler outer product representation (second-order tensor) suggested by Smolensky (1990). A predicate such as p(a,b) can be represented by the sum of role-filler products: $\mathbf{r}_1 \otimes \mathbf{a} + \mathbf{r}_2 \otimes \mathbf{b}$. Smolensky (1990) discusses two methods of decoding this role-filler binding. The first method provides exact decoding of bindings, but requires that the set of possible roles be linearly independent. It involves calculating decoding vectors $\mathbf{r}_i'$ for the roles, and then taking a tensor inner product with the binding: $(\mathbf{r}_1 \otimes \mathbf{a} + \mathbf{r}_2 \otimes \mathbf{b}) \cdot \mathbf{r}_1' = \mathbf{a}$ (which is equivalent to the vector-by-matrix multiplication $\mathbf{r}_1'^{\mathrm{T}}(\mathbf{r}_1\mathbf{a}^{\mathrm{T}} + \mathbf{r}_2\mathbf{b}^{\mathrm{T}}) = \mathbf{a}$). The disadvantage of requiring linearly independent role vectors is that the number of roles is limited to being less than or equal to the vector dimension, which means that the representation for roles cannot take advantage of the representational efficiency of distributed representations. The second method for decoding bindings allows the set of possible role vectors to be linearly dependent, but only provides approximate results. These results must be cleaned up by a post-processing system that finds the best match among candidate results. In this method the decoding vectors are the same as the encoding vectors: $(\mathbf{r}_1 \otimes \mathbf{a} + \mathbf{r}_2 \otimes \mathbf{b}) \cdot \mathbf{r}_1 \approx \mathbf{a}$. Care must be taken if the vectors are not normalized, as results will be scaled. Roles can also be decoded by taking an inner product in a different direction, which in matrix-vector terms corresponds to $(\mathbf{r}_1^{\mathrm{T}}\mathbf{a} + \mathbf{r}_2^{\mathrm{T}}\mathbf{b})\mathbf{a} \approx \mathbf{r}_1^{\mathrm{T}}$.

Dolan and Smolensky (1989) suggest that predicates can be represented by a sum of third-order tensor products of predicate names, roles, and fillers. For example, their tensor-product representation of p(a,b) would be $\mathbf{p} \otimes \mathbf{r}_1 \otimes \mathbf{a} + \mathbf{p} \otimes \mathbf{r}_2 \otimes \mathbf{b}$, where the $\mathbf{r}_1$ and $\mathbf{r}_2$ are the roles of p. This representation is very similar to plain role-filler bindings – it is in fact equivalent to taking the tensor product of the frame name and the set of bindings: $\mathbf{p} \otimes \mathbf{r}_1 \otimes \mathbf{a} + \mathbf{p} \otimes \mathbf{r}_2 \otimes \mathbf{b} = \mathbf{p} \otimes (\mathbf{r}_1 \otimes \mathbf{a} + \mathbf{r}_2 \otimes \mathbf{b})$.

Fillers can be decoded by taking an inner product between tensors: $(\mathbf{p} \otimes \mathbf{r}_1 \otimes \mathbf{a} + \mathbf{p} \otimes \mathbf{r}_2 \otimes \mathbf{b}) \cdot (\mathbf{p} \otimes \mathbf{r}_1) \approx \mathbf{a}$. The predicate name or the role can be decoded in a similar fashion by taking an inner product in the appropriate direction.

There is not much difference between these two methods for representing predicates. Including the predicate name in the tensor product might be useful if different predicates were to share the same roles and it were desired that the representations of different predicates be distinct. However, one can always view the inclusion of the predicate name in the binding as a way of making roles of different predicates distinct – $\mathbf{p} \otimes \mathbf{r}_1$ is distinct from $\mathbf{q} \otimes \mathbf{r}_1$. With both of these methods, multiple predicates can be represented in a single tensor as a sum of bindings. However, multiple occurrences of the same predicate cause problems in both representations, because bindings from one predicate are not grouped together. For example, a single tensor representing eat(John, fish) and eat(Mark, chips) is indistinguishable from one representing eat(John, chips) and eat(Mark, fish).

We can represent hierarchical structure by using higher-order tensors as fillers. The resulting tensor is of even higher-order – the order increases with each level of embedding. For example, if the tensors P and Q are second-order tensors representing predicates p(a,b) and q(c,d), then the third-order tensor $\mathbf{r}_1 \otimes P + \mathbf{r}_2 \otimes Q$ could represent the predicate cause(p(a,b), q(c,d)). Although this method does provide a general scheme for representing hierarchical structure, it has two serious drawbacks. The first is that different components of a structure can be represented by tensors of different orders. The most immediate consequence of this is the difficulty of adding tensors of different ranks, as would be required if one filler were a predicate and another a simple object. Smolensky et al. (1992) overcome this problem by multiplying lower-order tensors by *place-holder* vectors to bring all tensors up to the same rank. The second and more severe drawback is that the rank of the tensor, and hence the number of elements in it, grows exponentially with the depth of the structure. Smolensky et al. (1992) suggest that this problem could be overcome by projecting higher-order tensors onto lower-order tensors. This would produce a reduced description of the higher-order tensor. However, they do not discuss what sort of projections would be suitable, or what the encoding and decoding properties would be. The danger with using projections onto lower-dimensional spaces is that the information in the null space of the projection is completely lost. If the difference between two structures is in this null space, the two structures will be given the same reduced description.

Dolan: CRAM

Dolan (1989) describes a story understanding system called *CRAM*, which uses a role-filler tensor-product representation scheme. CRAM builds a representation of a simple story and finds the story schema in memory that best matches it. CRAM takes variable bindings into account during the matching process, and can perform simple reasoning about the story by rebinding variables in predicates from the retrieved schema.

CRAM uses a superimposed third-order tensor-product representation (roles, fillers, and predicate names) for stories and story schemas. Each story schema in long-term memory has specific hardware to perform variable matching. It is necessary to do variable matching to retrieve the correct schema because some schemas consist of the same predicates and only differ in their variable instantiation patterns, e.g., the schemas for flattery, boasting, and recommendation.

While CRAM can deal with multiple predicates, it is not able to properly handle schemas in which predicates form a hierarchical structure. CRAM does not have a satisfactory method for forming reduced descriptions of predicates. Predicate names can be used as fillers, but this is not an adequate representation if a predicate occurs more than once in a schema. In any case, the static binding hardware used in the retrieval process is not able to properly match hierarchical predicate structure.

Halford *et al*: component product representation for predicates

Halford et al. (1994) propose a different way of using tensor products to represent predicates. They want a memory system that can store multiple predicates and retrieve one component of a predicate (the name or a filler) given its remaining components. They represent a predicate by the tensor product of all the components of the predicate. The role of a filler determines its position in the product. For example, the representation of `mother-of(woman, baby)` is **mother** $\otimes$ **woman** $\otimes$ **baby**. They represent a collection of predicates by the sum of tensors for individual predicates. This representation allows them to solve analogy problems of the form "Woman is to baby as mare is to what?" For example, suppose T is a sum of predicates, including `mother-of(woman, baby)` and `mother-of(mare, foal)`. The analogy can be solved by first taking the appropriate inner product between the tensors T and **woman** $\otimes$ **baby**,[19] yielding **mother** (provided T does not contain other

---

[19] Care must be exercised to take the appropriate inner product, which depends upon the position of the unknown component in the third-order tensor.

predicates relating `mother` and `baby`). Having discovered that the relevant predicate is `mother-of` we next take the inner product between **mother** $\otimes$ **mare** and T, yielding the answer **foal**.

Halford et al. propose this alternative representation for both psychological and computational reasons. The psychological reasons have to do with their claim that people can process approximately four independent dimensions in parallel. Consequently, they use tensors with a maximum order of four. The computational reason stems from their belief that it is impossible to retrieve one component of a predicate if the other predicates are represented as a sum of role-filler bindings. This is true if multiple predicates are stored as superposition of predicates. However, this has more to do with the inadequacy of superposition as a method for composing the representations of multiple predicates than with the adequacy of the role-filler representation for single predicates. Role-filler bindings are an adequate representation for this task if predicates are stored as chunks in an auto-associative memory, as I show in Appendix I. Storing predicates as chunks resolves the ambiguity about which bindings come from the same predicate and actually results in a more versatile memory system – a predicate can be retrieved given any number of its components (provided the components distinguish a particular predicate). Role-filler representations have two other advantages over component product representations: they do not necessitate the imposition of an order on the components of a predicate and they have no difficulty dealing with missing arguments.

Halford et al. do not give much consideration to how hierarchical structure might be represented. They do mention chunking as a way of coping with more than four dimensions and with nested predicates, but do not say how vectors representing chunks, which would be akin to reduced descriptions, might be constructed.

2.4.4 Convolution-based models

The outer product is not the only operation on which a distributed associative memory can be based. Before matrix memories were conceived of, light holography was proposed as an analogy for human memory. A number of authors, including Gabor (1968), Willshaw et al. (1969), and Borsellino and Poggio (1973), considered distributed associative memory models based on convolution and correlation (the mathematical operations underlying holography).

More recently, Liepa (1977), Murdock (1982, 1983, 1993), and Metcalfe Eich (1982, 1985), Metcalfe (1991) have used convolution-based memories for qualitative and quantitative modeling of human memory performance. Slack (1984b,a, 1986) proposed a convolution-based representation for parse trees.

Discrete convolution combines two vectors into one. Like the outer product, it can be used to bind (associate) two vectors. Suppose $\mathbf{x}$ and $\mathbf{y}$ are two n-dimensional vectors. For notational convenience I assume n that is odd and that vector indices are centered about zero, so $\mathbf{x} = (x_{-(n-1)/2}, \ldots, x_{(n-1)/2})$ and $\mathbf{y} = (y_{-(n-1)/2}, \ldots, y_{(n-1)/2})$. The convolution operation, denoted by "$*$", is defined as

$$\mathbf{z} = \mathbf{x} * \mathbf{y} \quad \text{where} \quad z_j = \sum_{k=-(n-1)/2}^{(n-1)/2} x_k y_{j-k} \quad \text{for } j = -(n-1) \text{ to } n-1$$

Like the outer product, convolution stores information about the association of $\mathbf{x}$ and $\mathbf{y}$ in a distributed fashion over the elements of $\mathbf{z}$. Unlike the outer product, convolution is commutative, i.e., $\mathbf{x} * \mathbf{y} = \mathbf{y} * \mathbf{x}$.[20] Convolution can in fact be viewed as a compression of the outer product. Figure 28 shows the outer product of two 3-dimensional vectors, and Figure 29 shows how the elements of the outer product are summed to form the convolution. Convolution does increase the dimensionality of vectors, but not as drastically as the outer product: $\mathbf{z} = \mathbf{x} * \mathbf{y}$ has $2n - 1$ elements. Convolution can be applied recursively – the above definition is easily modified to handle $\mathbf{x}$ and $\mathbf{y}$ with different numbers of elements. The dimension of convolution products increases with the number of vectors in the product: $\mathbf{w} * \mathbf{x} * \mathbf{y}$ has $3n - 2$ elements. In general a k-way convolution has $k(n - 1) + 1$ elements.[21] Convolution is associative, i.e., $(\mathbf{w} * \mathbf{x}) * \mathbf{y} = \mathbf{w} * (\mathbf{x} * \mathbf{y})$. This together with commutativity means that the order of vectors in a convolution product does not matter.

The convolution of two vectors can be decoded by correlation. The correlation operation, denoted by "$\#$", is defined as:

$$\mathbf{w} = \mathbf{x} \# \mathbf{z} \quad \text{where} \quad w_j = \sum_{k=-(n-1)/2}^{(n-1)/2} x_{k-j} z_k \quad \text{for } j = -(n-1) \text{ to } n-1$$

Suppose $\mathbf{z} = \mathbf{x} * \mathbf{y}$. Then, under certain conditions on the elements of $\mathbf{x}$ and $\mathbf{y}$, correlating $\mathbf{x}$ with $\mathbf{z}$ reconstructs $\mathbf{y}$, with some noise:[22]

$$\mathbf{x} \# \mathbf{z} \approx \mathbf{y}$$

---

[20]The commutativity of convolution has consequences for psychological models. See Pike (1984) for a discussion.

[21]In Chapter 3 I describe a version of convolution that does not increase vector dimensionality.

[22]The *noise* in the decoding is not stochastic noise – for a particular choice of random vectors the noise in decoding is always the same. However, over different choices of random vectors, this noise can be treated as random noise.

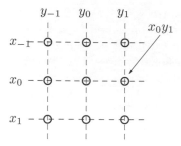

FIGURE 28 The outer product of two vectors. Each of the small circles at the intersection of a pair of lines represents a component of the outer product of **x** and **y**.

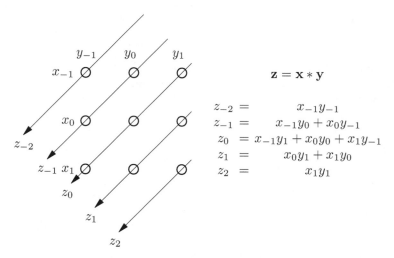

$$z = x * y$$

$$
\begin{aligned}
z_{-2} &= x_{-1}y_{-1} \\
z_{-1} &= x_{-1}y_0 + x_0 y_{-1} \\
z_0 &= x_{-1}y_1 + x_0 y_0 + x_1 y_{-1} \\
z_1 &= x_0 y_1 + x_1 y_0 \\
z_2 &= x_1 y_1
\end{aligned}
$$

FIGURE 29 Convolution represented as a compressed outer product for $n = 3$. The convolution of **x** and **y** consists of sums (along the lines) of outer product elements. Vector indices are centered on zero for notational convenience – vectors grow in dimensionality (at both ends) with recursive convolution.

The noise is lower with vectors of higher dimension. A sufficient condition for this reconstruction to hold is that the elements of **x** and **y** are independently distributed as $N(0, 1/n)$ (i.e., normally distributed with mean zero and variance $1/n$). Under this condition the expected Euclidean length of vectors is 1. Under other conditions the reconstruction is exact – I discuss these conditions and other properties of convolution and correlation in Chapter 3. Correlation is closely related to convolution: $\mathbf{x}\#\mathbf{z} = \mathbf{x}^* *\mathbf{z}$, where $\mathbf{x}^*$ is the mirror image of **x** (around the zero'th element), i.e., $x_i^* = x_{-i}$. Writing expressions with $\mathbf{x}^*$ and convolution instead of correlation makes them easier to manipulate, because convolution is associative and commutative, whereas correlation is neither.

As with outer products in matrix memories, convolution products can be superimposed to give a set of associations. This is often referred to as a memory *trace,* and sometimes has other information superimposed as well. The individual associations in a trace can be decoded separately, provided that the vectors in different associations are not too similar. For example, suppose $t = x * y + z * w$, where the elements of x, y, z and w are independently distributed as $N(0, 1/n)$. Then, any member of a pair can be extracted from t given the other member of the pair, e.g.:

$$x^* * t \approx y \quad \text{and} \quad w^* * t \approx z.$$

The noise in the extracted vectors is quite large and increases as more associations are added to the trace. The signal-to-noise ratio is usually less than 1 even when there is only one association in the trace. However, if the dimension of the vectors is sufficiently large, extracted vectors can be reliably recognized and cleaned up. To recognize vectors we need a measure of similarity. The dot product (vector inner product) is usually used for this. The dot product is defined as:

$$x \cdot y = \sum_i x_i y_i$$

If x and y are chosen so that elements are independently distributed as $N(0, 1)$, then the expected value of $x \cdot x$ is one, and the expected value of $x \cdot y$ is zero. If the vectors are normalized (so that $x \cdot x = 1$) the dot product is equal to the cosine of the angle between them. To recognize and clean up extracted vectors we must have all vectors stored in an error-correcting clean-up memory. The clean-up memory should find and output the most similar matching vector for a given input (i.e., the one with the highest dot product). For example, we clean up the result y' of extracting what is bound to x in $t = (x * y + z * w)$ $(y' = x^* * t)$ by passing y' to the clean-up memory. If we are lucky (and if the dimension is high enough the odds will be good) the vector in clean-up memory most similar to y' will be y, and y can be considered the result of the clean-up operation. This recognition process is the *matched filter* used by Anderson (1973) to identify components of a superposition of random vectors.

Higher-order convolutions can be decoded in a similar manner. For example, if $t = x * y * z$, then pairwise convolutions or items can be extracted from it:

$$x^* * t \approx y * z, \quad (x * y)^* * t \approx z, \quad (x * z)^* * t \approx y.$$

Convolution is a versatile operation for associating vectors. Associations of different orders, as well as plain unconvolved vectors, can be superimposed in a single memory trace. Although associations of different orders have different numbers of elements, lower-order associations can be padded with zeros. Generally, associations of different orders do not interfere with each other – the expected similarity (dot product) of $\mathbf{x}$ and $\mathbf{x} * \mathbf{y}$ is zero.

Human memory modeling: models and tasks

Liepa (1977), Murdock (1982, 1983, 1993), and Metcalfe Eich (1982, 1985), Metcalfe (1991) have proposed various models of human memory for sequences and lists of paired-associates, all based on convolution storage methods. I mention the various storage schemes here, but omit many of the details and intricacies of psychological data that motivate differences among them. For the sake of simplicity, I just give an example of how a storage scheme stores a short sequence or small set of pairs, unless it is unclear how the scheme generalizes to longer sequences or lists. Most of these schemes have scalar parameters that control how much weight each component is given in the trace. I omit these parameters where they are unimportant to the gross characteristics of the scheme.

These models are designed to perform various recall and recognition tasks. For example, a subject might be asked to memorize the list "cow-horse, car-truck, dog-cat, and pen-pencil" and then answer such questions as "Did 'car' appear in the list?" (recognition), or "What was 'cat' associated with?" (cued recall). In a sequence recall task the subject might be asked to recall the entire sequence, or recall what item followed another, or recognize whether an item appeared in the sequence at all. Subjects' relative abilities to perform these and other tasks under different conditions, and the types of errors they produce, give insight into the properties of human memory. Some commonly varied conditions are: the number of pairs or length of sequences, the familiarity of items, and the similarity of items (both within and across pairs).

Liepa: CADAM models

Liepa (1977) describe various schemes for storing lists of paired-associates and sequences, under the name of *Content-Addressable Distributed Associative Memory* (CADAM). His scheme for storing paired associates is unadorned pairwise convolution. For example, the two pairs $(\mathbf{a}, \mathbf{b})$ and $(\mathbf{c}, \mathbf{d})$ are stored as:

$$\mathbf{T} = \mathbf{a} * \mathbf{b} + \mathbf{c} * \mathbf{d}$$

With this scheme, it is easy to model cued recall ("What was paired with **b**?"), but it is not so easy to do other things such as recognition ("Did **a** appear in the list"), because there is no information about individual items in the trace. Liepa's scheme for sequences is more interesting, each item is stored by associating it with the convolution of all previous items. The sequence **abcd** is stored as:

$$\mathbf{T} = \mathbf{a} + \mathbf{a} * \mathbf{b} + \mathbf{a} * \mathbf{b} * \mathbf{c} + \mathbf{a} * \mathbf{b} * \mathbf{c} * \mathbf{d}$$

This scheme supports sequential recall in the following manner:

$$
\begin{aligned}
\mathbf{T} &= \underline{\mathbf{a}} + \mathbf{a} * \mathbf{b} + \mathbf{a} * \mathbf{b} * \mathbf{c} + \mathbf{a} * \mathbf{b} * \mathbf{c} * \mathbf{d} \\
&\approx \mathbf{a} \\
\mathbf{a}^* * \mathbf{T} &= \mathbf{a}^* * \mathbf{a} + \underline{\mathbf{a}^* * \mathbf{a} * \mathbf{b}} + \mathbf{a}^* * \mathbf{a} * \mathbf{b} * \mathbf{c} \\
&\quad + \mathbf{a}^* * \mathbf{a} * \mathbf{b} * \mathbf{c} * \mathbf{d} \\
&\approx \mathbf{b} \\
(\mathbf{a} * \mathbf{b})^* * \mathbf{T} &= (\mathbf{a} * \mathbf{b})^* * \mathbf{a} + (\mathbf{a} * \mathbf{b})^* * \mathbf{a} * \mathbf{b} \\
&\quad + \underline{(\mathbf{a} * \mathbf{b})^* * \mathbf{a} * \mathbf{b} * \mathbf{c}} + \dots \\
&\approx \mathbf{c} \\
(\mathbf{a} * \mathbf{b} * \mathbf{c})^* * \mathbf{T} &= (\mathbf{a} * \mathbf{b} * \mathbf{c})^* * \mathbf{a} + \dots + \underline{(\mathbf{a} * \mathbf{b} * \mathbf{c})^* * \mathbf{a} * \mathbf{b} * \mathbf{c} * \mathbf{d}} \\
&\approx \mathbf{d}
\end{aligned}
$$

The decoding cues must be built up out of retrieved items as the sequence is unraveled. Each of these equations holds (approximately) because the underlined terms, such as $\mathbf{a}^* * \mathbf{a} * \mathbf{b} (\approx \mathbf{b})$, are similar to items in the clean-up memory. The other terms, such as $\mathbf{a}^* * \mathbf{a}$ and $\mathbf{a}^* * \mathbf{a} * \mathbf{b} * \mathbf{c}$, are not likely to be similar to anything in clean-up memory, assuming all the vectors have been chosen randomly. This scheme is not subject to the obvious pitfall of chaining schemes, which is that repeated items could cause jumps or loops. However, Liepa's scheme does not support sequential decoding starting from a named item or subsequence, or item recognition without decoding. This makes it somewhat unsatisfactory as a model of how the human brain stores sequences, because people can perform both of these tasks quite well.

Murdock: TODAM

Murdock (1982, 1983) proposes a *Theory of Distributed Associative Memory* (TODAM) in which both item and associative information are superimposed in the memory trace. TODAM has different schemes for storing sequences and lists of paired-associates. The scheme for paired-associates (Murdock, 1982) stores $(\mathbf{a}, \mathbf{b})$ and $(\mathbf{c}, \mathbf{d})$ as:

$$\mathbf{T} = \mathbf{a} + \mathbf{b} + \mathbf{a} * \mathbf{b} + \mathbf{c} + \mathbf{d} + \mathbf{c} * \mathbf{d}$$

Here, the item information is $\mathbf{a} + \mathbf{b} + \mathbf{c} + \mathbf{d}$ and the pair information is $\mathbf{a} * \mathbf{b} + \mathbf{c} * \mathbf{d}$. Murdock uses several parameters to control the relative contributions of item and pair information and the decay of the trace as more pairs are added in. This representation supports both cued recall and item recognition. The processes for these two tasks are different. Cued recall involves correlating the trace with the cue and cleaning up the result, whereas item recognition involves calculating the dot product of the cue and the trace and comparing the result against a threshold.

The scheme for serial information (Murdock, 1983) is similar. The memory trace for the series $\{\mathbf{f}_1, \ldots, \mathbf{f}_k\}$ is built up iteratively using chaining:

$$\begin{aligned} \mathbf{M}_1 &= \mathbf{f}_1 \\ \mathbf{M}_j &= \alpha \mathbf{M}_{j-1} + \gamma \mathbf{f}_j + \omega \mathbf{f}_j * \mathbf{f}_{j-1} \quad \text{(for } j \geq 2) \end{aligned}$$

where $\mathbf{M}_j$ is the representation for the sequence up to $\mathbf{f}_j$. I show the weighting parameters because correct recall of the first item in the series depends on the relative weighting of the items. The intermediate and final traces for the sequence $\{\mathbf{a}, \mathbf{b}, \mathbf{c}, \mathbf{d}\}$ are the following:

$$\begin{aligned} \mathbf{M}_1 &= \mathbf{a} \\ \mathbf{M}_2 &= \gamma \mathbf{b} + \omega(\mathbf{b} * \mathbf{a}) + \alpha \mathbf{a} \\ \mathbf{M}_3 &= \gamma \mathbf{c} + \omega(\mathbf{c} * \mathbf{b}) + \alpha \gamma \mathbf{b} + \alpha \omega(\mathbf{b} * \mathbf{a}) + \alpha^2 \mathbf{a} \\ \mathbf{M}_4 &= \gamma \mathbf{d} + \omega(\mathbf{d} * \mathbf{c}) + \alpha \gamma \mathbf{c} + \alpha \omega(\mathbf{c} * \mathbf{b}) + \alpha^2 \gamma \mathbf{b} + \alpha^2 \omega(\mathbf{b} * \mathbf{a}) + \alpha^3 \mathbf{a} \end{aligned}$$

This representation can support a number of recall and recognition tasks. Item recognition is the same as for the paired-associates scheme. Whole sequences can be recognized by forming a trace for the probe sequence in the same manner and comparing it (by the dot product) to the memorized trace. Similar sequences will have higher dot products than dissimilar sequences. Lewandowsky and Murdock (1989) use this model to explain human subjects' performance on a number of serial learning and recall tasks.

To do serial recall we must first find the item with the highest weight (parameters must be chosen so that $\alpha^{k-1} > \gamma$). For the above trace ($\mathbf{M}_4$) this will be $\mathbf{a}$ (assuming that superimposing the items and pairs has not upset the relative weights of items). Then we follow the chain of pairs, correlating the trace with the current item to retrieve the next. The commutativity of convolution results in a minor problem in decoding. When we correlate with an interior item the result is a superposition of the previous and next items. For example, correlating $\mathbf{M}_4$ with $\mathbf{b}$ yields the superposition of $\mathbf{a}$ and $\mathbf{c}$. The decoding process must take this into account. It seems this scheme will not be adequate for sequences that contain repeated items. The above serial recall process could jump or loop on encountering a repeated item, and there is no obvious way in which this could be fixed.

Murdock remarks that TODAM memory traces can be regarded as memory chunks. Traces can be treated as items in their own right, and composed in a hierarchical fashion. Murdock does not give any examples, but here is how one might look. For clarity, I omit the weighting factors. Suppose we have the two chunks (traces) for the sequences $\{\mathbf{a}, \mathbf{b}\}$ and $\{\mathbf{c}, \mathbf{d}, \mathbf{e}\}$:

$$
\begin{aligned}
\mathbf{C}_1 &= \mathbf{a} + \mathbf{b} + \mathbf{a} * \mathbf{b} \\
\mathbf{C}_2 &= \mathbf{c} + \mathbf{d} + \mathbf{e} + \mathbf{c} * \mathbf{d} + \mathbf{d} * \mathbf{e}
\end{aligned}
$$

A sequence composed of these two chunks, and its expansion, would be stored as:

$$
\begin{aligned}
\mathbf{C} &= \mathbf{C}_1 + \mathbf{C}_2 + \mathbf{C}_1 * \mathbf{C}_2 \\
&= \mathbf{a} + \mathbf{b} + \mathbf{a} * \mathbf{b} + \mathbf{c} + \mathbf{d} + \mathbf{e} + \mathbf{c} * \mathbf{d} + \mathbf{d} * \mathbf{e} \\
&\quad + (\mathbf{a} + \mathbf{b} + \mathbf{a} * \mathbf{b}) * (\mathbf{c} + \mathbf{d} + \mathbf{e} + \mathbf{c} * \mathbf{d} + \mathbf{d} * \mathbf{e})
\end{aligned}
$$

This brings up the possibility that TODAM traces could function as a reduced description. The only problem with this is that the dimension of vectors grows with recursive convolution – not as fast as tensor products grow, but they still grow. It is not inconceivable that some chunks could be nested quite a few levels deep, and it is somewhat inelegant (and impractical) for vectors representing high-level chunks to be several times wider than vectors representing low-level chunks.

Murdock (1983) briefly discusses how predicates might be represented in the TODAM model. He suggests three different ways of storing the predicate $\mathbf{p}(\mathbf{a}, \mathbf{b})$:

$$
\begin{aligned}
\mathbf{P}_1 &= \mathbf{p} * \mathbf{a} + \mathbf{a} * \mathbf{b} \\
\mathbf{P}_2 &= \mathbf{p} * \mathbf{a} + \mathbf{p} * \mathbf{b} \\
\mathbf{P}_3 &= \mathbf{p} * \mathbf{a} * \mathbf{b}
\end{aligned}
$$

The first two of these methods are simple chaining representations, the first in the order $\{\mathbf{p}, \mathbf{a}, \mathbf{b}\}$ and the second in the order $\{\mathbf{a}, \mathbf{p}, \mathbf{b}\}$. The third stores the predicate as a triple. None of these methods is entirely satisfactory. The first and second method assume some ordering on the arguments of a predicate. The second and third methods lose argument order information – p(a,b) and p(b,a) have the same representation. With the third method it is difficult to retrieve the arguments knowing only the predicate name – it is only easy to decode one argument if we already know the predicate name and one other argument. All three methods fare poorly if some arguments are optional – the retrieval processes for a particular argument changes according to which other arguments are present. These problems are not insurmountable, but as Murdock points out, there are many ways predicates can be represented using convolution, and other ways could be superior.

Metcalfe: CHARM

Metcalfe Eich (1982, 1985), Metcalfe (1991) proposes another convolution-based representation for paired-associates lists. She uses this representation in her *Composite Holographic Associative Recall Model* (CHARM). CHARM differs from Murdock's TODAM in that item information is stored in the memory trace in the form of auto-convolutions. For example, the pairs $(\mathbf{a}, \mathbf{b})$ and $(\mathbf{c}, \mathbf{d})$ are stored as:

$$\mathbf{T} = \mathbf{a} * \mathbf{a} + \mathbf{b} * \mathbf{b} + \mathbf{a} * \mathbf{b} + \mathbf{c} * \mathbf{c} + \mathbf{d} * \mathbf{d} + \mathbf{c} * \mathbf{d}$$

The significance of this is that the recognition process is nearly identical to the recall process. Testing whether $\mathbf{a}$ is present in the trace involves correlating the trace with $\mathbf{a}$, and computing similarity of the result to $\mathbf{a}$. This leads to CHARM and TODAM making different predictions about the dependence of recall and recognition in the presence of similarity among items in the trace. Metcalfe (1991) claims that the data on human performance is more in line with the predictions derived from CHARM.

Murdock: TODAM2

Murdock (1992, 1993), in response to some failings of the TODAM model, proposes a more general and more complex scheme for storing sequences and lists of paired associates. Murdock calls this new model TODAM2. I will not describe TODAM2 in full – I will only explain the *chunking* idea that is a central component of it.

A *chunk* is a representation for a sequence of items. The chunk for the sequence $\{\mathbf{f}_1, .., \mathbf{f}_k\}$ is:

$$\mathbf{C}_k = \sum_{i=1}^{k} \left(\sum_{j-1}^{i} \mathbf{f}_j \right)^i,$$

where the i'th power of a vector is the vector convolved with itself i times ($\mathbf{a}^2 = \mathbf{a} * \mathbf{a}$). Some examples for the chunks of $\{\mathbf{a}, \mathbf{b}, \mathbf{c}, \mathbf{d}\}$ make this clearer:

$$
\begin{aligned}
\mathbf{C}_1 &= \mathbf{a} \\
\mathbf{C}_2 &= \mathbf{a} + (\mathbf{a} + \mathbf{b})^2 \\
&= \mathbf{a} + (\mathbf{a} + \mathbf{b}) * (\mathbf{a} + \mathbf{b}) \\
&= \mathbf{a} + \mathbf{a} * \mathbf{a} + 2\mathbf{a} * \mathbf{b} + \mathbf{b} * \mathbf{b} \\
\mathbf{C}_3 &= \mathbf{a} + (\mathbf{a} + \mathbf{b})^2 + (\mathbf{a} + \mathbf{b} + \mathbf{c})^3 \\
\mathbf{C}_4 &= \mathbf{a} + (\mathbf{a} + \mathbf{b})^2 + (\mathbf{a} + \mathbf{b} + \mathbf{c})^3 + (\mathbf{a} + \mathbf{b} + \mathbf{c} + \mathbf{d})^4
\end{aligned}
$$

For representing sequences, TODAM2 uses one chunk for the entire sequence, unless the sequence is broken down into subsequences. For paired associates, TODAM2 uses a chunk for each pair. Chunks contain all the convolution products used in CADAM, TODAM, and CHARM, thus the access processes of these models can be used with chunks.

Murdock uses chunks for two reasons: to support recall of missing items, and to create higher-order associations, the need for which is argued by Humphreys et al. (1989).

Recall of missing items involves recalling the items from an original list that are not in a new list. For example, given an original list $\{\mathbf{a}, \mathbf{b}, \mathbf{c}\}$ and a new list $\{\mathbf{a}, \mathbf{c}\}$, the missing item is $\mathbf{b}$. This information can be extracted from the chunk for $\{\mathbf{a}, \mathbf{b}, \mathbf{c}\}$ by correlating it with $\mathbf{a} * \mathbf{c}$:

$$
(\mathbf{a} * \mathbf{c})^* * \mathbf{C} = (\mathbf{a} * \mathbf{c})^* * (\mathbf{a} + (\mathbf{a} + \mathbf{b})^2 + (\mathbf{a} + \mathbf{b} + \mathbf{c})^3)
$$

Most of the terms in the expansion of this turn out to be noise, except for:

$$
(\mathbf{a} * \mathbf{c})^* * (6\mathbf{a} * \mathbf{b} * \mathbf{c} + 3\mathbf{a} * \mathbf{c} * \mathbf{c} + 3\mathbf{a} * \mathbf{a} * \mathbf{c}) \approx 6\mathbf{b} + 3\mathbf{c} + 3\mathbf{a},
$$

which can be cleaned up to give $\mathbf{b}$.

A possible problem with Murdock's chunks is that they introduce many higher-order associations for which there is no obvious need, such as $\mathbf{a}^2 * \mathbf{b}$. These dilute the useful associations, which has the effect of adding noise to decoded vectors. This means that a very high vector dimension is required to achieve acceptable levels of reliability. The problem worsens when chunks are composed of more than three items. One wonders whether the reasons for using chunks could be satisfied by some other more economical storage scheme. For example, another way to do missing item recall is to compute the difference of superpositions, as do Hadley et al. (1992):

$$
(\mathbf{a} + \mathbf{b} + \mathbf{c}) - (\mathbf{a} + \mathbf{c}) = \mathbf{b}.
$$

Doing missing item recall in this way does not require any more convolution products or vectors than are already required for other tasks such as item recognition. On the other hand, the higher-order convolution products present in the chunks of TODAM2 might help avoid some of the problems with crosstalk that can arise in memory systems that use superpositions of bindings, as identified by Rachkovskij and Kussul (2001) (see Section 3.11.5).

2.4.5 Binary Spatter Codes

Kanerva's (1996) *Binary Spatter Code* is a scheme for encoding complex compositional structures using role-filler bindings and binary distributed representations (see also Kanerva, 2001). Binary Spatter Codes use dense binary vectors[23] as patterns, elementwise exclusive-or for encoding and decoding bindings, and a thresholded sum for superposition. Both roles and fillers are represented by binary vectors of the same length. Hierarchical structures can be encoded because the representation of a complete frame, i.e., the superposition of several role-filler bindings, is the same length as the representation of any other filler, and can be used as a filler.

It turns out that Binary Spatter Codes have very similar properties to HRRs. Indeed, Binary Spatter Codes are equivalent to HRRs in the frequency domain (which can be accessed through the Fourier transform) with constant power in each frequency and with phase angles quantized to 0 and pi. This relationship is discussed further in Section 4.3.

2.4.6 Associative Projective Neural Networks

Sparse distributed representations (i.e., those in which patterns have relatively few non-zero values) have considerable advantages over more dense representations. Associative memory schemes are more efficient when used to store sparse binary vectors (Willshaw et al., 1969, Baum et al., 1988, Kanerva, 1988).[24] Additionally, some neurophysiological evidence suggests that the neural codes in the brain are quite sparse (Földiák, 2002). However, it is not straightforward to use sparse binary patterns in compositional encoding schemes because commonly used composition operations, especially superposition, can easily create non-sparse patterns.

Rachkovskij and Kussul (2001) present solutions to this problem in their *Associative Projective Neural Networks* (APNNs) scheme (see also

---

[23]In a dense binary vector, around half the elements have value 0 and half have value 1.

[24]Further discussion of the benefits of sparse representations can be found in Olshausen and Field (1996) and Hinton and Ghahramani (1997). These ideas are briefly discussed in Section 2.5.4.

Rachkovskij, 2001). This enables APNNs to encode complex compositional structure in sparse binary distributed representations. Rather than using a binding operation and superposition to create compositional representations (as in most of the schemes described above) APNNs use a family of composition operations that are carefully designed to maintain constant density in code vectors. Each composition operation (which binds several patterns together) is comprised of superposition followed by a *Context Dependent Thinning* operation, which brings the density of the superposition back down to the density of its inputs. For example, the sentence "Sam cooks eggs" could be represented as

$$^2 \langle \mathbf{cook} \vee {}^1 \langle \mathbf{cook}_{agt} \vee \mathbf{Sam} \rangle \vee {}^1 \langle \mathbf{cook}_{obj} \vee \mathbf{eggs} \rangle \rangle$$

where $\vee$ is binary-OR (superposition) and ${}^1 \langle \cdot \rangle$, ${}^2 \langle \cdot \rangle$, etc. are Context Dependent Thinning operations (different thinning operations are used at different levels of nesting.) Given an n-bit vector $\mathbf{z}$ and a target density of m ones ($\mathbf{z}$ might be the superposition of two n-bit vectors $\mathbf{x}$ and $\mathbf{y}$, each having approximately m ones), a context dependent thinning operation removes ones from $\mathbf{z}$ in a way that depends on $\mathbf{z}$ so that the result has approximately m ones. One context dependent thinning operation described by Rachkovskij and Kussul (2001) is *additive thinning*. This uses a series of permutations to thin $\mathbf{z}$ as follows:

$$^i \langle \mathbf{z} \rangle = \mathbf{z} \wedge ({}^i\mathbf{P_1}\mathbf{z} \vee {}^i\mathbf{P_2}\mathbf{z} \vee \cdots \vee {}^i\mathbf{P_k}\mathbf{z})$$

where the ${}^i\mathbf{P_j}$ are matrices that permute the elements of a vector, and k is chosen dependent on $\mathbf{z}$ so that the density of ${}^i \langle \mathbf{z} \rangle$ is as desired (k can be calculated based on the number and density of vectors that are superposed to form $\mathbf{z}$.) The permutation matrices ${}^i\mathbf{P_j}$ are arbitrary random permutations, but are always the same for the same i and j. The composition of vectors is similar to any of its components (i.e., ${}^i \langle \mathbf{x} \vee \mathbf{y} \rangle$ is similar to $\mathbf{x}$ and to $\mathbf{y}$.) This makes it simple to decode structures, provided that all chunks and compositions are stored in an auto-associative memory. For example, $^2 \langle \mathbf{cook} \vee {}^1 \langle \mathbf{cook}_{agt} \vee \mathbf{Sam} \rangle \vee {}^1 \langle \mathbf{cook}_{obj} \vee \mathbf{eggs} \rangle \rangle$ is similar to $\mathbf{cook}$, ${}^1 \langle \mathbf{cook}_{agt} \vee \mathbf{Sam} \rangle$, and ${}^1 \langle \mathbf{cook}_{obj} \vee \mathbf{eggs} \rangle$, and in turn ${}^1 \langle \mathbf{cook}_{obj} \vee \mathbf{eggs} \rangle$ is similar to $\mathbf{cook}_{obj}$ and $\mathbf{eggs}$.

Rachkovskij (2001) shows that APNNs have very similar capabilities to HRRs and Binary Spatter Codes with respect to structure representation and processing.

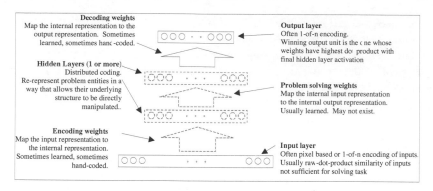

FIGURE 30   Levels of representation in an archetypal feedforward neural network.

2.5   Learning distributed representations

One of the basic problems with distributed representations is coming up with the codes for the particular objects to be represented. A distributed representation that is useful for solving a particular problem is usually a re-representation of the raw input (possibly sensory data). It represents, in a salient manner, the *semantic* features of the input (i.e., features that are relevant to solving the problem). The raw inputs to a neural network often carry few or no clues, in terms of simple dot-product similarity of activity in the input units, as to which inputs should be treated as similar or identical, and which should be treated as different. For a feedforward neural network such as the one in Figure 30 to solve such a problem in a parsimonious fashion the inputs must be re-represented, in the hidden layers, in a manner such that semantically similar, but neurally dissimilar, inputs evoke neurally similar activation patterns in hidden layers. E.g., if input patterns A and B are neurally dissimilar (i.e., have low dot-product similarity) but should produce the same output from the network, then one way for a network to do that is to have the weights entering the hidden layer transform the neurally dissimilar input layer patterns A and B into the neurally similar hidden-layer patterns A' and B'.

The techniques used in the literature for developing distributed representations can be classified into five broad categories: (1) random; (2) hand constructed; (3) learned in a supervised neural network from examples of input-output mappings; and (4) learned in an unsupervised neural network from examples of typical inputs (with no outputs presented); and (5) derived mathematically from summary statistics of data. Unfortunately, there have not been any successful attempts to systematically learn, on a large scale, distributed representations for objects with complex structure.

2.5.1 Hand-constructed representations

Many researchers have constructed distributed representation by hand, often based on features of inputs that are known or suspected to be useful. For example, Rumelhart and McClelland's (1986a) past-tense acquisition model used a hand-constructed distributed representation based on *Wickelfeatures.* To code a word in Wickelfeatures one first builds an unordered set of its Wickelphones, which are the triples of three consecutive phonemes in the word. For example, the word *came* contains three Wickelphones: #kA, kAm, and Am# (its three phonemes are k, A, and m, and # is used as a start and end symbol). The second step in representing a word was to turn on all the Wickelfeatures that responded to any of the Wickelphones in the word. Rumelhart and McClelland devised a set of 460 Wickelfeatures. Each responded to Wickelphones that had a certain subset of features. For example, one particular Wickelfeature responded to Wickelphones whose preceding context phoneme was an interrupted consonant, whose central phoneme was a vowel, and whose following context phoneme was an interrupted consonant. This Wickelfeature would respond to the Wickelphones kAm , bid , mAp , and many others. The set of 460 Wickelfeatures was chosen so that each Wickelphone would activate 16 Wickelfeatures. This meant that a word with three phonemes would activate 48 or fewer Wickelfeatures, because some Wickelphones might activate the same Wickelfeatures. Order of phonemes within a word is only represented implicitly in both Wickelphone and Wickelfeature representations. Although it is possible to find pairs of words that have the same set of Wickelphones (and/or Wickelfeatures), these are very unusual and did not occur in vocabulary of the model. The patterns of activation over the 460 Wickelfeatures formed a distributed coarse conjunctive code that captured much of the phonemic structure of words that was important to mapping the phonemic root form of an English verb to its phonemic past-tense form. The code was conjunctive because Wickelfeatures responded to conjunctions of features in adjacent phonemes, and was coarse because any particular Wickelfeature responded to many different Wickelphones.

In this book, I use of combination of random and manually constructed distributed representations in order to demonstrate the feasibility of HRRs. A concept (e.g., Fido) is represented by a small set of features (e.g., animal, mammal, dog, the name *Fido*). Each feature is represented by a vector of numbers randomly chosen from a Gaussian distribution. A concept is represented as the normalized superposition of its features. This gives representations for concepts that have many of the statistical properties of random Gaussian vectors, but which also reflect underlying similarities of the domain.

Developing a good distributed code by hand is often time consuming and is generally regarded as a stopgap measure suitable only for demonstrating the potential of a technique.

2.5.2 Representations derived from statistical summaries of data

Latent Semantic Analysis (LSA) (Deerwester et al., 1990) has achieved some remarkable successes in extracting the hidden structure of text documents. LSA can be viewed as a statistical technique for developing distributed representations for words and documents. LSA works by first constructing a term-document frequency matrix X for a collection of documents. The matrix has one row for each document and one column for each word in the collection. Element X_{ij} of the matrix is the count of the number of times word j appears in document i (or some monotonically-nondecreasing function of the count). This results in a very large matrix with many zeros. The next step in LSA is to compress the information in this matrix by applying Singular Value Decomposition and discarding all but the k (typically several hundred) most important dimensions. This results in a k-dimensional vector (pattern) representation for words and for documents. In general, similar words are represented by similar patterns, as are similar documents. The representation is dense, in that each element of the pattern usually takes on a real value from a Gaussian distribution. It also has superpositional properties, in that the pattern representing a document is approximately equal to the superposition of the patterns representing the words the document contains. By compressing the information in the term-document frequency matrix, LSA succeeds in discarding the noise regarding exactly which words were used to express the meanings of each document while retaining the underlying semantic similarity structure of the terms and documents. LSA has been applied to many tasks with a surprising degree of success, from document retrieval (by picking documents with patterns most closely matching the superposition of patterns for words in the query), to learning material from a textbook (it passed the exam!) to grading essays.

2.5.3 Backpropagation for learning representations

One of the most intriguing properties of the backpropagation algorithm applied to multilayer neural networks (such as the one in Figure 30) is its ability to learn distributed representations in its hidden layer that capture the underlying structure of the domain. Hinton's (1989) family trees network is an excellent example of this. For training, this network was presented with an incomplete set of examples of person/relationship/person (e.g., Penelope/Daughter-of/Margaret) from two isomorphic English and Italian family trees, each involving 12 people from three generations. The objective was to see whether, using backpropagation, the network could learn appropriate features in the hidden layers that would allow it to generalize to the relations not included in the training set. There were two groups of input units, one for person (24 units) and one for relationship (12 units), and one group of output units for person (24 units). Each input and output group used a 1-of-n encoding, thus betraying no information about how a particular input should be treated. The network had multiple hidden layers, with fewer units than in the input layer in order to encourage a componential encoding, and was trained using backpropagation with weight decay. After training, the network was able to generalize to unseen relations. Examination of the representations the network developed for the hidden layers indicated that it had used units in the hidden layers to encode underlying important features such as sex, nationality and generation, which were not explicitly present in the input or output.

Other good demonstrations of backpropagation's ability to learn useful internal distributed representations are Le Cun et al. (1989) (handwritten digit recognition), Elman (1991) (learning the structure of sentences generated by a simple artificial grammar for a subset of English), and Pollack (1990) (learning to represent hierarchical data structures).

2.5.4   Learning sparse representations

For some types of input with rich structure, e.g., natural images, useful distributed representations may be learned using unsupervised techniques. These typically work by learning an internal neural code from which the inputs can be reconstructed with a low degree of error. A typical architecture for such a net is shown in Figure 31. Early work with these types of autoencoder networks used the backpropagation algorithm and fewer hidden units than there were input units. This forced the network to learn a compact code to represent the inputs. Bourlard and Kamp (1988) and Baldi and Hornik (1989) showed that for a linear autoencoder network, training to minimize mean-square reconstruction error is equivalent to finding the first k principal components (where k is the number of hidden units). This makes linear autoencoders of limited interest, as it proves that the codes they will develop depend only on the pairwise covariance structure of the input. For example,

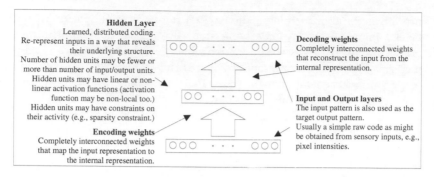

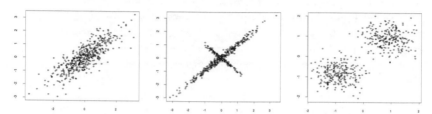

FIGURE 31   Typical autoencoder network. The network attempts to learn weights that map the input patterns an internal representation and then back again to patterns identical to the inputs.

FIGURE 32   Three data sets that have the same pairwise statistics. Each example in each data set is a point in 2-d space. These have the same principal components, and a linear autoencoder network will learn identical encodings for them.

they will develop the same codes for the two-dimensional data sets illustrated in Figure 32, which obviously have quite different underlying structure; (a) is Gaussian; (b) and (c) are non Gaussian.

For higher-dimensional data, e.g., images with binary pixels, this limitation is crippling. Even simple features such as lines and edges of varying contrast and orientation cannot be extracted with a linear mapping from input activations to hidden activations, which is the same as saying they cannot be identified through their pairwise covariance statistics.

If one imposes some constraint on the internal codes, i.e., the activations in the hidden layer, and allows hidden-layer activations to be a nonlinear function of input activations, more interesting results can be obtained. One potentially useful constraint is that internal codes be sparse, i.e., that most activation values in the internal code be zero. This allows the use of overcomplete codes, in which there are more units in the internal code than are used in the input representation. Overcomplete codes require nonlinear computation of hidden-layer activation values from inputs (the reconstruction weights from the hidden layer to the outputs can still be linear). Olshausen and Field (1996) used a network in which the incoming weights to a hidden unit are the same as its outgoing weights, augmented with connections among hidden units and having a settling phase during which the hidden units compete for the right to represent the inputs. The settling phase is in effect a search for a set of hidden-unit activations that maximizes an objective function that trades off sparsity of hidden-unit activation against accuracy of output reconstruction. Outputs are computed from hidden-unit activations in a straightforward linear fashion. Their training algorithm slowly modified the hidden-to-output weights to better allow the network to find sparse hidden-layer activations that could accurately reconstruct a set of natural images. This resulted in an overcomplete set of image features (the weights from one hidden unit to all the output units) that could describe the natural images. This set of image features had the characteristics of localized, oriented, bandpass receptive fields (i.e., receptive fields for short edges or bars of different sizes at different angles). The advantage of being an overcomplete set of image features is that it allows any particular image to be represented with a relatively small set of features well suited to representing that particular image. In this way it also captures some of the higher-order statistical structure of typical inputs that cannot be captured by a more compact principal components representation.

Olshausen and Field's (1996) approach is closely related to Independent Component Analysis (Hyvärinen and Oja, 2000). Hinton and Ghahramani (1997) and Zemel and Hinton (1995) explore other approaches to unsupervised learning of sparse distributed representations that efficiently encode inputs and capture the higher-order statistical structure in a set of inputs. Hinton and Ghahramani see sparse representations as a point on the spectrum between localist hidden-unit representations and principal-component hidden-unit representations. Localist hidden-unit representations have the advantage that they can capture any statistics of the data (each distinct input pattern can be assigned to a single hidden unit) and can represent multiple concepts simultaneously but have the twin disadvantages that they are a very inefficient representation and do not support generalization. Principal-component hidden-unit representations have the advantages that they are compact and efficient and support generalization, but have the disadvantages that they can only capture pairwise input statistics and can only represent a single concept at once. Sparse representations have the potential for blending the advantages of both approaches.

2.5.5 Kernel-based learning methods

Although kernel-based learning methods (Haussler, 1999, Collins and Duffy, 2002) are not commonly considered to use distributed representations, they have enough in common with distributed representations to deserve a mention in this section. In kernel-based methods, entities are represented by high-dimensional vectors. For example, a representation for sequences might use a vector that has an element for every possible subsequence. The dimensionality of the representational space is usually extremely large, and often infinite. Kernel-based methods use clever algorithms to avoid ever explicitly enumerating even the non-zero features of the representational space. The high-dimensional vectors that represent entities could be considered as a variety of sparse distributed representation. Learning with kernel-based methods involves computing statistics over examples and learning which features of the representational space are important. The relationship between kernel-based methods and HRRs is further explored in Section 6.7.8.

3

Holographic Reduced Representation

Nearly all of the schemes for the distributed representation of hierarchical structure reviewed in the previous chapter have serious flaws.[25] In the remainder of this book I present and discuss a scheme, called *Holographic Reduced Representation* (HRR) which I believe overcomes these flaws. HRRs support the useful properties of distributed representations that were identified in Section 1.4.2: explicitness, explicit similarity, redundancy, continuity, and efficiency. They satisfy Hinton's four desiderata for reduced descriptions: they are representationally adequate, the reduced descriptions are represented over fewer units, reduced and full descriptions are related in a systematic manner, and the reduced descriptions give some information about the contents of the full description.

HRRs incorporate ideas and techniques from several fields of research. HRRs are a concrete implementation of Hinton's (1990) notion of *reduced descriptions*. HRRs use the role-filler representation for predicates suggested by Hinton et al. (1986), but bind roles and fillers with convolution instead of the outer product. HRRs are based on convolution, like Murdock's (1982) and Metcalfe Eich's (1982) models, but use a version of convolution (circular convolution) which does not increase the dimensionality of vectors. Hierarchical structure is represented by recursively composing role-filler bindings in similar manner to Smolensky's (1990) recursively composed tensor products, but unlike the tensor product, circular convolution does not increase vector dimensionality.

---

[25]The exceptions are the two recent schemes: Kanerva's (1996) Binary Spatter Codes, and Rachkovskij and Kussul's (2001) *Associative Projective Neural Networks*.

HRRs are constructed in a simple and regular manner using primarily linear operations, as with Smolensky's tensor products (to which HRRs are closely related). This makes it possible to analyze and understand the properties of HRRs, including how well HRRs will scale to larger systems.

The biggest advantage of HRRs is that they make it easy to represent structure. This means that a learning system that uses HRRs does not need to expend computational resources learning how to represent structure – it is free to concentrate on the truly difficult task of learning the important relationships among objects in the task.

3.1 Circular convolution and correlation

Tensor products and ordinary convolution are recursively applicable associative operators, which makes them candidates for the representation of hierarchical structure. However, both increase the dimensionality of vectors, which makes them somewhat impractical for this purpose (although convolution increases dimensionality far less than the tensor product). *Circular convolution* is a version of convolution that does not increase vector dimensionality. It is well known in signal processing (sometimes as *wrapped* convolution, e.g., Gabel and Roberts (1973)) but its only use in associative memories has been by Willshaw et al. (1969) in their *nonlinear correlograph*. The result of the circular convolution of two vectors of n elements has just n elements – there is no expansion of dimensionality. Like ordinary convolution, circular convolution can be regarded as a compression of the outer product of two vectors, as illustrated in Figure 33.

Circular convolution can be regarded as a multiplication operator for vectors. It has many properties in common with both scalar and matrix multiplication. It is commutative: $\mathbf{x} \circledast \mathbf{y} = \mathbf{y} \circledast \mathbf{x}$; associative: $\mathbf{x} \circledast (\mathbf{y} \circledast \mathbf{z}) = (\mathbf{x} \circledast \mathbf{y}) \circledast \mathbf{z}$; and bilinear[26]: $\mathbf{x} \circledast (\alpha \mathbf{y} + \beta \mathbf{z}) = \alpha \mathbf{x} \circledast \mathbf{y} + \beta \mathbf{x} \circledast \mathbf{z}$. There is an identity vector: $\bar{\mathbf{I}} \circledast \mathbf{x} = \mathbf{x}$, $\bar{\mathbf{I}} = [1, 0, 0, \ldots]$; and a zero vector: $\bar{0} \circledast \mathbf{x} = \bar{0}$ and $\mathbf{x} + \bar{0} = \mathbf{x}$, $\bar{0} = [0, 0, 0, \ldots]$. For nearly all vectors $\mathbf{x}$, an exact inverse exists: $\mathbf{x}^{-1} \circledast \mathbf{x} = \bar{\mathbf{I}}$. For vectors from certain distributions, there is a stable approximate inverse that is generally more useful than the exact inverse. In algebraic expressions I give convolution the same precedence as multiplication, so that $\mathbf{x} \circledast \mathbf{y} + \mathbf{z} = (\mathbf{x} \circledast \mathbf{y}) + \mathbf{z}$, and higher precedence than the dot product, so that $\mathbf{x} \circledast \mathbf{y} \cdot \mathbf{w} \circledast \mathbf{z} = (\mathbf{x} \circledast \mathbf{y}) \cdot (\mathbf{w} \circledast \mathbf{z})$.

There is also a circular version of correlation, which under certain conditions is an approximate inverse of circular convolution. Circular correlation, $\circledcirc$, can also be regarded as a compression of the outer

---

[26] *Bilinear* means that the operation is linear in both operands.

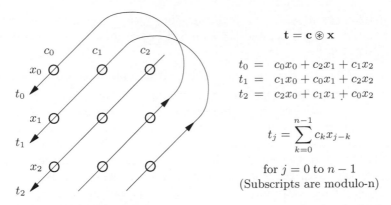

$$\mathbf{t} = \mathbf{c} \circledast \mathbf{x}$$

$$
\begin{aligned}
t_0 &= c_0 x_0 + c_2 x_1 + c_1 x_2 \\
t_1 &= c_1 x_0 + c_0 x_1 + c_2 x_2 \\
t_2 &= c_2 x_0 + c_1 x_1 + c_0 x_2
\end{aligned}
$$

$$t_j = \sum_{k=0}^{n-1} c_k x_{j-k}$$

for $j = 0$ to $n - 1$
(Subscripts are modulo-n)

FIGURE 33 Circular convolution ($\circledast$) represented as a compressed outer product for $n = 3$. The circles represent the elements of the outer product of $\mathbf{x}$ and $\mathbf{c}$. The elements of the convolution are the sum, along the wrapped diagonals, of the elements of the outer product.

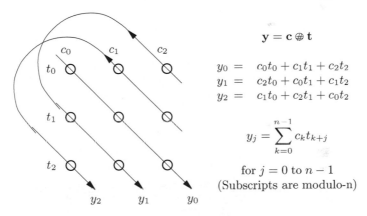

$$\mathbf{y} = \mathbf{c} \oplus \mathbf{t}$$

$$
\begin{aligned}
y_0 &= c_0 t_0 + c_1 t_1 + c_2 t_2 \\
y_1 &= c_2 t_0 + c_0 t_1 + c_1 t_2 \\
y_2 &= c_1 t_0 + c_2 t_1 + c_0 t_2
\end{aligned}
$$

$$y_j = \sum_{k=0}^{n-1} c_k t_{k+j}$$

for $j = 0$ to $n - 1$
(Subscripts are modulo-n)

FIGURE 34 Circular correlation ($\oplus$) represented as a compressed outer product for $n = 3$.

product, as illustrated in Figure 34.

Suppose we have a trace that is the convolution of a cue with another vector, $\mathbf{t} = \mathbf{c} \circledast \mathbf{x}$. Correlation of $\mathbf{c}$ with $\mathbf{t}$ reconstructs a distorted version of $\mathbf{x}$: $\mathbf{y} = \mathbf{c} \oplus \mathbf{t}$ and $\mathbf{y} \approx \mathbf{x}$.

Multiple associations, as in a paired-associates memory, can be represented by the sum of the individual associations. Upon decoding, the contribution of the irrelevant terms can be ignored as distortion. For example, if $\mathbf{t} = \mathbf{c}_1 \circledast \mathbf{x}_1 + \mathbf{c}_2 \circledast \mathbf{x}_2$, then the result of decoding of $\mathbf{t}$ with $\mathbf{c}_1$ is $\mathbf{c}_1 \oplus \mathbf{c}_1 \circledast \mathbf{x}_1 + \mathbf{c}_1 \oplus \mathbf{c}_2 \circledast \mathbf{x}_2$. If the vectors have been chosen randomly the second term will, with high probability, have low correlation with all of $\mathbf{c}_1, \mathbf{c}_2, \mathbf{x}_1$ and $\mathbf{x}_2$ and the sum will be recognizable as a distorted version of $\mathbf{x}_1$.

3.1.1 Distributional constraints on the elements of vectors

A sufficient condition for correlation to decode convolution is that the elements of each vector (of dimension n) be independently and identically distributed with mean 0 and variance $1/n$. This results in the expected Euclidean length of a vector being 1. Examples of suitable distributions for elements are the normal distribution and the discrete distribution with values equiprobably $\pm 1/\sqrt{n}$. The reasons for these distributional constraints should become apparent in the next subsection.

The tension between these constraints and the conventional use of particular elements of vectors to represent meaningful features in distributed representations is discussed in Section 3.5.

3.1.2 Why correlation decodes convolution

It is not immediately obvious why correlation decodes convolution. However, it is not hard to see if an example is worked through. Consider vectors with three elements, $\mathbf{c} = (c_0, c_1, c_2)$ (the cue), and $\mathbf{x} = (x_0, x_1, x_2)$, where the c_i and x_i are independently drawn from $N(0, 1/n)$ (i.e., a normal distribution with mean 0 and variance $1/n$, $n = 3$ in this example). The convolution of $\mathbf{c}$ and $\mathbf{x}$ is:

$$\mathbf{c} \circledast \mathbf{x} = \begin{bmatrix} c_0 x_0 + c_1 x_2 + c_2 x_1 \\ c_0 x_1 + c_1 x_0 + c_2 x_2 \\ c_0 x_2 + c_1 x_1 + c_2 x_0 \end{bmatrix}$$

We can reconstruct $\mathbf{x}$ from this trace by correlating with the cue $\mathbf{c}$:

$$\mathbf{c} \oplus (\mathbf{c} \circledast \mathbf{x})$$

$$= \begin{bmatrix} x_0(c_0^2 + c_1^2 + c_2^2) + x_1 c_0 c_2 + x_2 c_0 c_1 + x_1 c_0 c_1 \\ \quad + x_2 c_1 c_2 + x_1 c_1 c_2 + x_2 c_0 c_2 \\ x_1(c_0^2 + c_1^2 + c_2^2) + x_0 c_0 c_1 + x_2 c_0 c_2 + x_0 c_0 c_2 \\ \quad + x_2 c_1 c_2 + x_0 c_1 c_2 + x_2 c_0 c_1 \\ x_2(c_0^2 + c_1^2 + c_2^2) + x_0 c_0 c_1 + x_1 c_1 c_2 + x_0 c_1 c_2 \\ \quad + x_1 c_0 c_2 + x_0 c_0 c_2 + x_1 c_0 c_1 \end{bmatrix}$$

$$= \begin{bmatrix} x_0(1 + \zeta) + \eta_0 \\ x_1(1 + \zeta) + \eta_1 \\ x_2(1 + \zeta) + \eta_2 \end{bmatrix} = (1 + \zeta)\mathbf{x} + \bar{\eta}$$

where ζ and the η_i can be treated as zero-mean noise. The variances of ζ and the η_i are inversely proportional to n. The distributions of the ζ and η_i are normal in the limit as n goes to infinity, and the approximation to the normal is excellent for n as small as 16. In general, it is safe to use the normal approximations because typical values for n in convolution-based associative memory systems are in the hundreds and thousands.

Using the central limit theorem, and assuming the c_i and x_i are independent and distributed as $N(0, 1/n)$, the distributions of ζ and the η_i for large n are as follows:

$\zeta \overset{d}{=} N(0, \frac{2}{n})$, since $\zeta = (c_0^2 + c_1^2 + \ldots + c_n^2) - 1$, and the c_i^2 are independent and have mean $1/n$ and variance $2/n^2$.

$\eta_i \overset{d}{=} N(0, \frac{n-1}{n^2})$, since the $n(n-1)$ terms like $x_j c_k c_l$ ($k \neq l$) have mean 0 and variance $1/n^3$, and the pairwise covariances of these terms are zero.

It is more useful to calculate the variance of the dot product $\mathbf{x} \cdot (\mathbf{c} \oplus (\mathbf{c} \circledast \mathbf{x}))$ than the variances of the elements of $\mathbf{c} \oplus (\mathbf{c} \circledast \mathbf{x})$, because this can be used to calculate the probability of correct decoding. This in turn allows us to calculate the minimum dimension (n) for which the probability of correct decoding associations is acceptable. However, calculating these variances is not simple, because one must take into account the covariances of the noise terms in the different elements. Extensive tables of variances for dot products of various convolution products have been compiled by Weber (1988) for unwrapped convolution. Unfortunately, these do not apply exactly to circular convolution. The means and variances for dot products of some common circular convolution products will be given in Table 3 in Section 3.6.1.

3.1.3 Relationship of convolution to correlation

The correlation of $\mathbf{c}$ and $\mathbf{t}$ is equivalent to the convolution of $\mathbf{t}$ with the *involution* of $\mathbf{c}$ (Schönemann, 1987). The involution of $\mathbf{c}$ is the vector $\mathbf{d} = \mathbf{c}^*$ such that $d_i = c_{-i}$, where subscripts are modulo-n.[27] For example, if $\mathbf{c} = (c_0, c_1, c_2, c_3)$, then $\mathbf{c}^* = (c_0, c_3, c_2, c_1)$. Writing $\mathbf{c}^* \circledast \mathbf{t}$ is preferable to writing $\mathbf{c} \oplus \mathbf{t}$ because it simplifies algebra, since correlation is neither associative nor commutative whereas convolution is both. Involution distributes over addition and convolution, and is its own inverse:

$$(\mathbf{a} + \mathbf{b})^* = \mathbf{a}^* + \mathbf{b}^*, \quad (\mathbf{a} \circledast \mathbf{b})^* = \mathbf{a}^* \circledast \mathbf{b}^*, \quad \mathbf{a}^{**} = \mathbf{a}$$

In analogy to inverse matrices, it is sometimes convenient to refer to $\mathbf{c}^*$ as the *approximate inverse* of $\mathbf{c}$. The exact inverse of vectors under

---

[27] *Involution* has a more general meaning, but in this paper I use it to mean a particular operation.

convolution (i.e., $\mathbf{c}^{-1}$) will be discussed in Section 3.6.3.

3.1.4 How much information is stored in a convolution trace?

Since a convolution trace only has n numbers in it, it may seem strange that several pairs of vectors can be stored in it, since each of those vectors also has n numbers. The reason is that the vectors are stored with very poor fidelity. The convolution trace stores enough information to recognize the vectors in it, but not enough to reconstruct them accurately. For recognition, we only need to store enough information to discriminate an item from other possible items. Suppose we have M equiprobable items, each represented by an n-dimensional vector. About $2k \log_2 M$ bits of information are needed to represent k pairs of those items for the purposes of recognition.[28] The dimensionality of the vectors does not enter into this calculation – only the number of vectors matters.

For example, if we have 1024 items (each represented by a different vector), then the number of bits required to identify four pairs of those items is slightly less than $2 \times 4 \times \log_2 1024 = 80$ bits (this is a slight overestimation because the pairs are unordered). A convolution memory using random vectors with 512 elements can reliably store four pairs of these items (see Appendix D). Storing 80 bits of information in 512 floating-point numbers is not particularly efficient. However, for the storage of complex structure this is not a critical issue because the scaling is linear and there are potentially many ways to improve the efficiency. For example, the floating-point numbers could be stored in reduced precision. Consider the nonlinear correlograph of Willshaw et al.'s (1969). This is the most information-efficient convolution-based associative memory, and all vector elements are stored with one binary digit of precision, i.e., 0 or 1.

3.2 Superposition Memories

One of the simplest ways to store a set of vectors is to superimpose them (i.e., add them together). In general, such storage does not allow for recall or reconstruction of the stored items, but it does allow for recognition, i.e., determining whether a particular item has been stored or not. Anderson (1973) described and analyzed a memory model based on simple superposition of random vectors.

Superposition memory works because adding together two high-dimensional vectors gives a vector that is similar to each and not very

---

[28]Actually, slightly less than $2k \log_2 M$ bits are required if the pairs are unordered.

similar to anything else.[29] This principle underlies the ability to super-impose traces in both convolution and matrix memories.

It is not necessary for elements of vectors to have continuous values for superposition memories to work. Also, their capacity can be improved by applying a suitable nonlinear (e.g., threshold) function to the trace. Touretzky and Hinton (1988) and Rosenfeld and Touretzky (1988) discuss binary distributed memories, in which representations are superimposed by elementwise binary-OR. However, I do not use binary representations in this book because of difficulties with maintaining constant density (see Section 3.5.2).

3.2.1 The probability of correct recognition with superposition memories

It is simple to calculate the probability of correct recognition of a random vector stored in a superposition memory. I do this here because the same techniques are used to calculate the probabilities of correct reconstruction from convolution-based memories. This analysis is essentially the same as that given in Anderson (1973). In this section I give an expression for the probability of correct recognition, but do not give an analytic solution for it, because it involves an optimization. In Appendix B, I report results for the numerical optimization of this equation. In Appendix C I give a lower bound for the solution. The analysis presented here uses concepts from signal detection theory (Green and Swets, 1966).

Suppose we have a superposition memory with the following parameters:

- n: the dimensions of the vectors.
- A set $\mathbb{E}$ of m vectors, $\mathbf{a}, \mathbf{b}, \mathbf{c}, \mathbf{d}$ etc, with elements independently distributed as $N(0, 1/n)$.
- A memory trace $\mathbf{t}$, which is the superposition of k distinct vectors from $\mathbb{E}$. For the purposes of this analysis, normalization is unimportant, so I do not normalize the trace.
- Pr(All Correct), the probability of correctly determining which vectors are and are not stored in the memory trace.
- s_a and s_r, the accept and reject signals (see below).

To test whether a particular vector $\mathbf{x}$ from $\mathbb{E}$ is in the trace $\mathbf{t}$, we compute the dot product of $\mathbf{x}$ and $\mathbf{t}$. The resulting signal will be from one of two distributions; the accept distribution S_a (if $\mathbf{x}$ is in the trace), or the reject distribution S_r (if $\mathbf{x}$ is not in the trace). The means and

---

[29]This applies to the degree that the elements of the vectors are randomly and independently distributed.

variances of these distributions can be calculated by expanding $\mathbf{x} \cdot \mathbf{t}$. For example, consider the trace $\mathbf{t} = \mathbf{a} + \mathbf{b} + \mathbf{c}$, and a signal from the accept distribution:

$$s_a = \mathbf{a} \cdot \mathbf{t} = \mathbf{a} \cdot \mathbf{a} + \mathbf{a} \cdot \mathbf{b} + \mathbf{a} \cdot \mathbf{c}.$$

Consider typical vector elements x_i and y_j, which are independently distributed as $N(0, 1/n)$. It is easy to show that $E[x_i^2] = 1/n$ and $\text{var}[x_i^2] = 2/n^2$, and $E[x_i y_j] = 0$ and $\text{var}[x_i y_j] = 1/n^2$. By the central limit theorem, the terms like $\mathbf{a} \cdot \mathbf{a}$ are distributed as $N(1, 2/n)$, and the terms like $\mathbf{a} \cdot \mathbf{b}$ are distributed as $N(0, 1/n)$. Since these terms all have zero covariance, we can add means and variances to get $s_a \overset{d}{=} N(1, (k+1)/n)$ and $s_r \overset{d}{=} N(0, k/n)$.

The value of the dot product $\mathbf{x} \cdot \mathbf{t}$ (the signal) tells us whether or not the item $\mathbf{x}$ is present in the trace. If the signal is greater than some threshold t we assume that it is from the accept distribution and thus the item is in the trace, and if it is less we assume it is not.

Using cumulative distribution functions, we can work out the probability of correctly deciding an item was stored in a trace ($\text{Pr}(\text{Hit}) = \text{Pr}(s_a > t)$), and the probability of correctly deciding an item was not stored in a trace ($\text{Pr}(\text{Reject}) = \text{Pr}(s_r < t)$). The threshold t can be chosen to maximize the probability of correctly identifying all the items stored (and not stored) in a particular trace:

$$\text{Pr}(\text{All Correct}) = \text{Pr}(\text{Hit})^k \, \text{Pr}(\text{Reject})^{m-k} \tag{3.1}$$
$$= \max_t \; \text{Pr}(s_a > t)^k \, \text{Pr}(s_r < t)^{m-k} \tag{3.2}$$

The probability density functions (pdfs) for s_a and s_r and the optimal single threshold are shown in Figure 35, for an example with $n = 64$, $m = 100$, and $k = 3$ (for which $\text{Pr}(\text{All Correct}) = 0.68$). This threshold was found by numerical optimization of the expression for $\text{Pr}(\text{All Correct})$. We can actually achieve better discrimination by using a double-threshold scheme. In general, the optimal scheme for deciding which of two normal distributions a signal comes from involves testing whether the signal is in a region around the distribution with the smaller variance. However, the improvement gained by using two thresholds is small when misclassification probabilities are low.

This decision procedure is not infallible, but n can be chosen to make the probability of error acceptably low, since the variances of the signals are inversely proportional to n. When the variances of the signals are smaller, the probability of error is lower.

This analysis here treats signal values as random variables, but their

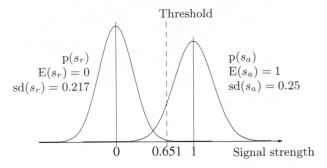

FIGURE 35   Probability density functions for accept (s_a) and reject (s_r) signals for recognition in a linear superposition memory, with $n = 64$ and $k = 3$. The threshold shown maximizes Pr(All Correct) for $m = 100$.

randomness is only a consequence of the random choice of the original vectors. For any particular trace with a particular set of vectors, the signal values are deterministic. This style of analysis is consistently used throughout this paper: there are no stochastic operations, only randomly chosen vectors.

3.2.2   The use of thresholds

Fixed thresholds are helpful in the analysis of probability of correct retrieval but they are not very good for determining the result of a similarity match in practice. The main reason for this is that the optimal threshold varies with both the composition of the trace and with the particular objects that comprise the trace (see Section 3.10.4 for an example). Consequently, no single fixed threshold will be appropriate for choosing the winning matches in all situations, and it is impractical to compute a new threshold for every situation. A simpler scheme is just to choose the most similar match, though this is of limited versatility. A possible enhancement is a no-decision region; if the highest score is not more than some fixed amount greater than the next highest score, then the result is considered unclear.

3.3   The need for clean-up memories

Linear convolution-based memories are not able to provide accurate reconstructions. If a system using convolution representations is to do some sort of recall (as opposed to recognition), it must have an additional error-correcting auto-associative item memory. This is needed to clean up the noisy vectors retrieved from the convolution traces. This clean-up memory must store all the items that the system can produce. When given as input a noisy version of one of those items it must either

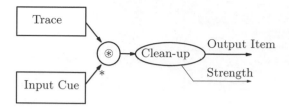

FIGURE 36   A heteroassociator machine. The "*" on the operand to the convolution indicates the approximate inverse is taken.

output the closest item or indicate that the input is not close enough to any of the stored items. Note that one convolution trace stores only a few associations or items, and the clean-up memory stores many items.

For example, suppose the system is to store pairs composed of the random vectors $\mathbf{a}, \mathbf{b}, \ldots, \mathbf{z}$. The clean-up memory must store these 26 vectors and must be able to output the closest item for any input vector (the *clean-up* operation). Such a system is shown in Figure 36. The trace is a sum of convolved pairs, e.g., $\mathbf{t} = \mathbf{a} \circledast \mathbf{b} + \mathbf{c} \circledast \mathbf{d} + \mathbf{e} \circledast \mathbf{f}$. The system is given one item as an input cue and its task is to output the associated item from the trace. It should also output a scalar value (the strength) which is high when the input cue was a member of a pair, and low when the input cue was not a member of a pair. When given the above trace $\mathbf{t}$ and $\mathbf{a}$ as a cue it should produce $\mathbf{b}$ and a high strength. When given $\mathbf{g}$ as a cue it should give a low strength. The item it outputs is unimportant when the strength is low.

Many of systems mentioned in Chapter 2 use some type of clean-up memory. For example, BoltzCONS uses *pull-out* networks, CRAM, and DCPS use *clean-up circuits*, and TODAM uses an *R-system*. The exact method of implementation of the clean-up memory is unimportant. Hopfield networks are probably not a good candidate because of their low capacity in terms of the dimension of the vectors being stored. *Sparse Distributed Memory* networks (Kanerva, 1988) have sufficient capacity, but can only store binary vectors. For the simulations reported in this book I store vectors in a conventional list data structure and compute all dot products in order to find the closest match.

3.4   Representing complex structure

Pairs of items are easy to represent in many types of associative memory, but convolution memory is also suited to the representation of more complex structure, namely sequences, predicates, and recursive predicates (hierarchical structure).

3.4.1 Sequences

Sequences can be represented in a number of ways using convolution encoding. An entire sequence can be represented in one memory trace, with the probability of error increasing with the length of the stored sequence. Alternatively, chunking can be used to represent a sequence of any length in a number of memory traces.

Murdock (1983, 1987), and Lewandowsky and Murdock (1989) propose a chaining method of representing sequences in a single memory trace, and model a large number of psychological phenomena with it. The technique used stores both item and pair information in the memory trace, for example, if the sequence of vectors to be stored is **abc**, then the trace is

$$\alpha_1 \mathbf{a} + \beta_1 \mathbf{a} \circledast \mathbf{b} + \alpha_2 \mathbf{b} + \beta_2 \mathbf{b} \circledast \mathbf{c} + \alpha_3 \mathbf{c},$$

where the α_i and β_i are weighting parameters, with $\alpha_i > \alpha_{i+1}$. The retrieval of the sequence begins with retrieving the strongest component of the trace, which will be **a**. From there the retrieval is by chaining – correlating the trace with the current item to retrieve the next item. The end of the sequence is detected when the correlation of the trace with the current item is not similar to any item in the clean-up memory. This representation of sequences has the properties that a sequence is similar to all of the items in it, retrieval can start from any given element of the sequence, and similar sequences will have similar representations. It has the disadvantage that some sequences with repeated items cannot be properly represented.

Another way to represent sequences is to use the entire previous sequence as context rather than just the previous item (Liepa, 1977). This makes it possible to store sequences with repeated items. To store **abc**, the trace is:

$$\mathbf{a} + \mathbf{a} \circledast \mathbf{b} + \mathbf{a} \circledast \mathbf{b} \circledast \mathbf{c}.$$

This type of sequence can be retrieved in a similar way to the previous, except that the retrieval cue must be built up using convolutions.

The retrieval of later items in both these representations could be improved by subtracting off prefix components as the items in the sequence are retrieved.

Yet another way to represent sequences is to use a fixed cue for each position of the sequence. I call this method for storing sequences *trajectory association*, because each element of the sequence is associated with a point along a predetermined trajectory. To store **abc**, the trace is:

$$\mathbf{p}_1 \circledast \mathbf{a} + \mathbf{p}_2 \circledast \mathbf{b} + \mathbf{p}_3 \circledast \mathbf{c}.$$

The retrieval (and storage) cues $\mathbf{p}_i$ can be arbitrary or generated in some manner from a single vector, e.g., $\mathbf{p}_i = (\mathbf{p})^i$, i.e., $\mathbf{p}$ raised to the i th convolution power (Section 3.6.5). Convolution powers provide an easy way of generating a sequence of uncorrelated vectors from a single vector. In Chapter 5 I describe how trajectory-associated sequences can be decoded by a recurrent network. Trajectory-association can also be applied to representing continuous trajectories by using fractional powers of $\mathbf{p}$. Fractional convolution powers are also discussed in Section 3.6.5. The choice of $\mathbf{p}$ is important, as the length of $(\mathbf{p})^i$ can increase exponentially with i. It is best to make $\mathbf{p}$ a unitary vector (Section 3.6.3), because if $\mathbf{p}$ is unitary, $|(\mathbf{p})^i| = 1$ for all i.

Multiple methods can be combined, e.g., we can combine positional cues and Liepa's context method to store **abc** as:

$$\mathbf{p}_1 \circledast \mathbf{a} + (\mathbf{p}_2 + \mathbf{a}) \circledast \mathbf{b} + (\mathbf{p}_3 + \mathbf{a} \circledast \mathbf{b}) \circledast \mathbf{c}.$$

Either cue can be used to decode the sequence, but the reconstruction noise will be lowest when both cues are used together.

These methods for representing sequences can also be used to represent stacks. For example, a stack of n items, $\mathbf{x}_1 \cdots \mathbf{x}_n$, with $\mathbf{x}_1$ on top, can be represented by

$$\mathbf{s} = \mathbf{x}_1 + \mathbf{p} \circledast \mathbf{x}_2 + \mathbf{p} \circledast \mathbf{p} \circledast \mathbf{x}_3 + \cdots + \mathbf{p}^n \circledast \mathbf{x}_n.$$

The functions for manipulating such a stack are as follows:

$$
\begin{aligned}
\text{push}(\mathbf{s}, \mathbf{x}) &= \mathbf{x} + \mathbf{p} \circledast \mathbf{s} && \text{(function value is the new stack)} \\
\text{top}(\mathbf{s}) &= \text{clean-up}(\mathbf{s}) && \text{(function value is the top item)} \\
\text{pop}(\mathbf{s}) &= (\mathbf{s} - \text{top}(\mathbf{s})) \circledast \mathbf{p}^* && \text{(function value is the new stack)}
\end{aligned}
$$

An empty stack is noticed when the clean-up operation finds nothing similar to $\mathbf{s}$.

A problem with this type of stack implementation is that

$$\text{pop}(\text{push}(\mathbf{s}, \mathbf{x})) = \mathbf{s} \circledast \mathbf{p} \circledast \mathbf{p}^*$$

is only approximately equal to $\mathbf{s}$. This is because $\mathbf{p}^*$ is an approximate inverse. A consequence is that successive pushes and pops at one level lead to the continual degradation of the lower-level items. After a pair of push-pop actions, the stack will be $\mathbf{s} \circledast \mathbf{p} \circledast \mathbf{p}^*$, which is only approximately equal to $\mathbf{s}$. Additional push-pop pairs further corrupt the remaining part of the stack. There are two possible solutions to this problem – use chunking (see next section) or restrict $\mathbf{p}$ to be a vector for which the exact inverse is equal to the approximate inverse, in which case $\mathbf{s} \circledast \mathbf{p} \circledast \mathbf{p}^* = \mathbf{s}$ (see Section 3.6.3).

3.4.2 Chunking of sequences

All of the above methods have soft limits on the length of sequences that can be stored. As the sequences get longer the noise in the retrieved items increases until the items are impossible to identify. This limit can be overcome by chunking – creating new non-terminal items representing subsequences.

The second sequence representation method is more suitable for chunking. Suppose we want to represent the sequence **abcdefgh**. We can create three new items representing subsequences:

$$s_{abc} = \mathbf{a} + \mathbf{a} \circledast \mathbf{b} + \mathbf{a} \circledast \mathbf{b} \circledast \mathbf{c}$$

$$s_{de} = \mathbf{d} + \mathbf{d} \circledast \mathbf{e}$$

$$s_{fgh} = \mathbf{f} + \mathbf{f} \circledast \mathbf{g} + \mathbf{f} \circledast \mathbf{g} \circledast \mathbf{h}$$

These new items must be added to the clean-up memory because they are new chunks. The creation of new chunks is what gives this method the ability to represent sequences of arbitrary length. The representation for the whole sequence is:

$$s_{abc} + s_{abc} \circledast s_{de} + s_{abc} \circledast s_{de} \circledast s_{fgh}.$$

Decoding this chunked sequence is slightly more difficult, requiring the use of a stack and decisions on whether an item is a non-terminal that should be further decoded.

3.4.3 Variable binding

It is simple to implement variable binding with convolution: convolve the variable representation with the value representation. For example, the binding of the value **a** to the variable **x** and the value **b** to the variable **y** is

$$\mathbf{t} = \mathbf{x} \circledast \mathbf{a} + \mathbf{y} \circledast \mathbf{b}.$$

Variables can be unbound by convolving the binding with the approximate inverse of the variable. This binding method allows multiple instances of a variable in a trace to be substituted for in a single operation (approximately). It also allows us to find out what variable is bound to a given value.

3.4.4 Holographic Reduced Representations for simple predicates

Predicates or relations can be represented as simple frame-like structures using convolution encoding, in a manner analogous to the outer products of roles and fillers in Hinton (1981) and Smolensky (1990) and the frames of DUCS (Touretzky and Geva, 1987). A frame consists of a frame name and a set of roles, each represented by a vector.

An instantiated frame is the superposition of the frame name and the role-filler bindings (roles convolved with their respective fillers). This instantiated frame is a reduced description for the frame, I call it a Holographic Reduced Representation (HRR). For example, suppose we have a (very simplified) frame for eating. The vector for the frame name is **eat** and the vectors for the roles are $\mathbf{eat}_{agt}$ and $\mathbf{eat}_{obj}$. This frame can be instantiated with the fillers **mark** and **the_fish**, to represent "Mark ate the fish":[30]

$$\mathbf{s}_1 = \mathbf{eat} + \mathbf{eat}_{agt} \circledast \mathbf{mark} + \mathbf{eat}_{obj} \circledast \mathbf{the\_fish}$$

Fillers (or roles) can be retrieved (decoded) from the instantiated frame by convolving with the approximate inverse of the role (or filler). The role vectors for different frames can be frame specific, i.e., $\mathbf{eat}_{agt}$ can be different from $\mathbf{see}_{agt}$, or they can be the same (or just similar). The frame name is included as a retrieval cue; it is not necessary for role-filler binding and unbinding. It makes all eat-frames somewhat similar to the **eat** vector (and thus to each other). Eat-frames can be retrieved from clean-up memory by probing with the **eat** vector.

A role-filler binding such as $\mathbf{eat}_{agt} \circledast \mathbf{mark}$ is not similar to either the role or the filler, because the expected value of $\mathbf{x} \circledast \mathbf{y} \cdot \mathbf{x}$ is zero. It is also not similar to a binding of **mark** with a dissimilar role, because the expected value of $\mathbf{x} \circledast \mathbf{y} \cdot \mathbf{x} \circledast \mathbf{z}$ is zero. This means that two different frames with the same fillers can have no similarity. If this is not desired, it is easy to make such frames similar by including the fillers in the frame:

$$\mathbf{s}'_1 = \mathbf{eat} + \mathbf{mark} + \mathbf{the\_fish} + \mathbf{eat}_{agt} \circledast \mathbf{mark} + \mathbf{eat}_{obj} \circledast \mathbf{the\_fish}$$

This makes the representation for a frame somewhat similar to its fillers and to other frames involving the same fillers. It also allows fillers to be used as retrieval cues, because $\mathbf{s}'_1$ is similar to $\mathbf{mark} + \mathbf{the\_fish}$. Including fillers in the frame is not without cost – additional vectors in a convolution trace always increase the noise in recognition and reconstruction.

3.4.5 Holographic Reduced Representations for hierarchical structure

The vector representation of a frame is of the same dimension as the vector representation of a filler and can be used as a filler in another frame. In this way, convolution encoding affords the representation of

---

[30]I do not attempt to represent tense in any of the examples in this book. All the examples are in the past tense, and I use the infinitive forms of verbs for vector names.

hierarchical structure in a fixed-width vector.[31]

For example, we can use an instantiated frame from the previous section as a filler in another frame representing "Hunger caused Mark to eat the fish":

$$s_2 = \mathbf{cause} + \mathbf{cause}_{agt} \circledast \mathbf{hunger} + \mathbf{cause}_{obj} \circledast \mathbf{s}_1$$
$$= \mathbf{cause} + \mathbf{cause}_{agt} \circledast \mathbf{hunger} + \mathbf{cause}_{obj} \circledast \mathbf{eat}$$
$$+\mathbf{cause}_{obj} \circledast \mathbf{eat}_{agt} \circledast \mathbf{mark} + \mathbf{cause}_{obj} \circledast \mathbf{eat}_{obj} \circledast \mathbf{the\_fish}$$

Normalization of Euclidean lengths of the subframes becomes an issue. In this example s_1 has a Euclidean length of $\sqrt{3}$ but in s_2 it probably should be given the same weight as **hunger** because in s_2, **hunger** and s_1 have arguably the same importance. I discuss the issue of normalization further in Section 3.5.3.

This HRR will be similar to other HRRs that have similar role-filler bindings or frame names. This HRR can be made similar to other frames that involve similar subframes or fillers in different roles by adding the filler vectors into the HRR:

$$s_2' = \mathbf{cause} + \mathbf{mark} + \mathbf{the\_fish} + \mathbf{hunger} + \mathbf{s}_1$$
$$+\mathbf{cause}_{agt} \circledast \mathbf{hunger} + \mathbf{cause}_{obj} \circledast \mathbf{s}_1$$

These hierarchical representations can be manipulated with or without chunking. Without chunking, we could extract the agent of the object by convolving with $(\mathbf{cause}_{obj} \circledast \mathbf{eat}_{agt})^* = \mathbf{cause}_{obj}{}^* \circledast \mathbf{eat}_{agt}{}^*$. Using chunking, we could first extract the object, clean it up, and then extract its agent, giving a less noisy result. There is a tradeoff between accuracy and speed – if intermediate chunks are not cleaned up the retrievals are faster but less accurate. I discuss the decoding of frames and give results from a simulation in Section 3.10.

The commutativity of the circular convolution operation can cause ambiguity in some situations. This results from the fact that $\mathbf{t} \circledast \mathbf{r}_1^* \circledast \mathbf{r}_2^* = \mathbf{t} \circledast \mathbf{r}_2^* \circledast \mathbf{r}_1^*$. The ambiguity is greatly alleviated by using frame-specific role vectors rather than generic role vectors (e.g., a generic *agent* vector.) A situation where ambiguity can still arise is when two instantiations of the same frame are nested in another instantiation of that same frame. E.g., "(A causes B) causes (C causes D)" (this is a contrived example). In the HRR encoding of such such cases the agent of the object (C) cannot be distinguished from the object of the agent (B), because $\mathbf{cause}_{antc} \circledast \mathbf{cause}_{cnsq} = \mathbf{cause}_{cnsq} \circledast \mathbf{cause}_{antc}$,

---

[31]Slack (1984b,a, 1986) suggests a distributed memory representation for trees involving convolution products that is similar to the representation suggested here, except that it uses non-circular convolution, and thus does not work with fixed-width vectors.

due to the commutivity of convolution. Thus the HRR encoding for "(A causes B) causes (C causes D)" is identical to the HRR encoding for "(A causes C) causes (B causes D)". Whether this would cause problems with the types of knowledge structures encountered in real-world information processing tasks (by human or machine) is unclear – it is difficult to conceive of realistic examples that lead to complete ambiguity as in the above example. However, commutativity could lead to related problems decoding other more realistic structures. If this does turn out to be a problem, there are variants of circular convolution that are not commutative (Section 3.6.7) and which could be used to avoid this problem.

Holographic reduced representations provide a way of realizing Hinton's (1990) hypothetical system that could, in the same physical set of units, either focus attention on constituents or have the whole meaning present at once. Furthermore, the systematic relationship between the representations for components and frames (i.e., reduced descriptions) means that frames do not need to be decoded to gain some information about the components (see Section 3.10.2).

3.4.6 Equivalence of first-order and higher-order representations for roles

In Section 2.4.3 I reviewed two tensor-product role-filler representations for predicates. Smolensky (1990) suggests that the predicate p(a,b) can be represented as a second-order tensor $\mathbf{r}_1 \otimes \mathbf{a} + \mathbf{r}_2 \otimes \mathbf{b}$. Dolan and Smolensky (1989) suggest a third-order tensor: $\mathbf{p} \otimes \mathbf{r}_1 \otimes \mathbf{a} + \mathbf{p} \otimes \mathbf{r}_2 \otimes \mathbf{b}$. The difference between these two representations is that the first uses a first-order tensor for the roles (e.g., $\mathbf{r}_1$), whereas the second uses a second-order tensor for the roles (e.g., $\mathbf{p} \otimes \mathbf{r}_1$). With HRRs, this difference is largely immaterial – $\mathbf{p} \circledast \mathbf{r}_1$ is just a vector, like $\mathbf{r}_1$. In most circumstances the use of these will be equivalent, though it is conceivable that the higher-order role representation could support cleverer ways of decoding HRRs.

The same remarks apply to the predicate name. The two styles of representations, exemplified by

$$\mathbf{s}_1 = \mathbf{eat} + \mathbf{eat}_{agt} \circledast \mathbf{mark} + \mathbf{eat}_{obj} \circledast \mathbf{the\_fish}$$

and

$$\mathbf{s}_1' = \mathbf{framename} \circledast \mathbf{eat} + \mathbf{eat}_{agt} \circledast \mathbf{mark} + \mathbf{eat}_{obj} \circledast \mathbf{the\_fish},$$

where **framename** is common to all frames, have the same characteristics. Different instantiations of the same predicate will be similar, and different predicates will be different. The only difference is in how the frame name can be accessed. The second style of representation ($\mathbf{s}_1'$) al-

lows one to decode the frame name from the HRR with **framename**[*],
giving the frame name superimposed with noise, which is easy to clean
up. The first style of representation (s_1) has the frame name superimposed with the role-filler bindings, which can be more difficult to clean
up, unless frame names are kept in a separate clean-up memory.

3.4.7 What can we do with reduced representations?

There are two ways we can use reduced representations of sequences
and predicates. One way is to decode them in order to reconstruct full
representations, which involves either reading out a sequence, or finding
the fillers of roles. If accurate results are required, the decoded vectors
must be cleaned up, which involves more computation. The other way
to use HRRs is in *holistic processing*, that is without decoding. An
example is computing the similarity between HRRs. Similarity can be
used as the criterion for retrieval from clean-up memory (long-term
memory), if the clean-up memory is content-addressable. If we want to
use undecoded HRRs to compute the similarity of items, then we must
make sure that the dot product of HRRs is an adequate measure of
similarity. This is the justification for adding vectors such as fillers and
predicate names into HRRs. In Chapter 6 I describe how to incorporate
additional bindings that improve the degree to which the similarity of
HRRs reflects the analogical similarity of structures. However, we must
be judicious in adding more vectors to HRRs, because each additional
vector creates more noise in both decoding and similarity judgments.

3.5 Constraints on the vectors and the representation of features and tokens

In many connectionist systems, the vectors representing items are analyzed in terms of the individual vectors representing *microfeatures*.
For example, Hinton's *Family trees* network (Hinton, 1989) apparently
learned microfeatures representing concepts such as age and nationality
(Section 2.2.2). The requirement of HRRs that elements of vectors be
randomly and independently distributed seems at odds with this view
– microfeatures should be distributed meaningfully, not randomly. Furthermore, if every element of a vector is regarded as a microfeature
it is unclear how to use the large number of microfeatures that the
vectors of HRRs provide. It turns out that these issues do not pose
any difficulties because the elements of HRR vectors do not correspond
directly to features (or microfeatures). The vector elements can have
the desired statistical properties while items have their features.

3.5.1 The representation of features, types, and tokens

There is no requirement that single semantic features be represented by single elements in a distributed representation vector. Features of an item can be represented by high-dimensional distributed representations as wide as the representation of the whole item. An item having some features can be partly the superposition of vectors representing those features. Tokens of a type can be distinguished from each other by the superposition, in each token, of some *random identity vector* that is unique for that token. Features can be represented by random vectors. For example, the person *Mark* can be represented by **mark** = **being** + **human** + $\mathbf{id}_{mark}$, where $\mathbf{id}_{mark}$ is some random identity vector that distinguishes **mark** from representations of other people. Each component feature can be weighted according to its importance or salience, if necessary.

This scheme has the following advantages over a localist microfeature representation:

- The representation of any feature of an item will degrade gracefully as the elements of the vector representing the item are corrupted.
- The number of features in an item is only loosely related to the dimensionality of the vectors representing items.
- The vectors can be of as high a dimension as desired, and higher-dimensionality will give better fidelity in the representation of features.
- The vectors representing items can be expressed as sums of vectors with random independently distributed elements.

When a set of vectors representing items is constructed from distributed features in this way the elements of the vectors are not guaranteed to be consistent with being drawn from independent distributions. However, if linear superposition and circular convolution are used to construct representations, all the expressions describing the recall and matching of vectors can be expanded in terms of the random feature vectors. Thus the means and variances for the signals in a system with non-random vectors, and consequently the probabilities of correct retrieval, can be analytically derived. This allows analysis of the crosstalk induced by having similar vectors representing similar entities (e.g., **mark** = **being** + **human** + $\mathbf{id}_{mark}$, and **john** = **being** + **human** + $\mathbf{id}_{john}$). This analysis is done in Sections 3.10.4 and 3.10.5.

The idea of distributing features over the entire vector representing an item is not new. It is a linear transform and has been suggested by other authors under the name *randomization* or *random maps*

Schönemann (1987, e.g.,).

Care must be taken that the ownership of features is not confused when using this method to represent features (or attributes) of objects. Ambiguity of feature ownership can arise when multiple objects are stored in a superposition memory. For example, suppose color and shape are encoded as additive components. If the representations for *red circle* and *blue triangle* were summed, the result would be the same as for the sum of *red triangle* and *blue circle*. However, note that if the representations were convolved with distinct vectors (e.g., different role vectors) before they were added the results would not be ambiguous:

$$(\textbf{red} + \textbf{triangle}) \circledast \textbf{role}_1 + (\textbf{blue} + \textbf{circle}) \circledast \textbf{role}_2$$

is distinct from

$$(\textbf{red} + \textbf{circle}) \circledast \textbf{role}_1 + (\textbf{blue} + \textbf{triangle}) \circledast \textbf{role}_2.$$

In any case, it sometimes may be necessary to convolve features with objects to avoid ambiguity, e.g., to use $\textbf{red} + \textbf{circle} + \textbf{red} \circledast \textbf{circle}$ for a *red circle*, and $\textbf{human} + \textbf{id}_{john} + \textbf{human} \circledast \textbf{id}_{john}$ for *John*. The disadvantages of doing this are lower similarity of an entity and its features (e.g., *red circle* and *red*), lower similarity of similar entities (e.g., *red circle* and *red square*), and slightly greater complexity. I did not find it necessary to do this in any of the examples in this book. Problems involving crosstalk are discussed further in Section 3.11.5.

3.5.2 Why binary distributed representations are difficult to use

Binary distributed representations have some advantages over distributed representations in $\mathcal{R}^n$. They use fewer bits to store the same amount of information (in terms of numbers of items), and can be used with nonlinear memories (e.g., Willshaw et al.'s (1969) nonlinear correlograph), which are more information-efficient and give reconstructions with higher signal-to-noise ratios.

However, systems that use binary distributed representations and superposition must deal with the major problem of maintaining uniform density in vectors. This is important because uniform density is essential for the correct functioning of many other memory techniques we might like to use, such as the nonlinear correlograph (a convolution-based memory for binary vectors, see Willshaw et al. (1969) or Willshaw (1989b)). For an example of how superposition make maintaining uniform density difficult, consider the superposition of the two vectors (01001100) and (00100101). There is no simple operation one can perform on the superposition (01101101) that results in a binary vector with density 3/8. Thus binary HRRs cannot be implemented by merely combining the thresholded convolution operations of the nonlinear cor-relograph with superposition. Hence, in this book I use real-valued dis-tributed representations.[32]

3.5.3   Normalization of vectors

The magnitude (Euclidean length) of all vectors (HRRs, tokens, and base vectors) should be equal, or close to, 1. There are two reasons for this. The first is that we want the dot product to reflect similarity rather than vector magnitude. The second is that when we superimpose two vectors, we want each to be equally represented in the result (we can use scalar weights if we want one vector to be more prominent in the sum).

There are two ways to make the magnitude of vectors close to 1: *normalization* and *scaling by expected magnitude*. Normalization makes the magnitude of vectors exactly 1, and careful scaling by expected magnitude makes the expected magnitude of vectors equal to 1.

The normalized version of the vector $\mathbf{x}$ is denoted by $\langle \mathbf{x} \rangle$ and is defined as follows (the denominator is the Euclidean length of $\mathbf{x}$):

$$\langle \mathbf{x} \rangle = \frac{\mathbf{x}}{\sqrt{\sum_{i=0}^{n-1} x_i^2}}$$

The expected magnitude of a vector can be made equal to 1 by scaling:

$$\mathbf{x}' = \frac{\mathbf{x}}{\mathrm{E}[\|\mathbf{x}\|]}$$

This differs from normalization in two ways. The magnitude of the scaled vector is not guaranteed to be equal to 1, but it has an expected value of 1. Also, only information about the distributions of the x_i and not their actual values, enters into the computation of the scaling factor.

New vectors can be created in three different ways: as a random base vector, as the convolution product of several vectors, or as the superposition of several vectors. Superposition is the main concern, because the magnitude of a superposition of several vectors is nearly always greater than the magnitudes of the individual vectors (the only time this is not true is when the vectors share components, and have opposite signs on those components).

The expected magnitude of vectors with 512 elements chosen inde-

---

[32]Since the bulk of the research described in this book was completed, Kanerva (1996, 2001) and Rachkovskij and Kussul (2001) have discovered representational schemes closely related to HRRs that work with binary distributed representations (see Sections 2.4.5 and 2.4.6).

pendently from $N(0, 1/512)$ (i.e., base vectors) is 1. For high-dimensional vectors the variance is small, e.g., with 512-dimensional vectors, and standard deviation of the vector magnitude will be $\sqrt{(2/512)} = 0.0625$.

The expected magnitude of a convolution product is equal to the product of the magnitudes, provided that the vectors do not have common components (i.e., their expected dot product is zero). If two vectors have expected magnitudes of 1, then their convolution product will have an expected magnitude of 1. The expected magnitude of an auto-convolution product, e.g., $\mathbf{a} \circledast \mathbf{a}$, is equal to $\sqrt{2}$ if the a_i are independently distributed as $N(0, 1/n)$ (see Table 3 in Section 3.6.1). For this reason, I avoid using the auto-convolution product.

The expected magnitude of a superposition of vectors is equal to the square root of the sum of the squares of the magnitudes, again provided that the vectors do not have common components. If we have a superposition of M independently chosen vectors, then we scale by $\sqrt{M}$ to make the expected magnitude of the superposition equal to 1. For example, we scale $\mathbf{a}+\mathbf{b}$ by $\sqrt{2}$. The only way to scale correctly when vectors are not chosen independently is to decompose the vectors to a set of independently chosen ones. For example, suppose $\mathbf{x} = (\mathbf{a}+\mathbf{b})/\sqrt{2}$ and $\mathbf{y} = (\mathbf{a}+\mathbf{c})/\sqrt{2}$ (where $\mathbf{a}$, $\mathbf{b}$ and $\mathbf{c}$ are independently chosen). The correct way to scale $\mathbf{z} = \mathbf{x} + \mathbf{y}$ is by expressing it as $\mathbf{z} = 2\mathbf{a}/\sqrt{2} + \mathbf{b}/\sqrt{2} + \mathbf{c}/\sqrt{2}$: the scaling factor is $\sqrt{3}$.

In general, normalization is both simpler to use and produces more reliable results, because it reduces the variance of dot products (see Appendix G). However, using normalization invalidates the simple capacity analyses presented in this book, so in cases where I analyze capacity I use scaling. These capacity analyses provide a lower bound – performance improves if normalization is substituted for scaling.

3.5.4 Are the constraints on vectors reasonable?

Fisher et al. (1987) argue that holographic memories would be difficult to use in practice because of the constraints that must be imposed on vectors in order to make them function well. They claim that most vectors produced by sensory apparatus or other components of a physical system would be unlikely to satisfy these constraints. Other types of associative memory can handle a wider range of vectors, and provide reconstructions with higher signal-to-noise ratios. Some researchers conclude from this that holographic memories are probably not worthy of further study.

However, this argument is made only in the context of considering the properties of different schemes for storing associations between pairs of items. HRRs do more than this. Other types of associative memories have many problems when applied to representing complex structure, and thus do not provide a clearly superior alternative as they do in the case of storing pairwise associations.

If it is desired to interface a system that uses HRRs with another system that uses vector representations that do not conform to the constraints (e.g., a perceptual system), a different associative memory can be used to translate between representations. The combination of a convolution-based memory (for HRRs) and another associative memory (for mapping between non-conforming and conforming representations) allows the representation of complex associations that are difficult to represent without using a convolution-based memory.

3.6 Mathematical Properties

Circular convolution may be regarded as a multiplication operation over vectors: two vectors multiplied together (convolved) result in another vector. A finite-dimensional vector space over the real numbers, with circular convolution as multiplication and the usual definitions of scalar multiplication and vector addition, forms a commutative linear algebraic system. This is most easily proved using the observation that convolution corresponds to elementwise multiplication in a different basis, as described in Section 3.6.2. All the rules that apply to scalar algebra (i.e., associativity and commutativity of addition and multiplication, and distributivity of multiplication over addition) also apply to this algebra. This makes it very easy to manipulate expressions containing additions, convolutions, and scalar multiplications.

This algebra has many of the same properties as the algebra considered by Borsellino and Poggio (1973) and Schönemann (1987), which had unwrapped convolution as a multiplication operation over an infinite-dimensional vector space restricted to vectors with a finite number of non-zero elements. Schönemann observed that representing the correlation of **b** and **a** as a convolution of **a** with an involution of **b** made expressions with convolutions and correlations easier to manipulate.

3.6.1 Statistical distribution of vector dot products

The distributions of the dot products of vectors and convolutions of vectors can be analytically derived. I have calculated distributions for some dot products; these are shown in Table 3. Note that as n (the number of elements in vectors) goes to infinity, means remain constant while variances go to zero. This is good because it means that a HRR system that uses higher-dimensional vectors will be more reliable and accurate, and that the reliability and accuracy can be increased without

	Expression	mean	variance
(1)	$\mathbf{a} \cdot \mathbf{a}$	1	$\frac{2}{n}$
(2)	$\mathbf{a} \cdot \mathbf{b}$	0	$\frac{1}{n}$
(3)	$\mathbf{a} \cdot \mathbf{a} \circledast \mathbf{b}$	0	$\frac{2n+1}{n^2}$
(4)	$\mathbf{a} \cdot \mathbf{b} \circledast \mathbf{c}$	0	$\frac{1}{n}$
(5)	$\mathbf{a} \circledast \mathbf{a} \cdot \mathbf{a} \circledast \mathbf{a} = \mathbf{a} \circledast \mathbf{a} \circledast \mathbf{a}^* \cdot \mathbf{a}$	$2 + \frac{2}{n}$	$\frac{40n+112}{n^2}$
(6)	$\mathbf{a} \circledast \mathbf{b} \cdot \mathbf{a} \circledast \mathbf{b} = \mathbf{a} \circledast \mathbf{b} \circledast \mathbf{a}^* \cdot \mathbf{b}$	1	$\frac{6n+4}{n^2}$
(7)	$\mathbf{a} \circledast \mathbf{b} \cdot \mathbf{a} \circledast \mathbf{a} = \mathbf{a} \circledast \mathbf{b} \circledast \mathbf{a}^* \cdot \mathbf{a}$	0	$\frac{6n+18}{n^2}$
(8)	$\mathbf{a} \circledast \mathbf{b} \cdot \mathbf{a} \circledast \mathbf{c} = \mathbf{a} \circledast \mathbf{b} \circledast \mathbf{a}^* \cdot \mathbf{c}$	0	$\frac{2n+2}{n^2}$
(9)	$\mathbf{a} \circledast \mathbf{b} \cdot \mathbf{c} \circledast \mathbf{c} = \mathbf{a} \circledast \mathbf{b} \circledast \mathbf{c}^* \cdot \mathbf{c}$	0	$\frac{2n+2}{n^2}$
(10)	$\mathbf{a} \circledast \mathbf{b} \cdot \mathbf{c} \circledast \mathbf{d} = \mathbf{a} \circledast \mathbf{b} \circledast \mathbf{c}^* \cdot \mathbf{d}$	0	$\frac{1}{n}$

TABLE 3 Means and variances of dot products of common convolution expressions for vectors with elements distributed as $N(0, 1/n)$, where n is the dimensionality of the vectors. These expressions assume no normalization or scaling. The dot products are normally distributed in the limit as n goes to infinity.

bound.

These calculations are based on the assumption that the elements for the vectors $\mathbf{a}, \mathbf{b}, \mathbf{c}$, and $\mathbf{d}$ are independently distributed as $N(0, 1/n)$ (the expected length of these vectors is 1). The Central Limit Theorem tells us that these dot products are normally distributed in the limit as n goes to infinity because they are the sum of products of individual vector elements.[33] The equivalent expressions in rows (5) to (10) are derived from the following identity of convolution algebra:

$$\mathbf{a} \circledast \mathbf{b} \circledast \mathbf{x}^* \cdot \mathbf{y} = \mathbf{a} \circledast \mathbf{b} \circledast \mathbf{y}^* \cdot \mathbf{x} = \mathbf{a} \circledast \mathbf{b} \cdot \mathbf{x} \circledast \mathbf{y}$$

The variances for decoding circular-convolution bindings are slightly higher than the variances for decoding unwrapped-convolution bindings (see Murdock (1985) for a table similar to Table 3). However, the difference is only a small constant factor (1.3 to 1.5), and is probably due to to the fact that circular-convolution bindings are represented over n elements rather than the $2n - 1$ elements for wrapped-convolution bindings.

These means and variances are used as follows: Suppose that $\mathbf{a}, \mathbf{b}, \mathbf{c}, \mathbf{d}$, and $\mathbf{e}$ are random vectors with elements drawn independently from $N(0, 1/n)$. Then the value of $\mathbf{a}^* \circledast (\mathbf{a} \circledast \mathbf{b} + \mathbf{c} \circledast \mathbf{d}) \cdot \mathbf{b}$ will have an

---

[33] Although there are some correlations among these products, there is sufficient independence for the Central Limit Theorem to apply for even quite small n.

expected value of 1 and a variance of $\frac{7n+4}{n^2}$ ($=\frac{6n+4}{n^2}+\frac{1}{n}$ using rows 6 and 10 in Table 3). The value of $\mathbf{a}^* \circledast (\mathbf{a} \circledast \mathbf{b} + \mathbf{c} \circledast \mathbf{d}) \cdot \mathbf{e}$ will have an expected value of 0 and a variance of $\frac{3n+2}{n^2}$ ($=\frac{2n+2}{n^2}+\frac{1}{n}$ using rows 8 and 10 in Table 3).

Of some interest is the distribution of the elements of $\mathbf{a} \circledast \mathbf{b}$. If the elements of $\mathbf{a}$ and $\mathbf{b}$ are independently distributed as $N(0, 1/n)$ then the mean of the elements of $\mathbf{a} \circledast \mathbf{b}$ is 0 but the variance is higher than $1/n$ and the covariance of the elements is not zero. The expected length of $\mathbf{a} \circledast \mathbf{b}$ is still 1 (provided that the elements of $\mathbf{a}$ are distributed independently of those of $\mathbf{b}$ since the expected length of $\mathbf{a} \circledast \mathbf{a}$ is $\sqrt{2 + 2/n}$). Thus, the variance of $(\mathbf{a} \circledast \mathbf{b}) \circledast \mathbf{c} \circledast (\mathbf{a} \circledast \mathbf{b})^* \cdot \mathbf{c}$ is higher than that of $\mathbf{a} \circledast \mathbf{c} \circledast \mathbf{a}^* \cdot \mathbf{c}$. A consequence of this is that some care must be taken when using $\mathbf{a} \circledast \mathbf{b}$ as a storage cue, because the statistics of decoding and detection are different than when using $\mathbf{a}$ as a storage cue. This is especially true in cases where $\mathbf{a}$ and $\mathbf{b}$ are not independent. This is particularly relevant to the storage capabilities of HRRs because when hierarchical frames are stored, convolution products, e.g., $\mathbf{cause}_{obj} \circledast \mathbf{eat}_{agt}$, are the storage cues.

These means and variances are different if normalization is used. In Appendix G, I report experiments that investigate this. The results show that variances are significantly lower and more uniform when normalization is used. In Chapter 4, I describe a different type of normalization that results in even lower and more uniform variances.

3.6.2 Using Fast Fourier Transforms to compute convolution

The fastest way to compute convolution is via Fast Fourier Transforms (FFTs) (Brigham, 1974). The computation involves a transformation, an elementwise multiplication of two vectors, and an inverse transformation. Computing convolution via these three steps takes $O(n \log n)$ time, whereas the obvious implementation of the convolution equation $c_i = \sum_j a_j b_{i-j}$ takes $O(n^2)$ time.[34]

The discrete Fourier transform, $\mathbf{f} : \mathcal{C}^n \rightarrow \mathcal{C}^n$ ($\mathcal{C}$ is the field of complex numbers), is defined as:

$$f_j(\mathbf{x}) = \sum_{k=0}^{n-1} x_k e^{-i2\pi jk/n},$$

where $i^2 = -1$ and $f_j(\mathbf{x})$ is the jth element of $\mathbf{f}(\mathbf{x})$. The discrete Fourier transform is invertible and defines a one-to-one relationship between

---

[34]Computing convolution via FFTs takes about the same time as the $O(n^2)$ method for $n = 32$. It is faster for $n > 32$ and slower for $n < 32$.

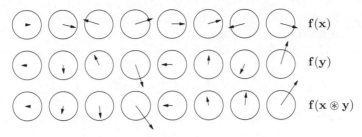

$\mathbf{f}(\mathbf{x})$

$\mathbf{f}(\mathbf{y})$

$\mathbf{f}(\mathbf{x} \circledast \mathbf{y})$

FIGURE 37   The convolution of 8-dimensional vectors $\mathbf{x}$ and $\mathbf{y}$ in the frequency domain. Each arrow represents a complex number in a unit circle. The angle of a component of $\mathbf{f}(\mathbf{x} \circledast \mathbf{y})$ is equal to the sum of the angles of the corresponding components of $\mathbf{f}(\mathbf{x})$ and $\mathbf{f}(\mathbf{y})$. The magnitude of a component of $\mathbf{f}(\mathbf{x} \circledast \mathbf{y})$ is equal to the product of the magnitudes of the corresponding components of $\mathbf{f}(\mathbf{x})$ and $\mathbf{f}(\mathbf{y})$.

vectors in the spatial and frequency domains. It can be computed in $O(n \log n)$ time using the Fast Fourier Transform (FFT) algorithm. The inverse discrete Fourier transform is similar:

$$f_j^{-1}(\mathbf{x}) = \frac{1}{n} \sum_{k=0}^{n-1} x_k e^{i2\pi jk/n}$$

and can also be computed in $O(n \log n)$ time using the FFT algorithm. The equation relating convolution and the Fourier transform is:

$$\mathbf{x} \circledast \mathbf{y} = \mathbf{f}^{-1}(\mathbf{f}(\mathbf{x}) \odot \mathbf{f}(\mathbf{y})),$$

where $\odot$ is the elementwise multiplication of two vectors. Figure 37 illustrates the elementwise multiplication of the transforms of two vectors $\mathbf{x}$ and $\mathbf{y}$. The constraints on the Fourier transforms of real vectors are apparent in this figure: the angles of $f_0(\mathbf{x})$ and $f_{n/2}(\mathbf{x})$ are zero, and $f_{i+n/2}(\mathbf{x})$ is the complex conjugate of $f_i(\mathbf{x})$ (for $1 \le i < n/2$).[35]

In the following sections, I shall refer to the original space as the *spatial domain*, and to the range of Fourier transform as the *frequency domain*. Both domains are n-dimensional vector spaces, and both the forward and inverse Fourier transforms are linear. In Chapter 4, I describe how all the operations required for HRRs can be performed solely in the frequency domain.

---

[35]If a vector in the frequency domain does not satisfy these constraints, then it is the Fourier transform of a complex vector. Put another way, if $\mathbf{X} \in \mathcal{C}^n$ (the frequency domain) does not satisfy these constraints, then $\mathbf{f}^{-1}(\mathbf{X})$ is a complex-valued vector.

3.6.3 Approximate and exact inverses in the frequency domain

Since convolution in the spatial domain is equivalent to elementwise multiplication in the frequency domain we can easily find convolutive inverses using the frequency domain. By definition, $\mathbf{y}$ is the inverse of $\mathbf{x}$ if $\mathbf{x} \circledast \mathbf{y} = 1$ and we can write $\mathbf{y} = \mathbf{x}^{-1}$. The convolutive identity vector is $\mathbf{1} = (1, 0, \ldots, 0)$. Transforming this into the frequency domain gives

$$\mathbf{f}(\mathbf{x}) \odot \mathbf{f}(\mathbf{x}^{-1}) = \mathbf{f}(\mathbf{1}).$$

The transform of the identity is

$$\mathbf{f}(\mathbf{1}) = (e^{0i}, e^{0i}, \ldots, e^{0i}) = (1, 1, \ldots, 1).$$

This gives independent relationships between the corresponding elements of $\mathbf{f}(\mathbf{x})$ and $\mathbf{f}(\mathbf{x}^{-1})$ which can be expressed as

$$f_j(\mathbf{x}^{-1}) f_j(\mathbf{x}) = 1,$$

where $f_j(\mathbf{x})$ is the j'th element of $\mathbf{f}(\mathbf{x})$.

Expressing $\mathbf{f}(\mathbf{x})$ in polar coordinates gives

$$f_j(\mathbf{x}) = r_j e^{i\theta_j}$$

and we can see that the Fourier transform of the exact inverse of $\mathbf{x}$ must be

$$f_j(\mathbf{x}^{-1}) = \frac{1}{r_j} e^{-i\theta_j}.$$

Now consider the approximate inverse. It can be seen from the definition of the Fourier transform that the transform of the involution of $\mathbf{x}$ is

$$f_j(\mathbf{x}^*) = r_j e^{-i\theta_j}.$$

In the frequency domain, the elements of the approximate inverse have the same magnitudes as the original elements, whereas the elements of the exact inverse have magnitudes equal to the reciprocals of the original elements. It follows that the approximate inverse is equal to the exact inverse if and only if the magnitude of all frequency components is 1 (i.e., $r_j = 1$ for all j). I refer to this class of vectors as *unitary* vectors.[36] Put another way, $\mathbf{x}$ is a unitary vector if and only if $\mathbf{x} \circledast \mathbf{x}^* = \mathbf{I}$ (i.e., $\mathbf{x} \oplus \mathbf{x} = \mathbf{I}$). Figure 38 shows the approximate and exact inverses of a vector.

Vectors that have zero magnitudes for one or more frequency components have no exact inverse, so I refer to these as *singular* vectors.

---

[36] By analogy to unitary matrices, for which the conjugate transpose is equal to the inverse.

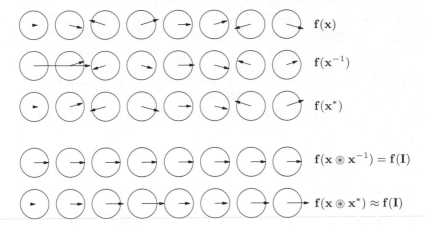

FIGURE 38 The exact and approximate inverses of a vector in the frequency domain ($\mathbf{f}(\mathbf{x}^{-1})$ and $\mathbf{f}(\mathbf{x}^*)$ respectively. $\mathbf{f}(\mathbf{x} \circledast \mathbf{x}^{-1})$ is the identity vector, and $\mathbf{f}(\mathbf{x} \circledast \mathbf{x}^*)$ is an approximation to it.

Unitary vectors and vectors with elements distributed as $N(0, 1/n)$ in the spatial domain are closely related. The mean of frequency-component magnitudes for the latter is 1 (except for the two components with zero angle), and the phase angles are uniformly distributed. Transformed into the spatial domain, the elements of unitary vectors are distributed as $N(1/n, 1/n)$. The elements are not independent – there are only $(n/2 - 1)$ degrees of freedom.

3.6.4   Why the exact inverse is not always useful

Since $\mathbf{x}^{-1}$ can be used to decode $\mathbf{x} \circledast \mathbf{y}$ exactly, it might seem to be a better candidate for the decoding vector than the approximate inverse $\mathbf{x}^*$. However, using the exact inverse results in a lower signal-to-noise ratio in the retrieved vector when the memory trace is noisy or when there are other vectors added into it.[37] This problem arises because the exact inverse is unstable. For vectors with elements independently distributed as $N(0, 1/n)$, $|\mathbf{x}^{-1}|$ (the magnitude of $\mathbf{x}^{-1}$) is often significantly greater than $|\mathbf{x}|$ (except when $\mathbf{x}$ is unitary). However, $|\mathbf{x}^*|$ is always equal to $|\mathbf{x}|$. The reason for this can be understood by considering the inverses in the frequency domain. The relationship between the vector magnitude and the magnitudes of the frequency components is given by Parseval's theorem:

$$|\mathbf{x}|^2 = \sum_k x_k^2 = \frac{1}{n} \sum_k |f_k(\mathbf{x})|^2.$$

---

[37]Inverse filters are well known to be sensitive to noise (Elliot, 1986).

Taking the approximate inverse does not change the magnitude of the frequency components, so $|\mathbf{x}^*|$ is always equal to $|\mathbf{x}|$. However, taking the exact inverse involves the reciprocals of the magnitudes, so if the magnitude of a frequency component of $\mathbf{x}$ is close to zero (which can happen), the magnitude of the corresponding frequency component of $\mathbf{x}^{-1}$ will be very large magnitude. If exact inverses are used for decoding a noisy trace, the high-magnitude frequency components magnify the noise in the trace without contributing much signal to the reconstruction.

3.6.5   The convolutive power of a vector

The convolutive power of a vector (exponentiation) can be straightforwardly defined by exponentiation of its elements in the frequency domain, i.e.,

$$f_j(\mathbf{x}^k) = (f_j(\mathbf{x}))^k.$$

It is easy to verify that this definition satisfies $\mathbf{x}^0 = \bar{\mathbf{I}}$, and $\mathbf{x}^i \circledast \mathbf{x} = \mathbf{x}^{i+1}$ for $i \geq 0$. For negative and fractional exponents powers are most easily expressed using polar coordinates. Let $f_j(\mathbf{x}) = r_j e^{i\theta_j}$, where $r_j \leq 0$ and $-\pi < \theta \leq \pi$. Then

$$f_j(\mathbf{x}^k) = r_j^k e^{ik\theta_j}.$$

Note that for any vector $\mathbf{x} \in \mathcal{R}^n$, and $k \in \mathcal{R}$, $\mathbf{x}^k$ is also in $\mathcal{R}^n$, because exponentiation as defined above does not affect the conditions that make a vector in the frequency domain the transform of a real vector in the spatial domain (see Section 3.6.2). (This would not be true if in the above definition we used $0 \leq \theta < 2\pi$, or allowed r to be negative.) Also, unitary vectors are closed under exponentiation: any power of a unitary vector is a unitary vector.

Integer powers are useful for generating some types of encoding keys (cf. Section 3.4.1) and fractional powers can be used to represent trajectories through continuous space, as done in Chapter 5.

3.6.6   Matrices corresponding to circular convolution

The convolution operation can be expressed as matrix multiplication of a vector:

$$\mathbf{a} \circledast \mathbf{b} = M_a \mathbf{b}$$

where M_a is the matrix corresponding to convolution by $\mathbf{a}$. It has elements $m_{a_{ij}} = a_{i-j}$ (where the subscripts on $\mathbf{a}$ are interpreted modulo n). Such matrices are known as *circulant matrices* (Davis, 1979). This shows that convolution is a linear operation. Furthermore, since the mapping computed by the connections between two layers in a feedforward network is matrix-vector multiplication, it is possible for such a mapping to correspond to convolution by a fixed vector.

The algebra of convolution carries through with matrix multiplication: $M_{a \circledast b} = M_a M_b$. Transposition corresponds to the approximate inverse, i.e., $M_{a^*} = M_a^T$. Also, if $\mathbf{a}$ is a unitary vector, then M_a is a real unitary matrix (i.e., an orthonormal matrix). The eigenvalues of M_a are the individual (complex-valued) elements of the Fourier transform of $\mathbf{a}$. The corresponding eigenvectors are the inverse transforms of the frequency components, i.e., $[1, 0, 0, \ldots]$, $[0, 1, 0, \ldots]$, etc, in the frequency domain.

3.6.7 Non-commutative variants and analogues of convolution

The commutativity of convolution can cause ambiguity in the representations of some structures. If this is a problem, non-commutative variants of circular convolution can be constructed by permuting the elements of the argument vectors in either the spatial or frequency domain. The permutations applied to right and left vectors must be different. The resulting operation is neither commutative nor associative, but is bilinear (and thus distributes over addition and preserves similarity) and has an easily computed approximate inverse.

An alternative operation that is non-commutative but still associative is matrix multiplication. This could be used to associate two vectors by treating each vector as a square matrix. The dimension of the vectors would have to be a perfect square. I am unaware of what the scaling and interference properties of such an associative-memory operation would be. It would be similarity preserving and vectors corresponding to orthogonal matrices would have simple inverses.

Another possibility is to use a random convolution-like compression of the outer product, as mentioned in Section 7.4.

3.6.8 Partial derivatives of convolutions

Convolution operations can be used in feedforward networks[38] and values can be propagated forward in $O(n \log n)$ time (on serial machines). Derivatives can also be backpropagated in $O(n \log n)$ time. Suppose we have a network in which the values from two groups of units are convolved together and sent to a third group of units. The relevant portion of such a feedforward network is shown in Figure 39. Suppose we have the partial derivatives $\frac{\partial E}{\partial c_i}$ of outputs of the convolution with respect to an objective function E. Then the partial derivatives of the inputs to the convolution can be calculated as follows:

---

[38] For an introduction to feedforward networks see Rumelhart et al. (1986a).

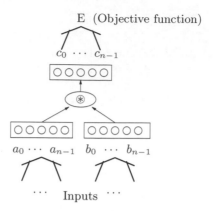

FIGURE 39 A convolution operation in a backpropagation network.

$$\frac{\partial E}{\partial a_k} = \sum_i \frac{\partial E}{\partial c_i} \frac{\partial c_i}{\partial a_k}$$
$$= \sum_i \frac{\partial E}{\partial c_i} b_{i-k}$$
$$= \sum_i \frac{\partial E}{\partial c_i} [\mathbf{b}^*]_{k-i}$$
$$= [\partial_c \circledast \mathbf{b}^*]_k$$

where ∂_c is the vector with elements $\frac{\partial E}{\partial c_i}$, and $[\cdot]_k$ is the kth element of a vector.

This means that it is possible to incorporate a convolution operation in a feedforward network and do the forward and backpropagation computations for the convolution in $O(n \log n)$ time. One reason one might want to do this could be to use a backpropagation network to learn good vector representations for items for some specific task. This is pursued in Chapter 5.

3.7   Faster comparison with items in clean-up memory

Computing the dot product of the probe with each item in clean-up memory can be expensive if there are a large number of items in clean-up memory, especially on a serial machine. This computation can be reduced by computing a fast estimate of the dot product and then only computing the floating-point dot product for the most promising candidates. The fast estimate is the count of matching bits in binary versions of the vectors. To make this practical, we must store a binary version along with each item in clean-up memory. The binary version is an n-bit vector, and the nth bit is 1 if the nth element of the item vector is

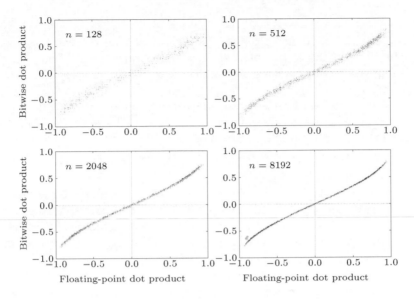

FIGURE 40 Bitwise dot products (vertical axis) versus floating-point dot products (horizontal axis) for various vector dimensions.

positive, and 0 otherwise. The dot product of quantized binary vectors (the *bitwise dot product*) can be computed many times faster, using full-word XOR operations, than the dot product of floating-point vectors. The bitwise dot product is highly correlated with the floating-point dot product – for $n = 2048$ the correlation coefficient was measured to be 0.997 (for 4096 pairs of vectors). This of course depends on HRR vector elements having a mean of 0, but this will be true if the HRRs are constructed following the descriptions in this chapter.

Figure 40 shows some simulation results. These plots show the bitwise dot product versus the floating-point dot product. It is clear that the correlation between the floating-point and the bitwise dot products increases with vector dimension. This means that the bitwise dot product is increasingly useful with higher dimension vectors. In Appendix I, I report some simulations in which this technique significantly reduced the amount of computation done by the clean-up operation.

The data in Figure 40 was generated by repeatedly choosing a random similarity value r in $[-1, 1]$, and two vectors $\mathbf{x}$ and $\mathbf{y}$ with elements randomly selected from $N(0, 1/n)$. Using $\mathbf{x}$ and $\mathbf{y}$ it is easy to construct two vectors $\mathbf{a}$ and $\mathbf{b}$ so that $\mathbf{a} \cdot \mathbf{b} = r$:

$$\mathbf{a} = \langle \mathbf{x} \rangle$$

$$\mathbf{b} \;=\; \langle r\mathbf{a} + \sqrt{1 - r^2}\,\mathbf{y}\rangle.$$

(Recall that $\langle \mathbf{x} \rangle$ denotes the normalized version of $\mathbf{x}$.) The floating-point dot product $\mathbf{a} \cdot \mathbf{b}$ is plotted against the scaled count of matching bits in the binary versions of $\mathbf{a}$ and $\mathbf{b}$. Each plot contains 4096 data points.

When searching for the vector in clean-up memory that is the closest to some vector $\mathbf{x}$, the following algorithm reduces the number of floating-point dot products that must be computed:

1. Compute and record the bitwise dot product of $\mathbf{x}$ with all the vectors in clean-up memory.
2. Let the maximum bitwise dot product be t. Calculate the lower bound on what the floating-point dot product corresponding to t could be, let this be t'. Calculate the lower bound on the bitwise dot product of vectors that have a floating-point dot product of t'; let this be t''.
3. Compute and record the floating-point dot products of $\mathbf{x}$ with all the vectors in clean-up memory that had a bitwise dot product of t'' or greater.

This scheme saves computation by not computing the floating-point dot product for vectors that could not possibly be the best match. The lower bounds must be derived from some statistical model of the differences between bitwise and floating-point dot products. Some preliminary analysis of simulation data (such as is shown in Figure 40) indicates that we can use

$$t'' = t - s, \quad \text{where} \quad s = 6e^{-0.505 \log n}.$$

This corresponds to an interval at least 8 standard deviations wide.

Seidl and Kriegel (1998) present algorithms for this kind of problem. Their algorithms suggest a somewhat obvious modification of the above algorithm that will improve its efficiency: in step 2, let t' be the actual floating-point dot product of $\mathbf{x}$ and the vector whose bitwise dot product with $\mathbf{x}$ is t.

3.8   The capacity of convolution memories and HRRs

In Appendices B through E, I investigate the capacities of superposition memory and paired-associates convolution memory. For superposition and pairwise (variable-binding) convolution memories, I demonstrate the following scaling properties:

- The number of pairs (items) that can be stored in a single trace is approximately linear in n.

- The probability of error is negative exponential in n.
- The number of items that can safely be stored in clean-up memory is exponential in n.

For example, if we use vectors with 4096 elements, and have $100,000$ items in clean-up memory, where 100 of those are similar to each other (with dot product 0.5), then we can store approximately a dozen bindings in a single trace, and have a 99% chance of decoding the trace correctly (from Figure 64).

If some items in clean-up memory are similar to each other, as they will be if they are tokens or HRRs constructed according to the suggestions in this book, then the capacity equation tends to be dominated by the number of similar items rather than by the total number of items in clean-up memory. Thus the simulations described, which mostly have a small number of similar items, could still work with a much larger number of items in clean-up memory (provided that there was not any one item in clean-up memory was similar to a large number of others.)

In Appendices D and E I only consider the capacity of paired-associates convolution memory. In order to predict the capacity of a system using HRRs, it is necessary to consider the effect of higher-order bindings. If unnormalized vectors are used, the results of decoding higher-order bindings will be much noisier than the results of decoding pairwise associations (i.e., the lowest-order of associations), and thus the capacity will be lower. This is because the variance for decoding higher-order convolution products is higher than that for decoding lower-order convolution products. For example, the variance of $(\mathbf{a} \circledast \mathbf{b} \circledast \mathbf{c}) \circledast (\mathbf{b} \circledast \mathbf{c})^{*} \cdot \mathbf{a}$ is greater than the variance of $(\mathbf{a} \circledast \mathbf{b}) \circledast \mathbf{b}^{*} \cdot \mathbf{a}$. If normalized vectors are used, the results will be only slightly noisier, and the capacity slightly lower. If unitary vectors are used, as discussed in Chapter 4, the results will not be any noisier than for pairwise associations.

Thus, if normalization is used the size of a structure that can be encoded in a HRR, i.e., the number of terms in the expanded convolution expression, can be expected to increase almost linearly with the vector dimension. The results of decoding deep structures will be noisier, but if this becomes a critical problem it can be overcome by storing sub-structures as separate chunks, and cleaning up intermediate results. In fact, if chunking is used, structures of unlimited size can be stored, as long as all the component chunks are not too large. Note that this does not imply that an unlimited amount of information can be encoded in a single HRR – when a large structure is chunked into a number of HRRs each HRR represents a limited portion of the structure and must be stored in a clean-up memory. Thus the total representational resources required to fully represent the structure is proportional to the size of the structure.

3.9 Convolution-based memories versus matrix-based memories

Convolution- and matrix-based memories have long been considered alternative ways of implementing associative distributed memory (e.g., see Willshaw et al. (1969), Willshaw (1989b), Pike (1984), and Fisher et al. (1987)). The focus has usually been on storing pairwise associations, though Pike does consider higher-order associations. Convolution-based memories were invented first, inspired by holography (Reichardt, 1957, Gabor, 1968, Longuet-Higgins, 1968, Willshaw et al., 1969, Borsellino and Poggio, 1973). Matrix memories were proposed by Willshaw et al. (1969) as a way of improving on the properties of convolution-based memories, while retaining their distributed associative character. Since then, convolution-based memories have fallen out of favor. Willshaw (1989a), commenting on his earlier work on convolution-based memory, writes:

> The prominence given to the newly emerging field of holography in the 1960s made it likely that before long the suitability of the hologram as a distributed associative memory would be explored. But as seen from today's viewpoint, a study of the hologram may seem an irrelevant diversion. This was, however, one of the routes to the particular associative memory that we investigated, the well-known matrix, or correlation, memory, to which holographic models bear a formal, mathematical similarity.

Matrix memories have gone on to be widely studied, e.g., in the form of Hopfield nets (Hopfield, 1982). In this book I return to convolution-based memories because they are more suitable for forming the higher-order associations necessary to represent complex structure, and their weaknesses can be compensated for by using them in conjunction with auto-associative clean-up memories.

3.9.1 Comparison of convolution and matrix-based memories

Matrix- and convolution-based memories have much in common – they share the following properties (where **a**/**b** means the association of **a** and **b**):

- Storage of an association is a one-shot process – an association can be stored after a single presentation, in contrast to schemes involving iterative feedback.[39]

- The framework involves three operations: a bilinear encoding operation to create associations, superposition to combine associations, and a bilinear decoding operation.
- Incorporating nonlinearities in the form of thresholds on the three operations improves performance and capacity (Willshaw, 1989b).
- Nonlinear versions have the same information efficiency under optimal conditions (Willshaw, 1989b), and linear versions also have similar information efficiency (Pike, 1984).
- Association preserves similarity: If items $\mathbf{a}$ and $\mathbf{a}'$ are similar, then the traces $\mathbf{a}/\mathbf{b}$ and $\mathbf{a}'/\mathbf{b}$ will also be similar (to approximately the same degree). This is useful because, if the representations of items make similarity explicit (Section 1.4.2), then structures composed of those items will also make similarity explicit.
- Association has a randomizing effect: If items $\mathbf{x}$ and $\mathbf{y}$ are not similar, then the traces $\mathbf{x}/\mathbf{a}$ and $\mathbf{y}/\mathbf{a}$ will also not be similar. This is useful because it allows superimposing multiple associations without getting false cross-associates.
- The encoding operation involves pairwise products of the elements of each vector.

The differences between convolution- and matrix-based memories are as follows:

- Convolution-based memories are symmetric, and matrix memories are not. This is because convolution is commutative $(\mathbf{a} \circledast \mathbf{b} = \mathbf{b} \circledast \mathbf{a})$, whereas the outer product is not.
- In matrix memories the dimensionality of the trace is the square of the dimensionality of the vectors being associated, whereas in convolution memories, the dimensionality of the trace can be made the same as that of the vectors being associated.
- Matrix memories can store a larger number associations of vectors of a given dimensionality (though the size of the traces are correspondingly larger).
- Reconstructions from linear matrix memories have higher signal-to-noise ratios than those from linear convolution-based memories.
- It is easier to build error correction into matrix memories, so that if the association $\mathbf{a}/\mathbf{b}$ is decoded with $\mathbf{a}'$ (a noisy version of $\mathbf{a}$), the reconstructed version of $\mathbf{b}$ will be more similar to $\mathbf{b}$ than $\mathbf{a}'$ is to $\mathbf{a}$.

---

[39]This is not to say that iterative schemes cannot improve performance. On the contrary, in Chapter 5 I describe how such a scheme enables the use of lower-dimensional vectors.

3.9.2 Convolution as a low-dimensional projection of a tensor product

The convolution operation can be seen as a realization of Smolensky et al.'s (1992) suggestion for solving the expanding-dimensionality problem of tensor products by projecting higher-order tensor products onto a lower-dimensional space. The projection matrix P such that $P\,\mathbf{x} \otimes \mathbf{y} = \mathbf{x} \circledast \mathbf{y}$ is easily derived. The 3×9 matrix P that projects a 9-element tensor $\mathbf{x} \circledast \mathbf{y}$ (represented as a 3×3 matrix) onto three elements is shown below. P has a regular structure: each its 3×3 blocks contains one shifted diagonal.

$$
P\,\mathbf{x} \otimes \mathbf{y} = \begin{bmatrix} 1 & 0 & 0 & 0 & 0 & 1 & 0 & 1 & 0 \\ 0 & 1 & 0 & 1 & 0 & 0 & 0 & 0 & 1 \\ 0 & 0 & 1 & 0 & 1 & 0 & 1 & 0 & 0 \end{bmatrix} \begin{bmatrix} x_1 y_1 & x_1 y_2 & x_1 y_3 \\ x_2 y_1 & x_2 y_2 & x_2 y_3 \\ x_3 y_1 & x_3 y_2 & x_3 y_3 \end{bmatrix}
$$

$$
= \begin{bmatrix} x_1 y_1 + x_3 y_2 + x_2 y_3 \\ x_2 y_1 + x_1 y_2 + x_3 y_3 \\ x_3 y_1 + x_2 y_2 + x_1 y_3 \end{bmatrix}
$$

$$
= \mathbf{x} \circledast \mathbf{y}
$$

In general, the dimensionality-reducing projection P has a null space that interferes minimally with associations. For any non-singular vector $\mathbf{x}$, there are no distinct vectors $\mathbf{y}$ and $\mathbf{y}'$ such that $P\,\mathbf{x} \otimes \mathbf{y} = P\,\mathbf{x} \otimes \mathbf{y}'$ (i.e., such that $\mathbf{x} \circledast \mathbf{y} = \mathbf{x} \circledast \mathbf{y}'$). It is true that there are an infinite number of distinct pairs $\mathbf{x}, \mathbf{y}$ and $\mathbf{x}', \mathbf{y}'$ such that $P\,\mathbf{x} \otimes \mathbf{y} = P\,\mathbf{x}' \otimes \mathbf{y}'$ (for which also $\mathbf{x} \circledast \mathbf{y} = \mathbf{x}' \circledast \mathbf{y}'$), but this does not cause problems if either we know one of the items in the association, or we choose vectors randomly so that this type of collision has low probability.

3.10 An example of encoding and decoding HRRs

An example of HRR frame construction and decoding is presented in this section. The types and tokens representing objects and concepts are constructed according to the suggestions in Section 3.5. Results from a simulation of the example using 512-dimensional vectors are reported.

This example is intended to serve two purposes: (1) to demonstrate the mechanics of constructing and decoding HRRs, and (2) to illustrate how the choices of vectors representing lower-level objects (e.g., that the vector representing the person *Mark* is similar to the vector representing the person *John*, but is not similar to the vector representing *the fish*) has consequences for the behavior of HRRs constructed from these vectors.

Frame names	Object features		Role features
cause	being	food	object
eat	human	fish	agent
see	state	bread	

TABLE 4 Base vectors. Vector elements are all independently chosen from $N(0, 1/512)$.

$$\mathbf{mark} = (\mathbf{being} + \mathbf{human} + \mathbf{id}_{mark})/\sqrt{3}$$
$$\mathbf{john} = (\mathbf{being} + \mathbf{human} + \mathbf{id}_{john})/\sqrt{3}$$
$$\mathbf{paul} = (\mathbf{being} + \mathbf{human} + \mathbf{id}_{paul})/\sqrt{3}$$
$$\mathbf{luke} = (\mathbf{being} + \mathbf{human} + \mathbf{id}_{luke})/\sqrt{3}$$
$$\mathbf{the\_fish} = (\mathbf{food} + \mathbf{fish} + \mathbf{id}_{the\_fish})/\sqrt{3}$$
$$\mathbf{the\_bread} = (\mathbf{food} + \mathbf{bread} + \mathbf{id}_{the\_bread})/\sqrt{3}$$
$$\mathbf{hunger} = (\mathbf{state} + \mathbf{id}_{hunger})/\sqrt{2}$$
$$\mathbf{thirst} = (\mathbf{state} + \mathbf{id}_{thirst})/\sqrt{2}$$
$$\mathbf{eat}_{agt} = (\mathbf{agent} + \mathbf{id}_{eat\_agent})/\sqrt{2}$$
$$\mathbf{eat}_{obj} = (\mathbf{object} + \mathbf{id}_{eat\_object})/\sqrt{2}$$

TABLE 5 Token and role vectors constructed from base vectors and random identity vectors. The identity vectors (e.g., $\mathbf{id}_{mark}$) are chosen in the same way as the base vectors. The denominators are chosen so that the expected length of a vector is 1.0. Other roles (e.g., $\mathbf{see}_{agt}$) are constructed in an analogous fashion.

3.10.1 Representation and similarity of tokens

The suggestion in Section 3.5 for token vectors (representing an instance of a type) was that they be composed of the sum of features and a distinguishing vector giving individual identity. In this example the base vectors (the features other vectors are composed of) have elements chosen independently from $N(0, 1/512)$. The base vectors are listed in Table 4. The token and role vectors are constructed by summing the relevant feature vectors and a distinguishing *random identity vector*. The random identity vector is unique to each instance of a type and gives the vector representing each instance a distinct identity. Scale factors are included in order to make the expected length of the vectors equal to 1. These token vectors and a representative pair of role vectors are listed in Table 5.

	mark	john	paul	luke	the_fish	the_bread	hunger	thirst
mark	1.07							
john	0.78	1.08						
paul	0.76	0.75	1.08					
luke	0.73	0.68	0.74	1.01				
the_fish	0.01	0.00	-.02	-.03	1.16			
the_bread	0.02	0.01	0.06	0.01	0.35	0.97		
hunger	0.01	0.06	0.05	0.03	0.10	0.03	0.93	
thirst	0.01	0.11	0.04	0.06	0.07	0.02	0.48	1.04

TABLE 6 Similarities (dot products) among some of the tokens. The diagonal elements are the squares of the vector lengths. Tokens sharing feature vectors (see Table 5) have higher similarity.

s_1 Mark ate the fish.
s_2 Hunger caused Mark to eat the fish.
s_3 John ate.
s_4 John saw Mark.
s_5 John saw the fish.
s_6 The fish saw John.

TABLE 7 Sentences.

The similarity matrix of the tokens is shown in Table 6. Tokens with more features in common have higher similarity (e.g., **mark** and **john**), and tokens with no features in common have very low similarity (e.g., **john** and **the_fish**).

I weighted vectors to make their expected length equal to 1 rather than normalizing them because normalization invalidates the analysis of expectations and variances of dot products. In practice, it is better to normalize vectors, although this makes the analysis of expectations no longer exact.

3.10.2   Representation and similarity of frames

The six sentences listed in Table 7 are represented as HRR frames. The expressions for these HRRs are listed in Table 8. Again, scale factors are included to make the expected length of the vectors equal to 1.

The similarities of the HRRs are shown in Table 9. Some similarities between instantiated frames can be detected without decoding. The HRRs for similar sentences (s_4, s_5, and s_6 form one group of similar

$$s_1 = (\text{eat} + \text{eat}_{agt} \circledast \text{mark} + \text{eat}_{obj} \circledast \text{the\_fish})/\sqrt{3}$$

$$s_2 = (\text{cause} + \text{cause}_{agt} \circledast \text{hunger} + \text{cause}_{obj} \circledast s_1)/\sqrt{3}$$

$$s_3 = (\text{eat} + \text{eat}_{agt} \circledast \text{john})/\sqrt{2}$$

$$s_4 = (\text{see} + \text{see}_{agt} \circledast \text{john} + \text{see}_{obj} \circledast \text{mark})/\sqrt{3}$$

$$s_5 = (\text{see} + \text{see}_{agt} \circledast \text{john} + \text{see}_{obj} \circledast \text{the\_fish})/\sqrt{3}$$

$$s_6 = (\text{see} + \text{see}_{agt} \circledast \text{the\_fish} + \text{see}_{obj} \circledast \text{john})/\sqrt{3}$$

TABLE 8 HRR frame vectors representing the sentences in Table 7

	s_1	s_2	s_3	s_4	s_5	s_6
s_1	1.14					
s_2	0.02	0.98				
s_3	0.81	0.01	1.11			
s_4	0.11	0.12	0.25	1.13		
s_5	0.30	0.05	0.31	0.73	0.99	
s_6	-.01	0.14	0.01	0.65	0.35	1.14

TABLE 9 Similarities (dot products) among the frames.

sentences, s_1 and s_3 form another group) are similar because convolution preserves similarity. One role-filler binding is similar to another to the extent that their respective roles and fillers are similar. This is investigated in more detail in Section 3.10.5.

The HRRs for two frames that have identical constituents but different structure are distinct. Consequently, s_5 and s_6 are distinct. Having the same filler in the same role causes more similarity between frames than having the same filler in a different role. Consequently, s_4 is more similar to s_5 than to s_6 because **john** fills the agent role in s_4 and s_5, and the object roles in s_6.

3.10.3 Extracting fillers and roles from frames

The filler of a particular role in a frame is extracted as follows: the frame is convolved with the approximate inverse of the role and the result is cleaned up by choosing the most similar vector in the clean-up memory. The clean-up memory contains all feature, token, role, and frame vectors (i.e., all the vectors listed in Tables 4, 5, and 8).

The extraction of various fillers and roles is shown in Table 10. For each extraction, the three vectors in clean-up memory that are most similar to the result are shown. In all cases the most similar object is

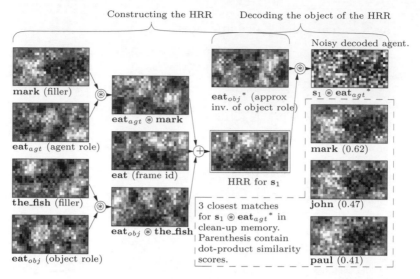

FIGURE 41 Construction and decoding of a HRR for the sentence "Mark ate the fish." (s_1 in Section 3.10). The instantiated frame, labeled s_1, is the sum of role-filler bindings and a frame id (shown in the second column). It is the same dimensionality as all other objects and may be used as a filler in another frame (e.g., as in s_2 in Section 3.10). A filler of the HRR can be extracted by convolving the HRR with the approximate inverse of its role. The extraction of the agent-role filler of this sentence is shown on the right (also see Table 10). Of the items in clean-up memory, the actual filler, **mark**, is the most similar (shown in the region enclosed by the dashed lines). The next two most similar items are also shown, with the dot-product match value in parentheses. The dot products of the decoded agent with **john** and **paul** might seem high, but these values are expected because the expected similarity of **mark** to other people is 2/3 (and $2/3 \times 0.62 \approx 0.41$). In this high-dimensional space these differences in similarity (0.62 to 0.47) are significant. See Section 3.10.3 for discussion.

the correct one.

As shown in Row (1), the expression to extract the agent of s_1 is

$$\mathbf{x} = \mathbf{s}_1 \circledast \mathbf{eat}_{agt}{}^*.$$

The three objects in clean-up memory most similar to $\mathbf{x}$ (with their respective dot products) are **mark** (0.62), **john** (0.47), and **paul** (0.41). The filler of the agent role in s_1 is indeed **mark**, so the extraction has been performed correctly.

The construction of s_1 and the determination of the filler of its object role, on row (1) in Table 10, is illustrated in Figure 41. In order to enable the perception of similarities among vectors in this figure,

Item to extract	Expression	Similarity scores (dot product)		
(1) Agent of s_1	$s_1 \circledast eat_{agt}^*$	**mark** (0.62)	john (0.47)	paul (0.41)
(2) Agent of s_1	$s_1 \circledast agent^*$	**mark** (0.40)	john (0.34)	human (0.30)
(3) Object of s_1	$s_1 \circledast eat_{obj}^*$	**the_fish** (0.69)	fish (0.44)	food (0.39)
(4) Agent of s_2	$s_2 \circledast cause_{agt}^*$	**hunger** (0.50)	state (0.39)	thirst (0.31)
(5) Object of s_2	$s_2 \circledast cause_{obj}^*$	s_1 (0.63)	s_3 (0.46)	eat (0.43)
(6) Agent of object of s_2	$s_2 \circledast cause_{obj}^* \circledast eat_{agt}^*$	**mark** (0.27)	paul (0.23)	luke (0.22)
(7) Object of object of s_2	$s_2 \circledast cause_{obj}^* \circledast eat_{obj}^*$	**the_fish** (0.39)	fish (0.24)	food (0.23)
(8) Object of s_3	$s_3 \circledast eat_{obj}^*$	**food** (0.07)	the_bread (0.06)	mark (0.06)
(9) John's role in s_4	$s_4 \circledast john^*$	**see$_{agt}$** (0.66)	agent (0.50)	see$_{obj}$ (0.47)
(10) John's role in s_5	$s_5 \circledast john^*$	**see$_{agt}$** (0.58)	agent (0.41)	eat$_{agt}$ (0.36)

TABLE 10 Results of extracting items from the frames. In all cases shown the item most similar to the result is the correct one. The similarity comparisons are all with the entire set of features, tokens, roles, and frames. See the text for discussion of each row.

the 512-element vectors were laid out in rectangles with dimensions permuted (on all vectors simultaneously) so as to reduce the total sum of variance between neighboring elements. This was done using a simulated annealing program. The reader should not take the visual similarities of the vectors too seriously – dot-product similarity is what is important and is very difficult to judge from merely looking at figures like these.

Row (2) illustrates that the agent of s_1 can also be extracted using the generic agent role (**agent**) rather than the agent role specific to the eat frame ($\mathbf{eat}_{agt}$). The results are stronger when the specific agent is used.

In s_2 the object role is filled by another frame. There are two alternative methods for decoding the components of this subframe. The first method, which is slower, is to clean up the subframe in clean-up memory (row 5) and then extract its components, as in rows (1) to (3). The second (faster) method, is to omit the clean-up operation and directly convolve the result with the approximate inverses of the roles of s_1. The expressions for the fast method are shown in rows (6) and (7). The first method is an example of using chunking to clean up intermediate results, and gives more reliable results at the expense of introducing intermediate clean-up operations. The second method is an example of holistic processing. With the intermediate clean-up omitted, the chances of error are higher; in row (6) the correct vector is only very slightly stronger than an incorrect one. However, the high-scoring incorrect responses are similar to the correct response; it is clear that the subframe-object-role filler is a person.

Row (8) shows what happens when we try to extract the filler of an missing role. The frame s_3 ("John ate.") has no object. As expected, $s_3 \circledast \mathbf{eat}_{obj}{}^*$ is not particularly similar to anything. Although **food** might seem an appropriate guess, all the responses are weak and it is just a coincidence that **food** gives the strongest response.

It is possible to determine which role a token is filling, as in rows (9) and (10). In s_4, on row (9), the correct role for **john** is $\mathbf{see}_{agt}$, but $\mathbf{see}_{obj}$ also scores quite highly. This is because **john** is a person, and a person (**mark**) also fills the object role in s_4. Compare this with s_5, where the object-role filler (**the_fish**) is not at all similar to the agent-role filler (**john**). The extracted role for **john** is not at all similar to the object role, as shown on row (10).

3.10.4 Probabilities of correct decoding

The expectations and variances of the dot products

$$\mathbf{s}_1 \circledast \mathbf{eat}_{agt}^* \cdot \mathbf{mark} \quad \text{and} \quad \mathbf{s}_1 \circledast \mathbf{eat}_{agt}^* \cdot \mathbf{p}$$

are calculated in this section (where $\mathbf{p}$ is a vector for a person that is not **mark**). This allows us to calculate the probability that the agent of $\mathbf{s}_1$ will be extracted correctly, as in row (1) of Table 10. It must be emphasized that, under the operations described here, the behavior of any particular system (i.e., set of vectors) is deterministic. A particular frame in a particular system always will or always will not be decoded correctly. The probabilities calculated in this section are those that a randomly chosen system will behave in a particular way.

Let $\mathbf{d} = \mathbf{s}_1 \circledast \mathbf{eat}_{agt}^*$, then

$$\mathbf{d} \cdot \mathbf{mark} = \mathbf{d} \cdot (\mathbf{being} + \mathbf{human} + \mathbf{id}_{mark})/\sqrt{3}, \text{ and}$$

$$\mathbf{d} \cdot \mathbf{p} = \mathbf{d} \cdot (\mathbf{being} + \mathbf{human} + \mathbf{id}_p)/\sqrt{3}.$$

The vector $\mathbf{p}$ is used here as a generic *incorrect person* filler. The extraction is judged to have been performed correctly if $\mathbf{d} \cdot \mathbf{mark} > \mathbf{d} \cdot \mathbf{p}$ for all vectors representing people in the clean-up memory. We can limit the consideration to people-vectors in clean-up memory, because it is extremely unlikely that other vectors will be more similar to $\mathbf{d}$ than the vectors representing people.

It is important to note that these two dot products are correlated because they share the common term $\mathbf{d} \cdot (\mathbf{being} + \mathbf{human})/\sqrt{3}$. To calculate the probabilities accurately it is necessary to take into account the value of this term when choosing the threshold. Let

$$X_{mark} = \mathbf{d} \cdot \mathbf{id}_{mark}/\sqrt{3},$$

$$X_p = \mathbf{d} \cdot \mathbf{id}_p/\sqrt{3}, \text{ and}$$

$$Z = \mathbf{d} \cdot (\mathbf{being} + \mathbf{human})/\sqrt{3}.$$

X_{mark}, X_p, and Z can be regarded as uncorrelated, normally distributed variables, which are derived from the random vectors.

The calculation of the means and variances of X_{mark}, X_p, and Z is presented in Appendix F. For $n = 512$, they are as follows:

	mean	variance	std dev
X_{mark}	0.192	0.00116	0.0341
X_p	0	0.000867	0.0294
Z	0.385	0.00246	0.0496

A lower estimate [40] for the probability P that $Z + X_{mark} > Z + X_p$

---

[40] $P' \leq P$ because it can be the case that $Z + X_{mark} < t$ and $Z + X_{mark} >$

for all p is given by

$$P' = \Pr(Z + X_{mark} > t) \cdot \Pr(Z + X_p < t \ \forall \ p \neq \mathbf{mark}),$$

where t is a threshold chosen to maximize this probability.[41]
  In this example there are three other people, so

$$P' = \Pr(X_{mark} + Z > t) \cdot \Pr(X_p + Z < t)^3.$$

This has a maximum value of 0.996 for $t = Z + 0.0955$. Thus the probability of correctly identifying the filler of agent role as **mark** in s_1 is at least 0.996. If there were 100 vectors representing people in the clean-up memory, the probability of correctly identifying the decoded agent as **mark** would drop to 0.984.

  The reason for calculating means and variances of signals is to estimate the minimum vector dimension that will result in an acceptable probability of error. It is not necessary to calculate the means and variances of all signals, it is sufficient to consider just those pairs whose means are close and whose variances are large.

3.10.5 Similarity-preserving properties of convolution

Convolution is similarity preserving – two convolution bindings are similar to the degree that their components are similar. For example, the two role-filler bindings $\mathbf{eat}_{agt} \circledast \mathbf{mark}$ and $\mathbf{eat}_{agt} \circledast \mathbf{john}$ are similar because **mark** and **john** are similar.

  The bilinearity and randomizing properties of convolution make it possible to calculate analytically the expectation and variance of dot products of convolution sums and products. The calculation is simple, if somewhat laborious. We use several facts (from Table 3) about the dot products of convolutions of vectors with elements chosen randomly from $N(0, 1/n)$:

$$E[(\mathbf{a} \circledast \mathbf{b}) \cdot (\mathbf{a} \circledast \mathbf{b})] \ = \ 1$$
$$E[(\mathbf{a} \circledast \mathbf{b}) \cdot (\mathbf{a} \circledast \mathbf{c})] \ = \ 0$$

Let $\mathbf{B}_1$ and $\mathbf{B}_4$ be two role-filler bindings involving similar entities:

$$\mathbf{B}_1 \ = \ \mathbf{eat}_{agt} \circledast \mathbf{mark}$$
$$\mathbf{B}_4 \ = \ \mathbf{eat}_{agt} \circledast \mathbf{john}$$
$$\mathbf{mark} \ = \ (\mathbf{being} + \mathbf{human} + \mathbf{id}_{mark})/\sqrt{3}$$
$$\mathbf{john} \ = \ (\mathbf{being} + \mathbf{human} + \mathbf{id}_{john})/\sqrt{3}$$

$Z + X_p \ \forall \ p \neq \mathbf{mark}$.
[41]t is chosen with knowledge of Z but not of X_{mark} or X_p.

Compared with	Similarity of filler		
mark $\circledast$ eat$_{agt}$	1	2/3	0
Similarity 1	mark $\circledast$ eat$_{agt}$ 1	john $\circledast$ eat$_{agt}$ 2/3	the_fish $\circledast$ eat$_{agt}$ 0
of role 1/2	mark $\circledast$ see$_{agt}$ 1/2	john $\circledast$ see$_{agt}$ 1/3	the_fish $\circledast$ see$_{agt}$ 0
0	mark $\circledast$ eat$_{obj}$ 0	john $\circledast$ eat$_{obj}$ 0	the_fish $\circledast$ eat$_{obj}$ 0

TABLE 11 Expected similarity of **mark** $\circledast$ **eat**$_{agt}$ to other role-filler bindings. One binding is similar to another to the degree that its components are similar.

where **being, human, eat**$_{agt}$, **id**$_{mark}$, and **id**$_{john}$ are random base vectors with elements from $N(0, 1/n)$. The scaling factor $1/\sqrt{3}$ makes the expected lengths of **mark** and **john** equal to 1. The vectors **mark** and **john** are similar – their expected dot product is $2/3$. The arithmetic is simpler if we replace **being** + **human** by $\sqrt{2}$**person**, where **person** is a random base vector.

The expected dot product of $\mathbf{B}_1$ and $\mathbf{B}_4$ is:

$$E[(\mathbf{eat}_{agt} \circledast \mathbf{mark}) \cdot (\mathbf{eat}_{agt} \circledast \mathbf{john})]$$
$$= E[(\mathbf{eat}_{agt} \circledast (\mathbf{person} + \mathbf{id}_{mark})/\sqrt{3})$$
$$\cdot (\mathbf{eat}_{agt} \circledast (\mathbf{person} + \mathbf{id}_{john})/\sqrt{3})]$$
$$= 2/3 E[\mathbf{eat}_{agt} \circledast \mathbf{person} \cdot \mathbf{eat}_{agt} \circledast \mathbf{person}]$$
$$+ \sqrt{2}/3 E[\mathbf{eat}_{agt} \circledast \mathbf{person} \cdot \mathbf{eat}_{agt} \circledast \mathbf{id}_{john}]$$
$$+ \sqrt{2}/3 E[\mathbf{eat}_{agt} \circledast \mathbf{id}_{mark} \cdot \mathbf{eat}_{agt} \circledast \mathbf{person}]$$
$$+ 1/3 E[\mathbf{eat}_{agt} \circledast \mathbf{id}_{mark} \cdot \mathbf{eat}_{agt} \circledast \mathbf{id}_{john}]$$
$$= 2/3 + 0 + 0 + 0 = 2/3$$

The expected similarity of two role-filler bindings is equal to the product of the expected similarities of the roles and of the fillers (provided that there is no similarity between roles and fillers).[42] The similarity of a binding to others with varying role and filler similarity is shown in Table 11.

So far I have only mentioned the expected dot product of two vectors, whereas what is usually important is the actual dot product. The dot product is a fixed value for a particular pair of vectors. However, we can usefully treat it as a random value that depends on the choice of random base vectors. The dot products of convolution products and sums are normally distributed, and their variance is inversely proportional to n. The observed values of the dot products in Table 11, for 200 choices of random base vectors of dimension 512, are shown in Fig-

---

[42]Care must be taken that one base vector does not appear in both components of a binding, because $E[\mathbf{a} \circledast \mathbf{a} \cdot \mathbf{a} \circledast \mathbf{a}] = 2 + 2/n$.

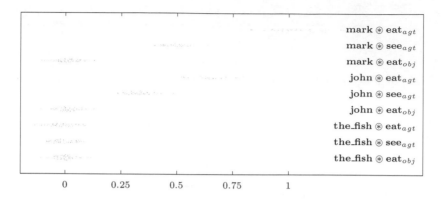

FIGURE 42 Similarities between $\mathbf{x} = \mathbf{mark} \circledast \mathbf{eat}_{agt}$ and various role-filler bindings (see Table 11) from 200 choices of random base vectors. The dimension of vectors is 512. There are 200 samples in each cluster. The variances of the points in each cluster are inversely proportional to the vector dimension. Density-dependent random vertical displacements were added to make the density of points clear.

ure 42. Although some of the clusters overlap, e.g., $\mathbf{mark} \circledast \mathbf{see}_{agt}$ and $\mathbf{john} \circledast \mathbf{eat}_{agt}$ (the ones with means at 0.5 and 0.66), these dot products are rarely out of order in a single run (114 times in 10,000 runs). The reason is that they are correlated – when one is high, the other tends to be high.

In Appendix A, I derive expressions for the means and variances of the similarities shown in Figure 42, and compare them to the observed means and variances. They match closely.

3.11 Discussion

3.11.1 Learning and HRRs

One of the attractions of distributed representations is that they can be used in neural networks and trained by example. Hinton's (1989) *Family trees* network demonstrated how a neural network could simultaneously learn a task and the representations for objects in the task. In Chapter 5 I will describe how a recurrent neural network can implement the trajectory-association method for storing sequences. The network learns item representations that are superior to randomly chosen ones.

3.11.2 HRRs and Hinton's reduced descriptions

HRRs are not an exact implementation of Hinton's (1990) reduced descriptions (Section 1.5), but they do capture their spirit, and satisfy the four desiderata for reduced descriptions – adequacy, reduction, systematicity, and informativeness about components. A HRR is a reduced description for a frame – the full representation is the set of fillers and predicate name (and roles). HRRs are not an exact implementation for two reasons: roles are not fixed (as is implied in Figure 1), and the full representation need not be laid out in parallel on several groups of units – it can be composed and decomposed iteratively. The issue of how (or whether) the full representation should be represented is not addressed in this book.

3.11.3 Chunking

The idea of chunking, or breaking large structures into pieces of manageable size, fits together very well with HRRs. Chunking makes it possible for systems based on HRRs to store structures of unlimited size, and HRRs provide a way of doing chunking that has some very attractive properties.

As more items and bindings are stored in a single HRR the noise on extracted items increases. If too many associations are stored, the quality will be so low that the extracted items will be easily confused with similar items or, in extreme cases, completely unrecognizable. The number of items and bindings in a HRR grows with both the height and width of the structure being represented – s_1 (representing "Mark ate the fish") has 3, while s_2 (representing "Hunger caused Mark to eat the fish") has 5. The number of items and bindings that can be stored for a given degree of quality of decoding grows linearly with the vector dimension (Section 3.8), so one way to store larger structures would be to increase vector dimensionality. However, using vectors with very high dimension is not a satisfactory way to store large structures because there will always be a structure too large to store in any particular dimensionality. A far superior way is to store a large structure as a number of chunks. This involves storing the HRRs for substructures (i.e., chunks) in the clean-up memory, and using them when decoding components of complex structures. Thus, a large structure is represented by a number of HRRs. For example, sentence (2) can represented using two chunks: s_2 and s_1, both of which should be stored in the clean-up memory. To decode the agent of the cause antecedent of s_2 we first extract the cause antecedent. This gives a noisy version of s_1, so we then clean it up by accessing clean-up memory and retrieving the closest match (which should be the chunk s_1). This gives an accurate version of s_1 from which we can extract the filler of the agent role. Storing HRRs for intermediate structures makes it possible to store structures of practically unlimited size in systems based on HRRs (though of course the number of chunks in clean-up memory grows with the size of the structure).

Any system that uses chunks must also have a way of reconstructing the contents of a chunk given the label for a chunk, and a way of creating a label for a new chunk. In conventional symbolic data structures a chunk is reconstructed by retrieving a record (i.e., the contents of a chunk) given the the pointer to the record (i.e., the label for the chunk). A label for a new record is created by finding the address of a suitable free block of memory. With HRRs a chunk is reconstructed by decoding its roles and/or fillers. The distinguishing aspect of HRRs is that a label for a chunk is created by systematic operations on the contents of the chunk. Consequently, a HRR is a representationally rich label for structure it encodes. This is what the *reduced* in *Holographic Reduced Representation* refers to – a HRR is a compressed, or reduced, version of the structure it represents. The advantage of having a label that encodes some information about its referent is that this makes holistic processing possible, i.e., processing without unpacking and reconstructing the contents of the structure. This can potentially provide new primitive operations for cognitive machines. For example, we can decode nested fillers quickly if very noisy results are acceptable, or we can get an estimate of the similarity of two structures without decoding the structures. In Chapter 6, I investigate how HRRs can be used to compute fast estimates of analogical similarity.

3.11.4 Comparison to other distributed representations for predicates

HRRs have much in common with Smolensky's (1990) tensor-product role-filler representation for predicates. The advantage HRRs have over tensor products is that the dimensions of HRRs do not expand when they are composed recursively. The natural way of constructing reduced descriptions and chunks in HRRs follows from this. The advantage tensor products have over HRRs is lower noise (zero under some conditions) in decoding. With tensor products, one can do such things as rebind multiple variables in parallel. One can also do this with HRRs, but the noise is considerable.

HRRs differ from Murdock's (1983) and Halford et al.'s (1994) predicate representations in that HRRs do not require that any ordering be imposed on the roles, and in their ease of coping with missing fillers. Some common types of decoding, such as finding the filler of a given role, appear to be easier with HRRs. Furthermore, HRRs seem to provide a more natural similarity structure for predicates (see Chapter 6). The type of access that Halford et al. claim is impossible with role-filler representations (finding one component of a predicate when provided with all the others) can actually be done quite easily with HRRs if a clean-up memory is used. I give an example of this in Appendix I. HRRs are actually more versatile for this type of retrieval because a HRR can be retrieved with fewer than all-but-one components.

Compared to Pollack's (1990) RAAMs, HRRs have the following computational advantages:

- No lengthy training is required for HRRs.
- The retrieval properties of HRRs are simple and predictable, and amenable to analysis.
- Arbitrary structures of arbitrary vectors can be stored in HRRs. The only structures and vectors that one can be confident a RAAM will encode are those it was trained (or tested) on.
- HRRs shed information about nested components, whereas with deeper structures, RAAMs must pack more and more information into the vector. Not all the information about the items in a complex association is stored in the HRR memory trace. Information storage is shared between the convolution memory trace and the associative clean-up memory.
- Many types of structures can be stored in HRRs. HRRs are not constrained to representing trees of a particular degree.
- HRRs have an infinite variety of roles, whereas RAAMs are limited to a small fixed number of positional roles.
- HRRs degrade gracefully in the presence of noise. HRRs normally work with a lot of noise. The effect of adding more noise can be quantified and compensated for by using higher-dimensional vectors. The effect of adding noise to RAAMs is difficult to quantify because they involve nonlinear transformations. Also, RAAMs are unlikely to work well in the presence of noise because they require values to be represented with high precision.
- HRRs do not depend upon representing floating-point values with high precision. Rounding to lower-precision values has much the same effect as adding noise.
- Construction and decomposition of HRRs can be done in $O(n \log n)$ time, using FFTs, whereas RAAMs take $O(n^2)$ time. However, this advantage is probably offset by the high vector dimensions that HRRs require.

HRRs have several disadvantages compared to RAAMs:

- The association operation in HRRs cannot take advantage of the possibility that some structures and items are commonly represented and others rarely. In RAAMs, the association operation is tuned to efficiently represent common structures and items.
- HRRs require very high dimensional vectors.
- For the statistical analysis of HRRs to be valid the elements of the basic vectors must be randomly independently distributed.

3.11.5   Crosstalk in HRRs

Because of their extensive use of superposition, HRRs are subject to some problems of crosstalk (also known as ghosting) – where some item that was not actually intended to have been stored was however apparently stored. The simplest example of this occurs with representations for entities and their features. For example, one convenient way to represent entities with features is to have independent random vectors for each possible feature value, and to represent an entity by the superposition of feature value vectors. Thus, *small circle* could be represented by **small** + **circle**, and *large triangle* by **large** + **triangle**, where **small**, **circle**, **large**, and **triangle** are all independently chosen random vectors. If sets of two or more entities are represented as the superposition of the representations of the entities, then crosstalk is possible: the representation for the set containing the two entities *small circle* and *large triangle* will appear to contain also the representation for the entity *small triangle* and for the entity *large circle*. This problem is not critical provided that representations include some convolution bindings involving the entities (e.g., role-filler bindings) that help to indicate which features belong to which entities, as do the representations used in Chapter 6. One can also ameliorate the problem by adding bindings between features. For example, *small circle* could be represented by **small** + **circle** + **small** ⊛ **circle**. Using this type of representation makes it possible to superimpose the representation for *small circle* and *large triangle* without ghosts of *small triangle* or *large circle* appearing. Including bindings with random identity vectors (see Section 3.5.1) provides further amelioration (i.e., some particular instance of *small circle* could be represented by $\mathbf{id}_{739} + \mathbf{small} + \mathbf{circle} + \mathbf{small} \circledast \mathbf{circle} + \mathbf{id}_{739} \circledast \mathbf{small} + \mathbf{id}_{739} \circledast \mathbf{circle}$).

One should be aware that including some convolution bindings does not automatically solve all crosstalk problems. Consider the following example, which is a reworded version of an example in Rachkovskij and Kussul (2001). Suppose we use a representation that includes bindings between every pair of features, but does not use any identity vectors.

Then we would have representations as follows:

small blue circle	:	**small** ⊛ **blue** + **small** ⊛ **circle** + **blue** ⊛ **circle**
large blue triangle	:	**large** ⊛ **blue** + **large** ⊛ **triangle** + **blue** ⊛ **triangle**
small red triangle	:	**small** ⊛ **red** + **small** ⊛ **triangle** + **red** ⊛ **triangle**

Superimposing these three vectors causes the ghost of *small blue triangle* to appear (because the superposition contains the bindings **small** ⊛ **blue**, **small** ⊛ **triangle**, and **blue** ⊛ **triangle**). This particular problem can be avoided by including higher-order bindings, such as **small** ⊛ **blue** ⊛ **circle** (along the lines of *chunks* in TODAM2 as described in Section 2.4.4). It can also be avoided by including bindings between the features and random identity vectors. Rachkovskij and Kussul's (2001) APNN sparse binary distributed representation (see Section 2.4.6) is partly motivated by desire to avoid these types of problems with crosstalk.

3.12 Summary

Memory models using circular convolution provide a way of representing complex structure in distributed representations. They implement Hinton's (1990) suggestion that reduced descriptions should be systematically derived from their constituents. HRRs preserve natural similarity structure – similar frames are represented by similar HRRs. The operations involved are mostly linear and the properties of the scheme are relatively easy to analyze, especially compared to schemes such Pollack's (1990) RAAMs. No learning is required and the scheme works with a wide range of vectors. Systems employing HRRs must have an error-correcting auto-associative memory to clean up the noisy results produced by convolution decoding. Convolution-based memories have low capacity compared to matrix memories, but the storage capacity is sufficient to be usable and scales almost linearly with vector dimension.

HRRs are intended more as an illustration of how convolution and superposition can be used to represent complex structure than as a strict specification of how complex structure should be represented. The essential features of HRRs are as follows:

- HRRs are a distributed representation.
- They represent frames as the superposition of role-filler bindings (and possibly some additional information).
- The representation of a compositional object has the same dimension as the representation of each of its components.

- Roles and fillers are bound together with associative memory operations, like circular convolution, which do not increase dimensionality and which are randomizing and similarity preserving.

In any particular domain or application, choices must be made about what will and will not be included in the representation, and about how the representation will be structured. For example, in the *contextualized HRRs* used in Chapter 6 bindings derived from the context of fillers are included in the representations for some entities. In other domains, fewer or different HRR components might be appropriate.

4

HRRs in the frequency domain

The fact that convolution is equivalent to elementwise complex multiplication in the frequency domain suggests that it might be possible to work with complex numbers and avoid convolution and Fourier transforms altogether. Indeed, this is the case, and I refer to HRRs computed in this system as *circular HRRs*. Circular HRRs have two major advantages over standard HRRs. The first is that binding (i.e., convolution) can be computed in $O(n)$ time. The second is that it is simple to force all vectors to be unitary, i.e., to force all frequency components to have a magnitude of 1. This is a particularly effective type of normalization: it makes it possible to use the exact inverse, it normalizes the Euclidean length of vectors, it reduces noise in decoding and comparison, and it results in simpler analytic expressions for the variance of dot products of bindings. The only difficulty with working with unitary vectors is that there is no operation that corresponds exactly to superposition: I define a substitute operation in this chapter.

4.1 Circular vectors

In order to work with unitary vectors in the frequency domain, the major representational change required is the use of distributed representations over complex numbers. I define an n-dimensional *circular vector* as a vector of n angles, each between $-\pi$ and π. Each angle can be viewed as the phase of a frequency component. The magnitude of each frequency component is 1, which means that circular vectors are unitary. I use the bar symbol to denote a vector of angles: $\bar{\phi} = [\phi_1, \ldots, \phi_n]^{\mathrm{T}}$. In a *random circular vector*, each of the angles is independently distributed as $\mathrm{U}(-\pi, \pi)$, i.e., the uniform distribution over $(-\pi, \pi]$.

The reader may recall from Section 3.6.2 that there are several constraints on the components of the Fourier transform of real-valued vectors: the angles of $f_0(\mathbf{x})$ and $f_{n/2}(\mathbf{x})$ are zero, and for $0 < i < n/2$, $f_{i+n/2}(\mathbf{x})$ is the complex conjugate of $f_i(\mathbf{x})$. When working with circular vectors it is unnecessary to maintain these constraints, since we can work entirely in the frequency domain without regard to what vectors these might be Fourier transforms of. Thus, each angle in a circular vector is allowed to take on any value in $(-\pi, \pi]$ without constraint.

4.2 HRR operations with circular vectors

HRRs require three operations: comparison, association (and decoding), and superposition. With the standard representation (real-valued vectors with elements distributed as $N(0, 1/n)$), we use the dot product, convolution, and addition. Using straightforward correspondences between operations in the frequency and spatial domains of the Fourier transform, we can derive comparison and association operations for circular vectors. Superposition is a little more tricky, because in general the sum of unit complex values does not lie on the unit circle.

As explained in Section 3.6.2, convolution in the spatial domain is equivalent to elementwise multiplication in the frequency domain. When all values in the frequency domain lie on the unit circle, this is equivalent to modulo-2π addition of angles. I use $\odot$ to denote this operation.

The similarity of two circular vectors can be measured by the mean of the cosines of the differences between corresponding angles:

$$\bar{\psi} \cdot \bar{\phi} = \frac{1}{n} \sum_i \cos(\psi_i - \phi_i)$$

This exactly corresponds to the dot product in the spatial domain, because of the identity

$$\mathbf{x} \cdot \mathbf{y} = \frac{1}{n} \sum_j \cos(\theta_j(\mathbf{x}) - \theta_j(\mathbf{y})),$$

where $\theta_j(\mathbf{x})$ is the phase angle of the jth component of the discrete Fourier transform of $\mathbf{x}$. This identity is easily proved by substituting $(\mathbf{z} - \mathbf{y})$ for $\mathbf{x}$ in the discrete version of Parseval's theorem, which states that $\sum_k x_k^2 = \frac{1}{n} \sum_k |f_k(\mathbf{x})|^2$, where $f_k(\mathbf{x})$ is the kth component of the discrete Fourier transform of $\mathbf{x}$.

The most obvious way to define superposition with circular vectors is as the angle of the rectangular sum of complex numbers. This requires storing both the angle and magnitude (or the real and the imaginary components) of the complex values during computation of the superposition. At the end of the computation the magnitudes are discarded. This corresponds to computing the sum in the spatial domain and normalizing the frequency magnitudes of the result. It is possible to use weights in superpositions by multiplying each vector by a weight before adding it into the superposition. Thus, we can define the circular superposition function sp() for k angles (i.e., complex values on the unit circle) with weights w_i as

$$\mathrm{sp}(w_1, \ldots, w_k, \phi_1, \ldots, \phi_k) = \theta$$

such that $\cos(\theta) = \sum_{i=1}^{k} w_i \cos \phi_i$ and $\sin(\theta) = \sum_{i=1}^{k} w_i \sin \phi_i$.

This definition is easily extended to vectors of angles by performing the same operation with corresponding elements of the vectors. For notational convenience, I omit the weights when they are all the same. I use the symbol $\oplus$ to denote the circular superposition of two vectors: $\theta \oplus \phi = \mathrm{sp}(\theta, \phi)$.

The circular superposition operation differs from standard superposition in that it is not strictly associative. In general,

$$((\theta \oplus \phi) \oplus \psi) \neq (\theta \oplus (\phi \oplus \psi)).$$

This is due to the normalization of magnitudes, which leads to ψ having a larger contribution to $(\theta \oplus \phi) \oplus \psi$ than θ or ϕ. However, this is not likely to be a serious problem – if it is desired to have a equally-weighted circular superposition of more than two vectors, the function $\mathrm{sp}(\cdot)$ as defined above can be used. Note also that the same is true for the standard HRR system when normalization is used.

Table 12 summarizes the corresponding entities and operations for standard and circular systems. In order to predict how well circular vectors and the associated operations will perform as a basis for HRRs, we need to know the means and variances of the similarity and decoding operations. In Appendix H I derive means and variances for some combinations, and report experimental results. It turns out that the variances for decoding bindings of circular vectors are lower and more uniform than for normalized or unnormalized standard vectors, which means that the circular system should be less noisy. However, the means for dot products of similar vectors (such as $\bar{\theta} \cdot (\bar{\theta} \oplus \bar{\phi})$) are also lower, which to some extent balances the advantage of lower variances. Tables 13 and 14 show the means and variances of dot products of various expressions for circular and unnormalized standard vectors. In Appendix H, I also compare the circular system to the normalized standard system. Overall, it appears that the circular system is far superior to the unnormalized standard system, and slightly superior to the normalized standard system in terms of signal-to-noise ratios.

Entity/Operation	Circular system	Standard system
Random vector	Elements iid as $U(-\pi, \pi)$	Elements iid as $N(0, 1/n)$
Superposition	Angle of sum $\theta \oplus \phi$, sp()	Addition $\mathbf{x} + \mathbf{y}$
Weights in superposition	Weights in angle of sum	Scalar multiplication
Additive zero	No corresponding object	$\overline{0} = [0, 0, \ldots, 0]^{\mathsf{T}}$
Association	Modulo-2π sum of angles $\bar{\theta} \odot \bar{\phi}$ (Element-wise complex multiplication)	Convolution $\mathbf{x} \circledast \mathbf{y}$
Associative identity	Vector of zero angles	Convolutive identity: $\bar{\mathbf{I}} = [1, 0, \ldots, 0]^{\mathsf{T}}$
Exact inverse	Negation (modulo-2π) $-\theta$	Inverse $\mathbf{x}^{-1}$
Approximate inverse	Same as exact inverse	Involution $\mathbf{x}^{*}$
Similarity	Sum of cosine of differences $\bar{\theta} \cdot \bar{\phi}$	dot product $\mathbf{x} \cdot \mathbf{y}$
Normalization	Not needed – circular vectors are normalized	$\langle \mathbf{x} \rangle$

TABLE 12 Corresponding entities and operations in the circular and standard systems. *iid* means *independently and identically distributed.*

4.3   Relationship to binary spatter codes

As Kanerva (1996) notes, there is an interesting relationship between Kanerva's binary spatter codes and circular HRRs: binary spatter codes are identical to circular HRRs working on unitary vectors with phase angles quantized to 0 and π.[43] Such quantized circular HRRs store one bit of information in each vector element – the two possible values are $(r = 1, \theta = 0)$ and $(r = 1, \theta = \pi)$ in polar coordinates, i.e., $1 + 0i$ and $-1 + 0i$. Recall that binary spatter codes use exclusive-OR for binding binary vectors, and the majority rule for the superposition of a set of vectors. It is straightforward to see that elementwise multiplication of complex vectors whose elements can be $(r = 1, \theta = 0)$ or $(r = 1, \theta = \pi)$ is equivalent to exclusive-OR, and that the sum of such vectors followed by elementwise quantization to $(r = 1, \theta = 0)$ or $(r = 1, \theta = \pi)$ is equivalent to computing the elementwise majority.

---

[43]This observation is due to Pentti Kanerva (personal communication).

Expression	Circular system		Standard system	
	mean	variance	mean	variance
(1) $\mathbf{a} \cdot \mathbf{a}$	1	0	1	$\frac{2}{n}$
(2) $\mathbf{a} \cdot \mathbf{b}$	0	$\frac{1}{2n}$	0	$\frac{1}{n}$
(3) $\mathbf{a} \cdot \mathbf{a} \odot \mathbf{b}$	0	$\frac{1}{2n}$	0	$\frac{2n+1}{n^2}$
(4) $\mathbf{a} \cdot \mathbf{b} \odot \mathbf{c}$	0	$\frac{1}{2n}$	0	$\frac{1}{n}$
(5) $\mathbf{a} \odot \mathbf{a} \cdot \mathbf{a} \odot \mathbf{a} = \mathbf{a} \odot \mathbf{a} \odot \mathbf{a}^* \cdot \mathbf{a}$	1	0	$2 + \frac{2}{n}$	$\frac{40n+112}{n^2}$
(6) $\mathbf{a} \odot \mathbf{b} \cdot \mathbf{a} \odot \mathbf{b} = \mathbf{a} \odot \mathbf{b} \odot \mathbf{a}^* \cdot \mathbf{b}$	1	0	1	$\frac{6n+4}{n^2}$
(7) $\mathbf{a} \odot \mathbf{b} \cdot \mathbf{a} \odot \mathbf{a} = \mathbf{a} \odot \mathbf{b} \odot \mathbf{a}^* \cdot \mathbf{a}$	0	$\frac{1}{2n}$	0	$\frac{6n+18}{n^2}$
(8) $\mathbf{a} \odot \mathbf{b} \cdot \mathbf{a} \odot \mathbf{c} = \mathbf{a} \odot \mathbf{b} \odot \mathbf{a}^* \cdot \mathbf{c}$	0	$\frac{1}{2n}$	0	$\frac{2n+2}{n^2}$
(9) $\mathbf{a} \odot \mathbf{b} \cdot \mathbf{c} \odot \mathbf{c} = \mathbf{a} \odot \mathbf{b} \odot \mathbf{c}^* \cdot \mathbf{c}$	0	$\frac{1}{2n}$	0	$\frac{2n+2}{n^2}$
(10) $\mathbf{a} \odot \mathbf{b} \cdot \mathbf{c} \odot \mathbf{d} = \mathbf{a} \odot \mathbf{b} \odot \mathbf{c}^* \cdot \mathbf{d}$	0	$\frac{1}{2n}$	0	$\frac{1}{n}$

TABLE 13 Means and variances of dot products for decoding and comparing bindings. The first two columns of numbers are for the circular system (reproduced from Table 33), and the last two columns are for the corresponding operations (i.e., using $\circledast$ instead of $\odot$) in the unnormalized standard system (reproduced from Table 3). n is the dimensionality of the vectors. The dot products are normally distributed in the limit as n goes to infinity.

Circular system			Standard (unnormalized) system		
Expression	mean	variance	Expression	mean	variance
$\mathbf{a} \cdot \mathbf{a}$	1	0	$\mathbf{a} \cdot \mathbf{a}$	1	$\frac{2}{n}$
$\mathbf{a} \cdot \mathbf{b}$	0	$\frac{1}{2n}$	$\mathbf{a} \cdot \mathbf{b}$	0	$\frac{1}{n}$
$\mathbf{a} \cdot (\mathbf{a} \oplus \mathbf{b})$	$\frac{2}{\pi} = 0.637\ldots$	$\frac{-8+\pi^2}{2\pi^2 n} = \frac{0.0947\ldots}{n}$	$\mathbf{a} \cdot \frac{1}{\sqrt{2}}(\mathbf{a}+\mathbf{b})$	$\frac{1}{\sqrt{2}}$	$\frac{3}{2n}$

TABLE 14 Means and variances for comparing similar, dissimilar, and half-similar vectors. $\mathbf{a}$ and $\mathbf{b}$ are random vectors. The formula for the circular system are from Appendix H.

4.4   Comparison with the standard system

Overall, circular HRRs appear to be superior to standard HRRs. Advantages of the circular relative to the standard system are as follows:

- Variances of dot products are lower, which means that there is less noise in decoding and in similarity comparisons.
- Variances of dot products of convolution expressions are simpler and more uniform, which makes variances easier to calculate (compare Table 33 in Appendix H with Table 3).

- The involution (which is the approximate inverse in the standard system) of a unitary circular vector is equal to its exact inverse.
- It is easy to create lower-precision representations by quantizing angles. Furthermore, with quantized angles the superposition, association, and similarity operations could possibly be speeded up by using lookup tables.
- Encoding and decoding bindings can be done in $O(n)$ time, compared to $O(n \log n)$ time for the standard system.

Disadvantages of the circular relative to the standard system are these:

- The means of similarity comparisons are lower (but the lower variances compensate for this.)
- Superposition is slower to compute, because the calculations are more complex. It still can be done in $O(n)$ time, but the constant is higher.
- The dot-product calculation is slower to compute because it involves n cosines (however, these could be computed by a fast table lookup, so this is not very important.)
- The scalar values in the distributed representation are angles rather than magnitudes, which makes it more difficult to use with common neural networks.

The two system are equivalent with respect to scaling properties, because the variance of decoding and similarity operations is inversely proportional to n.

For the remainder of this book I use normalized standard vectors rather than circular vectors, for two reasons. The first is that I expect standard vectors to be more accessible to researchers familiar with popular connectionist representations. The second is that the computational advantage of using circular vectors is less than it might appear. Encoding and decoding bindings is faster: it takes $O(n)$ time, as opposed to $O(n \log n)$ for the standard representation. However, the computational cost of simulations tends to be dominated by the clean-up memory, and the circular vector similarity operation is more expensive to compute.[44] In any case, all the experiments in this book could be replicated with circular vectors, although the results would not be identical. Furthermore, neural networks can be easily adapted to work with complex numbers. The most complex experiments performed with ordi-

---

[44]If table lookup were used for the cosines, the amount of computation for clean-up would be the same in the two systems.

nary HRRs in this book are replicated with circular HRRs in Appendix H.

5

Using convolution-based storage in systems that learn

Hinton (1989) and Miikkulainen and Dyer (1989) showed that useful distributed representations of objects could be learned using gradient descent in feedforward (backpropagation) network. Pollack (1990) showed that an autoencoder network could even learn representations for hierarchical structures. This ability to learn representations has two important applications: developing new representations and fine-tuning existing ones.

Given the difficulties encountered in learning representational schemes for compositional structures (such as Pollack's), and given that there are simple convolution-based methods for representing compositional structures, it is interesting to consider how convolution-based storage schemes might be incorporated into networks that could learn representations using gradient descent training. In this chapter I describe how the trajectory-association method for representing sequences (Section 3.4.1) can be incorporated into a recurrent network. I report some experiments in which these networks develop representations for objects and sequences, and compare their performance with that of more conventional recurrent networks.

5.1 Trajectory-association

A simple method for storing sequences using circular convolution is to associate elements of the sequence with points along a predetermined trajectory. This is akin to the memory aid called the *method of loci*, which instructs us to remember a list of items by associating each term with a distinctive location along a familiar path. Elements of the sequence and loci (points) on the trajectory are all represented by n-dimensional vectors. For example, the sequence "abc" can be stored as:

$$s_{abc} = p_0 \circledast a + p_1 \circledast b + p_2 \circledast c,$$

where the p_i are vectors representing the loci, which should not be similar to each other, and a, b, and c are the vectors representing the items. This representation of a sequence can be decoded by convolving it with the approximate inverses of the p_i in the appropriate order.

An easy way to generate a suitable sequence of loci is to use convolutive powers of a random unitary vector k, i.e., $p_i = k^i$. Convolutive powers are defined in the obvious way: k^0 is the identity vector and $k^{i+1} = k^i \circledast k$. Unitary vectors (Section 3.6.3) have unit magnitude in each of their frequency components – thus the magnitude of each of their eigenvalues is one. They are the class of vectors for which the exact inverse is equal to the approximate inverse. Restricting k to be unitary ensures that k does not blow up or disappear when raised to high powers because, for any unitary vector k, and for all t, $\|k^t\| = 1$;

Using convolutive powers for the loci, the trajectory-association representation for the sequence "abc" is:

$$s_{abc} = a + b \circledast k + c \circledast k^2.$$

Raising a unitary vector to some power t corresponds to multiplying the phase angles of its frequency components by t. (Fractional convolutive powers are easily defined in this way.) The series $k^1, k^2, k^3, \ldots$ where k is a unitary vector does not converge (except in the case where all phase angles are zero). Because the magnitude of each frequency component is one (from the definition of a unitary vector), the magnitude of each frequency component of k^t is also one. As t increases, one can think of the phase angles in k spinning around at different rates – for each increment of t the phase angle of frequency component j increases by $\theta_j(k)$. In effect, the series $k^1, k^2, k^3, \ldots$ maps out a pseudo-random trajectory through the space of unitary vectors. The starting point of this path (i.e., k) determines the entire path. We can use this path as a series of cues for storing and recalling a sequence.

It is useful to consider how close (i.e., how similar) points along this path are. Recall that the similarity of two unitary vectors depends on how well their corresponding phase angles match – the dot product is proportional to the sum of the cosines of the differences of the angles:

$$x \cdot y = \frac{1}{n} \sum_j \cos(\theta_j(x) - \theta_j(y)),$$

where $\theta_j(x)$ is the phase angle of the jth (frequency) component of the discrete Fourier transform of x.[45] Since the phase angles are randomly

---

[45]This identity is easily proved by substituting $(z - y)$ for x in the discrete version

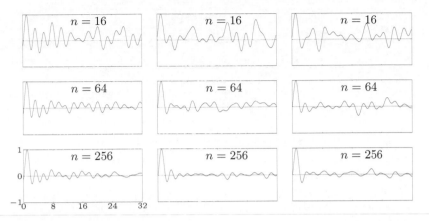

FIGURE 43 Example trajectory similarities. Each plot shows the similarity (vertical axis) of $\mathbf{k}$ to $\mathbf{k}^t$, for $t = 0$ to 32 (horizontal axis), for randomly selected unitary vectors $\mathbf{k}$ of dimension n. All plots are to the same scale. The first peak in each graph is for $t = 1$ (because $\mathbf{k}^1 = \mathbf{k}$). For large n, randomly chosen $\mathbf{k}$, and $t > 2$, the expected similarity of $\mathbf{k} \cdot \mathbf{k}^t$ is $2/n$, and the variance decreases with n.

distributed in $(-\pi, \pi]$, different integer powers of the same unitary vector have low expected similarity. Of course, for unitary $\mathbf{k}$ with phase angles that are rational fractions of π, there is always some t such that $\mathbf{k}^t = \mathbf{k}$. However, this t is almost always extremely large. Figure 43 shows some plots of the similarity of $\mathbf{k}^t$ to $\mathbf{k}$, for unitary vectors of various dimensions. For higher dimensions, the similarity of $\mathbf{k}$ and $\mathbf{k}^t$ for $t \geq 2$ has lower variance. Note that for t between 0 and 2, $\mathbf{k}$ and $\mathbf{k}^t$ become more similar as t becomes closer to 1. Also, it is easy to show that the similarity of two vectors is invariant under translation in power: $\mathbf{k} \cdot \mathbf{k}^t = \mathbf{k}^{1+\alpha} \cdot \mathbf{k}^{t+\alpha}$ for all α. This means that the similarity of $\mathbf{k}^6$ and $\mathbf{k}^8$ is the same as the similarity of $\mathbf{k}$ and $\mathbf{k}^3$, for example.

The waveforms in figure 43 are actually the superpositions of $n/2 - 1$ equally-weighted sine waves, and a constant $2/n$.[46] Each sine wave is generated by one frequency component of $\mathbf{k}$, and its period is $2\pi/\alpha$, where α is the phase angle (in $(-\pi, \pi]$).

---

of Parseval's theorem, which states that $\sum_k x_k^2 = \frac{1}{n} \sum_k |f_k(\mathbf{x})|^2$, where $f_k(\mathbf{x})$ is the k component of the discrete Fourier transform f $\mathbf{x}$.

[46]The constant of $2/n$ comes from the two frequency components that have a phase angle of zero for real vectors.

Direct		Recursive		Expansion			Result
$\mathbf{k}^0 \circledast \mathbf{s}_{abc}$	$=$	$\mathbf{s}_{abc}$		$= \mathbf{a}$	$+\mathbf{b} \circledast \mathbf{k}$	$+\mathbf{c} \circledast \mathbf{k}^2$	$\approx \mathbf{a}$
$\mathbf{k}^{-1} \circledast \mathbf{s}_{abc}$	$=$	$\mathbf{k}^{-1} \circledast \mathbf{s}_{abc}$		$= \mathbf{a} \circledast \mathbf{k}^{-1}+\mathbf{b}$		$+\mathbf{c} \circledast \mathbf{k}$	$\approx \mathbf{b}$
$\mathbf{k}^{-2} \circledast \mathbf{s}_{abc}$	$=$	$\mathbf{k}^{-1} \circledast (\mathbf{k}^{-1} \circledast \mathbf{s}_{abc})$		$= \mathbf{a} \circledast \mathbf{k}^{-2}+\mathbf{b} \circledast \mathbf{k}^{-1}+\mathbf{c}$			$\approx \mathbf{c}$

TABLE 15   The direct and recursive methods of decoding a trajectory-associated sequence.

5.1.1   Decoding trajectory-associated sequences

Trajectory-associated sequences can be decoded by repeatedly convolving with the inverse of the vector that generated the encoding loci. As with all convolution-based associations, the results are noisy and must be cleaned up. This requires all possible items to be stored in the clean-up memory.

There are two equivalent methods for decoding a trajectory-associated sequence, which are shown in Table 15. Since the approximate inverses of the loci are equal to their exact inverses (i.e., $(\mathbf{k}^*)^i = \mathbf{k}^{-i}$), I use negative powers to indicate the inverses of the loci. In the direct access method, the inverses of each loci are used to probe the sequence representation:

$$\mathbf{r}_i = \mathbf{k}^{-i} \circledast \mathbf{s},$$

where $\mathbf{r}_i$ is the decoded ith element of the sequence represented by $\mathbf{s}$. In the recursive access method, the sequence representation is repeatedly convolved with $\mathbf{k}^{-1}$, which steps through the elements of the sequence:

$$\mathbf{r}_0 = \mathbf{s} \quad \text{and} \quad \mathbf{r}_i = \mathbf{k}^{-1} \circledast \mathbf{r}_{i-1}$$

These two methods are equivalent because convolution is associative.

For example, to retrieve the third element of the sequence $\mathbf{s}_{abc}$ we convolve twice with $\mathbf{k}^{-1}$, and the result expands to $\mathbf{a} \circledast \mathbf{k}^{-2}+\mathbf{b} \circledast \mathbf{k}^{-1}+\mathbf{c}$. The first two terms are unlikely to be correlated with any items in the clean-up memory, so the most similar item will probably be $\mathbf{c}$.

5.1.2   Capacity of trajectory-association

In Appendix D, I calculate the capacity of circular-convolution-based associative memory. I assume that the elements of all vectors (dimension n) are chosen randomly from a Gaussian distribution with mean zero and variance $1/n$ (giving an expected Euclidean length of 1.0). Even for short sequences, quite high vector dimensions are required to ensure a low probability of error in decoding. For example, with 512 element vectors and 1000 items in the clean-up memory, 4 pairs can be stored with about a 1% chance of an error in decoding. The scaling is nearly linear in n – with 1024 element vectors, 8 pairs can be stored

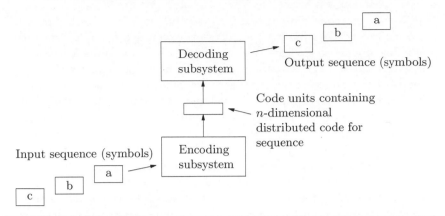

FIGURE 44 Subsystems to encode a sequence of symbols into a trajectory-associated code, and decode the code back into a sequence of symbols. The encoding and decoding subsystems must store internally the n-dimensional vectors that represent the symbols.

with about a 1% chance of error. This works out to an information capacity of about 0.16 bits per element. The elements are floating-point numbers, but high precision is not required.

These capacity calculations are roughly applicable to trajectory-association – the number of pairs corresponds to the length of sequences. They slightly underestimate its capacity because of the restriction that the encoding loci are unitary vectors, which results in lower decoding noise. Nonetheless this figure provides a useful benchmark against which to compare the capacity of the adaptive networks described in this chapter, which, on account of the training, should be able to store more.

5.2 Encoding and decoding systems for trajectory-associated sequences

Figure 44 shows the obvious way in which an encoding subsystem and a decoding subsystem can be composed to form a system that can store and recall sequences. In a system that uses trajectory-association to form distributed codes for sequences, there are at least two opportunities for learning representations. We can learn distributed representations for the individual items (à la Hinton (1989)), and we can fine-tune the distributed code for a sequence. The latter can be useful if errors occur during recall of the sequence – often we can adjust the code so that it is read out correctly.

If the error surfaces of the decoder are simple enough, the idea of adjusting the code for the sequence so that it is read out correctly can be extended to finding the code for a sequence from an arbitrary starting point. To do this, we instantiate the code units with some starting vector (e.g., a random vector), run the decoder to see what sequence it produces, compare that to the sequence we want to produce, backpropagate the errors, and adjust the code units to better produce the desired sequence. We repeat this until the code units contain the vector that produces the desired sequence.

In this chapter I only consider the decoding system, and investigate to what extent gradient descent methods can learn good representations for items and find codes for producing sequences of items. In some ways, this is the opposite of how recurrent networks are usually used to process sequences, in that the sequence is the output rather than the input. The reason I do this is that I wish to focus on representations for sequences. Decoding the sequence representation is a convenient way of ensuring that all the sequential information is present. Furthermore, at this preliminary stage I wish to avoid the complexity of constructing both encoding and decoding systems.

5.3 Trajectory-association decoding in a recurrent network

It is straightforward to build the trajectory-association decoding operations (Section 5.1.1) into a recurrent network. I call the resulting network a *Holographic Recurrent Network* (HRN).

This and the following sections describe some experiments that examine and compare the generic sequence-production ability of HRNs and Simple Recurrent Networks (SRNs) Elman (1991). These experiments with recurrent networks contrast with ones performed by Elman (1991) and others such as Tabor et al. (1997), which investigate the ability of recurrent neural networks to learn about the statistical structure of some particular set of sentences (e.g., the set of sentences that can be produced by a small, English-like grammar). The experiments described here were intended to give some insight into whether gradient descent learning techniques can be combined with the convolution-based techniques for representing conventional data structures (e.g., sequences) in fixed-width activation vectors. I focus here on the basic issues of representational adequacy and learnability in the belief that understanding these issues provides a foundation for understanding the potential and limitations of neural networks and distributed representations for more complex tasks involving complex data with rich statistical structure.

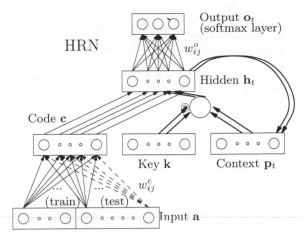

FIGURE 45 A Holographic Recurrent Network (HRN). The backwards curved arrows denote a copy of activations to the next time step. The hidden, code, context, and key layers all have the same number of units. The left block of input units is used during training, the right block during testing.

5.3.1 Architecture

The HRN used in the experiments described here is shown in Figure 45. The clean-up memory is easily implemented with a *softmax* output layer (see Section 5.3.2). The output layer does not actually hold distributed representations for symbols; instead it uses a localist representation. The softmax function ensures that the total activity in the output layer sums to 1, so that the output activities can be interpreted as probabilities. The output unit with maximum activation will be the one whose incoming weights best match the activations on the hidden units (the incoming weights on the outputs are the distributed representations of symbols). Using a localist output representation and the softmax function allows us to take derivatives of the error function. If we wanted to have distributed representations for symbols on the output, we could add an extra output layer and the weights to map the localist representation to the distributed one.

The key layer **k** has fixed activation and contains the generator for the inverse loci (**k** here corresponds to $\mathbf{k}^{-1}$ in Section 5.1, because **k** here is the decoding rather than the encoding key).

The input representation is also localist: only one input unit is active for each sequence. The outgoing weights from the single active input unit determine the activations at the code layer – these weights form a local-to-distributed map (as discussed in Section 2.2.2). The code layer injects activation into the hidden layer at the first step. After that the hidden-layer activations are cycled through the context layer, so the input and code units no longer affect the network.

Each sequence is produced independently – no residual activations from the production of previous sequences remain in the network.

5.3.2 Unit functions

The HRN computes the following functions. The activations of the input, code, and key layers remain constant during the production of a sequence. The parameter g is an adaptable input gain shared by all output units.

Code units:		$c_j = \sum_i a_i w^c_{ji}$
Hidden units:	(first time step)	$h_{1,j} = c_j$
	(subsequent steps)	$h_{t,j} = \sum_i p_i k_{j-i}$ $(\mathbf{h} = \mathbf{p} \circledast \mathbf{k})$
Context units:		$p_{t+1,j} = h_{t,j}$
Output units:	(total input)	$x_{t,j} = g \sum_i h_{t,i} w^o_{ji}$
	(output)	$o_{t,j} = \frac{e^{x_{t,j}}}{\sum_i e^{x_{t,i}}}$ (softmax)

On all sequences, the net is cycled for as many time steps as required to produce the target sequence. The outputs do not indicate when the net has reached the end of the sequence. However, other experiments have shown that it is a simple matter to add an extra output unit to indicate the end of the sequence.

The inputs and outputs to the network look like this:

		Output			
Sequence	Input	$t = 0$	$t = 1$	$t = 2$	$t = 3$
abc	1 0 0 0...0	1 0 0	0 1 0	0 0 1	
baac	0 1 0 0...0	0 1 0	1 0 0	1 0 0	0 0 1

5.3.3 Objective function

The objective function of the network is the asymmetric divergence between the activations of the output units $(o^s_{t,j})$ and the targets $(t^s_{t,j})$ summed over cases s and time steps t, plus two weight penalty terms:

$$E = - \left(\sum_{stj} t^s_{t,j} \log \frac{o^s_{t,j}}{t^s_{t,j}} \right) + \frac{0.0001}{n} \sum_{jk} (w^c_{jk})^2 + \sum_j \left(1 - \sum_k (w^o_{jk})^2 \right)^2$$

The first weight penalty term is a standard weight cost designed to penalize large weights (n is the number of hidden units). It is probably superfluous in the HRN, because the various operations from the w^c_{jk} to the total inputs of the output layer (x_j) are all linear, and scaling of the w^c_{jk} can be compensated for by the gain g. Later experiments without this weight cost term indicated that it has no effect on performance.

The second weight penalty term is designed to force the Euclidean length of the weight vector on each output unit to be one. This makes the output layer more like an ideal clean-up memory. The generalization performance with this special penalty term for the output weights is considerably better than that with a standard weight cost for the output weights (which is in turn better than that with no weight penalty). The reason for the worse performance with the standard weight cost is that the symbols that occur more frequently in the training set develop output weight vectors with higher magnitudes.

5.3.4 Derivatives

To do gradient descent learning, partial derivatives for all the adjustable parameters are required: $\frac{\partial E}{\partial w^o_{jk}}$, $\frac{\partial E}{\partial w^c_{jk}}$, and $\frac{\partial E}{\partial g}$. All of these can be easily calculated from the above equations using the chain rule and Rumelhart et al.'s (1986a) unfolding-in-time technique. The only partial derivatives not encountered in common backpropagation networks are those for the activations of the context units:

$$\frac{\partial E}{\partial p_j} = \sum_k \frac{\partial E}{\partial h_j} y_{k-j} \qquad (\equiv \nabla_{\mathbf{p}} = \nabla_{\mathbf{h}} \circledast \mathbf{y}^*)$$

When there are a large number of hidden units it is more efficient to compute this derivative via FFTs as the convolution expression on the right ($\nabla_{\mathbf{p}}$ and $\nabla_{\mathbf{h}}$ are the vectors of partial derivatives of E with respect to $\mathbf{p}$ and $\mathbf{h}$).

5.3.5 Training and testing productive capacity

To be useful, a trainable storage scheme for structures must be able to store a wide variety of novel structures without requiring adjustment of its basic parameters after initial training. In a HRN, the basic parameters are the weights on the output units. The novel structures are sequences the network was not exposed to in the initial training. I refer to the ability of the network to store novel sequences as its *productive capacity*.

I performed initial training on a small number of short sequences in order to find good values for the output weights w^o_{jk}, the output gain g, and the weights w^c_{ij} for all i in the training set. Each training (or testing case) uses one vector of weights from w^c_{ij}, which determines the activation values on the units 1 through j in the code layer. One the HRN was trained I froze the output weights w^o_{jk} and the output gain g. Next, I attempted to estimate the productive capacity of the trained HRNs. I did this by repeatedly choosing a longer novel sequence at random and testing whether a gradient descent search could find a vector of code activation values (i.e., a vector of weights w_{ij}^c for sequence i) that would cause the trained HRN to output the sequence.

For the initial training I used randomly chosen sequences of length 4 over various numbers of symbols. The number of symbols corresponds to the number of output units in the network. The number of sequences in the training set is 4 times the number of symbols, which means that on average each symbol occurs 16 times in a training set. For example, there are 12 sequences in the training set over three symbols. I initialized all weights to small random values, and the output gain to 1. I used conjugate-gradient minimization and stopped when all sequences were correctly produced (or when 400 steps had been taken). I judged a sequence to be correctly produced only if all its symbols are correct. I judged a symbol to be correct when the activation of the correct output unit exceeds 0.5 and exceeds twice any other output-unit activation.[47]

For estimating the productive capacity I used novel sequences of lengths 3 to 16 (32 sequences of each length, giving 448 novel sequences). I used a conjugate-gradient search to find a code (i.e., one row of the input to code layer weights w_{ij}^c) for each sequence. None of the other weights in the network was modified during this search. The search was started from small random values, and stopped when the sequence has been correctly produced, or when 100 steps have been taken, whichever happened first.

5.4   Simple Recurrent Networks

In this section, I compare HRNs to other more conventional recurrent networks, both to get some idea of their relative capacities and because the comparison gives some insight into various reported difficulties with recurrent networks. Elman (1991) and Servan-Schreiber et al. (1991) use Simple Recurrent Networks (SRNs) to process sequential input and induce small finite state grammars. However, their training times are extremely long, even for very simple grammars. Maskara and Noetzel (1992) report similar results and make the plausible suggestion that the long training times are due to the difficulty of finding a recurrent operation that preserves information in the hidden units over many time steps. Simard and LeCun (1992) report being unable to train a type of recurrent network to produce more than one trajectory through continuous space, a task that requires careful control over information

---

[47]Insisting that the winning unit have twice the activation of any other unit is not really necessary with softmax units, as the margin of winning can easily be made as large as desired by increasing the output gain.

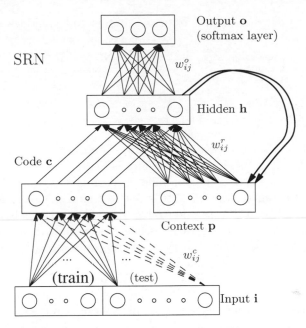

FIGURE 46   A Simple Recurrent Network (SRN). The backwards curved arrows denote a copy of activations to the next time step. The hidden, code, and context layers all have the same number of units. The left block of input units is used during training, the right block during testing.

in the hidden units.

Given these reported difficulties, I expected that SRNs would perform poorly at the sequence-production task, since it requires preserving and transforming information in the hidden units over many time steps. To test this, I built a version of the SRN for the sequence-production task. The architecture of this SRN differs from the HRN in that the hidden layer receives activation through a weight matrix from the context layer, as with the SRNs. The SRN is shown in Figure 46.

The only difference between the SRN and the HRN is in the computation of the activations of the hidden units:

$$h_j = \tanh(c_j + \sum_k w^r_{jk} p_k + b_j),$$

where b_j is a bias on each hidden unit. As with the HRN, the activations on the code units do not change during the production of a sequence. However, in contrast with the HRN, the activations of the code units flow to the hidden units at every time step.

The objective function for the SRN is the same as for the HRN, except for the inclusion of an extra penalty term for large recurrent weights (i.e., w_{ij}^r, the weights from the context to the hidden layer):

$$E = -\left(\sum_{stj} t_{t,j}^s \log \frac{o_{t,j}^s}{t_{t,j}^s}\right) + \frac{0.0001}{n}\left(\sum_{jk}(w_{jk}^r)^2 + \sum_{jk}(w_{jk}^c)^2\right)$$
$$+ \sum_j \left(1 - \sum_k (w_{jk}^o)^2\right)^2$$

The SRNs described here differ in two important ways from other SRNs described in the literature (besides being used to produce rather than process sequences): the tanh function (symmetric sigmoid) is used on the hidden units, rather than the non-symmetric logistic function, and full unfolding-in-time is used to calculate correct derivatives, rather than Elman's truncated derivative scheme. Experiments showed that both changes significantly improved training times and productive capacity.

In the experiments with SRNs, I used almost exactly the same training and testing regime as for HRNs. The only difference was that I also experimented with training sets containing more examples.

5.5 Training and productive capacity results

5.5.1 Holographic Recurrent Network results

HRNs prove to be easy to train, and to have good productive capacity. They also appear to have good scaling properties – as the number of hidden units increases they can store longer sequences or sequences over more symbols. Figure 47 shows the performance of HRNs with eight output units and varying numbers of hidden units. The points shown are averages of data from five runs, each starting with a randomization of all parameters. As the number of hidden units increases from 4 to 64 the productive capacity increases steadily. For a HRN with a fixed number of hidden units, the length of sequences that can be stored reliably drops as the number of symbols increases, as shown in Figure 48. This is expected because when there are more symbols, more information is required to specify them. For example, the same amount of information is required to specify a sequence of length eight over three symbols as a sequence of length four over nine symbols.

To make a rough guess at the information efficiency of HRN sequence codes we can calculation how much information is in the maximum-length sequence that can be reliably encoded. For example, Figure 47 shows that a HRN with 16 hidden units can reliably store sequences of length 5 over 8 symbols. Such a sequence contains 15 bits of information

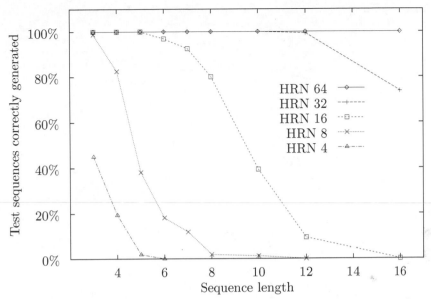

FIGURE 47 Percentage of novel sequences that can be produced, versus length of those sequences for HRNs with varying numbers of hidden units. The sequences are over 8 symbols. All points are averages of data from 5 different training runs.

(assuming all symbols are equally likely), which gives an information efficiency of nearly 1 bit per code element (15/16). This figure appears stable for different numbers of hidden units and for different numbers of symbols. This compares well with the 0.16 bit per element achieved by random vector circular convolution (Section 5.1.2). The increase in capacity can be attributed largely to the adaptive method of forming codes.

5.5.2 Simple Recurrent Network results

SRNs turned out to be better at this task than expected. Figure 49 shows how the performance varies with sequence length for various networks with 16 hidden units. SRNs required much more training data, which is not surprising since they have more parameters in the form of weights from the context to the hidden layer. The productive capacity for a SRN trained on 12 sequences of length 4 (the same amount of data as a HRN) was very poor – compare the bottom and top lines in the graph. However, with more training data consisting of longer sequences, the productive capacity was better, though never as high as that of HRNs. In the figure, "srn+" is the productive capacity of an

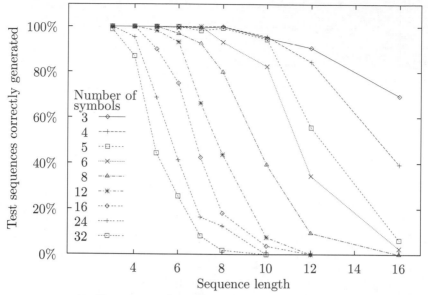

FIGURE 48 Percentage of novel sequences that can be produced by HRNs with 16 hidden units, versus length of those sequences, for varying numbers of symbols (i.e., varying numbers of output units). All points are averages of data from 5 different training runs.

SRN trained on 48 sequences of length 8 (8 times as much training data) and "SRN++" is one trained on 192 sequences of length 8 (32 times as much training data). The length of training sequences appeared to have a significant effect on productive capacity. Experiments not shown here indicated that the increase in productive capacity obtained by doubling the length of training sequences (4 to 8) was greater than that obtained by doubling the number of training sequences.

Interestingly, freezing the recurrent weights at random values results in a significant increase in productive capacity for a SRN trained on the small training set ("SRNZ" in the figure). Random values for all the weights coming into the hidden units are chosen from a Gaussian distribution with mean zero and the same variance as those from a sample trained SRN (0.2 for a net with 16 hidden units). These weights are frozen at the beginning of training and never changed. The productive capacity achieved with these weights tends to suggest that the recurrent weights are not doing much more than a random mapping. The performance would probably improve further if the weight matrix were chosen so that all its eigenvalues were of equal magnitude (like the

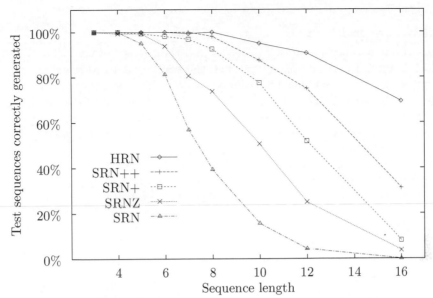

FIGURE 49 Percentage of novel sequences that can be produced versus length of those sequences, for various types of networks (all with 16 hidden units and 3 symbols). "SRN+" is the SRN with 8 times as much training data and "SRN++" is the SRN with 32 times as much. "SRNZ" is the SRN with frozen random recurrent weights. All points are averages of data from 5 different training runs.

recurrent operation in HRNs).

In general, modifications to SRNs that make them more like HRNs seem to improve performance. As mentioned before, early experiments with the standard non-symmetric sigmoid operation on the hidden layer had very poor performance. The symmetric sigmoid (tanh), which is more like the linear transfer function in the HRN, gives much better performance. Freezing the hidden weights at random values also improves performance (for nets with a small training set). Other experiments showed that removing the bias on the hidden units usually improves performance. Changing the hidden-unit transfer function of the SRN from tanh to linear improves performance on shorter novel sequences, but not on longer novel sequences. This is probably because the linear transfer function allows eigenvectors with large eigenvalues to grow exponentially, whereas the tanh function limits their growth. The only change that makes the SRN more like the HRN, and that consistently harms performance, is making the code units inject activation into the hidden units at the first time step only.

5.5.3 General training and testing issues

The training times for both the HRNs and the SRNs are very short. Both require around 30 passes through the training data to train the output and recurrent weights. Finding a code for test sequences of length 8 takes the HRN an average of 14 passes, and the SRN an average of 57 passes (44 with frozen recurrent weights). The SRN trained on more data takes much longer for the initial training (average 281 passes) but the code search is shorter (average 31 passes).

Local minima in the space of codes for trained networks are not a significant problem for either HRNs or SRNs. Experiments with restarts for failed searches for a sequence code (during testing) show that allowing one restart improves the productive capacity figures by only 0.3% for HRNs and 1.3% for SRNs.

5.6 Trajectories in continuous space

Simard and LeCun (1992) devise a *Reverse Time-Delay Neural Network* for producing trajectories through a continuous space. They train the network to produce pen trajectories for writing the characters "A" to "Z". One reported motivation for the complex architecture of their network is the difficulty they had with training a simpler recurrent network to produce more than one trajectory. HRNs can be adapted to produce trajectories and have a much simpler architecture than Reverse Time-Delay Neural Networks. Only two modifications need be made: change the function on the output units to sigmoid and add biases, and use a fractional power of a random vector for the key vector. The hidden-unit activations are still $\mathbf{k} \circledast \mathbf{c}$, where $\mathbf{c}$ is the code vector. The fractional-power key vector $\mathbf{k}$ is derived by taking a random unitary vector $\mathbf{x}$ and multiplying the phase angle of each frequency component by some fraction α, i.e., $\mathbf{k} = \mathbf{x}^{\alpha}$. The result is that $\mathbf{k}^i$ is similar to $\mathbf{k}^j$ when the difference between i and j is less than $1/\alpha$, and the similarity is greater when i and j are closer. This is good for generating smooth trajectories because the decoding key at one step is similar to the decoding key at the next step. This means that the contents of the hidden layer will be similar at successive time steps. The rate at which the output trajectory is traversed can be adjusted by changing α – smaller values result in a slower rate of change.

I tested a trajectory producing HRN on a task similar to Simard and Le Cun's: producing pen trajectories for the digits zero to nine. The HRN has 16 hidden units and a key vector with $\alpha = 0.06$. The trajectories have 100 steps in three dimensions (X, Y, and pen up/down). As

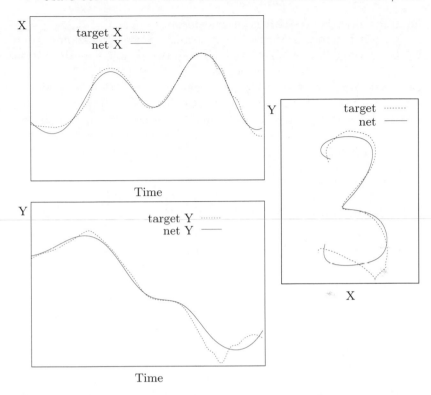

FIGURE 50 Targets and outputs of a HRN trained to produce trajectories through continuous space. The trajectory was not one that the network was trained on.

with other HRNs, there are two sets of parameters: the input-to-code weights and the output weights. I trained the network on 20 instances of handwritten digits and then froze the output weights. With the output weights frozen, the network could easily find codes that produce trajectories for novel digit instances. Figure 50 shows the X and Y target trajectories and the output of the network for one instance. The HRN does not reproduce trajectories exactly – the code has a very limited number of parameters and can be expected to impose some sort of regularization on the trajectory.

The code that produces a trajectory is a 16-element vector. One would expect the codes that produce similar trajectories to be similar. This does seem to be the case: 40 codes for producing the trajectories for 40 digits clustered into the digit classes with only one exception. The code vector is potentially useful wherever a compact representation for trajectories is needed, e.g., in classification.

It is possible to vary the rate of trajectory traversal by adding a unit to the network that exponentiates the key vector. Let ζ be the output of this unit. The hidden-layer activations will be $\mathbf{k}^\zeta \circledast \mathbf{c}$. The network can be set up so that the value of ζ changes during the production of a trajectory. The base-line value for ζ should be one. To progress more rapidly through the trajectory ζ should be greater than one, and to progress more slowly, ζ should be less than one. It is not difficult to calculate partial derivatives for ζ, and preliminary experiments showed that a HRN could learn to control ζ dynamically so as to align the network output with a target sequence.

5.7 Hierarchical HRNs

The main attraction of circular convolution as an associative memory operator is its potential for representing hierarchical structure. In order to investigate whether gradient descent training could be used to find hierarchical codes for sequences I built a two-level HRN. It consists of two HRNs with the outputs of one (the main HRN) supplying the code for the other (the sub-HRN). Figure 51 shows the overall architecture of this system. The subsequence decoder (at the top of the figure) produces sequences of symbols from the codes it receives from the main sequence generator. When the subsequence decoder has finished a subsequence it signals the main sequence decoder to produce the next subsequence code. Each decoder is similar to one of the HRNs already described. The clean-up memory for the subsequence decoder, i.e., its output units, contains symbol codes. The clean-up memory for the main sequence decoder contains subsequence codes. The clean-up memory uses a localist representation, so the output of the main sequence decoder must be transformed back to a distributed representation (the subsequence codes) by a local-to-distributed mapping.

For example, suppose the encoding key for the subsequence generator is $\mathbf{k}$, and the key for the main sequence generator is $\mathbf{j}$. Suppose that "abc", "de", and "fgh" are chunks the main sequence generator knows about. Then the sequence "abcdefgh" can be stored as

$$(\mathbf{a} + \mathbf{b} \circledast \mathbf{k} + \mathbf{c} \circledast \mathbf{k}^2) + (\mathbf{d} + \mathbf{e} \circledast \mathbf{k}) \circledast \mathbf{j} + (\mathbf{f} + \mathbf{g} \circledast \mathbf{k} + \mathbf{h} \circledast \mathbf{k}^2) \circledast \mathbf{j}^2.$$

This two-level HRN was able to produce sequences given appropriate codes. However the network was not able to find main sequence codes by using gradient descent with backpropagated errors from target symbols – there were too many local minima. This was the case even when the components of the network were trained separately and frozen. The local minima are most likely due to the presence of an intermediate

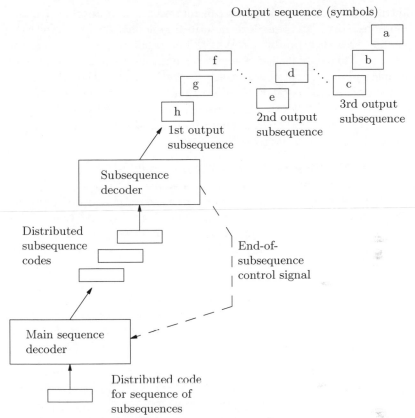

FIGURE 51 A two-level system for decoding nested sequences. The main system outputs a series of codes for subsequences, which are input to the subsequence decoder. When the subsequence decoder has completed a subsequence it signals the main sequence decoder to produce the next subsequence.

clean-up memory.

5.8   Discussion

5.8.1   Application to processing sequential input

An issue in processing sequential data with neural networks is how to present the inputs to the network. One approach has been to use a fixed window on the sequence, e.g., as in Sejnowski and Rosenberg's (1986) NETtalk. A disadvantage of this is that any fixed-size window may not be large enough in some situations. Instead of a fixed window, Elman (1991) and Servan-Schreiber et al. (1991) used a recurrent net to retain information about previous inputs. A disadvantage of this is the difficulty that recurrent nets have in retaining information over many time steps. HRNs and the SRNs described here offer another approach: use the codes that produce a sequence as input rather than the raw sequence. This would allow a fixed-size network to take sequences of variable length as inputs (as long as they were finite), without having to use multiple input blocks or windows. This would not be immediately applicable to networks that process sequences without any beginning or end, but some modification could be made along the lines of using a code that produces the recent relevant inputs.

5.8.2 Application to classification of sequences

The codes that produce sequences have similarity structure, e.g., the code for producing "abc" is more similar to the code for "acc" than the code for "cab". This is also true for the codes for producing trajectories through continuous space. Any similarity structure in the vectors representing the individual symbols would also be expressed in the similarity of codes for sequences, e.g., the code for "abc" would be more similar to the code for "avc" than "axc" if the representation for "b" were more similar to that for "v" than for "x". This leads to the possibility powerful vector-based classification techniques (e.g., neural networks, decision trees, etc.) could be applied to variable-length sequences by representing each sequence by its fixed-width vector code.

5.8.3 Improving the capacity of convolution-based memory

Adapting the representations of objects and traces in a system using the trajectory-association method gave a five-fold increase in the productive capacity. Experiments with networks having many more output units showed that the information capacity was not affected by the number of different symbols used in the sequences.

The improvement in capacity is encouraging because it suggests that the capacity of other types of convolution-based memory could be improved by adapting representations, and also that traces that fail to decode correctly could be corrected by a simple gradient descent procedure.

5.9 Conclusion

It is straightforward to build the decoding operations for trajectory-associated sequences into a recurrent network. The resulting HRN can be trained using standard neural network methods. During training, the network simultaneously discovers memory traces for sequences and good representations for the objects. My experiments with HRNs demonstrate four points:

1. Non-nested representations of sequences can be learned quickly and reliably in HRNs using gradient descent techniques.
2. The productive (storage) capacity of HRNs can be increased by adapting representations of sequences and objects using gradient descent techniques. By extension, these techniques can probably be used to improve the storage capacity of any convolution-based memory.
3. For the task of producing sequences and trajectories, HRNs are as good as, if not better than, more conventional recurrent networks. They have fewer parameters, and consequently require less training data. The convolution operation appears to be ideal for the recurrent operation in situations where information must be preserved but transformed in the hidden layer, because all the eigenvalues of the recurrent operation have a magnitude of one.
4. It is possible to construct multi-level HRNs that produce sequences in a hierarchical manner, but gradient descent techniques cannot easily learn the representations that drive these multi-level HRNs to produce particular sequences.

These experiments demonstrate that gradient descent learning techniques can be combined with convolution-based representations to learn representations for non-hierarchical structures. Such techniques can also probably be used to fine-tune existing representations for more complex structures, either to improve capacity or to reduce errors. However, it appears that it is not a simple matter (if it can be done at all) to combine gradient descent learning with convolution-based representations for hierarchical structures.

6

Estimating analogical similarity

One of the advantages of reduced descriptions is the ability to use them
for holistic processing. Such computations can be very fast, since they
do not require time-consuming reconstruction of the full representation.
The power and usefulness of this type of computation is determined by
what information is made explicit in the reduced representation and
what operations can be performed on this information.

Estimation of similarity between structured objects is one potentially
useful computation that can could be performed with reduced representations. The vector dot product is an efficiently computable measure
of similarity between two vectors. The usefulness of this computation
depends on the usefulness of the similarity structure this measure induces over the objects being represented. This in turn depends upon
which aspects of the objects and their structure are made explicit in
the reduced representation.

Gentner and Markman (1993) suggested that the ability to deal with
analogy would be a "watershed or Waterloo" for connectionist models.
They observed that connectionist models had difficulty dealing with
complex structure and tasks such as *structural alignment*, which is the
matching of corresponding components of two structures in a manner
that preserves their relationships. They identified structural alignment
as the central aspect of analogy making, and noted the apparent ease
with which people perform structural alignment in a wide variety of
tasks. Gentner and Markman wondered whether there could be a connectionist representation of structured objects whose surface forms were
similar to the degree that the underlying structures were similar. Such
a representation would allow structural alignment to be performed by
merely comparing the surface forms of representations. Gentner and
Markman saw little prospect for the development of such a representation.

In fact, Holographic Reduced Representations provide such a representation. As we have seen, a HRR is a high-dimensional vector. The vector dot product of HRRs can be computed very quickly and is a measure of the similarity of the surface forms of HRRs. Throughout this chapter, I will refer to the dot product of HRRs as *HRR similarity*. HRR similarity can be used as an estimate of the overall similarity of structures represented by HRRs. HRR similarity is influenced by the superficial or surface similarity of the represented structures and by some aspects of their structural similarity,[48] even though structural correspondences are never explicitly computed.

This chapter investigates the similarity structure induced on structured objects by HRR similarity. It turns out that HRR similarity captures some aspects of analogical similarity as embodied in two models of human performance on analogical-reasoning tasks: ACME (Analog Constraint Mapping Engine) (Holyoak and Thagard, 1989) and SME (Structure-Mapping Engine) (Falkenhainer et al., 1989). As an introduction to the use of HRRs for estimating analogical similarity and modeling human similarity judgments, Section 6.1 uses a simple example with shape configurations, such as "small triangle above large circle." The vector dot product of HRR encodings of these shape configurations corresponds to people's intuitive judgment of the similarity of those shape configurations.

In Section 6.2 I briefly review theories and experimental evidence about how people perform various analogical-reasoning tasks. I concentrate on the *analog recall* task, which is the retrieval of analogs from long-term memory in response to some stimulus (a *probe*). Although peoples' ability to recall analogs of a probe story is mainly influenced by non structural aspects of similarity, structural aspects of similarity do seem to have some effect. Some existing psychological models of analog recall in people account for this finding by using two-stage models: a computationally-fast first stage that filters the large number of potential recall candidates based on non structural similarities between the candidates and the probe, and a computationally-slower second stage that filters the remaining candidates based on structural correspondences with the probe. Section 6.3 in this chapter demonstrates how a single-stage model based on HRR similarity could provide a simpler

---

[48] *Surface features* of structures (e.g., stories) are derived from the features of the entities and relation names involved, considering each entity or relation name independently. *Superficial* is a synonym for *surface*. *Structural features* are derived from the relationships among the relations and entities. *Surface similarity* is the result of shared surface features, and *structural similarity* is the result of shared structural features.

alternative model of human performance in analog recall experiments.

The remainder of this chapter explores in more depth how vector operations on HRRs can implement various analog processing tasks in a fast but approximate manner. These operations have potential applications both in cognitive models, where the goal is to reproduce and understand patterns of human performance, and in Artificial Intelligence models, where the goal is to process information efficiently and effectively. Section 6.3.2 uses more variations on examples in order to tease apart how different aspects of structural similarity influence, or fail to influence, HRR similarity, and thereby understand its strengths and weaknesses as an estimate of analogical similarity. Section 6.4 explains the mechanisms whereby HRR similarity reflects structural similarity and compares and contrasts HRR similarity with Kernel-based methods (Haussler, 1999) for computing the similarity between structures. Section 6.5 describes how HRRs can be augmented with additional structure features so that the HRR dot product reflects abstract structural similarity to a greater degree. Section 6.6 describes how vector operations on HRRs can provide fast, computational primitives for seemingly high-level operations such as finding corresponding entities between two structures. Finally, Section 6.7 discusses various issues including scaling, how well HRR similarity performs as an estimate of analogical similarity, and the relationship between HRR similarity and kernel-based methods for computing similarity between complex discrete structures.

6.1 An experiment with shape configurations

Markman et al. (1993) report a simple experiment that neatly demonstrates the importance of both superficial and structural commonalities to people's conscious and deliberate judgments of similarity (as opposed to less conscious processes like reminding and recall, which are also affected by similarity, but in a different way). Markman et al.'s materials allow for a simple demonstration that HRR similarity has many commonalities with people's judgments of similarity.

In their experiment Markman et al. asked people to judge the relative similarity of pairs of configurations of geometric shapes shown in Table 16. For a particular row, the participants were shown configuration A and then asked to say which of B or C was more similar to it. B and C were presented in a random order to each participant. The elements of each pair of comparisons are systematically varied in the different rows in order to investigate which aspects of the relations are important to similarity judgments. The item most frequently selected as more similar to A is shown in column B in all cases, and the number of times it was selected is shown as the top number beside (the numbers in the parentheses and brackets are from experiments with HRRs, explained later).

Markman et al. use the results of this experiment to make a number of mostly uncontroversial claims about the things that affect people's conscious, deliberate judgments of similarity:

1. Sharing objects (superficial similarity) contributes to similarity – hence 1A is more similar to 1B than to 1C.

2. Sharing relations (another example of superficial similarity) contributes to similarity – hence 2aA is more similar to 2aB (they share the relation *above*) than to 2aC (2aA involves the relation *above*, while 2aC involves the relation *beside*), and 2bA is more similar to 2bB than to 2bC (again because 2bB involves the same relation as 2bA, while 2bC involves a different relation).

3. Having similar objects in similar roles (structural similarity) contributes to similarity – hence 3A is more similar to 3B (same objects in same roles) than to 3C (same objects but roles switched). This is true even when only some objects are similar – hence 4aA is more similar to 4aB (both have a circle on the bottom) than to 4aC (circle on top) and 4bA is more similar to 4bB (both have a triangle on top) than to 4bC (triangle on the bottom).

4. Relational correspondences (structural similarity) contribute to similarity whether or not objects are similar. Rows 3, 4a, and 4b show that relational correspondences matter when objects are similar. Row 6 shows that relational correspondences matter even when objects do not match.

5. Multiple relations can contribute to similarity provided that the matching relations entail the same object correspondences – hence 6A (X above Y and X smaller-than Y) is more similar to 6B (X above Y and X smaller-than Y) than to 6C (X above Y and Y smaller-than X). (Row 5 is also an example of this, but with matching objects.)

All of these claims seem quite uncontroversial except perhaps for the one that rows 5 and 6 involve multiple relations. An alternative interpretation, and the one used here, is that row 6 shows that having similar but not identical objects in the same roles contributes to similarity (i.e., one instance of small-object above large-object is more similar to another instance of small-object above large-object than to an instance of large-object above small-object). The ramifications of these interpretations are discussed at more length in Section 6.7.2.

	A	B		C	
1			10 (0.223) [0.253 ± 0.031]		0 (0.108) [0.170 ± 0.031]
2a			8 (0.738) [0.752 ± 0.019]		2 (0.255) [0.255 ± 0.032]
2b			10 (0.675) [0.670 ± 0.019]		0 (0.128) [0.168 ± 0.031]
3			10 (1.000) [1.000 ± 0.000]		0 (0.738) [0.752 ± 0.019]
4a			9 (0.827) [0.835 ± 0.013]		1 (0.695) [0.711 ± 0.020]
4b			9 (0.845) [0.833 ± 0.012]		1 (0.715) [0.711 ± 0.016]
5			9 (1.000) [1.000 ± 0.000]		1 (0.745) [0.753 ± 0.017]
6			10 (0.630) [0.628 ± 0.020]		0 (0.375) [0.381 ± 0.030]

TABLE 16 Shape-configuration matching materials and results from Markman et al. (1993), and results from HRR comparisons. The number of Markman et al.'s human respondents who judged B or C to be more similar to A is shown with each row. The HRR similarity estimate (from one run) of B and C with A is shown in parentheses. The vector dimension was 1024. The means and standard errors over 100 runs are shown in square brackets.

The similarity judgments in this experiment can be simulated using HRRs by encoding each shape configuration as a HRR, and then computing HRR similarities between them.

Two relations were used to encode the shape configurations as HRRs: *are horizontal*, with roles *left* and *right*; and *are vertical*, with roles *above* and *below*.[49][50] These predicate names and roles are represented by the patterns **horizontal**, **left**, **right**, **vertical**, **above**, and **below**. All of these are *random base vectors* (vectors with elements chosen independently from $N(0, 1/n)$). The patterns for the small and large shapes are derived from the random base vectors **large**, **small**, **triangle**, **circle**, **square**, and **star** by superimposing the size and shape and normalizing, e.g.:

$$\textbf{smStar} \quad = \quad \langle \textbf{small} + \textbf{star} \rangle,$$
$$\textbf{lgSquare} \quad = \quad \langle \textbf{large} + \textbf{square} \rangle.$$

The configurations 1A ("small triangle above large circle") and 6A ("small triangle above large circle") were encoded in HRRs as follows:

$$\textbf{C1A} \quad = \quad \langle \textbf{vertical} + \langle \textbf{lgTriangle} + \textbf{lgCircle} \rangle$$
$$+ \textbf{above} \circledast \textbf{lgTriangle} + \textbf{below} \circledast \textbf{lgCircle} \rangle,$$
$$\textbf{C6A} \quad = \quad \langle \textbf{vertical} + \langle \textbf{smTriangle} + \textbf{lgCircle} \rangle$$
$$+ \textbf{above} \circledast \textbf{smTriangle} + \textbf{below} \circledast \textbf{lgCircle} \rangle.$$

HRRs for the other configurations were constructed in the same fashion.[51]

The HRR similarities from one run (with 1024-dimensional vectors) are shown in parentheses in Table 16 (e.g., 0.223 is the HRR similarity between A and B in the first row). The means and standard errors

---

[49]The somewhat clumsy predicate names are intended to avoid confusion between predicate names and role names.

[50]The representation used here is merely one of several possible simple propositional representations for shape configurations. One obvious alternative is to encode relative size with a predicate such as *larger than* (or *smaller than*) instead of the absolute features *large* and *small*. Given the variety of possible representations, the results reported here should be taken as an indicating that it is a possibility, and not a necessity, that HRRs will give human-like results.

[51]It is worth noting that there are several ways that HRRs can be constructed and normalized. The way consistently used in this chapter was to normalize the superposition of all fillers before adding that to the role-filler bindings and relation name. This results in expressing the superficial features of the relation with a lower weight than the bindings (because the fillers all together have about the same weight as one binding). Many other rules could be devised. Of various ones I tried, the results were slightly different but usually qualitatively similar to those reported here.

over 100 runs are shown in square brackets.[52] For all items, the pair chosen as more similar by most of Markman et al.'s participants also has higher HRR similarity. The reasons for the agreement between human and HRR ratings are that HRRs directly implement most of the claims that Markman et al. make about people's judgments of similarity:

- Item 1: Having similar objects makes two HRRs more similar.
- Item 2a and 2b: Having similar predicates make two HRRs more similar.
- Item 3: Having similar items involved in similar relational roles makes two HRRs more similar.
- Item 4a and 4b: Not all roles need to filled by similar items for other similar items in similar roles to have an effect.
- Item 5 and 6: Although the pattern of HRR similarity is the same as for humans, the reasons are different from those given by Markman et al.. In these HRRs, size has not been represented with a relation. The reason for the apparent "matching of multiple relations" has to do with binding the size features of objects with spatial roles (e.g., 6A and 6B contain the binding of the feature *small* with the spatial role *above*).

6.2 Models of analogy processing

Informally, two structures form a good analogy if the important objects or entities in each can be placed into correspondence in such a way that the relations also correspond. Most analogous situations are mundane in that they involve similar entities related in the same way. Reasoning about such mundane analogies is the stuff of straightforward generalization and inference, e.g., "Bill's dog likes 'Happy Dog' dog food," "Alex's dog likes 'Happy Dog' dog food," therefore "Most dogs like 'Happy Dog' dog food," and "Sam's dog will probably like 'Happy Dog' dog food." Analogical retrieval and processing become more challenging and interesting when the analog situations involve dissimilar entities – sometimes the relational similarities point to a deeper, more general principle that the situations share. For example, consider the following three situations "The surgeon successfully irradiated the tumor without damaging surrounding tissue by using multiple converging beams of radiation," "The technician welded the light-bulb filament without damaging the fragile bulb by using multiple converging lasers," and "The fort surrounded by a moat with narrow easily defended bridges was conquered by a general who attacked all bridges simultaneously."

---

[52]Different runs result in slightly different HRR similarities because of the different base vectors in each run.

Although these situations have little-to-no superficial similarity, they are analogous and share the principle of bringing a powerful force to bear on some protected object without damaging its fragile enclosure by using multiple converging weaker forces, each of which can individually pass through the enclosure without harm.

The human aptitude for analogy has received a significant amount of attention in the psychological literature. Much attention has been devoted to teasing apart the differing effects of superficial and structural similarity in the various analogy processing tasks. A very brief introduction to the concepts and tasks involved in analogy processing is given here; for more details, see Forbus et al. (1994), Thagard et al. (1990), and Hummel and Holyoak (1997).

Analog processing concerns the processes of retrieving stories or scenarios from long-term memory in response to another story or scenario, and relating or applying the retrieved story or scenario to the current one. In a typical experiment to test how people retrieve and process analogs, a person might be presented with a number of stories in the first session, and asked to reason about them, or merely to remember them for the future. In the second session, several days or weeks later, the same person would be presented with a new story and asked which of the previous stories they are reminded of. They might also be asked to rate how similar the retrieved stories are to the new one, or to point out which objects in a retrieved story correspond to which objects in the new story. The new story might also involve a problem for which the retrieved story can provide a valuable structural hint about the solution method (this is an analog inference task). The stories or scenarios used in experiments are typically specially written, one or several sentences long, involving up to a dozen entities, and having a number of relationships among the entities. In human experiments researchers have used material such as plot-synopses of Shakespeare's plays and Aesop's fables. For parallel experiments with computers, the same materials as in human experiments has often been used, usually encoded into a frame-like representation (i.e., predicates with no variables).

There are four broad categories of tasks in analogy processing:

- *Recall* (aka *retrieval*): the process of accessing potential analogs of some probe story from long-term memory.
- *Similarity judgment*: rating the similarity of one story to another, after conscious consideration.
- *Mapping*: finding the corresponding objects (i.e., the objects that fill the same structural roles) in two stories that share significant structure.

- *Inference*: proposing a novel solution or consequence in one story, based on the presence of a structurally equivalent solution or consequence in the other story.

Retrieval is usually regarded as not being under conscious control – in typical experiments people are merely asked to write down or indicate all the previous stimuli that the current stimulus reminds them of. Much evidence points to superficial similarities being the dominant, but not the only, influence on human performance. In contrast, the other three tasks (similarity judgment, mapping, and inference) are usually regarded as being under conscious, deliberative control, and adults are heavily influenced by structural correspondences in their performance of these tasks.

6.2.1 Psychological models of analogical similarity and reasoning

The criteria for good analogies in SME (Falkenhainer et al., 1989) and ACME (Holyoak and Thagard, 1989) are listed in Table 17. They share a strong emphasis on structural isomorphism, for which they have almost identical definitions. SME and ACME are intended to model analogical reasoning in people, so these criteria come from observations, experiments, and theories about how people judge and reason with analogies.

To investigate how well HRR similarity can estimate analogical similarity I used a set of one-sentence *episodes*, most involving three frames in a nested structure. The *memorized* episodes were similar in different ways to the probe episode.[53]

Together, the episodes involved dogs (*Fido*, *Spot*, and *Rover*), people (*Jane*, *John*, and *Fred*), a cat (*Felix*) and a mouse (*Mort*). Members of one species were assumed to be similar to each other but not to members of other species. The *probe* episode (denoted "P") to which the others are compared, was as follows:

P (Probe) "Spot bit Jane, causing Jane to flee from Spot."

There were five other *memorized* episodes to which the probe was compared, corresponding to five categories of analogical similarity often used in the literature. Collectively, these memorized episodes represent all possible combinations of presence or absence of object-attribute similarity and structural similarity with the probe (note however that all share predicates names with the probe):

---

[53]These episodes were adapted from an example in Thagard et al. (1990). I added higher-order relational structure and created new episodes. *Higher-order* relations involve other relations as their argument, i.e., the *cause* relation in these episodes.

SME	ACME
Systematicity: consistent mappings are required. This involves: • Presence of only one-to-one mappings. • Structural consistency – a relation can be in a mapping only if its arguments are consistently mapped. **Richness:** analogies with more correspondences are better. **Abstractness:** correspondences among abstract entities are better: • Attributes (one-place predicates) are not mapped (unless operating in literal similarity mode). • Higher-order relations are more important. **Clarity:** it is clear which objects in the two situations correspond to each other.	**Isomorphism:** Consistent mappings are required: • Mappings should be one-to-one. • Structural consistency – if a relation is mapped, then its arguments should be mapped consistently as well. **Semantic similarity:** Mapped elements should be similar. **Pragmatic centrality:** Either a particular correspondence holds or a particular element is involved in some correspondence.

TABLE 17 Criteria for good analogies in SME and ACME.

LS (*Literal Similarity*) "Fido bit John, causing John to flee from Fido." (Has both structural and superficial similarity to the probe.)

SS (*Superficial Similarity*) "John fled from Fido, causing Fido to bite John." (Has superficial similarity with the probe to the same degree as LS, but not structural similarity.)

AN (*Analogy*) "Mort bit Felix, causing Felix to flee from Mort." (Has structural similarity with the probe to the same degree as LS, but not superficial similarity.)

CM (*Cross-Mapped Analogy*) "Fred bit Rover, causing Rover to flee from Fred." (Has both structural and superficial similarity to the probe to the same degree as LS, but types of corresponding objects are switched.)

FA (*False Analogy* aka *First-Order-Relations only*) "Mort fled from Felix, causing Felix to bite Mort." (Has no structural similarity to the probe, and no superficial similarity to the probe other than shared predicate labels.)

	Type	Object attributes	First-order relation names	Higher-order structure	Frequency of reminding
		Commonalities with probe			
Literal Similarity	LS	✓	✓	✓	0.56
Surface Similarity (Surface Features match)	SS	✓	✓	×	0.53
Analogy	AN	×	✓	✓	0.12
Cross-Mapped Analogy	CM	×	✓	✓	–
False Analogy (First-Order Relation match)	FA	×	✓	×	0.09

TABLE 18 Types of match to a probe episode. The frequencies of reminding are from an experiment with people described in Table 2 in Forbus et al. (1994).

These categories of similarity are summarized in Table 18, along with the frequency of reminding from an analog recall experiment with people reported by Forbus et al. (1994).

There is much evidence that in adults, structural similarity plays a large role in conscious similarity judgments and in analogical mapping and inference (Gentner, 1983, Holyoak and Koh, 1987, Falkenhainer et al., 1989, Holyoak and Thagard, 1989). The role of structural similarity in retrieval is less clear: some researchers argue that structural similarity usually has little effect on retrieval (Gentner et al., 1993) while others argue that under some circumstances, structural similarity can influence retrieval (Wharton et al., 1994). Others suggest that structural similarity matters only when the entities involved in the situations share superficial features (Ross, 1989). There is strong evidence that cross mapping results in lower retrieval performance in adults compared to the literal similarity condition (Ross, 1989). Overall, the general consensus is that the pattern for retrievability of items from long-term memory seems to be LS > CM ≥ SS > AN ≥ FA. The primary disputes are about the conditions under which the inequalities are strict (if there are any).

Regarding human performance on mapping, a strong, if somewhat unsurprising, result is that people, especially children, are far more prone to making erroneous mappings in situations where cross mappings are present (Ross, 1989, Gentner et al., 1993). For example, in the cross-mapped episode above, the correct, class-crossing mappings

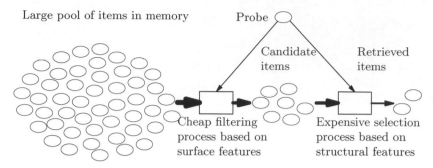

FIGURE 52 Two-stage models of analogy retrieval. The first stage selects potential analogies to the probe from the large pool of items in long-term memory, using fast but superficial comparisons. The bottleneck depicted here is not necessary – the computation required by the first stage could happen in parallel throughout long-term memory (e.g., in a content-addressable memory). The second stage performs a more expensive structural comparison between the probe and each potential analogy passed by the first stage.

are "dog to person" and "person to dog," while alternate, but incorrect, class-preserving mappings of "dog to dog" and "person to person" are available and often chosen. This supports the idea that there are two competing processes at work in analogical reasoning – one fast and more instinctual process that is influenced by superficial similarities, and another slower and more conscious learned process that can identify and make use of deeper structural similarities. The results presented in this chapter suggest that simple vector operations on HRRs could model the fast instinctual processes. At the same time, HRRs can adequately represent the complex structural information necessary for more structure-sensitive processing.

6.2.2 Psychological models of analog recall

Existing computational models of human performance on analog retrieval tasks such as ARCS (*Analog Retrieval by Constraint Satisfaction* Thagard et al., 1990) and MAC/FAC (*Many Are Called / Few Are Chosen* Forbus et al., 1994) have explained the effect of structural correspondences by invoking two processes. Figure 52 illustrates this type of model. The first stage is simple and computationally cheap, and only examines superficial features. This explains much of the human performance, but cannot account for effects of structural similarity (i.e., LS > SS, LS > CM, and AN ≥ FA). Thus, these models require a second stage that takes structural similarity into account, by proposing and evaluating structural correspondences. This is far more computationally expensive than the first stage.

In this chapter I will argue that it is possible to explain the pattern of retrieval ability observed in people with a single-stage model based on vector dot products of HRRs. Comparisons in this model will be primarily sensitive to superficial similarity, but will also be sensitive to structural similarity, thus mirroring the performance of people, i.e., LS > CM ≥ SS > AN ≥ FA. With HRRs it is also possible to make estimates of corresponding objects across representations that are usually correct except when dealing with cross-mapped analogies, again mirroring human performance.

The first stages of MAC/FAC and ARCS only inspect surface features. The first stage of MAC/FAC (MAC=*Many Are Called*) uses a vector representation of the surface features. Each location in the vector corresponds to a surface feature of an object, relation or function, and the value in the location is the number of times the feature occurs in the structure. The MAC first-stage estimate of the similarity between two structures is the dot product of their feature-count vectors. A threshold is used to select likely analogies. Among the dog-bites-human episodes, it would give the LS, CM, and SS episodes equal and highest similarity to the probe and select those to pass to the second stage. The first stage of ARCS is less selective than that of MAC/FAC. It selects all episodes that share a relation with the probe, ignoring ubiquitous relations such as *cause* and *if*. In the dog-bites-human episodes, it would select all memorized episodes to pass to the second stage (because all involve the *bite* and *flee* relations, as does the probe).

The second stages of MAC/FAC (FAC=*Few Are Chosen*) and ARCS detect structural correspondences. Although they use quite different implementation techniques to find and evaluate structural correspondences – ARCS uses a connectionist constraint-satisfaction network, while MAC/FAC uses a symbolic rule-based program called SME (Structure-Mapping Engine) – both implement very similar principles: mapped relations must match, all the arguments of mapped relations must be mapped consistently, and mapping of objects must be one-to-one. One difference between ARCS and MAC/FAC is that SME requires exact matches of relations, while ARCS allows mapping of similar relations. This is only a minor difference because similar relations can be decomposed into identical and dissimilar components and it would be straightforward to modify SME to cope with this. SME has two modes – literal similarity mode and analogy mode. In literal similarity mode, mappings between similar objects are favored over those between dissimilar objects, which gives literal similarity a higher score than analogy (*literal similarity* is analogy plus object attribute matches). Where it is relevant in this chapter, it is assumed that SME is operating in literal similarity mode.

These second stages of both MAC/FAC and ARCS are designed to give higher similarity ratings when structural correspondences are present. Although the interactions between the first and second stages are quite different in MAC/FAC and ARCS, the overall effect in both models is to retrieve episodes that have high superficial similarity with the probe, and to slightly favor those with more structural correspondences with the probe. This leads to overall retrieval performance that is the same as shown by people, i.e., $LS > CM \geq SS > AN \geq FA$.

6.3 Analogies between hierarchical structures

The comparisons of the shape configurations involve little structural complexity, as the configurations can be represented with single frames. To investigate how HRR similarity estimates the similarity of structures involving several predicates and more complex correspondences, I used the set of dog-bites-human episodes. Section 6.3.1 describes HRRs for these episodes, and MAC content vector and HRR similarity scores. This example illustrates how HRR similarity can reflect similarity of structural arrangements, as well as similarity of surface features, and demonstrates that a model based on HRR similarity alone could explain the pattern of retrieval observed in people ($LS > SS > AN \geq FA$ as described in Section 6.2.1).

Although these episodes are very simple, there are still quite a few ways their structure can vary within the standard LS, SS, AN, and FA categories. It is important to be aware of these variations because their existence means that extra care must be taken when categorizing experimental stimuli used with humans and attempting to fit the results to theoretical models. Section 6.3.2 investigates the effects of these different types of structural variations upon HRR similarities.

6.3.1 Experiment 1A: HRRs and the "dog bites human" episodes

The HRR for the probe episode, "Fido bit John, causing John to run from Fido" was constructed from three frames and object and predicate features, in the same way as in the shape-configuration experiments (Section 6.1):

$$\mathbf{P}_{bite} = \langle \mathbf{bite} + \langle \mathbf{spot} + \mathbf{jane} \rangle + \mathbf{bite}_{agt} \circledast \mathbf{spot} + \mathbf{bite}_{obj} \circledast \mathbf{jane} \rangle$$

$$\mathbf{P}_{flee} = \langle \mathbf{flee} + \langle \mathbf{spot} + \mathbf{jane} \rangle + \mathbf{flee}_{agt} \circledast \mathbf{jane} + \mathbf{flee}_{from} \circledast \mathbf{spot} \rangle$$

$$\mathbf{P} = \langle \mathbf{cause} + \langle \mathbf{P}_{bite} + \mathbf{P}_{flee} \rangle$$

Base vectors		Token vectors
person	bite	$\text{jane} = \langle \text{person} + \text{id}_{jane} \rangle$
dog	flee	$\text{john} = \langle \text{person} + \text{id}_{john} \rangle$
cat	cause	$\text{fred} = \langle \text{person} + \text{id}_{fred} \rangle$
mouse	stroke	$\text{spot} = \langle \text{dog} + \text{id}_{spot} \rangle$
	lick	$\text{fido} = \langle \text{dog} + \text{id}_{fido} \rangle$
bite_{agt}	bite_{obj}	$\text{rover} = \langle \text{dog} + \text{id}_{rover} \rangle$
flee_{agt}	flee_{from}	$\text{felix} = \langle \text{cat} + \text{id}_{felix} \rangle$
cause_{antc}	cause_{cnsq}	$\text{mort} = \langle \text{mouse} + \text{id}_{mort} \rangle$
stroke_{agt}	stroke_{obj}	
lick_{agt}	lick_{obj}	

TABLE 19 Base and token vectors. The average similarity (i.e., dot product) between any pair of persons is 0.5, as is the similarity between any pair of dogs. The average similarities between all other pairs are zero.

$$+ \, \mathbf{cause}_{antc} \circledast \mathbf{P}_{bite} + \mathbf{cause}_{cnsq} \circledast \mathbf{P}_{flee} \rangle$$

The HRRs for the other episodes were built in an analogous fashion. Patterns representing individuals (the token patterns) were constructed so that instances of the same type were represented by similar patterns. Each token was constructed as the superposition of a pattern representing the class of the individual and a unique identity pattern. The pattern in common between tokens of the same class results in an average similarity between individuals of 0.5. Thus Jane, John, and Fred, being people, were represented by similar patterns, as were the dogs Spot, Fido, and Rover. The different species, people, dogs, cats, and mice, were not considered similar at all – the example is simple enough to not require a hierarchy of types.[54] The complete set of base and token vectors used in this and later experiments is shown in Table 19. All base and identity (**id**) vectors are randomly chosen with elements independently distributed as $N(0, 1/n)$ (i.e., the normal distribution with mean zero and variance $1/n$).

Average HRR similarity scores are shown in Table 20. The MAC similarity scores are also shown. These are based on the dot product of normalized MAC *content vectors* over the following features: the entities **person**, **dog**, **mouse**, and **cat** and the predicates **cause**, **bite**, and **flee**. For example, the MAC content vector for the probe is $(1, 1, 0, 0, 1, 1, 1)/\sqrt{5}$, because it includes *person* and *dog*, excludes

---

[54]It is, however, easy enough to represent a class hierarchy using HRRs by making the representation of each class in the hierarchy the superposition of its parent and some random vector specific to the class. This is a generalization of the technique used to construct individual tokens.

Probe: Spot bit Jane, causing Jane to flee from Spot.	Object attributes	First-order relation names	Higher-order structure	Type	HRR	MAC
Commonalities with probe spanning					**Similarity scores**	
Episodes in long-term memory:						
E1: Fido bit John, causing John to flee from Fido.	✓	✓	✓	LS	0.71	1.0
E4: Mort bit Felix, causing Felix to flee from Mort.	✗	✓	✓	AN	0.42	0.6
E2: Fred bit Rover, causing Rover to flee from Fred.	✓	✓	✓	CM	0.47	1.0
E6: John fled from Fido, causing Fido to bite John.	✓	✓	✗	SS	0.46	1.0
E8: Mort fled from Felix, causing Felix to bite Mort.	✗	✓	✗	FA	0.30	0.6

TABLE 20 Results from Experiment 1A. The HRR similarities are averages from 100 runs with different random base and identity vectors, and a vector dimension of 2048. The standard deviation of the HRR similarities ranged between 0.016 and 0.026. The episodes are labeled non sequentially because they are a subset of the complete set, which is presented in Table 21 in the next section. These five episodes were selected from the complete set as representatives of the main types (LS, AN, etc.) of analogical similarity.

mouse and *cat*, and includes *cause*, *bite*, and *flee*, in that order.

The episodes **E1** (LS) and **E6** (SS) each have the same surface commonalities (object features and predicate names) with the probe. The difference between them is that **E1** (LS) is structurally isomorphic to the probe, whereas **E6** (SS) is not. Because there is no structural information (beyond the names of the higher-order predicates) encoded in MAC content vectors, the MAC similarity score of **E1** and **E6** to the probe is the same: MAC is insensitive to structural arrangement. On the other hand, the HRR similarity between **E1** (LS) and the probe is reliably higher than that between **E6** (SS) and the probe, because HRRs are sensitive to differences in structural match when episodes share similar objects arranged in a similar manner.

The episodes **E4** (AN) and **E8** (FA) behave in a similar fashion to **E1** and **E6**: although **E4** (AN) is isomorphic to the probe and **E8** (FA) is not, their MAC similarity scores with the probe are identical. However, the HRR similarity of **E4** (AN) is higher than that of **E8** (FA), because of the structural similarity between **E4** (AN) and the probe.

When episodes do not share similar objects, or when similar objects are not arranged in a similar manner, ordinary HRR similarities are low and do not reliably reflect structural match. **E2** (CM) demonstrates this – although it has the same structure as the probe, and has similar objects, those objects are not arranged in a similar manner (they are cross-mapped), and consequently the HRR similarity of **E2** (CM) to the probe is approximately the same as than that of **E6** (SS). Furthermore, although the HRR similarity score for **E4** (AN) is higher than for **E8** (FA) in Table 20 (due to the *bite* and *flee* frames filling the same roles as in the probe), it is possible to construct other FA and AN examples such that the FA examples have higher HRR similarity to the probe than do the AN examples (see Section 6.3.2). However, some of these deficiencies[55] of HRR similarity can be rectified – it is possible to enhance HRRs by adding further conjunctive features based on abstract structural relations, as described in Section 6.5. With these added features, HRR similarity more consistently reflects structural match even in the absence of similar objects.

6.3.2 Experiment 1B: Variations on surface and structural commonalities

Gentner et al. (1993) identified three possible types of commonalities between episodes: object attributes, first-order relation names, and higher-order relational structure.[56] Two of these types of commonalities, object attributes and higher-order relational structure, are varied systematically in the categories LS, SS, AN, and FA. However, there are subcategories of these and other additional possible commonalities. In particular, structural commonalities can be partitioned into three subcategories: common role-filler bindings (which have a large effect on HRR similarity); other object-level isomorphisms (which have no effect on HRR similarity under the encoding used here), and common higher-order structure (isomorphisms in the arrangement of higher-order relations, which has some effect on HRR similarity). Another possible superficial commonality is presence of higher-order relation names in common.

It is useful to describe and investigate these extra types of commonalities because they have differing impacts on HRR similarity. Experi-

---

[55]Whether or not these properties of HRR similarity are actually deficiencies depends on the goal of the model.

[56]*First-order* relations are relations whose arguments are objects (e.g., *bite* and *flee* in the examples), and *higher-order* relations are relations whose arguments are other relations (e.g., *cause* in the examples). Gentner et al. (1993) write of *First-order relational commonalities*, but by this they appear to mean merely first-order-relation names in common, thus I refer to it by the more precise term *first-order relation names*.

ment 1B includes six additional episodes that vary these commonalities with the probe. These episodes, along with their HRR and MAC similarity scores with respect to the probe, are shown in Table 21. (Standard deviations are not shown for MAC similarities because there is no random component to MAC similarities – hence they do not vary.) The superscripts on the category names are intended to be mnemonics with the following meanings:

$XX^{\times H}$: non matching higher-order structure – higher-order predicates have different predicates as arguments

XX^{-H}: missing higher-order structure – higher-order predicates are completely missing

$XX^{\times I}$: no object-level isomorphism – objects (**spot**, **jane**, etc.) cannot be mapped consistently

Table 21 reports the results of Experiment 1B. **E**10 ($OO^{\times H}$) and **E**11 (OO^{-H}) are objects-only matches: they share similar objects with the probe, but not any first-order relations. They have rather low HRR similarity. **E**11 has no relations at all in common with the probe and has the lowest HRR similarity to the probe out of all of the episodes.

E9 (SS^{-H}) is a surface-similarity match with the probe. It differs from the other SS episodes in that it does not have higher-order relations (it is missing the *cause* relation). Apart from the lack of the *cause* relation **E**9 is actually the same as **E**1 (LS). Despite the first-order role-filler bindings that are similar to those in the probe, **E**9 has the lowest HRR similarity to the probe of all the SS episodes. This demonstrates that first-order role-filler bindings are sufficient in themselves to result in high HRR similarity – the way they combine with higher-order structure is also important.

The difference between the **E**5 and the **E**6 episodes is that **E**5 lacks object-level isomorphism with the probe (no mapping that preserves the *bite* and *flee* relations), whereas **E**6 has a different higher-order structure to the probe (*flee* causes *bite*). **E**6 has a higher HRR similarity to the probe than **E**5, despite **E**5 having more first-order role-filler binding similarity with the probe. This again demonstrates the importance of higher-order structure in determining HRR similarity.

E7 ($FA^{\times I}$) does not have object-level isomorphism with the probe, in contrast to **E**8 ($FA^{\times H}$), which does not share higher-order structure with the probe. In the absence of common object attributes, the lack of object-level isomorphism does not affect HRR similarity, but the lack of common higher-order structure causes **E**8 ($FA^{\times H}$) to be less similar to the probe than **E**7 ($FA^{\times I}$).

E3 (AN) is analogous to the probe, like **E**4 (AN). However the ob-

P: Spot bit Jane, causing Jane to flee from Spot.

Episodes in long-term memory:

	Object attributes	First-order relation names	Higher-order relation names	Role-filler bindings	Higher-order structure	Object-level isomorphism	Type	HRR		MAC	
E1: Fido bit John, causing John to flee from Fido.	✓	✓	✓	✓	✓	✓	LS	0.71 ±0.016	(1)	1.0	(=1)
E2: Fred bit Rover, causing Rover to flee from Fred.	✓	✓	✓	✗	✓	✓	CM	0.54 ±0.022	(3)	1.0	(=1)
E3: Felix bit Mort, causing Mort to flee from Felix.	✗	✓	✓	✗	✓	✓	AN	0.42 ±0.025	(=5)	0.6	(=6)
E4: Mort bit Felix, causing Felix to flee from Mort.	✗	✓	✓	✗	✓	✓	AN	0.43 ±0.025	(=5)	0.6	(=6)
E5: Rover bit Fred, causing Rover to flee from Fred.	✓	✓	✓	½	✓	✗	SS$^{\times I}$	0.62 ±0.020	(2)	1.0	(=1)
E6: John fled from Fido, causing Fido to bite John.	✓	✓	✓	✓	✓	✓	SS$^{\times H}$	0.46 ±0.020	(4)	1.0	(=1)
E7: Mort bit Felix, causing Mort to flee from Felix.	✗	✓	✓	✗	✗	✗	FA$^{\times I}$	0.42 ±0.025	(=5)	0.6	(=6)
E8: Mort fled from Felix, causing Felix to bite Mort.	✗	✓	✓	✗	✗	✓	FA$^{\times H}$	0.30 ±0.026	(=9)	0.6	(=6)
E9: Fido bit John, John fled from Fido.	✓	✓	✗	✓	✗	✓	SS^{-H}	0.30 ±0.021	(=9)	0.89	(5)
E10: Fred stroked Rover, causing Rover to lick Fred.	✓	✗	✗	✗	✗	✗	OO$^{\times H}$	0.37 ±0.023	(8)	0.6	(=6)
E11: Fred stroked Rover, Rover licked Fred.	✓	✗	✗	✗	✗	✗	OO^{-H}	0.10 ±0.022	(11)	0.45	(11)

Commonalities with probe. Mean similarities, ±stddev and (ranks).

TABLE 21 Results from Experiment 1B.

jects map differently: cat maps to dog and person to mouse for **E3** and cat maps to person and dog to mouse for **E4**. If the patterns for cats and dogs were somewhat similar, these different mappings would result in different HRR similarities, but they are not in this experiment, and thus **E3** and **E4** have the same HRR similarity to the probe.

E2 (CM) is analogous to the probe, but is cross-mapped. It has the same objects and structure as the probe, but unlike **E1** (LS), the objects do not map to objects of the same class in the probe – in **E2** (CM) the dog maps to the person, and the person maps to the dog. Consequently, it does not have many role-filler bindings in common with the probe, and its HRR similarity to the probe is much lower than that of **E1** (LS),.

One of the three additional categories of commonalities, *role-filler binding* similarity is especially important to HRR similarity. This is because in HRRs, role-filler bindings are the primary source of conjunctive (i.e., structural) features.

In contrast, object-level isomorphism (the presence of one-to-one mapping of the objects that preserves first-order relations) has no independent effect on ordinary HRR similarities – the only way it can have any effect is through resulting in more similar role-filler bindings.

The HRR similarities shown in Table 21 vary from run to run because of the random choice of base vectors in each run, but the standard deviation of the similarities is small compared to the differences between the similarities. For example, the similarities to the probe of **E1** (LS) and **E5** ($SS^{\times I}$) differ by approximately four times their standard deviation. The ranking of the HRR similarities to the probe was consistent with the following order in 93 out of 100 runs with vector dimension 2048 (where the ordering within the curly braces varies):

$$LS > SS^{\times I} > CM > \{SS^{\times H}, AN, FA^{\times I}\}$$
$$> OO^{\times H} > \{FA^{\times H}, SS^{-H}\} > OO^{-H}.$$

The important features of this order are LS > all types of SS and LS > CM, which is consistent with observed human performance. The order violations in seven runs are due to variation in HRR similarities. The variance of the similarities decreases as the vector dimension increases. When this experiment was rerun with vector dimension 4096 there was only one violation of this order in 100 runs.

6.3.3 Weighting different aspects similarity

In order to reproduce the flexibility and context sensitivity of human cognition, methods for performing comparisons between complex structures need a simple way for varying what is considered important in the comparison. For example, in some contexts, object features might be more important, while in others, it might be structural features that matter. This is simple to implement with HRRs by weighting the appropriate components in the probe item. For example, if it were desired that object features should be the primary influence in the comparison between the probe and the items in memory, one could increase the contribution to the probe of the patterns **spot** and **jane**. Only one HRR involved in the comparison need be changed in order to produce an effect. This is computationally convenient – it means that in any retrieval task the importance of different aspects of similarity can be changed by just reweighting components of the probe, without changing any of the HRRs stored in memory.

To illustrate this, Experiment 1 was rerun with the objects given a much higher weight in the HRR for the probe, as follows:

$$\mathbf{P}'_{bite} = \langle \mathbf{bite} + 5\langle \mathbf{spot} + \mathbf{jane}\rangle + \mathbf{bite}_{agt} \circledast \mathbf{spot} + \mathbf{bite}_{obj} \circledast \mathbf{jane}\rangle$$

$$\mathbf{P}'_{flee} = \langle \mathbf{flee} + 5\langle \mathbf{spot} + \mathbf{jane}\rangle + \mathbf{flee}_{agt} \circledast \mathbf{jane} + \mathbf{flee}_{from} \circledast \mathbf{spot}\rangle$$

$$\mathbf{P}' = \langle \mathbf{cause} + \langle \mathbf{P}'_{bite} + \mathbf{P}'_{flee}\rangle$$
$$+ \mathbf{cause}_{antc} \circledast \mathbf{P}'_{bite} + \mathbf{cause}_{cnsq} \circledast \mathbf{P}'_{flee}\rangle$$

The HRRs for the *memorized* episodes were the same as in Experiment 1 (i.e., they did not have higher weight on the objects).

The results were that object-feature commonality became the dominant determiner of rank: episodes that shared object features with the probe scored higher than those that did not. Out of 100 runs, there were no violations of the following order:

$$\{LS, SS^{\times I}, SS^{-H}, SS^{\times H}, CM, OO^{\times H}, OO^{-H}\} > \{FA^{\times I}, FA^{\times H}, AN\}$$

It is worth noting again that in the HRRs described in this chapter, some relative weighting is accomplished by normalization. For example, in the original version of the probe, the contribution of the entire *bite* relation ($\mathbf{P}_{bite}$) was about the same as the contribution of the *cause* relation name (**cause**). Since the *bite* relation name (**bite**) was a component of $\mathbf{P}_{bite}$, its contribution to the probe was only approximately half that of the *cause* relation name (**cause**).

6.4   Why HRR similarity reflects structural similarity

Insight into why and when HRR similarity reflects structural similarity at all can be gained by considering the component patterns of HRRs. The HRR for an episode can be viewed as the superposition of a set of vectors and *binding chains* – convolutions of two or more vectors. The ordinary vector components of a HRR encode the superficial features of a structure – their contributions to the HRR depend only on the features present and not on the way the entities are related in the structure. Binding chains encode structural features – their contributions to the HRR depend on the way features are related in the episode. Binding chains can be thought of as conjunctive features of a structure. The binding chains for the probe are illustrated in Figure 53 and their formulae tabulated in Table 22.

Recall that circular convolution is randomizing, which means that for most vectors, $\mathbf{a} \circledast \mathbf{b}$ is not similar to $\mathbf{a}$ or $\mathbf{b}$ – it is akin to a new random vector. This means that binding chains are like brand-new features, and are not similar to any of the other features of the episode.

It is worth briefly noting that because of normalization and multiple occurrences, not all features will have the same weight in a HRR (weights are not shown in the figure or table). Furthermore, if it were desired to expand everything down to the level of *primitive* features (if those existed[57]), vectors in the HRR that were themselves HRRs or superpositions of other features could be expanded further. For example the binding chain $\mathbf{bite}_{agt} \circledast \mathbf{spot}$ could be expanded to the superposition of the features $\mathbf{bite}_{agt} \circledast \mathbf{dog}$ and $\mathbf{bite}_{agt} \circledast \mathbf{id}_{spot}$ (because $\mathbf{bite}_{agt} \circledast \mathbf{spot}$ = $\mathbf{bite}_{agt} \circledast (\mathbf{dog} + \mathbf{id}_{spot}) = \mathbf{bite}_{agt} \circledast \mathbf{dog} + \mathbf{bite}_{agt} \circledast \mathbf{id}_{spot}$). It is important to bear in mind that the algebraic expansion of a HRR is an activity that occurs totally at the whim of the external analyst and has no impact on the behavior of the system being investigated. It is only the value of the vector which is important to system behavior, not how it is construed by an external analyst.

The binding chains express structural features of a structured object as superficial features in a HRR vector. Consideration of the binding chains shows both why HRR similarity reflects structural similarity under some conditions and why it is an unreliable indicator when those conditions are not satisfied. Recall that superposition preserves similarity in an additive fashion. Thus HRRs for two episodes will be similar to the degree that they have similar vectors and binding chains; having a moderate fraction of similar vectors and binding chains will result in a moderate degree of similarity. However, because convolution preserves similarity in a multiplicative fashion, two binding chains are similar to the degree that *all* the vectors in them are similar. Any pattern that is present in one binding chain but absent from the other will cause those two binding chains to be dissimilar. Two structures

---

[57] In the examples used in this book, random base vectors are primitive features. However, if some learning procedure were used to construct vectors representing entities, in a way that similar entities were represented by similar vectors, there need not be any primitive features in the system. One possible such learning procedure is Latent Semantic Analysis (Deerwester et al., 1990).

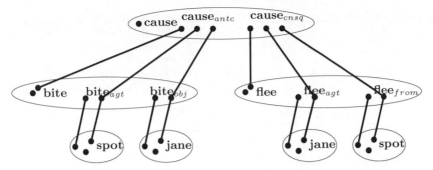

FIGURE 53 The HRR for the probe is the weighted sum of binding chains and vectors (weights not shown). Each ellipse is a relation or object. Each dot represents an instance of a vector (vector names are shown). The isolated dots are vectors, and the vertically connected dots are binding chains. For example, the vector **spot** occurs six times: twice by itself, and in four binding chains (on the left and on the right). Note that because of the way HRRs are constructed in this book, not all binding chains extend from the top-level relation down to the objects – there are binding chains that begin at lower-level relations.

that are structurally similar and have similar fillers in similar roles will have similar binding chains. Their HRRs are the superposition of those binding chains and the superficial features of the structures. Because the LS and SS example episodes involve objects of different types within each episode, and corresponding types between episodes, HRR similarity can reliably detect that the LS episode has higher structural similarity to the probe. This is due to the presence of binding chains such as $\mathbf{cause}_{antc} \circledast \mathbf{bite}_{agt} \circledast \mathbf{dog}$ in the LS episode and in the probe, but not in the $SS^{\times H}$ episode, whose corresponding binding chain is $\mathbf{cause}_{cnsq} \circledast \mathbf{bite}_{agt} \circledast \mathbf{dog}$. However, episodes that do not have similar fillers in similar roles, such as AN and FA episodes, cannot have many binding chains in common with the probe, no matter how structurally similar they are to the probe (because the different fillers at the ends of binding chains preclude the binding chains being similar). Thus, ordinary HRR similarity cannot always distinguish AN from FA episodes, both of which have low superficial similarity to the probe, because the dissimilarity of objects precludes having similar binding chains to the probe.[58] Additionally, ordinary HRR similarity cannot reflect struc-

---

[58]Note that in Experiment 1A, **E**4 (AN) and the probe share the structural conjunctive features $\mathbf{cause}_{antc} \circledast \mathbf{bite}$ and $\mathbf{cause}_{cnsq} \circledast \mathbf{flee}$ and consequently have a higher HRR similarity than the probe and **E**8 (FA). However, as discussed in Section 6.3.2, this difference between the HRR similarity of the AN and FA episodes

From $\mathbf{P}_{bite}$	From $\mathbf{P}_{flee}$	From $\mathbf{cause}_{antc} \circledast \mathbf{P}_{bite}$
spot	spot	$\mathbf{cause}_{antc} \circledast$ spot
jane	jane	$\mathbf{cause}_{antc} \circledast$ jane
bite	flee	$\mathbf{cause}_{antc} \circledast$ bite
$\mathbf{bite}_{agt} \circledast$ spot	$\mathbf{flee}_{agt} \circledast$ jane	$\mathbf{cause}_{antc} \circledast \mathbf{bite}_{agt} \circledast$ spot
$\mathbf{bite}_{obj} \circledast$ jane	$\mathbf{flee}_{from} \circledast$ spot	$\mathbf{cause}_{antc} \circledast \mathbf{bite}_{obj} \circledast$ jane

From $\mathbf{cause}_{cnsq} \circledast \mathbf{P}_{flee}$	From $\mathbf{P}$
$\mathbf{cause}_{cnsq} \circledast$ spot	cause
$\mathbf{cause}_{cnsq} \circledast$ jane	
$\mathbf{cause}_{cnsq} \circledast$ flee	
$\mathbf{cause}_{cnsq} \circledast \mathbf{flee}_{agt} \circledast$ jane	
$\mathbf{cause}_{cnsq} \circledast \mathbf{flee}_{from} \circledast$ spot	

TABLE 22 Vectors and binding chains in the probe.

tural similarity in the case where different objects in an episode are of the same type, e.g., all fillers are dogs, because that makes all binding chains similar.

6.4.1   Evaluation of HRR similarity as an estimate of analogical similarity

Under certain conditions HRR similarity provides a good indication of analogical similarity. However, it has two weaknesses:

1. It overestimates when structural similarity is low and there are many similar role-filler bindings.
2. It underestimates when structural similarity is high and there are few similar role-filler bindings.

These weaknesses are in part due to ordinary HRRs' not encoding multiple occurrences of a single entity as an explicit surface feature. Each occurrence is treated as a separate object and no links are made among multiple occurrences. This has several consequences for the fidelity of HRR similarity as an estimate of analogical similarity. One consequence is that HRRs are insensitive to object-level isomorphism in the absence of object-attribute similarity. Another consequence is that lack of object-level isomorphism is not detected if there are multiple objects of the same type. The HRR similarity of the probe $\mathbf{P}$ and an episode will be high as long as the episode involves a dog biting a person, causing a person to run away from a dog. It does not matter whether the first person is the same as the second person, or the first

---

to the probe is not reliable in general because there are other FA episodes that do have these conjunctive features in common with the probe.

dog the same as the second. For example, "Fido bit John, causing Fred to run away from Rover" would have the same HRR similarity to the probe as **E**1. Ordinary HRR similarity is only sensitive to object-level isomorphism by virtue of sensitivity to the presence of similar role-filler bindings.

This reliance on the presence of similar role-filler bindings as an indicator of structural similarity is the underlying reason for the failure of HRR similarity to reflect structural similarity when corresponding fillers are not similar. The next section presents an enhancement of HRRs intended to address this problem.

6.5 Contextualized HRRs

The effect of structural consistency on analog recall in people is not beyond controversy (see the discussion in Section 6.2.1). Some researchers maintain that structural similarity has only a small effect in general, while others maintain that structural similarity can have a large effect under certain conditions. The literature in the field supports the following claims:

- The effect of superficial similarity dominates any effect of structural consistency. (For summaries of the literature see Johnson and Seifert 1992, Wharton et al. 1994, Forbus et al. 1994, Hummel and Holyoak 1997.)
- In some situations there is no detectable effect of structural consistency on reminding (Rattermann and Gentner 1987, Gentner and Forbus 1991, Gentner et al. 1993).
- Structural consistency can affect retrieval when superficial features are shared (Holyoak and Koh 1987, Ross 1989, Wharton et al. 1994).
- Abstract structural features (i.e., structural consistency in the absence of superficial similarity) can affect retrieval when material is intensively studied and/or when participants are domain experts (Seifert et al. 1986, Catrambone and Holyoak 1989, Novick 1988, Gick and Holyoak 1983, Wharton et al. 1994).

These findings suggest that ordinary HRR similarity can probably account for human analog recall performance under most, but not all, conditions. In particular, ordinary HRR similarity is not sensitive to structural consistency in the absence of superficial similarity. This section describes how HRRs can be enhanced with additional conjunctive features (binding chains) so that HRR similarity is sensitive to structural consistency even in the absence of superficial similarity or the presence of cross mapping. Such an enhanced representation may be useful both in modeling human analog recall performance under more probing conditions (e.g., involving experts or intensive study) and in achieving higher levels of performance in AI systems.

6.5.1 Abstract structure and contextualization

HRR similarity can be influenced by structural consistency at all levels, from the consistency of higher-order relations among relations (e.g., "bite causes flee"), to the consistency of object mapping. However, there are conditions – ordinary HRRs are not sensitive to structural consistency when corresponding objects are dissimilar or cross-mapped, or when all objects are of the same type. This is revealed in some of the relative HRR similarities in the previous section. For example, the cross-mapped analogy $\mathbf{E}2$ (CM) scores lower than the superficially similar episode $\mathbf{E}5$ ($\mathrm{SS}^{\times \mathrm{I}}$), and the analogical episodes $\mathbf{E}3$ (AN) and $\mathbf{E}4$ (AN) score identically to the false analogy $\mathbf{E}7$ ($\mathrm{FA}^{\times \mathrm{I}}$). This is a potential deficiency for AI systems, and for cognitive models of analog retrieval behavior that shows an elevated sensitivity to structural similarity (such as that of domain experts).

HRRs can be made sensitive to more abstract structural properties by enhancing them with additional abstract structural features. One way of doing this is by constructing HRRs so that they include conjunctive features (binding chains) that carry information about which roles are filled by the same filler. These additional binding chains are abstract structural features because they do not involve filler patterns. In general, structurally consistent episodes will have more of these abstract structural features in common than will structurally inconsistent episodes. These abstract structural features can be introduced in a simple manner by *contextualizing* the representations of fillers. This involves making the representation for a filler in a particular episode incorporate information about the other roles that it fills in the episode. For example, in the probe episode "Spot bit Jane, causing Jane to flee from Spot," Spot is something that bites (a *biter*) and something that is fled from (a *fledfrom*). Vectors for these extra features such as *biter* and *fledfrom* are blended with the vector for the filler (*Spot*). Thus the contextualized representation of a filler in a particular episode involves both its identity and its contexts (the roles it fills) in the episode.

For example, consider contextualizing the HRR for the probe. In the **flee** relation in the probe the context for Spot can be represented by the pattern $\mathbf{bite}_{typagt}$ (a biter), and in the **bite** relation the context for Spot can be represented by the pattern $\mathbf{flee}_{typfrom}$. The contextualized

HRR for the probe is constructed as follows:[59]

$$\mathbf{P}_{bite} = \langle \mathbf{bite} + \langle \mathbf{spot} + \mathbf{jane} \rangle$$
$$+ \mathbf{bite}_{agt} \circledast \langle \kappa_o\mathbf{spot} + \kappa_c\mathbf{flee}_{typfrom} \rangle$$
$$+ \mathbf{bite}_{obj} \circledast \langle \kappa_o\mathbf{jane} + \kappa_c\mathbf{flee}_{typagt} \rangle \rangle$$

$$\mathbf{P}_{flee} = \langle \mathbf{flee} + \langle \mathbf{spot} + \mathbf{jane} \rangle$$
$$+ \mathbf{flee}_{agt} \circledast \langle \kappa_o\mathbf{jane} + \kappa_c\mathbf{bite}_{typobj} \rangle$$
$$+ \mathbf{flee}_{from} \circledast \langle \kappa_o\mathbf{spot} + \kappa_c\mathbf{bite}_{typagt} \rangle \rangle$$

$$\mathbf{P} = \langle \mathbf{cause} + \langle \mathbf{P}_{bite} + \mathbf{P}_{flee} \rangle$$
$$+ \mathbf{cause}_{antc} \circledast \mathbf{P}_{bite} + \mathbf{cause}_{cnsq} \circledast \mathbf{P}_{flee} \rangle$$

In these formulae, the constants κ_o and κ_c (where $\kappa_o^2 + \kappa_c^2 = 1$) control the relative importance of objects and contexts in the final representations for fillers: a high κ_c results in a highly contextualized HRR, and a zero κ_c results in an ordinary HRR.

6.5.2 Patterns for contexts

Although arbitrary patterns could be used to represent contexts, there is one particularly interesting choice of pattern: the product of the predicate name and the inverse role vector. For example, the pattern representing a biter is

$$\mathbf{bite}_{typagt} = \mathbf{bite} \circledast \mathbf{bite}_{agt}^*,$$

and the pattern representing something fled from is

$$\mathbf{flee}_{typfrom} = \mathbf{flee} \circledast \mathbf{flee}_{from}^*.$$

The pattern $\mathbf{bite}_{typagt}$ can be viewed as the feature of being a typical filler of the *bite* agent role, because it is a component of the result of decoding the agent of any *bite* frame:

$$(\mathbf{bite} + \mathbf{bite}_{agt} \circledast \mathbf{agent} + \mathbf{bite}_{obj} \circledast \mathbf{object}) \circledast \mathbf{bite}_{agt}^*$$
$$= \mathbf{bite} \circledast \mathbf{bite}_{agt}^* + \mathbf{bite}_{agt} \circledast \mathbf{agent} \circledast \mathbf{bite}_{agt}^*$$
$$+ \mathbf{bite}_{obj} \circledast \mathbf{object} \circledast \mathbf{bite}_{agt}^*$$

The second term in the RHS is the normally desired component of the result – it is approximately equal to **agent**. The other two

---

[59]It is beyond the scope of this book to describe how ordinary, let alone contextualized, HRRs might be constructed in a connectionist system. However, a system that did build contextualized HRRs would probably accumulate context patterns on the fillers, which would result in more context patterns appearing in the HRRs than are in the formulae here. For example, the context feature $\mathbf{bite}_{typagt}$ would appear in the *bite* agent binding (despite being superfluous) and as a component of $\mathbf{P}_{bite}$ (next to **spot**). These additional context patterns would have little affect on HRR similarity, as they would occur in the HRRs for all episodes.

terms have been treated as decoding noise up until here in this book. However, the first term term is always present when an agent is extracted from a *bite* frame, and thus seems to be a reasonable candidate for the contextual feature of being a typical filler of the *bite* agent role. Note that with this representation for contexts, it would be superfluous to blend the $\mathbf{bite}_{typagt}$ vector with the filler in the $\mathbf{bite}_{agt}$ role, because its contribution when convolved with the $\mathbf{bite}_{agt}$ role evaluates to the **bite** vector, which is already included in the HRR for the *bite* relation (because $\mathbf{bite}_{agt} \circledast (\mathbf{agent} + \mathbf{bite}_{typagt}) = \mathbf{bite}_{agt} \circledast \mathbf{agent} + \mathbf{bite}_{agt} \circledast \mathbf{bite} \circledast \mathbf{bite}^*_{agt} = \mathbf{bite}_{agt} \circledast \mathbf{agent} + \mathbf{bite}$). This is the reason why, in the experiments described here, a contextualized HRR for a particular frame only includes vectors for contexts outside of that frame.

As an aside, there is a potentially interesting connection between stereotyping and contextualization. Suppose that the long-term memory representation for Spot were somewhat malleable, and that Spot was often encountered when decoding the agent in *bite* frames. Then the pattern for Spot might over time incorporate this component, which represents a *typical biter*. This would stereotype Spot as being a biter. This type of stereotyping could be useful as it would provide a shortcut method for contextualizing. It is important to note that information resulting from stereotyping (e.g., the presence of the *biter* pattern in the pattern for Spot) would only provide correct contextual clues when the stereotyped object is filling a stereotypical role. In other situations it could result in incorrect recall, decoding or inferences. However, the implementation and consequences of this type of stereotyping is left for future research.

6.5.3 Flexible salience of abstract structural similarity

Human judgments of similarity tend to be flexible – in general the salience of different aspects of similarity can be changed by context or by explicit instructions to pay attention to a particular aspect of similarity (Tversky, 1977). In contextualized HRRs the degree to which abstract structural similarity affects HRR similarity can be adjusted by changing the degree of contextualization in just one episode of a pair. Hence, the items in memory can be encoded with fixed κ values (κ_o^m and κ_c^m) and the salience of role alignment can be changed by altering the degree of contextualization in the probe (κ_o^p and κ_c^p). This is fortunate as it would be impractical to recode all items in memory in order to alter the salience of abstract structural similarity in a particular comparison.

Note that not all episodes in memory need be encoded using contextualization, but the HRRs for those that are not will not have enhanced value of the dot product with the contextualized HRR for a structurally similar probe.

6.5.4 Experiments 2 and 3: Contextualized HRRs

Two experiments were performed with contextualized HRRs, with the same set of twelve episodes as used in Experiment 1B. In both experiments the memorized episodes were encoded with the same degree of contextualization ($\kappa_o^m = \sqrt{1/3}, \kappa_c^m = \sqrt{2/3}$). In Experiment 2 contextualization was used in the probe ($\kappa_o^p = \sqrt{1/3}, \kappa_c^p = \sqrt{2/3}$). In Experiment 3 the probe was non contextualized ($\kappa_o^p = 1, \kappa_c^p = 0$), to test (by comparison with the results of Experiment 2) whether the influence of structural commonalities could be controlled by how the probe was encoded, without changing how the memorized episodes were encoded. As before, each set of comparisons was run 100 times, and the vector dimension was 2048. The results are listed in Table 23. Only the means of the HRR similarities are shown – the standard deviations were again between 0.010 and 0.028.

The HRR similarities in Experiment 2 were consistent (in 97 out of 100 runs) with an ordering that ranks structurally isomorphic episodes strictly more similar to the probe than non isomorphic ones:

$$\text{LS} > \text{CM} > \text{AN} > \{\text{SS}^{\times I}, \text{SS}^{\times H}\}$$
$$> \{\text{SS}^{-H}, \text{FA}^{\times I}, \text{FA}^{\times H}, \text{OO}^{\times H}\} > \text{OO}^{-H}.$$

The HRR similarities in Experiment 3 were consistent (in 92 out of 100 runs) with the same order as given for Experiment 1B.

$$\text{LS} > \text{SS}^{\times I} > \text{CM} > \{\text{SS}^{\times H}, \text{AN}, \text{FA}^{\times I}\}$$
$$> \text{OO}^{\times H} > \{\text{FA}^{\times H}, \text{SS}^{-H}\} > \text{OO}^{-H}.$$

This shows that the influence of structural similarity can be controlled just by how the probe is encoded.

6.5.5 Discussion of results

When both the probe and memorized episodes are contextualized (Experiment 2), the episodes that are structurally isomorphic to the probe (**E1**, **E2**, **E3**, and **E4**, i.e., LS, CM, AN, and AN) have higher HRR similarity to the probe than the other episodes.

However, in Experiment 3 the ordering of HRR similarity between the non contextualized probe and contextualized episodes is the same as for Experiment 1B. This is because the extra conjunctive features in the contextualized episodes do not match up with any features in the probe and consequently do not affect the HRR similarities to the

P: Spot bit Jane, causing Jane to flee from Spot.

Episodes in long-term memory:	Object attributes	First-order relation names	Higher-order relation names	Role-filler bindings	Higher-order structure	Object-level isomorphism	Type	Ex 2		Ex 3	
								HRR similarity scores and (ranks)			
E1: Fido bit John, causing John to flee from Fido.	✓	✓	✓	✓	✓	✓	LS	0.83	(1)	0.64	(1)
E2: Fred bit Rover, causing Rover to flee from Fred.	✕	✓	✓	✕	✓	✓	CM	0.77	(2)	0.54	(3)
E3: Felix bit Mort, causing Mort to flee from Felix.	✕	✓	✓	✕	✓	✓	AN	0.66	(=3)	0.42	(=6)
E4: Mort bit Felix, causing Felix to flee from Mort.	✕	✓	✓	$\frac{1}{2}$	✓	✕	AN	0.66	(=3)	0.42	(=6)
E5: Rover bit Fred, causing Rover to flee from Fred.	✓	✓	✓	✓	✕	✓	SS×I	0.57	(5)	0.59	(2)
E6: John fled from Fido, causing Fido to bite John.	✓	✓	✓	✕	✓	✓	SS×H	0.49	(6)	0.44	(4)
E7: Mort bit Felix, causing Mort to flee from Felix.	✕	✓	✓	✕	✕	✕	FA×I	0.43	(7)	0.43	(=5)
E8: Mort fled from Felix, causing Felix to bite Mort.	✕	✓	✓	✓	✕	✓	FA×H	0.37	(8)	0.30	(9)
E9: Fido bit John, John fled from Fido.	✓	✓	✕	✕	✕	✓	SS−H	0.36	(=9)	0.25	(10)
E10: Fred stroked Rover, causing Rover to lick Fred.	✓	✕	✓	✕	✕	✕	OO×H	0.36	(=9)	0.36	(8)
E11: Fred stroked Rover, Rover licked Fred.	✓	✕	✕	✕	✕	✕	OO−H	0.10	(11)	0.10	(11)

Commonalities with probe

TABLE 23 Results from Experiments 2 and 3.

probe (other than making HRR similarities lower across the board, due to the greater number of features in the contextualized episodes).

The relative weights of the context and the object in a filler (i.e., $\kappa_c = \sqrt{2/3}$ and $\kappa_o = \sqrt{1/3}$) were chosen so that these structurally isomorphic episodes would be more similar to the probe than all the others. This choice of parameters was made in order to demonstrate that it is possible to design distributed representations such that structural similarity dominates object-level similarity in comparisons. When the context and object are weighted equally (i.e., $\kappa_c = \kappa_o$), **E5** ($SS^{\times I}$) is sometimes more similar to the probe than **E3** (AN) or **E4** (AN) (in 32 runs out of 100). This is because **E5** ($SS^{\times I}$) shares object features and some structure with the probe, whereas **E3** (AN) and **E4** (AN) share no object features but do share structure with the probe. In these cases the contribution from the object features balances the contributions from structural features, resulting in tied HRR similarity to the probe.

The example here shows the use of contextualization for objects, but it could also be used in cases where a single relation appeared in multiple higher-order relations. For example, if the probe had another higher-order relation and "Jane fled from Spot" filled a role in it (in addition to the *cause* antecedent role), then **cause**$_{typcnsq}$ could be the context used in that other relation.

6.5.6 Additional binding chains introduced by contextualization

Contextualization adds binding chains that represent more abstract structural features, such the "the filler of the agent role of *bite* is the filler of the *from* role of *flee*." Adding these structural features causes contextualized HRR similarity to better reflect structural similarity compared to ordinary HRR similarity, especially when corresponding objects have little or no similarity.

Contextualization nearly doubles the number of binding chains in the HRR for these episodes (and would increase their number even more if some entities were involved in more than two relations). Table 24 shows the binding chains in the contextualized probe that are in addition to those already tabulated in Table 22. Figure 54 shows the binding chains in the contextualized HRR for the probe.

6.5.7 Limits of contextualization

Contextualization is not a complete solution for detecting structural consistency. The features introduced into two different episodes by contextualization can match fully even when the episodes are not structurally consistent. This happens in situations where there are two dis-

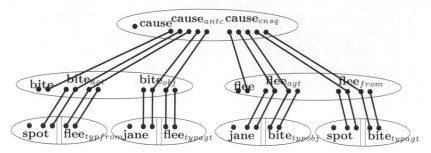

FIGURE 54 The binding chains in the contextualized HRR for the probe (compare with Figure 53). The incorporation of context almost doubles the number of binding chains.

From $\mathbf{P}_{bite}$	From $\mathbf{P}_{flee}$
$\mathbf{bite}_{agt} \circledast \mathbf{flee}_{typfrom}$	$\mathbf{flee}_{agt} \circledast \mathbf{bite}_{typobj}$
$\mathbf{bite}_{obj} \circledast \mathbf{flee}_{typagt}$	$\mathbf{flee}_{from} \circledast \mathbf{bite}_{typagt}$

From $\mathbf{cause}_{antc} \circledast \mathbf{P}_{bite}$	From $\mathbf{cause}_{cnsq} \circledast \mathbf{P}_{flee}$
$\mathbf{cause}_{antc} \circledast \mathbf{bite}_{agt} \circledast \mathbf{flee}_{typfrom}$	$\mathbf{cause}_{cnsq} \circledast \mathbf{flee}_{agt} \circledast \mathbf{bite}_{typobj}$
$\mathbf{cause}_{antc} \circledast \mathbf{bite}_{obj} \circledast \mathbf{flee}_{typagt}$	$\mathbf{cause}_{cnsq} \circledast \mathbf{flee}_{from} \circledast \mathbf{bite}_{typagt}$

TABLE 24 Binding chains in the contextualized HRR encoding for the probe that are in addition to those in the standard HRR encoding of the probe.

tinct instances of one type and the set of roles filled by one instance is the same as the set of roles filled by the other instance. Such situations are somewhat pathological (and somewhat confusing!), but by no means impossible. They can occur easily when there are multiple objects of the same type. Consider the situation where two boys are bitten by two dogs, and each flees from the dog that did not bite him. Contextualized HRRs will not be able to distinguish this from the situation where each boy flees from the dog that did bite him. In this case the structural context required to distinguish objects is more than the set of roles that the objects fill. This example with two boys and two dogs can be written as follows (where p is the *bite* relation and q is the *flee* relation):

$$
\begin{aligned}
S_1 &= p(x,y), p(w,z), q(z,x), q(y,w) \\
S_2 &= p(a,b), p(c,d), q(d,a), q(b,c) \\
S_3 &= p(a,b), p(c,d), q(b,a), q(d,c)
\end{aligned}
$$

S_2 is analogous to S_1, but S_3 is not. However, if objects are ignored, they all have the same contextualized representation (where c_{q_1} is the context pattern indicating a filler of the first role of q etc):

$$p(c_{q_2}, c_{q_1}), p(c_{q_2}, c_{q_1}), q(c_{p_2}, c_{p_1}), q(c_{p_2}, c_{p_1})$$

One could extend contextualization by incorporating yet more information into filler contexts, for example, by contextualizing John as "the fleer from the other dog," but the scheme does begin to lose its simplicity. Basic contextualization will usually make HRR similarity more sensitive to structural similarity and will fail to help only when there is a high degree of repetition and symmetry within episodes.

6.6 Interpretations of an analogy

Retrieval of analogies is only the first step in analogy processing tasks. After retrieving a potentially analogous episode we may want to access the structure in order to better evaluate the degree of structural consistency, or to use the episode for analogical reasoning. The structure of a HRR could be decoded using the techniques described in Section 3.10.3, and then used in a symbolic processor like SME or in some other connectionist architecture. However, some apparently more symbolic tasks, like finding corresponding entities in two episodes, can be computed directly on HRRs using only vector operations.

6.6.1 Finding correspondences without intermediate clean-up

Consider the probe **P** "Spot bit Jane, causing Jane to flee from Spot," and **E**1 "Fido bit John, causing John to flee from Fido." The object in **E**1 corresponding to Jane in the probe can be found in two steps with a single final clean-up operation:

1. Extract the roles Jane fills in the probe with the operation:

$$\mathbf{jane\text{-}roles_P} = \langle \mathbf{P} \circledast \mathbf{jane^*} \rangle.$$

The pattern **jane-roles$_P$** is a blend of various roles and other noise patterns. The following are the dot products of **jane-roles$_P$** with all role patterns (for one run, in order of similarity):

$$
\begin{aligned}
\mathbf{jane\text{-}roles_P} \cdot \mathbf{cause}_{antc} &= 0.20 \\
\mathbf{jane\text{-}roles_P} \cdot \mathbf{cause}_{cnsq} &= 0.18 \\
\mathbf{jane\text{-}roles_P} \cdot \mathbf{flee}_{agt} &= 0.13 \\
\mathbf{jane\text{-}roles_P} \cdot \mathbf{bite}_{obj} &= 0.12 \\
\mathbf{jane\text{-}roles_P} \cdot \mathbf{stroke}_{agt} &= -0.0052
\end{aligned}
$$

	Extraction using $R = \text{jane-roles}_P$	Extraction using $R_c = \text{clean-jane-roles}_P$
LS	$\langle \mathbf{E1} \circledast \mathbf{R}^* \rangle$ john 0.38 ✓ fido 0.07	$\langle \mathbf{E1} \circledast \mathbf{R}_c^* \rangle$ john 0.27 ✓ fido 0.20
CM	$\langle \mathbf{E2} \circledast \mathbf{R}^* \rangle$ fred 0.25 × rover 0.17	$\langle \mathbf{E2} \circledast \mathbf{R}_c^* \rangle$ rover 0.29 ✓ fred 0.20
AN	$\langle \mathbf{E3} \circledast \mathbf{R}^* \rangle$ mort 0.20 ✓ felix 0.05	$\langle \mathbf{E3} \circledast \mathbf{R}_c^* \rangle$ mort 0.29 ✓ felix 0.18
AN	$\langle \mathbf{E4} \circledast \mathbf{R}^* \rangle$ felix 0.16 ✓ mort 0.09	$\langle \mathbf{E4} \circledast \mathbf{R}_c^* \rangle$ felix 0.25 ✓ mort 0.20
$\text{SS}^{\times \text{I}}$	$\langle \mathbf{E5} \circledast \mathbf{R}^* \rangle$ fred 0.30 ? rover 0.11	$\langle \mathbf{E5} \circledast \mathbf{R}_c^* \rangle$ fred 0.26 ? rover 0.25
$\text{SS}^{\times \text{H}}$	$\langle \mathbf{E6} \circledast \mathbf{R}^* \rangle$ john 0.23 ? fido 0.07	$\langle \mathbf{E6} \circledast \mathbf{R}_c^* \rangle$ john 0.25 ? fido 0.17
$\text{FA}^{\times \text{H}}$	$\langle \mathbf{E8} \circledast \mathbf{R}^* \rangle$ mort 0.12 ? felix 0.06	$\langle \mathbf{E8} \circledast \mathbf{R}_c^* \rangle$ mort 0.26 ? felix 0.19

TABLE 25 Interpretation of an analogy: extraction of corresponding entities (for ordinary HRRs). Correct extractions have a check mark, incorrect extractions have a cross. Extractions where there is not a clear right or wrong answer have a question mark.

$$\text{jane-roles}_P \cdot \text{bite}_{agt} = -0.0097$$
$$\text{jane-roles}_P \cdot \text{stroke}_{obj} = -0.012$$
$$\text{jane-roles}_P \cdot \text{lick}_{obj} = -0.013$$
$$\text{jane-roles}_P \cdot \text{lick}_{agt} = -0.036$$
$$\text{jane-roles}_P \cdot \text{flee}_{from} = -0.039$$

2. Use **jane-roles**$_P$ to extract the fillers from **E**1 and compare (dot product) with the entities in **E**1:

$$\langle \mathbf{E1} \circledast \text{jane-roles}_P^* \rangle \cdot \text{john} = 0.38$$
$$\langle \mathbf{E1} \circledast \text{jane-roles}_P^* \rangle \cdot \text{fido} = 0.07$$

The most similar entity is John, which is in fact the entity in **E**1 corresponding to Jane in the probe.

The extraction of the entities corresponding to Jane in the various episodes is shown in Table 25(a). Correct extractions have a check mark. The correct answer is obtained in **E**1 (LS), where corresponding objects are similar, and in **E**3 (AN) and **E**4 (AN), where there is no object similarity. This extraction process has a bias towards choosing similar entities as the corresponding ones, which leads to a reasonable answer for **E5** ($SS^{\times I}$) and an incorrect answer for **E2** (CM). There is no correct answer for **E5** ($SS^{\times I}$), because there is no consistent mapping between **P** and **E5**. However, because of the bias for mapping similar items, **fred** is strongly indicated to be the one corresponding to **jane**. The wrong answer is given for the cross-mapped analogy **E2**, where again the more similar object is indicated to be the corresponding one. It is interesting to note that people, especially children, also tend to have difficulties in finding correspondences in the presence of cross mapping (Ross, 1989, Gentner et al., 1993).

Closer examination of the extraction process reveals the reason for this bias. Consider the expansion of **P** ⊛ **jane*** into some of its terms (omitting normalization and weighting factors):

$$
\begin{aligned}
\textbf{jane-roles}_\textbf{P} \;&=\; \textbf{P} \circledast \textbf{jane}^* \\
&=\; \ldots + \textbf{bite}_{obj} + \ldots + \textbf{flee}_{agt} \\
&\quad + \ldots + \textbf{cause} \circledast \textbf{jane}^* + \ldots .
\end{aligned}
$$

The roles **bite**$_{obj}$ and **flee**$_{agt}$ are desired – they are the roles of **jane** (they come from **bite**$_{obj}$ ⊛ **jane** ⊛ **jane*** and **flee**$_{agt}$ ⊛ **jane** ⊛ **jane***). The sources of the bias are other unwanted terms like **cause** ⊛ **jane***, which are not roles at all. Continuing with the algebra, the approximate inverse[60] of **jane-roles**$_\textbf{P}$ includes the following terms:

$$
\textbf{jane-roles}_\textbf{P}^* = \ldots + \textbf{bite}_{obj}^* + \ldots + \textbf{flee}_{agt}^* + \ldots + \textbf{cause}^* \circledast \textbf{jane} + \ldots
$$

When this is used to extract the fillers from **E2**, i.e. as

$$
\begin{aligned}
\textbf{jane-roles}_\textbf{P}^* \circledast \textbf{E2} \;&=\; \ldots + \textbf{bite}_{obj} \circledast \textbf{fido} \circledast \textbf{bite}_{obj}^* \\
&\quad + \textbf{flee}_{agt} \circledast \textbf{fido} \circledast \textbf{flee}_{agt}^* \\
&\quad + \ldots + \textbf{cause}^* \circledast \textbf{jane} \circledast \textbf{cause} + \ldots ,
\end{aligned}
$$

the result includes **fido** from **bite**$_{obj}$⊛**fido**⊛**bite**$_{obj}^*$ and **flee**$_{agt}$⊛**fido**⊛ **flee**$_{agt}^*$ as intended. However, this result also includes a component of **jane** (as **cause*** ⊛ **jane** ⊛ **cause**) from the other terms that are the same in **P** and **E2**. The **jane** component in this final result is larger than the **fido** component, and as **jane** is similar to **fred** the result ends up being more similar to **fred** than **fido** (and is also more similar to **jane** than **fred**, but we were never comparing to **jane** because we were limiting comparisons to objects in **E2**).

---

[60]Recall that the approximate inverse obeys the axioms $(a + b)^* = a^* + b^*$ and $(a \circledast b^*)^* = a^* \circledast b$.

6.6.2 Finding correspondences with intermediate clean-up

This bias towards mapping similar entities can be eliminated by performing an intermediate *multi-way* clean-up on the roles extracted by the operation $\mathbf{P} \circledast \mathbf{jane}^*$. This multi-way clean-up[61] should filter out non-role components like $\mathbf{cause} \circledast \mathbf{jane}^*$, and negative role components, while passing through all positive role components. For example, the cleaned-up version of $\mathbf{jane\text{-}roles_P} = \mathbf{P} \circledast \mathbf{jane}^*$ should be:

$$\mathbf{clean\text{-}jane\text{-}roles_P} = 0.20\mathbf{cause}_{antc} + 0.18\mathbf{cause}_{cnsq}$$
$$+ 0.13\mathbf{flee}_{agt} + 0.12\mathbf{bite}_{obj},$$

where the weights come from the dot products of $\mathbf{P} \circledast \mathbf{jane}^*$ with the roles (listed in step 1 at the beginning of this section). This clean-up can be viewed as a less competitive version of the standard clean-up. The corresponding objects extracted using role clean-up are shown in Table 25(b). The process gives the correct answers for all four episodes where there is a consistent mapping, and an ambiguous answer for the episode that has no consistent mapping with the probe.

There are two problems with these fast techniques for extracting corresponding entities. One is that each pair in the mapping is extracted independently. This matters when there is more than one consistent mapping. For example, if we have two possible mappings $\{X \leftrightarrow A, Y \leftrightarrow B\}$ and $\{X \leftrightarrow B, Y \leftrightarrow A\}$, then the choice of mapping for X should constrain the choice for Y, but this will not be the case with the above techniques. The other problem is that these techniques do not work well when two different objects have the same set of roles – ambiguous results can be produced. However, when this occurs it would probably confuse people too.

6.7 Discussion

6.7.1 HRR similarity as an estimate of analogical similarity

Table 17 presented criteria for good analogies, as specified by (Falkenhainer et al., 1989) and (Holyoak and Thagard, 1989). Ordinary and contextualized HRR similarity can be seen as conforming with these criteria to various degrees:

Clarity: In general, no. However, an indication of clarity could be obtained by computing corresponding objects and seeing if one possible mapping stands out clearly above the others.

Richness: Yes. A greater number of similar components, and greater

---

[61] As with the single-way clean up, the details of how it is performed are not important to the arguments in this book.

similarity of components both contribute to higher HRR similarity.

Abstractness: Not with ordinary HRRs, to some degree with contextualized HRRs. Having similar attributes on corresponding objects does contribute to HRR similarity, but can be made less important by using contextualization. Higher-order relations can be given more importance by using larger weights for them.

Semantic similarity: Yes. Semantic similarity between corresponding entities increases HRR similarity. (This is the opposite of abstractness.)

Systematicity (isomorphism):

- Structural consistency: Is detected to some degree with both ordinary and contextualized HRRs. Two instances of a higher-order relation will be more similar if their arguments are similar.
- One-to-one mappings: Not with ordinary HRRs, to some extent with contextualized HRRs.

Pragmatic centrality: Not investigated in this book. However, a simple approach with HRRs would be to give particularly important objects or relations be given a higher weight in the probe.

One important criterion omitted from this list is flexibility. Gentner and Markman (1993) and Goldstone et al. (1991) present convincing evidence that people are flexible in how they evaluate or use analogies. People can take different aspects of situations into account, depending on what is salient in the given context. In the HRR model all aspects are added together but flexibility is retained – different aspects in the representations can be weighted as appropriate. This requires only changing the representation of the probe; the representations of items in long-term memory can be fixed.

Forbus et al. (1994) list some additional criteria for computational models of similarity-based retrieval:

Structured representation: The model must be able to store structured representations.

Structured mapping: The model must incorporate processes of structural mapping (i.e., alignment and transfer) over its representations.

Primacy of the mundane: The majority of retrievals should be literal similarity matches, i.e., they should have many structural and surface commonalities.

Surface superiority: Retrievals based on surface similarity are frequent.

Rare insights: Relational remindings must occur at least occasionally, with lower frequency than literal similarity or surface remindings.

Scalability: The model must be plausibly capable of being extended to large memory sizes (large numbers of items in memory).

All of these criteria are satisfied by a simple HRR-based model of analog retrieval, with the exception of the one that states that the retrieval process must involve some type of structural mapping process. The fact that HRR similarity can reflect structural similarity without computing or considering any mappings shows that this criterion is unnecessary for retrieval. A HRR-based model manages to get away without needing to compute any mappings because of its use of conjunctive features (binding chains) that can indicate structural matches.[62]

6.7.2   Features or predicates?

In HRRs as described in this book, features and predicates are represented differently. This can create the problem of having to decide which to use. The choice is important because it can dramatically affect the similarity of ordinary HRRs, but has a lesser effect on the similarity of contextualized HRRs, as explained below.

Markman et al. (1993) claim that results involving Items 5 and 6 in the shape-configuration experiments demonstrate that multiple relations can be used in the same comparisons (an instance of "(X smaller-than Y) and (X above Y)" is more similar to another instance of the same than to "(Y smaller-than X) and (X above Y)", or, alternatively, "(X larger-than Y) and (X above Y)"). However, in the ordinary HRR encoding for the shape configurations I used features rather than binary relations to represent the relative sizes, and this gave acceptable results. It would in fact be possible to encode the relative sizes as a binary predicate *is-larger than* (with roles *larger* and *smaller*), rather than as features of the objects. If this were done, ordinary HRR similarity would not produce the correct answers for Item 6, because there would be no explicit relationship (binding) between *smaller* and *above*, or between *larger* and *below*. However, using contextualization and a *is-larger-than* predicate would have a very similar effect to using the features *large* and *small*, because contextualization would provide a *typical-larger-object* feature and a *typical-smaller-object* feature to be added to the shape features (circle, star, etc.) Note also that using

---

[62]A similar technique is used in the graph-matching literature. Finding isomorphism is an expensive global process. Many algorithms augment the vertices with attributes reflecting their local neighborhood. For example, see DePiero and Krout (2003).

single-place predicates *is-small* and *is-large* instead of *small* and *large* features would remove binding chains that are valuable for detecting structural similarity, but contextualization would add those binding chains back in. This suggests that there is something right about contextualization – it lessens the somewhat artificial distinction between features and predicates.

Note that features could also be represented as unary predicates in HRRs (i.e., as a frame with just one role). However, this choice is less important because the representations are quite similar. For example, the unary predicate representation of "small circle" would be $\langle$**is-small** + **circle** + **is-small**$_{arg}$ ⊛ **circle**$\rangle$. The only effective difference between this and the feature-based representation (i.e., $\langle$**small** + **circle**$\rangle$) is the role-filler binding **is-small**$_{arg}$ ⊛ **circle**. The unary predicate representation could quite possibly be a better way to represent features than mere superposition because it introduces a binding between the feature and the object it belongs too, which could help to avoid crosstalk regarding which features belong to which objects in a superposition involving other objects with their own features.

6.7.3 Inadequacy of vector dot-product models of similarity

Tversky (1977) pointed out the now well-known reasons why human similarity judgments cannot be modeled as a simple vector dot product. The problems arise because there are cases in which people's similarity judgments violate each of the three axioms of metric spaces (with $d(\cdot, \cdot)$ as the distance function): minimality, $d(x, x) = 0$; symmetry, $d(x, y) = d(y, x)$; and the triangle inequality, $d(x, z) \leq d(x, y) + d(y, z)$.

However, these problems do not preclude the use of vector dot products at some level in a model of similarity. Much of the problematic data could be easily explained by a vector dot-product model that allowed vectors to be transformed before computing the dot product. The transform would depend on the context of the comparison and possibly on the items to be compared. It could be something as simple as an adjustment of the weighting of various components in the vector.

6.7.4 Scaling to more memorized episodes

In the experiments reported here, the long-term (clean-up) memory held only 12 episodes. However, many more episodes could be added without any decrease in accuracy of retrieval, provided the new episodes were not very similar to the existing ones. Retrieval or rating errors are most likely to occur with similar episodes; errors are extremely unlikely with non-similar episodes because the Gaussian distribution of dot products ensures an infinitesimal chance of a non-similar episode having a higher HRR similarity to the probe than a similar one. Thus, as long as any one episode is similar to only a small number of others, the system with $n = 2048$ or $n = 4096$ will be able to store many thousands of episodes.

6.7.5 Scaling to larger structures

One problem with HRR similarity as a measure of analogical similarity is that it does not distinguish between a poorly matching pair of components and a well-matching but low-weighted pair of components. This could cause problems when attempting to match larger structures, because in the HRR for a structure with many components, most components will have low weights. Chunking (see Section 3.11.3) could help to solve this problem. Using chunking in an analog retrieval task would involve storing the HRRs for substructures of episodes in long-term memory, along with the top-level HRRs for episodes. It would also probably require using HRRs for substructures of the probe as additional retrieval cues. The process would retrieve from long-term memory those HRRs that had the highest density of overlap to the probe or its substructures. The retrieved HRRs could represent either entire episodes or just chunks of episodes. A potential problem with this if the probe were chunked in a different manner to a stored episode, the good match might be overlooked because none of the individual chunks match sufficiently well.

Eliasmith and Thagard (2001) present a different approach to analogical mapping that is well able to deal with larger structures. They combine HRRs and ACME to provide an impressive account of analogical mapping that is sensitive to structural details as well as to the nuances of meaning that can be captured in distributed representations.

6.7.6 Sketch of a model for analog mapping

The existence of a fast technique for computing good guesses at object correspondences suggests a new model for analogical mapping. Mapping could be done by *guessing* sets of correspondences and then stepping through the components of the two structures and verifying that the proposed correspondences are consistent. If an inconsistency were discovered, the process would need to be restarted, with the correspondence that resulted in the inconsistency inhibited from being in the set of guessed correspondences. To implement a model like this with HRRs would require several mechanisms or modules along the lines of the following:

- A mechanism that outputs a set of correspondences, given two structures and possibly a set of correspondences to inhibit. This could be built around the corresponding-entity operations described in Section 6.6.

- A mechanism for storing a set of correspondences, and checking whether correspondences are consistent. One instance of the mechanism could be used to store the guessed correspondences, and another instance used to store the inhibited correspondences. This could be based on a simple paired-associates memory, as described in Sections 2.4.4 and 3.1.

- A mechanism for traversing a structure, reading out each entity in the structure sequentially. Such a mechanism for HRRs is described in Plate (1995).

This is merely a sketch of a fully-fledged HRR-based model of analogical mapping – its full description and implementation is beyond the scope of this book. Such a model would differ from ones like ACME and SME in that it would put complex structure-sensitive processing at a different level. The top level involves simple sequential computation (traversing a structure and checking for mapping inconsistencies) rather than complex structural matching or construction of special networks, while the bottom level involves information-rich vector processing to measure similarities and estimate correspondences.

6.7.7 Deductive logic involves making analogies

Rule matching in deductive logic, such as in logic-based AI systems like logic programming and production systems, is a type of analogy making. For example, consider the production rule (or Horn clause)

$$p(X, Y) \wedge q(X, Y) \rightarrow r(X, Y).$$

Matching this rule to a database of (true) instantiated propositions is an instance of analogical reasoning. Each variable in the rule must map consistently to a symbol in the database of instantiated propositions. Although the variables in rules are often regarded as having very different status to grounded symbols, we can regard the variables just as symbols that have few or no constraints on what type of terms they can be mapped to (apart from the structural systematicity constraints). The example rule would match in the database containing $\{p(a, b), q(a, b)\}$, but would not match in the database containing $\{p(a, b), q(b, a)\}$ because there is no consistent mapping between the rule and the database. An additional constraint on the mapping is that all grounded (non variable) symbols in the rule must map identically to symbols in the database. This observation shows that analogical reasoning is not merely some esoteric task that appears as a component of tests and experiments, but is a common task, at least for people who consciously reason following explicit rules on a regular basis. A psychological model of rule following based on analogical-reasoning skills implemented with HRRs could provide a bridge between this human ability and its neural implementation.

6.7.8 Relationship between HRR similarity and kernels for discrete structures

Work in machine learning on kernel-based methods over discrete structures, such as strings and trees, uses a variety of *kernels* to measure similarity between structures (Haussler, 1999, Collins and Duffy, 2002, Bod, 1998). For example, a kernel for strings could count the number of matching substrings, and kernel for trees could count the number of matching subtrees. A kernel is always a dot product between two feature vectors, i.e., a function K where $K(x, y) = \mathbf{h}(x) \cdot \mathbf{h}(y) = \sum_i h_i(x)h_i(y)$. The function $\mathbf{h}$ is some mapping of structures onto numerical vectors – $h_i(x)$ is the value of the ith feature of structure x. For example, in a kernel for strings, $h_i(x)$ could be the number of times the ith substring (in some enumeration of all substrings in the data set of interest) occurs in string x. What makes kernel-based methods practical is that there are efficient methods for computing $K(x, y)$ that do not require $\mathbf{h}(x)$ (or $\mathbf{h}(y)$) to ever be explicitly represented or even enumerated. This is fortunate, as the length of $\mathbf{h}$-vectors can be exponential in the size of the structures being represented – even the number of non-zero elements in $\mathbf{h}(x)$ can be exponential in the size of x. These efficient algorithms are typically based on dynamic-programming techniques and calculate $K(x, y)$ in time polynomial in the size of x and y. For some kernels there are even algorithms with quadratic time and linear time complexity (e.g., Vishwanathan and Smola, 2003, Lodhi et al., 2000).

Kernel-based machine learning algorithms have shown some degree of success in challenging tasks, e.g., text classification (Lodhi et al., 2000), and natural language parsing (Collins and Duffy, 2002). Hence it is interesting to see how HRR similarity compares with kernels. In a straightforward but not particularly interesting way, HRR similarity is a kernel because it is the inner product of two vectors. However, there is a deeper sense also in which the HRR similarity is a kernel (approximately). Recall that a HRR can be viewed as a normalized superposition of vectors and binding chains (Sections 6.4 and 6.5.6). For the purposes of this discussion it is easier if we ignore normalization, and use symbols like $\mathbf{x}_1$ to denote binding chain vectors. Thus we can express the HRR for structure X as the superposition of m_x vectors, i.e.,

$$\mathbf{X} = \mathbf{x}_1 + \mathbf{x}_2 + \ldots + \mathbf{x}_{m_x},$$

and the HRR for the structure Y as the superposition of m_y vectors, i.e.,

$$\mathbf{Y} = \mathbf{y}_1 + \mathbf{y}_2 + \ldots + \mathbf{y}_{m_y}.$$

Then, using basic algebra, the dot product $\mathbf{X} \cdot \mathbf{Y}$ can be expressed as the sum of all pairwise similarities between the vectors in the HRRs for X and Y:

$$\mathbf{X} \cdot \mathbf{Y} = \sum_{i=1}^{m_x} \sum_{j=1}^{m_y} \mathbf{x}_i \cdot \mathbf{y}_j.$$

This expression shows that the dot product of HRRs is like a kernel over the feature space of all possible vectors and binding chains in the domain[63] – a massively larger feature space than the elements of the HRR vector.

This connection can be seen more clearly if we (somewhat unrealistically) assume that the binding chains and vectors comprising $\mathbf{X}$ and $\mathbf{Y}$ are constructed by convolving distinct and independently chosen random vectors. Then $\mathrm{E}[\mathbf{x}_i \cdot \mathbf{y}_j] = 0$, unless $\mathbf{x}_i$ and $\mathbf{y}_j$ are the same vector or binding chain, in which case the expected value is 1. Further, assume that the dimensionality of the HRRs is sufficiently large that the variance of the dot products of binding chains can be ignored, so that we can just say that if $\mathbf{x}_i$ and $\mathbf{y}_j$ are different then $\mathbf{x}_i \cdot \mathbf{y}_j = 0$, and if $\mathbf{x}_i$ and $\mathbf{y}_j$ are the same then $\mathbf{x}_i \cdot \mathbf{y}_j = 1$. Then $\mathbf{h}$ is the feature vector of the kernel and $h_k(\mathbf{X}) = 1$ if $\mathbf{X}$ contains the kth binding chain, and $h_k(\mathbf{X}) = 0$ otherwise. Consequently we can write the HRR dot product as the kernel over $\mathbf{h}$:

$$\mathbf{X} \cdot \mathbf{Y} = \sum_{i=1}^{m_x} \sum_{j=1}^{m_y} \mathbf{x}_i \cdot \mathbf{x}_j \approx \sum_k h_k(\mathbf{X}) h_k(\mathbf{Y}).$$

As noted, this should be regarded as an approximate relationship, since variances will not be zero with any finite-dimensional HRR vectors.

In summary we can say the following initial statements about the relationship between HRR dot products and kernels:

- The HRR dot product can be viewed as an approximate kernel over the feature space comprised of all possible vectors and binding chains. The vectors and binding chains are the appropriate level at which to take this view because they are independent features of the HRR.[64] (The randomizing property of convolution means that

---

[63] A sufficient condition for the dot product of HRRs to be a kernel over this space is that $\mathbf{x}_i \cdot \mathbf{y}_j$ equals one if $\mathbf{x}$ and $\mathbf{y}$ are the same vector or binding chain, and zero otherwise.

[64] This picture becomes more complicated when the vectors out of which HRRs are constructed are not independently chosen, but have some similarity structure,

a convolution of independently chosen random vectors is effectively a new independently chosen random vector.)

- This approximate kernel can be computed in time linear in the dimensionality of the HRR vectors for a set of structures that are already encoded as HRRs. For a particular accuracy of approximation, the dimensionality of the HRR vectors should be proportional to the number of binding chains (conjunctive features) present in structures. Thus, for some specified accuracy of approximation, the time complexity of the HRR dot product is linear in the number of binding chains in the HRRs.

- Unlike with most existing kernels over discrete structures, in which the features are either identical or different, with HRRs the features themselves (i.e., the binding chains) can have continuous degrees of similarity. Another way of saying this is that with HRRs the feature comparison need not bottom out at a level of discrete objects where similarity is either 0 or 1.

- The use of normalization while constructing HRRs will affect which binding chains are more important in the dot product of HRRs.

- In the HRRs described in this book, the binding chains for tree structures are mostly subpaths of paths from the root of the tree to the leaves (contextualized HRRs do have other types of binding chains). It could be possible that there are other ways of constructing binding chains for tree structures that could improve the performance of HRRs for cognitive modeling or Artificial Intelligence purposes.

6.7.9 Comparison to other distributed representation models

The results presented in this chapter should be readily duplicated with other methods for distributed representation of complex structure that use superposition and role-filler bindings and in which the binding operation is both randomizing and similarity preserving. For example, Kanerva's (1996) Binary Spatter Codes are closely related to HRRs and Kanerva (2001) shows how various analogical processing tasks can be performed with them. Another closely related scheme is presented by Gayler (1998). Rachkovskij (2001) shows how various analogical processing tasks can be performed with Rachkovskij and Kussul's (2001) APNN model, which uses sparse binary distributed representations.

Pollack's (1990) RAAMs are a type of backpropagation network that can learn to encode hierarchical structures in a fixed-width vector. Conceivably, one could get estimates of structural similarity by comparing

---

as in the examples in this book. I have not investigated the consequences of this.

the reduced representations discovered by RAAMs. Pollack shows some cluster diagrams that seem to have similar structures grouped together. However, the strength of this effect is unclear. One probable drawback of RAAMs for this application is that they require considerable learning time and the generalization appears weak – there is no guarantee that a new structure can be represented at all without extensive training. For example, if a RAAM were trained on episodes involving the predicates *cause*, *bite*, and *flee*, it might not even be able to represent episodes involving *stroke* or *lick*, let alone compare them to other episodes (see Blair 1997 for a discussion of generalization in RAAMs). Another potential disadvantage is that the nonlinear nature of RAAMs makes it possible for similar structures to have quite different representations, even when the structures are similar in both surface and structural features. On the other hand, the learning involved in RAAMs offers a potential advantage over HRRs – RAAMs could learn to devote more representational resources to commonly encountered structures and thus achieve better performance on them. The downside of this could be poorer performance on rarely encountered structures.

Smolensky's (1990) tensor-product representations are another method for encoding hierarchical structure in distributed representations. They have much in common with HRRs, and it would not be difficult to use them to replicate the results in this chapter. The main difference between the two methods is that the dimensionality of the tensor-product representation increases exponentially with the depth of the structure, while the dimensionality of HRRs remains constant. This could lead to unreasonable resource requirements for structures with several levels of nesting. An advantage of tensor-product representations is that they tend to be less noisy than HRRs in decoding, and would probably also give less noisy similarity estimates.

The results here would be difficult to replicate with Halford et al.'s (1994) representation for relations (Section 2.4.3). Their representation for a relation is the tensor product of its arguments and name. For example, the relation `bite(Spot, Jane)` would be represented as **bite**$\otimes$**spot**$\otimes$**jane**. One problem with this representation is that a pair of relations have zero similarity if any pair of corresponding arguments have zero similarity, no matter how similar the other arguments are. For example, **bite** $\otimes$ **spot** $\otimes$ **jane** is dissimilar to **bite** $\otimes$ **spot** $\otimes$ **fido** (assuming **jane** and **fido** are dissimilar). Another problem is that it is not clear how to represent episodes with multiple or nested predicates. Halford et al. mention chunking but do not give any details how it might be done.

Hummel and Holyoak (1997) present a very different model of analogical mapping that also uses distributed representations. What distinguishes their model is that they use temporal synchrony as the binding mechanism, instead of some static vector or matrix operation as in HRRs and the other schemes mentioned above. It is as yet unclear whether static or dynamic binding methods are more like what the human brain uses, or provide a better model of human performance.

6.8   Conclusion

While it would be overstating the importance of this work to describe it as a watershed for connectionist modeling, this work adds further evidence that complex structure and structural alignment is not the Waterloo for connectionist techniques (cf. Gentner and Markman, 1993). HRRs shows that it is not necessary to perform structural alignment in order to compute an estimate of analogical similarity – as Gentner and Markman recognized would be possible with the right type of connectionist representation. No explicit structural alignment is performed when computing HRR similarity, yet HRR similarity is sensitive to the degree of structural alignment that is possible. This is because HRRs express structural features of the structured objects they represent in the surface features of the representation.

HRR similarity (the dot product of HRRs) is not sufficiently sensitive to the details of structural correspondences to model deliberate human judgments of analogical similarity between large complex structures, but it could provide a very simple account of human performance on analog recall tasks. Furthermore, HRRs encode, in an easily retrievable manner, all the structural information that is needed for more complex analogy processing. HRRs can provide powerful primitive operations for higher-level analogy processing. For example, some of the basic operations needed for analogy processing, such as finding corresponding objects in two structures, can be implemented by fast vector operations on HRRs.

Contextualization is a way of adding more abstract structural features to HRRs. Contextualized HRR similarity is more sensitive to structural similarity, especially in the absence of similarity between corresponding entities.

7

Discussion

In this chapter I briefly discuss several issues that I have not had the opportunity to deal with elsewhere: how HRRs can be transformed without decomposition, conflicts between HRRs and some psychological notions of chunks, how other vector-space multiplication operations could be used instead of convolution, how a disordered variant of convolution might be implemented in neural tissue, and weaknesses of HRRs.

7.1 Holistic processing

One of advantages of reduced descriptions is the ability to perform structure-sensitive processing (i.e., *holistic processing*) on them without unpacking them. This provides a fast type of computation with no obvious parallel in conventional symbol manipulation.

Determining similarity is one of the simplest types of processing. In Chapter 6 I showed how HRRs can be used for fast (but approximate) detection of structural similarity without the need to unpack representations of structured objects. Chapter 6 also showed how HRR computations can be used to rapidly but imperfectly identify corresponding entities in two analogous situations, again without unpacking the representations of the situations. Also, Rachkovskij (2001) demonstrates that APNNs achieve performance similar to HRRs on simple analogy-matching tasks.

Various authors have demonstrated that a variety of more complex structure-sensitive manipulations can be performed on distributed representations without the need to unpack them. Pollack (1990) trained a feedforward network to transform reduced descriptions for propositions like (LOVED X Y) to ones for (LOVED Y X) where the reduced descriptions where found by a Recursive Auto-Associative Memory (RAAM), (and where X and Y were always instantiated with some actual pattern). Chalmers (1990) trained a feedforward network to transform reduced descriptions for simple passive sentences to one for active sentences, where again the reduced descriptions were found by a RAAM. Niklasson and van Gelder (1994) trained a feedforward network to do material conditional inference, and its reverse, on reduced descriptions found by a RAAM. This involves transforming reduced descriptions for formulae of the form $(A \rightarrow B)$ to ones of the form $(\neg A \vee B)$ (and vice-versa). Legendre et al. (1991) showed how tensor product representations for active sentences could be transformed to ones for passive sentences (and vice-versa) by a pre-calculated linear transform. Neumann (2001, 2002) trained networks to perform holistic transformations on a variety of representations, including RAAMs, HRRs, and Binary Spatter Codes.

It is easy to do holistic transforms with HRRs, using analytically derived linear transformations.[65] Consider Niklasson and van Gelder's (1994) task, which was to perform the following transformations:

$$
\begin{aligned}
p \rightarrow q &\;\Rightarrow\; (\neg p \vee q) \\
(\neg p \vee q) &\;\Rightarrow\; (p \rightarrow q) \\
(p \rightarrow (q \vee r)) &\;\Rightarrow\; (\neg p \vee (q \vee r)) \\
(\neg p \vee (q \vee r)) &\;\Rightarrow\; (p \rightarrow (q \vee r)) \\
(p \rightarrow (q \rightarrow r)) &\;\Rightarrow\; (\neg p \vee (q \rightarrow r)) \\
(\neg p \vee (q \rightarrow r)) &\;\Rightarrow\; (p \rightarrow (q \rightarrow r))
\end{aligned}
$$

We need two relations to represent these formulae: *implication* and *disjunction*. *Implication* has two roles, *antecedent* and *consequent*, and *disjunction* also has two roles, which I will call *negative* and *positive*. I use the following HRRs to represent $(\neg p \vee q)$ and $(p \rightarrow (q \vee r))$:

$$
\begin{aligned}
\mathbf{R}_{\neg p \vee q} &= \langle \mathbf{disj} + \mathbf{neg} \circledast \mathbf{p} + \mathbf{pos} \circledast \mathbf{q} \rangle \\
\mathbf{R}_{p \rightarrow (q \vee r)} &= \langle \mathbf{impl} + \mathbf{ante} \circledast \mathbf{p} \\
&\quad + \mathbf{cnsq} \circledast \langle \mathbf{disj} + \mathbf{pos} \circledast \mathbf{q} + \mathbf{pos} \circledast \mathbf{r} \rangle \rangle
\end{aligned}
$$

To transform an implication into a disjunction, we need to do three things: change **impl** to **disj**, change **ante** $\circledast$ **x** to **neg** $\circledast$ **x** (for any **x**), and change **cnsq** $\circledast$ **y** to **pos** $\circledast$ **y** (for any **y**). The first can be accomplished by convolving the implication with **impl*** $\circledast$ **disj**, the second by convolving with **ante*** $\circledast$ **neg**, and the third by convolving

---

[65]Recall that the convolution of vector **x** by another vector **y** is a linear operation because it is identical to multiplying the vector **x** by the matrix M_y, where M_y is the circulant matrix corresponding to **y** (see Section 3.6.6).

with $\mathbf{cnsq}^* \circledast \mathbf{pos}$. In all cases, there are other convolution products such as $\mathbf{impl}^* \circledast \mathbf{disj} \circledast \mathbf{ante} \circledast \mathbf{x}$, but these products can be treated as noise. These three vectors can be superimposed to give a vector that transforms implications to disjunctions:

$$\mathbf{t}_1 = \langle \mathbf{impl}^* \circledast \mathbf{disj} + \mathbf{ante}^* \circledast \mathbf{neg} + \mathbf{cnsq}^* \circledast \mathbf{pos} \rangle.$$

When we convolve $\mathbf{R}_{p \to q}$ with $\mathbf{t}_1$, we get a noisy version of $\mathbf{R}_{\neg p \lor q}$. A similar vector can be constructed to transform disjunctions to implications:

$$\mathbf{t}_2 = \langle \mathbf{disj}^* \circledast \mathbf{impl} + \mathbf{neg}^* \circledast \mathbf{ante} + \mathbf{pos}^* \circledast \mathbf{cnsq} \rangle.$$

The transformation vectors $\mathbf{t}_1$ and $\mathbf{t}_2$ can be superimposed to give one vector that will transform implications to disjunctions and disjunctions to implications:

$$\mathbf{t} = \langle \mathbf{t}_1 + \mathbf{t}_2 \rangle.$$

This results in more noise products, but these will not make the result unrecognizable if the vector dimension is high enough. The strength of non-noise components in the transformed HRR is $1/\sqrt{k}$ times their strength in the original HRR, where k is the number of components in the transformation vector ($k = 6$ for $\mathbf{t}$).

I simulated the above task, checking the result by decoding its various roles. For example, $\mathbf{t} \circledast \mathbf{R}_{p \to (q \to r)}$ should give $\mathbf{R}_{\neg p \lor (q \to r)}$, which should decode as follows:

$\mathbf{t} \circledast \mathbf{R}_{p \to (q \lor r)}$	$\approx$	disj
$\mathbf{t} \circledast \mathbf{R}_{p \to (q \lor r)} \circledast \mathbf{neg}^*$	$\approx$	p
$\mathbf{t} \circledast \mathbf{R}_{p \to (q \lor r)} \circledast \mathbf{pos}^*$	$\approx$	impl
$\mathbf{t} \circledast \mathbf{R}_{p \to (q \lor r)} \circledast \mathbf{pos}^* \circledast \mathbf{ante}^*$	$\approx$	q
$\mathbf{t} \circledast \mathbf{R}_{p \to (q \lor r)} \circledast \mathbf{pos}^* \circledast \mathbf{cnsq}^*$	$\approx$	r

I tried the various formulae with all possible instantiations of five different variables, which gave 550 different formulae, and 4800 retrieval tests. For 10 runs with $n = 4096$, there were an average of 1.2 retrieval errors per run (out of 4800). Five of the runs had no errors. With lower dimensions, there were more errors. For example, with $n = 2048$ there were an average of 58.5 retrieval errors per run (over 10 runs).

It turns out that the most difficult thing to do is to leave something untransformed. This is because any linear operation that leaves at least one component of a superposition untransformed must also leave all the other components untransformed as well. Consider what happens if we want to change all $\mathbf{x}$ to $\mathbf{y}$, but leave everything else that might be superimposed with $\mathbf{x}$ untransformed. Then we must have a transformation vector like this:

$$\mathbf{t} = \mathbf{x}^* \circledast \mathbf{y} + \bar{\mathbf{I}}.$$

The identity vector is included so that the result will have an untransformed component of the original. However, a linear operation like this cannot target particular bindings in the original – it applies generally. Thus, when we apply it to a HRR like

$$\mathbf{R} = \mathbf{x} \circledast \mathbf{a} + \mathbf{z} \circledast \mathbf{b}$$

we get

$$\mathbf{t} \circledast \mathbf{R} = \mathbf{y} \circledast \mathbf{a} + \mathbf{x} \circledast \mathbf{a} + \mathbf{z} \circledast \mathbf{b} + \text{noise}.$$

This problem does not arise when every component is transformed, because in that case, the cross terms are not similar to anything else we might be using. The only way to solve the problem is to do transformations separately, and clean up intermediate results. It would be interesting to see whether a similar difficulty arises with representations developed by RAAMs.

One thing to note when considering transformations on structures is that the result of a transformation will be noisy, and usually can only be cleaned up by decoding and reassembly. This is because the transformed structure will most likely be novel and thus cannot have been stored in clean-up memory. This is different from the situation where we decode chunked structures, and can clean up intermediate structures because they are stored in the clean-up memory.

7.2 Chunks and the organization of long-term memory

7.2.1 The organization of long-term memory

In this book, I have been concerned mainly with the internal organization of memory chunks, rather than with how long-term memory for a large set of chunks could be implemented. All I have assumed about long-term (clean-up) memory is that it can keep chunks distinct, and perform closest-match associative retrieval.

I only use superposition and convolution on the small scale, as ways of building chunks with a high degree of internal structure. It seems that we need a third auto-associative operation for long-term memory, if chunks are to be kept distinct. With HRRs, the clean-up memory provides this third auto-associative operation. Using the same operator for both the internal organization of chunks and the organization of long-term memory would seem to be prone to ambiguity.

Psychological matrix-based memory models, e.g., those of Halford et al. (1994), Humphreys et al. (1989), and Pike (1984), treat long-term memory as the superposition of chunks (which are the tensor products of their components). This type of scheme appears to have several disadvantages relative to HRRs: chunks have limited and inflexible internal organization, associative retrieval based on partial information is more complicated, and chunks must have very high dimensionality if many of them are to be superimposed and remain distinct. In any case, additional memory mechanisms may be necessary with these models – Halford et al. recognize the need to clean up the results of their analogy computations. They only need to clean up the representations of atomic objects, but it is hard to see how a principled distinction could be made between atomic and composite objects in anything more complex than a toy system.

7.2.2   The opacity of chunks

Some writers in the psychological literature, e.g., Johnson (1972), have regarded chunks as *opaque containers*. This means that an encoding of a chunk reveals nothing about the contents of the chunk until it is unpacked. It implies that the similarity of codes for chunks cannot reflect the similarity of their contents. If we regard chunks as equivalent to reduced descriptions, this is at odds with the desideratum for reduced descriptions that they should give information about their components without decoding, and with the idea that distributed representations should make similarity explicit.

Murdock (1992, 1993) describes the chunks in TODAM2 as opaque, and likens a chunk to objects in a suitcase: to find out what is inside you must open the suitcase. However, TODAM2 chunks are better described as at most semi-opaque, because they do reveal some of their contents without unpacking, and because the similarity of codes for chunks does reflect the similarity of their contents.

From a computational viewpoint, opacity seems to be an undesirable property. Opacity makes retrieval based on partial information about components difficult, and makes transformation without decomposition impossible.

The opacity of chunks has some consequences for the structure of long-term memory: if chunks are opaque, then it is more feasible to superimpose chunks in long-term memory.

7.3   Convolution, tensor products, associative operators, conjunctive coding, and structure

Hinton (1981) and Hinton et al. (1986) originally described conjunctive coding in terms of outer or tensor products. It is well known that both convolution and the tensor product can be used as the associative operator in pairwise and higher-order associative memories, but it has been less well known that conjunctive coding can also be based on convolution. It is interesting to consider whether other vector-space multiplication operations could serve as associative operators and as a basis for conjunctive coding. There are two reasons to consider other operations: it widens the space of available associative memory operators, and it allows us to view some existing network models in these terms.

The properties of convolution that make it a good basis for HRRs are as follows:

1. Bilinearity – $(\alpha\mathbf{a} + \beta\mathbf{b}) \circledast \mathbf{c} = \alpha\mathbf{a} \circledast \mathbf{c} + \beta\mathbf{b} \circledast \mathbf{c}$,[66] for all vectors $\mathbf{a}$, $\mathbf{b}$, and $\mathbf{c}$, and scalars α and β. This makes convolution similarity preserving – if $\mathbf{a}$ is similar to $\mathbf{a}'$ (i.e., $\mathbf{a}' = \mathbf{a} + \epsilon\mathbf{b}$ where ϵ is small) then $\mathbf{a} \circledast \mathbf{c}$ will be similar to $\mathbf{a}' \circledast \mathbf{b}$.

2. Invertibility – if vector elements are independently distributed as $N(0, 1/n)$ there is a simple stable approximate inverse of circular convolution.[67] This makes it possible to extract components from HRRs.

3. Randomization – the expected similarity of $\mathbf{a} \circledast \mathbf{b}$ to $\mathbf{a}$ or $\mathbf{b}$ is zero (provided that the expected similarity $\mathbf{a}$ (and $\mathbf{b}$) with the identity vector is zero). This helps to avoid unwanted correlations.

4. Closure (maps onto the same space) – the circular convolution of two vectors from $\Re^n$ is a vector in $\Re^n$. This allows easy representation of hierarchical structures.

5. Distribution preservation – if the elements of $\mathbf{a}$ and $\mathbf{b}$ are independently distributed as $N(0, 1/n)$, then the elements of $\mathbf{a} \circledast \mathbf{b}$ will be close to being distributed as $N(0, 1/n)$.[68] The distribution can be made closer by normalizing vectors after convolution. This is equivalent to saying that all the eigenvalues of the operation $\mathbf{f}_a(\mathbf{x}) = \mathbf{a} \circledast \mathbf{x}$ have a magnitude around 1. This property is important for the usability of higher-order associations.

6. Efficient computation – the circular convolution of n-dimensional vectors can be computed in $O(n \log n)$ time using Fast Fourier Transforms.

7. Commutativity and associativity – convolution has both these algebraic properties. While they make the algebra simple, they are not essential properties.

Table 26 lists various vector-space multiplication operations, all of which can be viewed as compressions of a tensor product.[69] I would

---

[66] Convolution is commutative, so $\mathbf{c} \circledast (\alpha\mathbf{a} + \beta\mathbf{b}) = \alpha\mathbf{c} \circledast \mathbf{a} + \beta\mathbf{c} \circledast \mathbf{a}$ is also true.

[67] An exact inverse also exists, but as explained in Section 3.6.4, it is less stable unless the vectors are constrained to be unitary.

[68] Distributions are exactly preserved for unitary vectors.

[69] See Plate (1997) for a more in-depth consideration of how various representa-

Range		Domain	Operations
vector×vector	→	matrix	outer product, tensor product
matrix×vector	→	vector	matrix-vector multiplication
matrix×matrix	→	matrix	matrix multiplication
vector×vector	→	vector	convolution, permuted convolution (Section 3.6.7), random convolution (Section 7.4)

TABLE 26 Vector-space multiplication operations.

expect that most of the results reported in this book could be achieved with any of the operators from this table taking the place of convolution. The implementation for those that expand vector dimensionality is not as elegant, but it is still possible. To do this, it would be necessary to find distributions of vectors (or matrices) which the operation preserved, and for which there were stable inverses.

It is possible to view Hinton's (1981) triple memory as conjunctive code based on matrix-vector multiplication, in which the PROP units are a reduced representation of the relation.

Smolensky [personal communication] observed that Pollack's (1990) RAAMs can be viewed as using association by matrix-vector multiplication. The fillers (input unit activations) are vectors, and the roles (the weights from input to hidden units) are matrices. The input to the hidden units is the superposition of matrix-vector products of roles and fillers. The weights from the hidden to output units must implement the inverse operation, and clean up output vectors as well. The nonlinearities on the hidden and output units probably help with the clean-up, but they also complicate this interpretation.

Recurrent networks can be viewed in a similar fashion, with the recurrent weights implementing a type of trajectory-association (Chapter 5), though again the nonlinearities complicate this interpretation.

7.4   Implementation in neural tissue

The highly-ordered nature of circular convolution seems to be a barrier to implementation of HRR computations in real neurons – how could the precise and regular connections required by circular convolution be developed among real neurons? The necessity for complementary decoding circuitry make the issue even more thorny.

This section shows that precise and regular connections are not necessary: a far more random network can suffice for convolution-like en-

---

tional schemes can be placed in a common framework.

coding operations. Furthermore, and the complementary decoding operations can be learned in an efficient manner using simple learning rules. This section gives a brief introduction to these ideas – for a full description see Plate (2000).

Recall that the circular convolution of $\mathbf{x}$ and $\mathbf{y}$ can be viewed as a compression of the outer product (Section 3.1). For $n = 4$, the circular convolution of $\mathbf{x}$ and $\mathbf{y}$ is:

$$
\begin{bmatrix} z_0 \\ z_1 \\ z_2 \\ z_3 \end{bmatrix} = \begin{bmatrix} x_0y_0 + x_1y_3 + x_2y_2 + x_3y_1 \\ x_0y_1 + x_1y_0 + x_2y_3 + x_3y_2 \\ x_0y_2 + x_1y_1 + x_2y_0 + x_3y_3 \\ x_0y_3 + x_1y_2 + x_2y_1 + x_3y_0 \end{bmatrix}
$$

Each z_i is the sum of n x_jy_k terms, and each x_j (and y_k) appears exactly once in the sum. Each product appears in the sum for only one z_i. Decoding by correlation works (when the x_i and y_i are independently distributed as $N(0, 1/n)$) because $\mathbf{x} \oplus \mathbf{z} \approx \mathbf{y}$, since

$$
\mathbf{x} \oplus \mathbf{z} = \begin{bmatrix} (x_0^2 + x_1^2 + x_2^2 + x_3^2)y_0 + \dots \\ (x_0^2 + x_1^2 + x_2^2 + x_3^2)y_1 + \dots \\ (x_0^2 + x_1^2 + x_2^2 + x_3^2)y_2 + \dots \\ (x_0^2 + x_1^2 + x_2^2 + x_3^2)y_3 + \dots \end{bmatrix} = (1 + \zeta)\mathbf{y} + \bar{\eta}
$$

where ζ and the η_i can be regarded as zero-mean Gaussian noise (Section 3.1.2).

It turns out that convolution-like operations can be performed by circuitry that does not compress the outer product in such a highly-ordered manner. Even if the terms in the sum for z_i are randomly selected, the resulting $\mathbf{z}$ vector is an association of $\mathbf{x}$ and $\mathbf{y}$ which has all the essential properties of convolution. The decoding noise is the same as for circular convolution if (a) each x_j (and y_k) appears exactly once in the sum for each z_i, and (b) each product appears in the sum for only one z_i. However, these conditions do not appear to be essential – breaking them will just result in more noise.

Consider the disordered outer product compression $\mathbf{z} = \mathbf{x} \circledast_d \mathbf{y}$ in Figure 55. The expressions for the z_i are as follows:

$$
\begin{bmatrix} z_0 \\ z_1 \\ z_2 \\ z_3 \end{bmatrix} = \begin{bmatrix} x_0y_3 + x_1y_2 + x_2y_0 + x_3y_1 \\ x_0y_2 + x_1y_1 + x_2y_3 + x_3y_0 \\ x_0y_0 + x_1y_3 + x_2y_1 + x_3y_2 \\ x_0y_1 + x_1y_0 + x_2y_2 + x_3y_3 \end{bmatrix}
$$

To reconstruct $\mathbf{y}$ from $\mathbf{z}$ ($= \mathbf{x} \circledast_d \mathbf{y}$) and $\mathbf{x}$, we need to find the appropriate compression, $\oplus_d$, of the outer product of $\mathbf{z}$ and $\mathbf{x}$ (i.e., the analogue of correlation), so that $\mathbf{x} \oplus_d \mathbf{z} \approx \mathbf{y}$. Call the elements of this

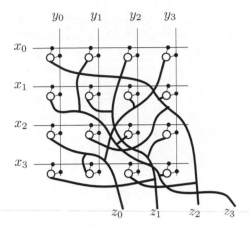

FIGURE 55 A disordered compression of the outer product of **x** and **y**.

vector $[\mathbf{x} \oplus_d \mathbf{z}]_i$. Then we want

$$[\mathbf{x} \oplus_d \mathbf{z}]_i = (x_0^2 + x_1^2 + x_2^2 + x_3^2)y_i + \ldots$$

where the dots are $x_j x_k y_l$ terms that can be treated as zero-mean Gaussian noise.

We can find this compression by selecting for $[\mathbf{x} \oplus_d \mathbf{z}]_i$ those terms in the outer product of **x** and **z** which contain $x_j^2 y_i$. For example, we want $[\mathbf{x} \oplus_d \mathbf{z}]_0 = x_2 z_0 + x_3 z_1 + x_0 z_2 + x_1 z_3$. The $x_2 z_0$ term is present because $x_2 y_0$ appears in z_0, the $x_3 z_1$ term because $x_3 y_0$ appears in z_1, the $x_0 z_2$ term because $x_0 y_0$ appears in z_2, and the $x_1 z_3$ term because $x_1 y_0$ appears in z_3. The whole expression for $\mathbf{x} \oplus_d \mathbf{z}$ is:

$$\mathbf{x} \oplus_d \mathbf{z} = \begin{bmatrix} x_2 z_0 + x_3 z_1 + x_0 z_2 + x_1 z_3 \\ x_3 z_0 + x_1 z_1 + x_2 z_2 + x_0 z_3 \\ x_1 z_0 + x_0 z_1 + x_3 z_2 + x_2 z_3 \\ x_0 z_0 + x_2 z_1 + x_1 z_2 + x_3 z_3 \end{bmatrix}$$

This expands to

$$\mathbf{x} \oplus_d \mathbf{z} = \begin{bmatrix} (x_0^2 + x_1^2 + x_2^2 + x_3^2)y_0 + \ldots \\ (x_0^2 + x_1^2 + x_2^2 + x_3^2)y_1 + \ldots \\ (x_0^2 + x_1^2 + x_2^2 + x_3^2)y_2 + \ldots \\ (x_0^2 + x_1^2 + x_2^2 + x_3^2)y_3 + \ldots \end{bmatrix} = (1 + \zeta)\mathbf{y} + \bar{\eta}$$

where ζ and $\bar{\eta}_i$ can be treated as zero-mean noise, assuming the x_i and y_i are independently distributed as $N(0, 1/n)$.

Turning to the matter of neural implementation, the sum-of-products could be computed by *sigma-pi* units. Feldman and Ballard (1982) proposed this type of unit and suggested the sum-of-product interactions might happen in the dendritic tree. In neural tissue, the encoding map could be fixed. The appropriate decoding map could be learned, provided one started with sigma-pi units that had a dense sampling of $z_j x_k$ products. The learning would attenuate the contribution of inappropriate $z_j x_k$ terms in $[\mathbf{x} \oplus_d \mathbf{z}]_i$. This could be done by simple Hebbian learning in an auto-associative framework – it would not require back-propagation of errors through multiple layers. A considerable amount of training would be required, since there would be n^3 parameters. However, auto-associations of random vectors would suffice for training examples, so there should be no problem getting enough training data.

7.5 Weaknesses of HRRs

HRRs have several weaknesses as a representation for nested relations. While these are not fatal, it is good to be aware of them.

- Representing types and tokens as a superposition of features (Section 3.5) makes superpositions of tokens subject to crosstalk (Section 3.11.5). To a large extent, this problem can be avoided by making sure that objects are bound to different roles. A further possible remedy is to give tokens more internal structure, e.g., by convolving features together.

- Relations that have identical or symmetric roles (e.g., conjunction, same-as, addition) have identical role vectors. In a HRR, this has the same effect and problems as superimposing the fillers of these roles.

- The decoding of binding chains for hierarchical structures can be ambiguous, because of the commutativity and associativity of convolution. This is mainly a problem when one relation appears more than once in a HRR – e.g., the agent of the object has the same binding chain as the object of the agent (since $\mathbf{r}_1 \circledast \mathbf{r}_2 \circledast \mathbf{x} = \mathbf{r}_2 \circledast \mathbf{r}_1 \circledast \mathbf{x}$). One solution to this problem is to use chunking. Another is to use a non-commutative version of convolution (Section 3.6.7).

- If there can be more than one object retrieved from clean-up memory (as happens when there are identical role vectors and the filler is decoded), we need to set cutoff threshold below which similarity is judged to be merely due to noise. It is possible to analyze a particular scenario to derive an appropriate threshold, but this is probably impractical in general.

In the literature, there are several claims about weaknesses of conjunctive codes and HRRs that I believe are not true. Hummel and Holyoak (1992) claim that the most serious limitation of conjunctive codes is that they lose the natural similarity structure of predicates and objects. By this, they mean that the proposition (chase Arnold Bill) is naturally more similar to (chase Bill Arnold) than to (says My-doctor Caffeine-makes-me-nervous). While this claim might be true for some implementations of conjunctive coding, I showed in Chapter 6 how the natural similarity structure of predicates and objects can be neatly captured by conjunctive coding in the form of HRRs. On the topic of how this is achieved, there is a tension between wanting the bindings of a filler with different roles (e.g., **bill** bound to **agent** versus **bill** bound to **object**) to be similar (to aid with the recognition of similarity) and wanting them to be different (to be able to tell which role the filler is bound to). In HRRs, different components are responsible for each of these (**bill** for the similarity to other predicates involving Bill, and **bill** ⊛ **agent** for the role binding), and they can be weighted appropriately.

Smolensky et al. (1992, pp21-22) remark that HRRs appeared to be an adequate representation, "at least for stimuli with only a small degree of structure." HRRs can in fact cope with quite a high degree of structure, both in depth and width. Without chunking, the width of structures is limited by the vector dimension (the relationship is linear). HRRs cope quite well with deep structures if vectors are either normalized or constrained to be unitary. With chunking, structures of unlimited depth and width can be stored, by breaking them up into chunks of manageable size.

7.6 Conclusion

HRRs provide a solution to the longstanding problem of how to encode hierarchical relational structure (i.e., compositional structure) in a fixed-width distributed representation. HRRs can be seen as an implementation of Hinton's reduced descriptions, and satisfy all the desiderata for reduced descriptions: adequacy, reduction, systematicity, and informativeness. HRRs inherit all the major advantages of distributed representations of atomic objects: they allow explicit representation of relevant aspects, they make similarity among composite objects explicit, they store information in a redundant fashion, they use representational resources efficiently, and they exist in a continuous vector space. HRRs are based on circular convolution, a bilinear associative memory operator. It is possible to analyze from first principles the properties of systems that use HRRs. The storage capacity and probabilities of correct operation can be derived from the analysis.

One of the major drawbacks of convolution-based memory is the low signal-to-noise ratio of the results of decoding. However this problem can be overcome by using HRRs in conjunction with an auto-associative clean-up memory to clean up decoding results. Storing HRRs and atomic objects[70] in the auto-associative clean-up memory allows for a complex network of relationships among the entities in memory.

HRRs encode hierarchical structures in such a way that many aspects of the underlying structure are made explicit in the surface form of the representation. This allows the degree of structural alignment (i.e., structural similarity) between two HRRs to be estimated by their dot product. Thus, the use of HRRs allows the results of an exponential-time computation (structure matching) to be estimated by a linear-time computation. This technique has possible applications as a filter in psychological models of memory retrieval, and in reasoning systems.

HRRs make it easy to encode structure in a distributed representation. The ability to represent complex data structures, and the ability to process them using powerful primitive operations offers the potential of building general-purpose computers that combine the power of symbolic manipulation with the robustness, learning and generalization ability of neural networks.

---

[70]Whether or not atomic, or base-level, objects are useful in sophisticated systems, or have any psychological reality, does not really matter in this scheme.

Appendix A

Means and variances of similarities between bindings

The means and variances of the dot-products of convolution bindings can be calculated using the expressions in Table 3. For the calculation of the variance of the dot-product of $\mathbf{B}_1$ and $\mathbf{B}_4$ from Section 3.10.5 we need the following two expressions from Table 3:

$$\mathrm{var}[(\mathbf{a} \circledast \mathbf{b}) \cdot (\mathbf{a} \circledast \mathbf{b})] = \frac{6n + 4}{n^2}$$

$$\mathrm{var}[(\mathbf{a} \circledast \mathbf{b}) \cdot (\mathbf{a} \circledast \mathbf{c})] = \frac{2n + 2}{n^2}$$

The variance of $\mathbf{B}_1 \cdot \mathbf{B}_4$ is:

$$
\begin{aligned}
&\mathrm{var}[(\mathbf{eat}_{agt} \circledast \mathbf{mark}) \cdot (\mathbf{eat}_{agt} \circledast \mathbf{john})] \\
&= \mathrm{var}[(\mathbf{eat}_{agt} \circledast (\mathbf{person} + \mathbf{id}_{mark})/\sqrt{3}) \\
&\qquad \cdot (\mathbf{eat}_{agt} \circledast (\mathbf{person} + \mathbf{id}_{john})/\sqrt{3})] \\
&= \mathrm{var}[2/3\mathbf{eat}_{agt} \circledast \mathbf{person} \cdot \mathbf{eat}_{agt} \circledast \mathbf{person}] \\
&\quad + \mathrm{var}[\sqrt{2}/3\mathbf{eat}_{agt} \circledast \mathbf{person} \cdot \mathbf{eat}_{agt} \circledast \mathbf{id}_{john}] \\
&\quad + \mathrm{var}[\sqrt{2}/3\mathbf{eat}_{agt} \circledast \mathbf{id}_{mark} \cdot \mathbf{eat}_{agt} \circledast \mathbf{person}] \\
&\quad + \mathrm{var}[1/3\mathbf{eat}_{agt} \circledast \mathbf{id}_{mark} \cdot \mathbf{eat}_{agt} \circledast \mathbf{id}_{john}] \\
&= \frac{4}{9}\frac{6n+4}{n^2} + \frac{2}{9}\frac{2n+2}{n^2} + \frac{2}{9}\frac{2n+2}{n^2} + \frac{1}{9}\frac{2n+2}{n^2} = \frac{34n + 26}{9n^2}
\end{aligned}
$$

The variances of the dot-products of $\mathbf{B}_1$ with other bindings from Section 3.10.5 can be calculated in a similar fashion and are shown in Table 27. The sample means and variances from $10,000$ trials are shown in the same table. The sample statistics agree with the derived expressions within the margin of error. (The standard deviation of a variance statistic for samples from a normal distribution is approxi-

	Statistics of $binding \cdot$ **mark** $\circledast$ **eat**$_{agt}$				
Binding	Exp. value	Variance	Variance $(n = 512)$	Sample mean	Sample variance
mark $\circledast$ **eat**$_{agt}$	1	$(6n + 4)/(n^2)$	0.0117	1.0009	0.0118
mark $\circledast$ **see**$_{agt}$	1/2	$(6xn + 5)/(2n^2)$	0.00586	0.5003	0.00586
mark $\circledast$ **eat**$_{obj}$	0	$(2n + 2)/(n^2)$	0.00391	0.0010	0.00385
john $\circledast$ **eat**$_{agt}$	2/3	$(34n + 26)/(9n^2)$	0.00739	0.6665	0.00749
john $\circledast$ **see**$_{agt}$	1/3	$(73n + 50)/(36n^2)$	0.00397	0.3328	0.00398
john $\circledast$ **eat**$_{obj}$	0	$(13n + 8)/(9n^2)$	0.00283	0.0003	0.00281
the_fish $\circledast$ **eat**$_{agt}$	0	$(2n + 2)/(n^2)$	0.00391	0.0009	0.00398
the_fish $\circledast$ **see**$_{agt}$	0	$(5n + 2)/(4n^2)$	0.00244	0.0004	0.00253
the_fish $\circledast$ **eat**$_{obj}$	0	$n/(n^2)$	0.00195	0.0000	0.00192

TABLE 27 Means and variances of the dot-products of the bindings. The sample statistics are from $10,000$ runs (i.e., $10,000$ different choices of base vectors) with 512-dimensional vectors.

mately $\sqrt{2/N}\sigma^2$, where N is the number of samples. This works out to about 1.4% of the variances here.)

Appendix B

The capacity of a superposition memory

In Section 3.2.1 I discussed how the probability of correct recognition in a superposition memory could be calculated. Knowing how to calculate this probability enables us to calculate the capacity, i.e., how many vectors can be stored, for a given dimension and probability of error. However, the formula for this probability involves an optimization, and it is difficult to find an analytic form for the solution. In the first section of this Appendix I report the results of numerical solutions of this formula. These results show how the number of vectors stored in the trace, and the number of vectors in the clean-up memory, scale with vector dimension. I call this a *simple* superposition memory because I assume that all the vectors in the clean-up memory are independently chosen, i.e., there is no systematic similarity among them. In Appendix C, I give an analytic lower bound on the capacity of a simple superposition memory.

In the second section of this Appendix I calculate the recognition probabilities and scaling properties for superposition memory in the case where there is similarity among the vectors in the clean-up memory.

B.1   Scaling properties of a simple superposition memory

I use the following symbols and definitions (which are the same as in Section 3.2.1):

- n is the vector dimension,
- *random* vectors have elements independently drawn from $N(0, 1/n)$,
- $\mathbb{E}$ is a set of m random vectors, $\mathbf{a}, \mathbf{b}, \mathbf{c}, \mathbf{d}$, etc. (these are the vectors stored in clean-up memory),

- **t** is a memory trace, which is the (unnormalized) superposition of k distinct vectors from $\mathbb{E}$, and
- Pr(All Correct) is the probability of correctly identifying the vectors in **t**, i.e., correctly determining for each vector in $\mathbb{E}$ whether or not it is stored in **t**.

Equation 3.2 in Section 3.2.1 gives the probability of correct recognition in a simple superposition memory:

$$\begin{aligned} \Pr(\text{All Correct}) &= \Pr(\text{Hit})^k \Pr(\text{Reject})^{m-k} \\ &= \max_t \; \Pr(s_a > t)^k \Pr(s_r < t)^{m-k} \end{aligned}$$

I wrote a computer program to find the threshold (t) that maximizes Pr(All Correct) for given values of k, m, and n. I used it to find the vector dimension (n) that gives Pr(All Correct) $= 0.99$ for various values of k and m. The results are plotted in Figures 56 and 57. The threshold was adjusted to maximize the capacity for each data point.

The scaling of k with n is slightly less than linear (Figure 56). This scaling is due to two factors. The linear part is due to the variances being equal to the ratio of k to n (in the limit). This means that if k is increased by some factor, then n should be increased by the same factor to keep the variance constant. The sublinear part is due to the exponentiation of Pr(Hit) by k in the equation for Pr(All Correct). When the threshold is chosen to optimize Pr(All Correct), Pr(Hit) is much smaller than $1 - \Pr(\text{False Alarm})$. If k increases, while the ratio k/n is held constant, Pr(All Correct) decreases.

The scaling of m with respect to n is very good. m can increase exponentially with n while maintaining Pr(All Correct) constant. This scaling is shown in Figure 57. The exponential nature of the scaling is due to the rapid drop-off of the area under the tail of the normal distribution.

The scaling of Pr(Error) with n is also very good. The probability of error drops exponentially with linear increase in n, as illustrated in Figure 58.

B.1.1   Computation involved

Computing the dot-product of the trace with all the vectors in $\mathbb{E}$ may seem like an unreasonable amount of computation. However, any process that does closest-match retrieval must effectively do this. If we have a particularly efficient closest-match process we can in most situations use it to quickly find all the vectors whose dot-product with the trace exceeds some threshold. Furthermore, this is a computation that is very amenable to implementation in parallel hardware.

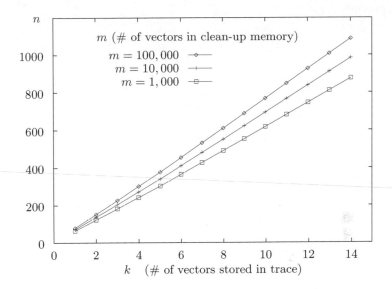

FIGURE 56   Scaling of n with k for $\mathrm{Pr}(\text{Error}) = 0.01$ with various m in a simple superposition memory. The threshold was adjusted to maximize the capacity for each data point.

B.2   A superposition memory with similarity among the vectors

When there is similarity among vectors the analysis becomes more complex, because recognition signals will come from more than two distributions. Having similarity among vectors is the rule rather than the exception, so it is important to know how similarity affects the scaling properties.

Suppose that in our set $\mathbb{E}$ of m vectors there is a subset $\mathbb{E}_p$ of m_p vectors that are similar to each other. Suppose the vectors in $\mathbb{E}_p$ have the general form $\mathbf{p}_i = \alpha\mathbf{p} + \beta\mathbf{d}_i$, where $\mathbf{p}$ is the component the vectors in $\mathbb{E}_p$ have in common, $\mathbf{d}_i$ is a random vector, and the scalars α and β are positive weighting constants such that $\alpha^2 + \beta^2 = 1$ (so that $\mathrm{E}[\|\mathbf{p}_i\|] = 1$). The expected value of the dot-product of $\mathbf{p}_i$ and $\mathbf{p}_j \in \mathbb{E}_p$ is α^2. The other $m - m_p$ vectors in $\mathbb{E}$ are randomly chosen. The expected value of the dot-product of two different vectors from $\mathbb{E}$ is zero, provided at least one them is not from $\mathbb{E}_p$.

Since the vectors in $\mathbb{E}_p$ are similar, they are much more likely to be

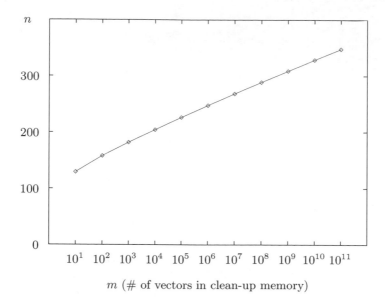

m (# of vectors in clean-up memory)

FIGURE 57 Scaling of n with m for $k = 3$ and $\Pr(\text{Error}) = 0.01$ in a simple superposition memory.

confused with each other than with random vectors. This results in a lower capacity for a superposition memory storing similar vectors than for a superposition memory storing random vectors.

In this analysis I consider only the situation in which all the vectors stored in the trace are from $\mathbb{E}_p$. The reasons for this are related to the limitations of superposition memories and will be explained later.

Suppose we have stored k distinct vectors from $\mathbb{E}_p$ in the trace, so that

$$\mathbf{t} = \sum_{i=1}^{k} \mathbf{p}_i \quad \mathbf{p}_i \in \mathbb{E}_p.$$

The signal for probing the trace with a vector $\mathbf{x}$ will be distributed in one of three ways, depending on whether $\mathbf{x}$ is one of the vectors stored in the trace, or is similar to the stored vectors (i.e., $\mathbf{x}$ is some other element of $\mathbb{E}_p$) or is some other non-similar element of $\mathbb{E}$.

Since $\mathbf{p}$ can be a component of both the trace and the probe, the value $\mathbf{p} \cdot \mathbf{p}$ appears in both the accept and the reject-similar signals. This value will be a constant for constant $\mathbf{p}$. Better discrimination can be achieved if this value is taken into account when the threshold is

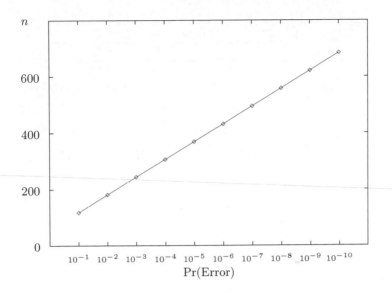

FIGURE 58 Scaling of n with $\Pr(\text{Error})$ for $k = 3$ and $m = 1000$ in a simple superposition memory.

chosen. One way of doing this is to choose $\mathbf{p}$ so that $\mathbf{p} \cdot \mathbf{p}$ is exactly equal to 1, which is what I assume in this analysis.

Let s_a (the accept signal) be the signal for probing with a vector stored in the trace. Without loss of generality, we can assume that $\mathbf{p}_1$ is in the trace and that the probe is equal to $\mathbf{p}_1$. Assuming that $\mathbf{p} \cdot \mathbf{p} = 1$ (and thus $\text{var}[\mathbf{p} \cdot \mathbf{p}] = 0$), the mean and variance of s_a are:

$$
\begin{aligned}
\mathrm{E}[s_a] &= \mathrm{E}[\mathbf{t} \cdot \mathbf{p}_1] \\
&= \mathrm{E}[\sum_{i=1}^{k} \mathbf{p}_i \cdot \mathbf{p}_1] \\
&= \mathrm{E}[(k\alpha\mathbf{p} + \sum_{i=1}^{k} \mathbf{d}_i) \cdot (\alpha\mathbf{p} + \beta\mathbf{d}_1)] \\
&= k\alpha^2 \mathrm{E}[\mathbf{p} \cdot \mathbf{p}] + k\alpha\beta \mathrm{E}[\mathbf{p} \cdot \mathbf{d}_1] + \alpha\beta \sum_{i=1}^{k} \mathrm{E}[\mathbf{d}_i \cdot \mathbf{p}]
\end{aligned}
$$

Signal	E	var
s_a	$k\alpha^2 + \beta^2$	$\frac{1}{n}(k(k+3)\alpha^2\beta^2 + (k+1)\beta^4)$
r_s	$k\alpha^2$	$\frac{1}{n}(k(k+1)\alpha^2\beta^2 + k\beta^4)$
r_d	0	$\frac{1}{n}(k^2\alpha^2 + k\beta^2)$

TABLE 28 Means and variances of signals for a superposition memory with similarity.

$$\begin{aligned}
& + \beta^2 \mathrm{E}[\mathbf{d}_1 \cdot \mathbf{d}_1] + \beta^2 \sum_{i=2}^{k} \mathrm{E}[\mathbf{d}_i \cdot \mathbf{d}_1] \\
=\ & k\alpha^2 + 0 + 0 + \beta^2 + 0 \\
=\ & k\alpha^2 + \beta^2 \\
\mathrm{var}[s_a] =\ & \mathrm{var}[\mathbf{t} \cdot \mathbf{p}_a] \\
=\ & \mathrm{var}[(k\alpha\mathbf{p} + \sum_{i=1}^{k} \mathbf{d}_i) \cdot (\alpha\mathbf{p} + \beta\mathbf{d}_1)] \\
=\ & k^2\alpha^4 \mathrm{var}[\mathbf{p} \cdot \mathbf{p}] + (k+1)^2\alpha^2\beta^2 \mathrm{var}[\mathbf{p} \cdot \mathbf{d}_1] \\
& + \alpha^2\beta^2 \sum_{i=2}^{k} \mathrm{var}[\mathbf{d}_i \cdot \mathbf{p}] + \beta^4 \mathrm{var}[\mathbf{d}_1 \cdot \mathbf{d}_1] + \beta^4 \sum_{i=2}^{k} \mathrm{var}[\mathbf{d}_i \cdot \mathbf{d}_1] \\
=\ & \frac{1}{n}(0 + (k+1)^2\alpha^2\beta^2 + (k-1)\alpha^2\beta^2 + 2\beta^4 + (k-1)\beta^4) \\
=\ & \frac{1}{n}((k^2 + 3k)\alpha^2\beta^2 + (k+1)\beta^4)
\end{aligned}$$

There are two other signals; the reject-similar signal r_s, for when the probe is from $\mathbb{E}_p$ but is not in the trace, and the reject-dissimilar signal r_d, for when the probe is not from $\mathbb{E}_p$. The means and variances of the three signals are listed in Table 28. The probability of correctly identifying all the vectors in the trace, for a threshold t, is:

$$\Pr(\text{All Correct}) = \Pr(s_a > t)^k \Pr(r_s < t)^{m_p - k} \Pr(r_d < t)^{m - m_p}.$$

The distributions of s_a, r_s, and r_d, for $n = 512$, $m = 1000$, $m_p = 100$, $\alpha^2 = 0.5$, and $k = 3$, are shown in Figure 59. For these parameter values, the optimal threshold is 1.79 and the probability of correctly identifying all the components of $\mathbf{t}$ is 0.906.

The way n must vary with α to give a constant $\Pr(\text{All Correct})$ is shown in Figure 60. As α gets larger the similarity between the elements of $\mathbb{E}_p$ grows, and it is necessary to use much higher-dimensional vectors to discriminate them.

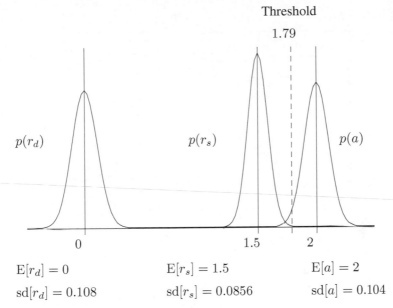

FIGURE 59 Probability density functions for signals in an superposition memory with similarity among vectors, with $n = 512$, $m = 1000$, $|\mathbb{E}_p| = 100$, $\alpha^2 = 0.5$, and $k = 3$.

The scaling of n with k is shown in Figure 61. The required dimensionality of the vectors is proportional to k^2. This is because the variances are proportional to the ratio of k^2 to n, which in turn is due to the component $k\alpha\mathbf{p}$ in the trace.

B.2.1 The effect of the decision process on scaling

It is possible to design more complex decision procedures that increase the probability of making correct decisions. This was done to some extent in the above analysis by assuming that $\mathbf{p} \cdot \mathbf{p} = 1$. This has nearly the same effect as taking into account the value of $\mathbf{p} \cdot \mathbf{p}$ when setting the threshold.

Another way to improve the decision procedure would be to take into account the value of $(\mathbf{a} + \mathbf{b} + \mathbf{c}) \cdot \mathbf{p}$ when setting the threshold. For a particular trace, s_a and r_s have the common term $\alpha\beta(\mathbf{a} + \mathbf{b} + \mathbf{c}) \cdot \mathbf{p}$. This will cause the values of s_a and r_s to be correlated, and their distributions will be tighter than shown in Figure 59 (the distributions in Figure 59 are for a randomly selected trace). This will increase the probability of making correct decisions, but the scaling of n with k will remain quadratic.

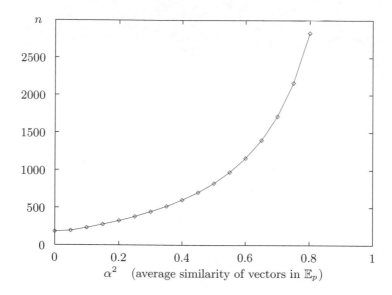

FIGURE 60 Scaling of n with α for $k = 3$, $m = 1000$, and $\Pr(\text{Error}) = 0.01$ in a superposition memory with similarity.

A way to more radically improve the decision procedure would be to subtract $k\alpha\mathbf{p}$ from the trace, and then probe it with the token parts of the vectors from $\mathbb{E}_p$, i.e., $\mathbf{a}$ rather than $\mathbf{p}_a$. This would not only increase the probability of making correct decisions, but would also make the scaling of n with k near to linear. However, it would be a far more complicated procedure.

Another point worth noting is that a k-closest-match procedure (i.e. choosing the k members of $\mathbb{E}$ that have the highest dot-product with $\mathbf{t}$) will give better results than a procedure using threshold tests. For any particular trace it is more likely that all the accept signals are greater than all the reject signals than that all the accept signals are greater than some threshold and all the reject signals are less than some threshold. A problem with this type of procedure is knowing the value of k. Unless there is some other way of knowing how many items to accept, some type of threshold is necessary.

B.3 Limitations of superposition memories

Superposition memories suffer badly from crosstalk when the vectors stored are similar. This is the reason that the means of s_a and r_s (in

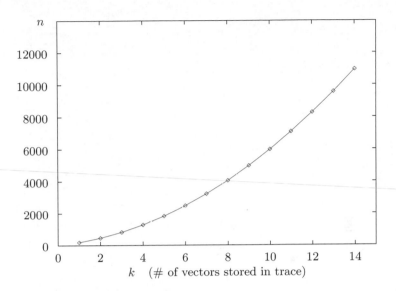

FIGURE 61 Scaling of n with k for $\alpha^2 = 0.5$, $m = 1000$, and $\Pr(\text{Error}) = 0.01$ in a superposition memory with similarity.

the previous section) are so high. The significance of this limitation becomes clear if we consider what happens when we try to store two vectors from $\mathbb{E}_p$ (whose average similarity $\alpha^2 = 0.5$) and one vector from $\mathbb{E} - \mathbb{E}_p$, e.g., $\mathbf{t} = \mathbf{p}_a + \mathbf{p}_b + \mathbf{c}$. There will be two distributions of accept signals – the accept similar (a_s) and the accept dissimilar signals (a_d). The problem is that the accept dissimilar signal ($a_d = (\mathbf{p}_a + \mathbf{p}_b + \mathbf{c}) \cdot \mathbf{c})$) will have the same mean ($=1.0$) as the reject similar signal ($r_s = (\mathbf{p}_a + \mathbf{p}_b + \mathbf{p}_x) \cdot \mathbf{x}, \mathbf{p}_x \in (\mathbb{E}_p - \{\mathbf{p}_a, \mathbf{p}_b\}))$. Thus, no single-threshold or k-closest-match procedure will be able to discriminate the signals. A possible solution is to use a high threshold when probing with a similar vector and a lower threshold when probing with a dissimilar vector. However, this makes for a very complex decision process. A better solution is to avoid the situation where vectors of high similarity are superimposed.

Appendix C

A lower bound for the capacity of superposition memories

In this Appendix I derive a lower bound (Inequality C.11) on the number of vectors that can be stored in a simple superposition memory for given vector dimension, probability of error, and total number of vectors in clean-up memory.

I use the following symbols and definitions (which are the same as in Section 3.2.1 and Appendix B):

- n is the vector dimension,
- *random* vectors have elements independently drawn from $N(0, 1/n)$,
- $\mathbb{E}$ is a set of m random vectors, $\mathbf{a}, \mathbf{b}, \mathbf{c}, \mathbf{d}$, etc. (these are the vectors stored in clean-up memory),
- $\mathbf{t}$ is a memory trace, which is the (unnormalized) superposition of k distinct vectors from $\mathbb{E}$,
- Pr(All Correct) is the probability of correctly determining for each vector in $\mathbb{E}$ whether or not it is stored in $\mathbf{t}$.
- $q = 1 - \text{Pr(All Correct)}$,
- s_a and s_r are the accept and reject signals ($s_a \overset{d}{=} N(1, (k+1)/n)$ and $s_r \overset{d}{=} N(0, k/n)$),
- $\text{erfc}(x)$ is the standard "error function": $\text{erfc}(x) = \dfrac{2}{\sqrt{\pi}} \displaystyle\int_x^\infty e^{-t^2}\, dt$, and
- $\text{tail}(x)$ is the area under the (normalized) normal probability density function beyond x (in one tail):

$$\text{tail}(x) = \frac{1}{\sqrt{2\pi}} \int_x^\infty e^{\frac{-t^2}{2}}\, dt = \frac{1}{2}\text{erfc}\left(\frac{x}{\sqrt{2}}\right)$$

Equation 3.2 in Section 3.2.1 gives the probability of correct recognition in a simple superposition memory:

$$
\begin{aligned}
\Pr(\text{All Correct}) \quad &= \quad \Pr(\text{Hit})^k \Pr(\text{Reject})^{m-k} \\
&= \quad \max_t \quad \Pr(s_a > t)^k \Pr(s_r < t)^{m-k}
\end{aligned}
$$

I use the following inequality from Abramowitz and Stegun (1965):

$$
\text{erfc}(x) \quad < \quad \frac{2}{\sqrt{\pi}} e^{-x^2} \frac{1}{x + \sqrt{x^2 + \frac{4}{\pi}}},
$$

(C.3)

and a simplification of it:

$$
\text{erfc}(x) \quad < \quad \frac{1}{x\sqrt{\pi}} e^{-x^2} \tag{C.4}
$$

The first step in finding a lower bound for $\Pr(\text{All Correct})$ is to use a threshold of 0.5. $\Pr(\text{All Correct})$ must be greater than the probability of correctly discriminating the signals using a non optimal threshold. The second step involves several applications of the inequality $(1-\epsilon)^k > 1 - k\epsilon$ (which is true for $0 \le \epsilon \le 1$).

$$
\begin{aligned}
\Pr(\text{All Correct}) \quad &= \quad \max_t \quad \Pr(s_a > t)^k \Pr(s_r < t)^{m-k} & \text{(C.5)} \\
&> \quad \Pr(s_a > 0.5)^k \Pr(s_r < 0.5)^{m-k} \\
&= \quad (1 - \Pr(s_a < 0.5))^k (1 - \Pr(s_r > 0.5))^{m-k} \\
&> \quad (1 - k\Pr(s_a < 0.5))(1 - (m - k)\Pr(s_r > 0.5)) \\
&> \quad 1 - k\Pr(s_a < 0.5) - (m - k)\Pr(s_r > 0.5) & \text{(C.6)}
\end{aligned}
$$

Now consider q, the probability of one or more errors. This can be simplified by first using Inequality C.6 to give Inequality C.7, then next replacing smaller variances with the maximum variance to give Inequality C.8. After that we use Inequality C.4 to give Inequality C.9 and finally replace the square root factor by one to give Inequality C.10, since it is safe to assume that that factor is less than 1.

$$
\begin{aligned}
q \quad &= \quad 1 - \Pr(\text{All Correct}) \\
&< \quad k\Pr(s_a < 0.5) + (m - k)\Pr(s_r > 0.5) & \text{(C.7)} \\
&= \quad k\,\text{tail}\left(\frac{1}{2}\sqrt{\frac{n}{k+1}}\right) + (m - k)\text{tail}\left(\frac{1}{2}\sqrt{\frac{n}{k}}\right) \\
&< \quad k\,\text{tail}\left(\frac{1}{2}\sqrt{\frac{n}{k+1}}\right) + (m - k)\text{tail}\left(\frac{1}{2}\sqrt{\frac{n}{k+1}}\right) & \text{(C.8)}
\end{aligned}
$$

$$= m \, \text{tail} \left(\frac{1}{2} \sqrt{\frac{n}{k+1}} \right)$$

$$= \frac{m}{2} \text{erfc} \left(\frac{1}{2} \sqrt{\frac{n}{2(k+1)}} \right)$$

$$< \frac{m}{\sqrt{\pi}} \sqrt{\frac{2(k+1)}{n}} \; e^{\frac{-n}{8(k+1)}} \qquad\qquad\qquad (C.9)$$

$$< m \, e^{\frac{-n}{8(k+1)}} \qquad\qquad \text{if } \sqrt{\frac{2(k+1)}{\pi n}} < 1 \quad (C.10)$$

Rearranging gives:

$$n \; < \; 8(k+1) \ln(\frac{m}{q}) \qquad \text{if } n > \frac{2(k+1)}{\pi}$$

$$\text{or} \qquad k \; > \; \frac{n}{8 \ln(m/q)} - 1 \qquad \text{if } k < \frac{n\pi}{2} - 1 \qquad (C.11)$$

This lower bound on the capacity (k) is reasonably close. Numerical solutions of the exact expression for Pr(All Correct) (Equation C.5) for k in the range (2..14), m in ($10^2 \dots 10^{10}$), and q in ($10^{-2} \dots 10^{-10}$) are reasonably well approximated by

$$n = 3.16(k - 0.25) \ln \frac{m}{q^3}.$$

Appendix D

The capacity of convolution-based associative memories

The simplest type of convolution memory is one that stores pairs of items. These could be variables and values, or any other kinds of items to be associated. In this appendix I analyze the capacity and scaling of this type of memory. In the first section I analyze the case where there is no systematic similarity among vectors. In the second section I analyze the case where there is some similarity. I will avoid reproducing derivations analogous to those in Appendix B.

D.1 A memory for paired-associates with no similarity among vectors

I use the following symbols and definitions:

- n is the vector dimension,
- "Random" vector have elements independently drawn from $N(0, 1/n)$,
- $\mathbb{E}$ is a set of m random vectors,
- $\mathbf{t}$ is a memory trace that is the (unnormalized) superposition of k distinct unordered pairs of vectors from $\mathbb{E}$, with the conditions that the two vectors in a pair must be different, and vectors in different pairs must be different:

$$\mathbf{t} = \sum_{i=1}^{k} \mathbf{x}_i \circledast \mathbf{y}_i, \quad \text{where} \quad \begin{cases} \mathbf{x}_i, \mathbf{y}_i \in \mathbb{E}, & \mathbf{x}_i \neq \mathbf{y}_j \forall i, j, \\ \mathbf{x}_i \neq \mathbf{x}_j \forall i \neq j, & \mathbf{y}_i \neq \mathbf{y}_j \forall i \neq j \end{cases}$$

- Pr(All Correct) is the probability of correctly identifying the vectors in $\mathbf{t}$, i.e., correctly determining for each vector in $\mathbb{E}$ whether or not it is stored in $\mathbf{t}$.

In this analysis I assume that we do not know what the appropriate cues are so, to find all the pairs, we must try every combination of cue

249

and probe. In order to allow the retrieval process to be simple I assume that it tests for an identical cue and probe, even though no such pair is stored in the trace.

To test for the presence of a pair $(\mathbf{c}, \mathbf{p})$ in $\mathbf{t}$ we first decode it with the *cue* $\mathbf{c}$, and calculate the dot-product with the *probe* $\mathbf{p}$. This gives a scalar signal:

$$s = \mathbf{t} \circledast \mathbf{c}^* \cdot \mathbf{p}$$

Calculating the dot-product of $\mathbf{t} \circledast \mathbf{c}^*$ with the probe corresponds to what a clean-up memory does, for each vector stored in it. Swapping the cue and probe gives identical results, as does probing the trace directly with $\mathbf{c} \circledast \mathbf{p}$, since

$$\mathbf{t} \circledast \mathbf{c}^* \cdot \mathbf{p} \;=\; \mathbf{t} \circledast \mathbf{p}^* \cdot \mathbf{c} \;=\; \mathbf{t} \cdot \mathbf{c} \circledast \mathbf{p}$$

are identities of convolution algebra.

There are five distributions of reject signals and one distribution of accept signals. The distribution of a reject signal depends on whether the cue or probe occur in the trace and on whether the cue is equal to the probe. Table 29 lists the six different signals, along with their means and variances, and the number of each of these signals that must be tested to probe exhaustively for each pair in the trace. The variances were calculated by adding the appropriate variances from Table 3, ignoring the terms of order $1/n^2$.

The derivations of all the signals are similar. I show the derivation of the signal (r_1) where one of the cue or probe is in the trace. Without loss of generality I assume the cue is equal to $\mathbf{x}_1$, and the probe is $\mathbf{z}$, where $\mathbf{z}$ is an element of $\mathbb{E}$ not in the trace.

$$
\begin{aligned}
r_1 \;&=\; \mathbf{t} \circledast \mathbf{x}_1^* \cdot \mathbf{z} \\[1mm]
&=\; \sum_{i=1}^{k} \mathbf{x}_i \circledast \mathbf{y}_i \circledast \mathbf{x}_1^* \cdot \mathbf{z} \\[1mm]
\mathrm{E}[r_1] \;&=\; \mathrm{E}\left[\sum_{i=1}^{k} \mathbf{x}_i \circledast \mathbf{y}_i \circledast \mathbf{x}_1^* \cdot \mathbf{z} \right] \\[1mm]
&=\; \sum_{i=1}^{k} \mathrm{E}[\mathbf{x}_i \circledast \mathbf{y}_i \circledast \mathbf{x}_1^* \cdot \mathbf{z}] \\[1mm]
&=\; \sum_{i=1}^{k} 0 = 0 \\[1mm]
\mathrm{var}[r_1] \;&=\; \mathrm{var}\left[\sum_{i=1}^{k} \mathbf{x}_i \circledast \mathbf{y}_i \circledast \mathbf{x}_1^* \cdot \mathbf{z} \right]
\end{aligned}
$$

Signal	Example	E	var	Number of tests	Description (referring to $\mathbf{t} \circledast \mathbf{c}^* \cdot \mathbf{p}$)
a	$\mathbf{t} \circledast \mathbf{x}_1{}^* \cdot \mathbf{y}_1$	1	$\frac{k+5}{n}$	k	$\mathbf{c} \neq \mathbf{p}$ and $(\mathbf{c}, \mathbf{p})$ is a pair in the trace.
$r_{1=}$	$\mathbf{t} \circledast \mathbf{x}_1^* \cdot \mathbf{x}_1$	0	$\frac{2k+4}{n}$	$2k$	$\mathbf{c} = \mathbf{p}$ and appears in the trace.
r_2	$\mathbf{t} \circledast \mathbf{x}_1^* \cdot \mathbf{x}_2$	0	$\frac{k+2}{n}$	$2k(k-1)$	$\mathbf{c} \neq \mathbf{p}$ and both $\mathbf{c}$ and $\mathbf{p}$ are in the trace (but are not members of the same pair).
r_1	$\mathbf{t} \circledast \mathbf{x}_1^* \cdot \mathbf{z}$	0	$\frac{k+1}{n}$	$2k(m-2k)$	$\mathbf{c} \neq \mathbf{p}$ and one of them is in the trace.
$r_{0=}$	$\mathbf{t} \circledast \mathbf{z}^* \cdot \mathbf{z}$	0	$\frac{2k}{n}$	$m-2k$	$\mathbf{c} = \mathbf{p}$ and does not appear in the trace.
r_0	$\mathbf{t} \circledast \mathbf{z}^* \cdot \mathbf{w}$	0	$\frac{k}{n}$	$\frac{(m-2k)(m-2k-1)}{2}$	$\mathbf{c} \neq \mathbf{p}$ and neither of them are in the trace.

TABLE 29 Means and variances of signals in a paired-associates convolution memory. The examples refer to the trace $\mathbf{t} = \sum_{i=1}^{k} \mathbf{x}_i \mathbf{y}_i$, and two vectors $\mathbf{z}$ and $\mathbf{w}$ from $\mathbb{E}$ not in the trace.

$$= \text{var}[\mathbf{x}_1 \circledast \mathbf{y}_1 \circledast \mathbf{x}_1^* \cdot \mathbf{z}] + \sum_{i=2}^{k} \text{var}[\mathbf{x}_i \circledast \mathbf{y}_i \circledast \mathbf{x}_1^* \cdot \mathbf{z}]$$

$$= \frac{2}{n} + k\frac{1}{n} = \frac{k+1}{n}$$

The variance of the sum is equal to the sum of the variance because the covariance between all the terms in the sum is zero (e.g., $\text{cov}[\mathbf{x}_1 \circledast \mathbf{y}_1 \circledast \mathbf{x}_1^* \cdot \mathbf{z}, \mathbf{x}_2 \circledast \mathbf{y}_2 \circledast \mathbf{x}_1^* \cdot \mathbf{z}] = 0$).[71] This is true for the sums of variances for all the signals in this scenario.

Since there are $2k(n-2k)$ cue-probe pairs that will generate a signal from this distribution, the r_1 signal must be rejected this many times.

For a threshold t the probability of correctly identifying all the pairs in the trace is:

$$\begin{aligned}
\text{Pr(All Correct)} \quad = \quad & \text{Pr}(a > t)^k + \text{Pr}(r_{1=} < t)^{2k} \\
& + \text{Pr}(r_2 < t)^{2k(k-1)} + \text{Pr}(r_1 < t)^{2k(m-2k)} \\
& + \text{Pr}(r_{0=} < t)^{m-2k} \\
& + \text{Pr}(r_0 < t)^{(m-2k)(m-2k-1)/2} \qquad \text{(D.12)}
\end{aligned}$$

---

[71]This would not be true if pairs of identical vectors were allowed in the trace, since $\text{cov}[\mathbf{x}_2 \circledast \mathbf{x}_2 \circledast \mathbf{x}_1^* \cdot \mathbf{z}, \mathbf{x}_3 \circledast \mathbf{x}_3 \circledast \mathbf{x}_1^* \cdot \mathbf{z}] \neq 0$.

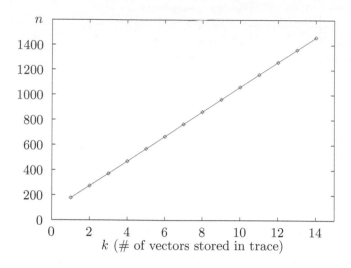

FIGURE 62 Scaling of n with k for $\Pr(\text{Error}) = 0.01$ and $m = 1000$ in a paired-associates convolution memory.

The scaling of k with n to give a constant $\Pr(\text{All Correct})$ is slightly less than linear. It is shown in Figure 62. This scaling is of the same nature as that of the simple superposition memory, for the same reasons. Likewise, the scaling of $\Pr(\text{Error})$ and m with n is exponential.

D.2 A memory for paired-associates with some similarity among vectors

I now consider a convolution memory used to store variable-value bindings, where there is similarity among some of the values. In order to avoid complicating the analysis, I assume variables and values come from different sets.

The following symbols are used:

- n, the vector dimension.
- *Random* vector have elements independently drawn from $N(0, 1/n)$.
- $\mathbb{E}_p$, a set of m_p value-vectors with average similarity α^2. They have the general form $\mathbf{p}_i = \alpha\mathbf{p} + \beta\mathbf{d}_i$, where $\mathbf{p}$ is the component the vectors in $\mathbb{E}_p$ have in common, $\mathbf{d}_i$ is a random vector, and the scalars α and β are positive weighting constants such that $\alpha^2 + \beta^2 = 1$ (so that $E[\|\mathbf{p}_i\|] = 1$). $\mathbf{p}$ is a random vector. In contrast with Appendix B, I do not assume that $|\mathbf{p}| = 1$.

Class	Value	E.g.	Variable	E.g.
1	$\in \mathbb{E}_p$ in the trace	$\mathbf{p}_1$		$\mathbf{x}_1$
2	$\in \mathbb{E}_p$ not in the trace	$\mathbf{p}_0$	N/A	
3	$\in \mathbb{E}_{-p}$ in the trace	$\mathbf{y}_1$		$\mathbf{x}_{j+1}$
4	$\in \mathbb{E}_{-p}$ not in the trace	$\mathbf{z}$	not bound	$\mathbf{x}_0$

TABLE 30 Classes of values and variables in a variable-binding memory with similarity. The class of a variable is determined by which (if any) value it is bound to. The example vectors refer to the typical trace shown above.

- $\mathbb{E}$, the set of m value-vectors, containing $\mathbb{E}_p$ and $(m - m_p)$ random vectors. The set $\{\mathbb{E} - \mathbb{E}_p\}$ is denoted by $\mathbb{E}_{-p}$.
- $\mathbb{V}$, a set of v variable vectors, all of which are random.
- $\mathbf{t}$, a trace with k variable-value bindings for similar values (from $\mathbb{E}_p$), and j variable-value bindings for dissimilar values (from $\mathbb{E}_{-p}$):

$$\mathbf{t} = \underbrace{\mathbf{x}_1 \circledast \mathbf{p}_1 + \mathbf{x}_2 \circledast \mathbf{p}_2 + \mathbf{x}_3 \circledast \mathbf{p}_3 + \cdots}_{\text{Similar values (k pairs)}} + \underbrace{\mathbf{x}_{k+1} \circledast \mathbf{y}_1 + \mathbf{x}_{k+2} \circledast \mathbf{y}_2 + \cdots}_{\text{Non-similar values (j pairs)}},$$

where $\mathbf{x}_i \in \mathbb{V}$, $\mathbf{p}_i \in \mathbb{E}_p$, and $\mathbf{y}_i \in \mathbb{E}_{-p}$. No value or variable appears more than once in the bindings in the trace.

Variables are unbound by using the variable as the cue and the possible values as the probes. To find out which value is associated with a variable $\mathbf{x}$ in the trace $\mathbf{t}$ we compute $\mathbf{t} \circledast \mathbf{x}^*$ and compare (using dot-product) the result to each of the vectors in $\mathbb{E}$. It is also possible to use a value as a probe to discover which variable it is bound to.

For the purposes of calculating the distributions of accept and reject signals, there are four classes of values and three classes of variables. These are given in Table 30. The example vectors in this table correspond to the vectors in the typical trace just mentioned, assuming that $\mathbf{p}_0$ is some value-vector in $\mathbb{E}_p$ that is not in the trace, $\mathbf{z}$ is some value-vector in $\mathbb{E}_{-p}$ that is not in the trace, and $\mathbf{x}_0$ is some variable-vector that is not in the trace. A signal is generated by a cue (variable) and a probe (value). Consequently there are two distributions of accept signals and twelve distributions of reject signals. These signals and their relationship to the classes are illustrated in Figure 63. The rows are the variable classes and the columns are the value classes. The means, variances, and the number of instances of each of the fourteen signals are shown in Table 31.

If nothing is known about what variables or values are stored in the trace, then the probability of correctly identifying all the variables and values is the probability that all reject signals are less than the

		m_p		Values	$m - m_p$	
		k		j		
k		a_{11} r_{11}	r_{12}	r_{13}	r_{14}	1
j		r_{31}	r_{32}	a_{33} r_{33}	r_{34}	3
v Variables $v - k - j$		r_{41}	r_{42}	r_{43}	r_{44}	4
		1	2	3	4	Class

FIGURE 63 The different signals in a variable-binding memory with similarity. The numbers of variables and values are shown beside the arrows. Each square is labeled with the name of the signal distribution that results from using a cue and probe from that row and column.

Signal	Mean	Variance	Number
a_{11}	1	$\frac{1}{n}(5 + k + j + (k-1)\alpha^4)$	k
a_{33}	1	$\frac{1}{n}(5 + k + j)$	j
r_{11}	α^2	$\frac{1}{n}(j + (k+2)(1 + \alpha^4))$	$k(k-1)$
r_{12}	α^2	$\frac{1}{n}((3+k)(1 + \alpha^4) + j - 2)$	$k(m_p - k)$
r_{13}	0	$\frac{1}{n}(k + j + 2)$	kj
r_{14}	0	$\frac{1}{n}(k + j + 1)$	$k(m - m_p - j)$
r_{31}	0	$\frac{1}{n}((k-1)(1 + \alpha^4) + j + 3)$	jk
r_{32}	0	$\frac{1}{n}(k(1 + \alpha^4) + j + 1)$	$j(m_p - k)$
r_{33}	0	$\frac{1}{n}(k + j + 2)$	$j(j-1)$
r_{34}	0	$\frac{1}{n}(k + j + 1)$	$j(m - m_p - j)$
r_{41}	0	$\frac{1}{n}((k-1)(1 + \alpha^4) + j + 2)$	$(v - j - k)k$
r_{42}	0	$\frac{1}{n}(k(1 + \alpha^4) + j)$	$(v - j - k)(m_p - k)$
r_{43}	0	$\frac{1}{n}(k + j + 1)$	$(v - j - k)j$
r_{44}	0	$\frac{1}{n}(k + j)$	$(v - j - k)(m - m_p - j)$

TABLE 31 Means, variances, and numbers of signals in a variable-binding memory with similarity.

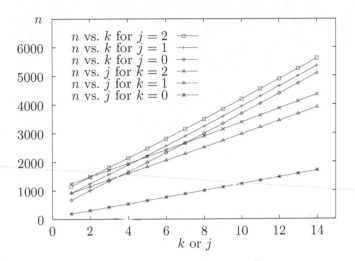

FIGURE 64 Scaling of n with k and j for $\Pr(\text{Error}) = 0.01$, $m = 100,000$, $v = 100,000$, $m_p = 100$, and $\alpha^2 = \beta^2 = 0.5$ in a variable-binding memory with similarity.

threshold and all accept signals are greater than the threshold. The signals can be assumed to be independent as in the previous models.[72]

The scaling of n with k and j, the numbers of items stored in the trace, is shown in Figure 64. The three steeper lines are for n versus k, the number of similar values stored. The three lines are for $j = 0$, 1, and 2. The three less steep lines are for n versus j, the number of non-similar values stored. The gradient for k is steeper because higher dimensionality is needed to discriminate similar vectors. Note that in all cases the relationship between n and k (or j) is near linear, just the gradient differs.

The scaling of n with α and k is shown in Figure 65. As in the

---

[72]This assumption is not entirely correct, as in any particular model there will be some correlations due to the similarity among the members of $\mathbb{E}_p$, e.g., $\mathbf{x}_1 \circledast \mathbf{p}_1 \circledast \mathbf{x}_1^* \cdot \mathbf{p}_2$ will be correlated with $\mathbf{x}_1 \circledast \mathbf{p}_1 \circledast \mathbf{x}_1^* \cdot \mathbf{p}_3$. This leads to a slight underestimation of $\Pr(\text{All Correct})$ because the expected number of errors is correct, but errors will tend to occur in clusters. Experiments give similar $\Pr(\text{All Correct})$ to those predicted by the model. For example, in $10,000$ trials with $n = 1024$, $m = 200$, $m_p = 100$, $v = 200$, $k = 3$, $j = 1$, $\alpha^2 = 0.5$, for 10 different sets $\mathbb{E}$, there were a total of 699 trials in which not all elements of the trace were correctly identified. The above analysis gives $\Pr(\text{All Correct}) = 0.907$, which predicts 930 failures (with standard deviation 9.2) out of $10,000$ trials.

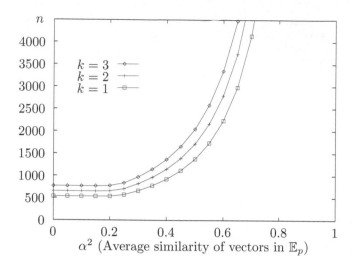

FIGURE 65 Scaling of n with α for various values of k for $\mathrm{Pr(Error)} = 0.01$, $m = 100,000$, $v = 100,000$, $m_p = 100$, and $j = 3$ in a variable-binding memory with similarity.

superposition memory model with similarity, the capacity is relatively unaffected by small values of α.

Figure 66 shows the scaling of n with the number of similar items in the clean-up memory. As with the previous scenarios, the number of items in clean-up memory (similar items in this case) can increase exponentially with the vector dimension.

Figure 67 shows the scaling of n with the number of non-similar items in the clean-up memory. This graph shows how the number of similar items dominates the capacity equation: n is nearly constant for less than 10^{28} non-similar items in memory. Beyond that, the number of non-similar items can increase exponentially with the vector dimension.

D.3 Comments on the variable-binding memory with similarity

Unlike in a simple superposition memory for similar vectors, the similar value-vectors stored in the variable-binding memory do not interfere with means of the accept and reject signals. This is due to the randomizing property of convolving with a random variable; $\mathbf{x}_1 \circledast \mathbf{a}$ and $\mathbf{x}_2 \circledast \mathbf{a}$ have an expected similarity of zero if $\mathbf{x}_1$ and $\mathbf{x}_2$ are random. Any combination of similar and non-similar values can be bound without affecting

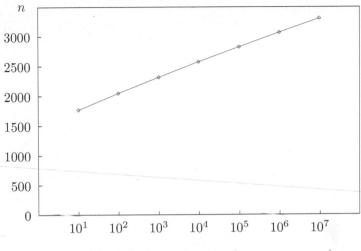

FIGURE 66 Scaling of n with m_p (the number of similar items in memory) for $\Pr(\text{Error}) = 0.01$, $m = 10^8$, $v = 100{,}000$, $k = 3$, $j = 3$, and $\alpha^2 = \beta^2 = 0.5$ in a variable-binding memory with similarity.

the means of signals. The similarity among values only acts to increase the signal variances. However, this is not the case when there is similarity among the variable vectors used in the trace. Furthermore, the signal variances will increase dramatically if the variables are similar to the values (due to the high variance of $\mathbf{x} \circledast \mathbf{x} \cdot \mathbf{x} \circledast \mathbf{x}$).

It is possible to associate the same value with two different variables, e.g., $\mathbf{t} = \mathbf{x}_1 \circledast \mathbf{y}_1 + \mathbf{x}_2 \circledast \mathbf{y}_2$. The same process as before can be used to find which value is bound to a given variable. The signal variances will be marginally higher, but the means will be the same.

If the same variable is associated with two different values, then correlating with that variable will give a blend of the two values, e.g., $(\mathbf{x}_1 \circledast \mathbf{y}_1 + \mathbf{x}_1 \circledast \mathbf{y}_2) \circledast \mathbf{x}_1^*$ will give a noisy version of $\mathbf{a} + \mathbf{b}$. This can be treated as a superposition memory trace.

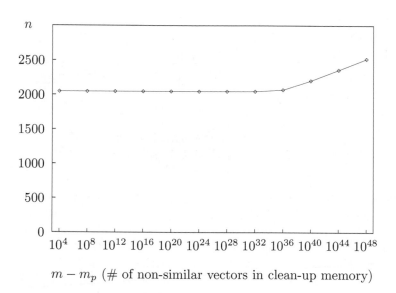

$m - m_p$ (# of non-similar vectors in clean-up memory)

FIGURE 67 Scaling of n with $m - m_p$ (the number of non-similar items in memory) for $\Pr(\text{Error}) = 0.01$, $m_p = 100$, $k = 3$, $j = 3$, and $\alpha^2 = \beta^2 = 0.5$ in a variable-binding memory with similarity.

Appendix E

A lower bound for the capacity of convolution memories

In this appendix I give an analytic lower bound on the capacity of a convolution memory in the case where there is not any systematic similarity among vectors.

I use the following symbols and definitions (which are the same as in Section D.1):

- n is the vector dimension,
- "Random" vector have elements independently drawn from $N(0, 1/n)$,
- $\mathbb{E}$ is a set of m random vectors,
- $\mathbf{t}$ is a memory trace that is the (unnormalized) superposition of k distinct unordered pairs of vectors from $\mathbb{E}$, with the conditions that the two vectors in a pair must be different, and vectors in different pairs must be different:

$$\mathbf{t} = \sum_{i=1}^{k} \mathbf{x}_i \circledast \mathbf{y}_i, \quad \left\{ \begin{array}{l} \mathbf{x}_i, \mathbf{y}_i \in \mathbb{E}, \quad \mathbf{x}_i \neq \mathbf{y}_j \forall i, j, \\ \mathbf{x}_i \neq \mathbf{x}_j \forall i \neq j, \quad \mathbf{y}_i \neq \mathbf{y}_j \forall i \neq j \end{array} \right.$$

- $\Pr(\text{All Correct})$ is the probability of correctly determining for each vector in $\mathbb{E}$ whether or not it is stored in $\mathbf{t}$.

Equation D.12 from Section D.1 gives the probability of correctly identifying all the pairs in the trace:

$$
\begin{aligned}
\Pr(\text{All Correct}) \quad = \quad & \Pr(a > t)^k + \Pr(r_{1=} < t)^{2k} \\
& + \Pr(r_2 < t)^{2k(k-1)} + \Pr(r_1 < t)^{2k(m-2k)} \\
& + \Pr(r_{0=} < t)^{m-2k} + \Pr(r_0 < t)^{(m-2k)(m-2k-1)/2}
\end{aligned}
$$

Using the same inequalities as in Appendix C we get:

$$q \;<\; \frac{m(m+1)}{2} \, \text{tail}(\frac{1}{2}\sqrt{\frac{2k+4}{n}})$$

$$<\; m^2 \, e^{\frac{-n}{16(k+2)}} \qquad \text{if } \; n > \frac{4(k+2)}{\pi}$$

$$\text{or} \quad n \;<\; 16(k+2)\ln\frac{m^2}{q} \qquad \text{if } \; n > \frac{4(k+2)}{\pi}$$

Numerical solutions of the Equation D.12 for k in the range $(2..14)$, m in $(10^2 \ldots 10^{10})$, and q in $(10^{-2} \ldots 10^{-10})$ are reasonably well approximated by

$$n = 4.5(k+0.7)\ln\frac{m}{30q^4}.$$

Appendix F

Means and variances of a signal

The detailed calculation of the mean and variance one of the components of one of the signals in Section 3.10.4 is presented in this appendix. The scalar value X_{mark} from that section (page 135) indicates the strength with which the $\mathbf{id}_{mark}$ vector is present in the decoded filler of the eat-agent role in the HRR $\mathbf{s}_1$. Expanding the expression for the signal X_{mark} gives the following:

$$
\begin{aligned}
X_{mark} &= \mathbf{s}_1 \circledast \mathbf{eat}_{agt}^* \cdot \frac{1}{\sqrt{3}}\mathbf{id}_{mark} \\
&= \frac{1}{\sqrt{3}}(\mathbf{eat} + \mathbf{eat}_{agt} \circledast \mathbf{mark} + \mathbf{eat}_{obj} \circledast \mathbf{the\_fish}) \\
&\quad \circledast \mathbf{eat}_{agt}^* \cdot \frac{1}{\sqrt{3}}\mathbf{id}_{mark} \\
&= \frac{1}{3}(\mathbf{eat} + \mathbf{eat}_{agt} \circledast \frac{1}{\sqrt{3}}(\mathbf{being} + \mathbf{person} + \mathbf{id}_{mark}) \\
&\quad +\mathbf{eat}_{obj} \circledast \mathbf{the\_fish}) \circledast \mathbf{eat}_{agt}^* \cdot \mathbf{id}_{mark} \\
&= \frac{1}{3}\mathbf{eat} \circledast \mathbf{eat}_{agt}^* \cdot \mathbf{id}_{mark} \\
&\quad +\frac{1}{3\sqrt{3}}\mathbf{eat}_{agt} \circledast \mathbf{being} \circledast \mathbf{eat}_{agt}^* \cdot \mathbf{id}_{mark} \\
&\quad +\frac{1}{3\sqrt{3}}\mathbf{eat}_{agt} \circledast \mathbf{person} \circledast \mathbf{eat}_{agt}^* \cdot \mathbf{id}_{mark} \\
&\quad +\frac{1}{3\sqrt{3}}\mathbf{eat}_{agt} \circledast \mathbf{id}_{mark} \circledast \mathbf{eat}_{agt}^* \cdot \mathbf{id}_{mark} \\
&\quad +\frac{1}{3}\mathbf{eat}_{obj} \circledast \mathbf{the\_fish} \circledast \mathbf{eat}_{agt}^* \cdot \mathbf{id}_{mark}
\end{aligned}
$$

The expectations and variances of these terms can be found by consulting Table 3. It is not necessary to expand the vectors $\mathbf{eat}_{agt}$, $\mathbf{eat}_{obj}$

261

or **the_fish**, as the components of these are independent of the other vectors appearing in the same terms. The expectation of the fourth term is $\frac{1}{3\sqrt{3}}$ (row 4 in Table 3), and the expectations of all the remaining terms are zero. These five terms are independent and thus the variance of the sum is the sum of the variances. The variance of the first term is $\frac{1}{9n}$ (row 3 in Table 3), the variance of the second and third terms is $\frac{2n+2}{27n^2}$ (row 8), the variance of the fourth term is $\frac{6n+4}{27n^2}$ (row 6), and the variance of the fifth term is $\frac{1}{9n}$ (row 10). These terms are uncorrelated, so their expectations and variances can be summed to give

$$\mathrm{E}[X_{mark}] = \frac{1}{3\sqrt{3}}, \quad \mathrm{var}[X_{mark}] = \frac{16n+8}{27n^2} \approx 0.593/n.$$

X_p and Z (also from page 135) are the strength with which the vectors $\mathbf{id}_p$ and **being** + **human** are present, respectively, in the decoded filler of the eat-agent role in the HRR $\mathbf{s}_1$. Their expectations and variances can be calculated in a similar manner; their values are as follows:

$$\mathrm{E}[X_p] = 0, \quad \mathrm{var}[X_p] = \frac{12n+6}{27n^2} \approx 0.444/n$$

$$\mathrm{E}[Z] = \frac{2}{3\sqrt{3}}, \quad \mathrm{var}[Z] = \frac{34n+20}{27n^2} \approx 1.26/n$$

Appendix G

The effect of normalization on dot-products

The retrieval and recognition performance of convolution- and HRR-based memories is usually improved by normalizing all vectors so that their magnitude is 1 (see Section 3.5.3). However, the means and variances of dot-products reported in Table 3 in Section 3.6.1 are not accurate when vectors are normalized. When using normalized vectors, means of dot-products are generally the same or slightly lower than with unnormalized vectors, and variances are generally the same or much lower. Both retrieval and recognition can be viewed as signal detection problems, so performance is improved when means increase or when variances decrease. Although means are often slightly lower with normalized vectors, the significantly lower variances result in an overall improvement in performance.

Recall that $\langle \mathbf{x} \rangle$ denotes the normalized version of $\mathbf{x}$ (so that $\langle \mathbf{x} \rangle \cdot \langle \mathbf{x} \rangle = 1$):

$$\langle \mathbf{x} \rangle = \frac{1}{\sqrt{\sum_{i=0}^{n-1} x_i}} \mathbf{x}$$

For the purposes of this section, a *random* vector of dimension n is one whose elements are chosen randomly from $N(0, 1/n)$.

G.1 Means and variances of dot-products of vectors with varying similarity

Consider the first two rows in Table 3 (page 115), for $\mathbf{x} \cdot \mathbf{x}$ and $\mathbf{x} \cdot \mathbf{y}$, where $\mathbf{x}$ and $\mathbf{y}$ have elements independently drawn from $N(0, 1/n)$. For scaled vectors the variances are:

$$\text{var}[\mathbf{x} \cdot \mathbf{x}] = 2/n \quad \text{and} \quad \text{var}[\mathbf{x} \cdot \mathbf{y}] = 1/n.$$

263

However, if we normalize the vectors, the variances are:[73]

$$\text{var}[\langle \mathbf{x} \rangle \cdot \langle \mathbf{x} \rangle] = 0 \quad \text{and} \quad \text{var}[\langle \mathbf{x} \rangle \cdot \langle \mathbf{y} \rangle] = 1/n.$$

Using these two rows in Table 3 we can calculate the expected value and variance of the dot-product of $\mathbf{x}$ with vectors that have varying similarity to $\mathbf{x}$ (if normalization is not used). For example, for $d = \mathbf{x} \cdot 1/\sqrt{3}(\mathbf{x} + \mathbf{a} + \mathbf{b})$ (where $\mathbf{x}$, $\mathbf{a}$, and $\mathbf{b}$ are random vectors) we have:

$$\text{E}[d] = 1/\sqrt{3} \quad \text{and} \quad \text{var}[d] = 4/3n.$$

The $1/\sqrt{3}$ scale factor makes the expected magnitude of $1/\sqrt{3}(\mathbf{x}+\mathbf{a}+\mathbf{b})$ equal to 1. In general, for

$$d_k = \tfrac{1}{\sqrt{k}}(\mathbf{x} + \textstyle\sum_{i=1}^{k-1} \mathbf{y}_i) \cdot \mathbf{x}$$

(where $\mathbf{x}$ and $\mathbf{y}_i$ are random vectors) we have

$$\text{E}[d_k] = \frac{1}{\sqrt{k}} \quad \text{and} \quad \text{var}[d_k] = \frac{1}{n}\frac{k+1}{k}.$$

G.1.1 Experimentally observed means and variances of dot-products

The expected and experimentally observed variances for dot-products of scaled vectors are shown in Figure 68. As expected, these are almost identical. The experimentally observed variances for dot-products of normalized vectors are also shown:

$$d_k = \left(\langle\langle \mathbf{x} \rangle + \textstyle\sum_{i=1}^{k-1} \langle \mathbf{y}_i \rangle\rangle \right) \cdot \langle \mathbf{x} \rangle,$$

These variances are considerably lower, though they tend to the same limit (1) as k tends to infinity. The experiments were done with $n = 1024$ and $10,000$ runs.

The experimentally observed means for dot-products of scaled and normalized vectors were indistinguishable from the expected values (i.e., $1/\sqrt{k}$).

G.2 Means and variances of dot-products of convolution expressions

Rows 3 through 10 in Table 3 concern the means and variances of dot-products that arise when convolution bindings are decoded or compared.

The experimentally observed means and variances for various dot-products of convolution products are shown in Table 32. The means and variances for the decoding and similarity expressions are reported

---

[73]I am indebted to Radford Neal for a proof that $\text{var}[\langle \mathbf{x} \rangle \cdot \langle \mathbf{y} \rangle] = 1/n$.

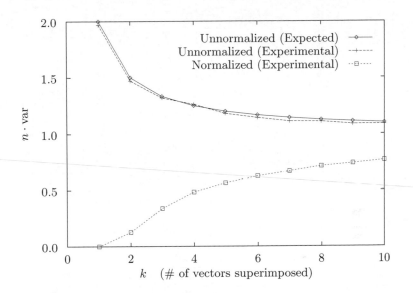

FIGURE 68 Variances of the dot-product of $\mathbf{x}$ with superpositions of $\mathbf{x}$ with (k-1) other vectors. The value on the vertical axis is $n \cdot \mathrm{var}[d_k]$. The experimental data are for $n = 1024$ and $10,000$ runs.

separately, since the decoding/similarity identity

$$\mathbf{a} \circledast \mathbf{b} \circledast \mathbf{c}^* \cdot \mathbf{d} \;=\; \mathbf{a} \circledast \mathbf{b} \cdot \mathbf{c} \circledast \mathbf{d}$$

does not hold if vectors are normalized. It turns out that in general

$$\langle\langle\langle\mathbf{a}\rangle \circledast \langle\mathbf{b}\rangle\rangle \circledast \langle\mathbf{c}\rangle^*\rangle \cdot \langle\mathbf{d}\rangle \;\neq\; \langle\langle\mathbf{a}\rangle \circledast \langle\mathbf{b}\rangle\rangle \cdot \langle\langle\mathbf{c}\rangle \circledast \langle\mathbf{d}\rangle\rangle,$$

and the expected values are the same only when they are zero.

The variances are significantly lower with normalization. The non-zero means for decoding convolution bindings with normalization are also lower. For example, the sample mean of $\langle\langle\langle\mathbf{a}\rangle \circledast \langle\mathbf{b}\rangle\rangle \circledast \langle\mathbf{a}\rangle^*\rangle \cdot \langle\mathbf{b}\rangle$ is 0.7088, whereas without normalization the mean of this is 1. However, the decrease in variance outweighs the decrease in means – performance is generally superior when normalization is used.

	Unnormalized Expected (Analytic)		Unnormalized Experimental		Normalized Experimental Decoding		Normalized Experimental Similarity	
Expression	mean	$n \cdot$ var	mean	$n \cdot$ var	mean	$n \cdot$ var	mean	$n \cdot$ var
(1) $\mathbf{a} \cdot \mathbf{a}$	1	2	1.0003	2.0094	1.0000	0.0000	1.0000	0.0000
(2) $\mathbf{a} \cdot \mathbf{b}$	0	1	-0.0007	1.0251	0.0002	0.9952	0.0000	0.9842
(3) $\mathbf{a} \cdot \mathbf{a} \circledast \mathbf{b}$	0	2.0001	-0.0002	2.0122	-0.0001	1.9897	-0.0002	2.0480
(4) $\mathbf{a} \cdot \mathbf{b} \circledast \mathbf{c}$	0	1	0.0006	1.0014	-0.0004	0.9995	-0.0001	0.9926
(5) $\mathbf{a} \circledast \mathbf{a} \circledast \mathbf{a}^* \cdot \mathbf{a}$	2.0020	40.109	2.0038	39.9667	1.0000	0.0000	0.8201	0.5014
(6) $\mathbf{a} \circledast \mathbf{b} \circledast \mathbf{a}^* \cdot \mathbf{b}$	1	6.0039	0.9998	5.9699	1.0000	0.0000	0.7088	0.4524
(7) $\mathbf{a} \circledast \mathbf{b} \circledast \mathbf{a}^* \cdot \mathbf{a}$	0	6.0176	-0.0015	6.1133	0.0003	2.9795	0.0002	2.9631
(8) $\mathbf{a} \circledast \mathbf{b} \circledast \mathbf{a}^* \cdot \mathbf{c}$	0	2.0020	-0.0003	2.0184	-0.0001	1.9378	-0.0001	0.9974
(9) $\mathbf{a} \circledast \mathbf{b} \circledast \mathbf{c}^* \cdot \mathbf{c}$	0	2.0020	-0.0004	1.9866	0.0000	1.0049	0.0006	1.9434
(10) $\mathbf{a} \circledast \mathbf{b} \circledast \mathbf{c}^* \cdot \mathbf{d}$	0	1	0.0006	1.0073	-0.0001	1.0135	0.0003	1.0149

TABLE 32 Experimentally observed means and variances of dot-products of common convolution expressions for normalized and unnormalized versions. In the normalized version, normalization is performed at every step. For example, for (10), the expression for normalized decoding is $\langle\langle\langle \mathbf{a} \rangle \circledast \langle \mathbf{b} \rangle\rangle \circledast \langle \mathbf{c} \rangle^*\rangle \cdot \langle \mathbf{d} \rangle$ and the expression for normalized similarity is $\langle\langle \mathbf{a} \rangle \circledast \langle \mathbf{b} \rangle\rangle \cdot \langle\langle \mathbf{c} \rangle \circledast \langle \mathbf{d} \rangle\rangle$. The statistics are for $n = 1024$ over $10,000$ runs. The variances are multiplied by n to make them easier to read and compare.

Appendix H

HRRs with circular vectors

In this appendix, I present analytic and experimental results concerning the means and variances for dot-products of superpositions and bindings in the *circular* system described in Chapter 4. In this system, each vector element is a point on the unit circle in the complex plane, i.e., each vector element is normalized to have unit magnitude. I also compare the circular system with unnormalized and normalized versions of the standard system.

H.1 Means and variances of dot-products of vectors with varying similarity

For the standard system, it is easy to show that the similarity of $\mathbf{x}$ and the scaled (but not normalized) superposition of $\mathbf{x}$ with $k - 1$ other vectors $(1/\sqrt{k+1}(\mathbf{x} + \sum_{i=1}^{k-1} \mathbf{y}_i))$ is $1/\sqrt{k}$. This remains true if vectors are normalized rather than scaled. Variances are also easily calculated, at least in the unnormalized version. For circular vectors, these calculations are more difficult. I present simulation results for $k = 1 \ldots 10$ and analytic derivations for means and variances in the cases of $k = 0$ and $k = 1$.

Figures 69 and 70 show the experimentally observed means and variances of

$$s_c = \bar{\theta} \cdot \mathrm{sp}(\bar{\theta}, \bar{\phi}_1, \ldots \bar{\phi}_{k-1})$$

for $k = 0$ to 10, where $\bar{\theta}$ and the $\bar{\phi}_i$ are random vectors. For comparison, the corresponding observations for unnormalized and normalized standard vectors are also plotted. These observations are for

$$s_u = \mathbf{x} \cdot \sqrt{\frac{1}{k}} (\mathbf{x} + \sum_{i=1}^{k-1} \mathbf{y}_i)$$

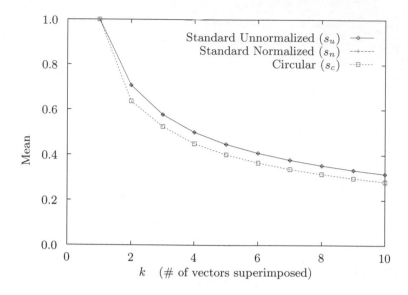

FIGURE 69 Means of the dot-product of a random vector with superpositions of it and $(k-1)$ other random vectors. The data are for $n = 512$ and $10,000$ runs. The results for the normalized and unnormalized systems overlap on this plot.

and

$$s_n = \langle \mathbf{x} \rangle \cdot \langle \langle \mathbf{x} \rangle + \sum_{i=1}^{k-1} \langle \mathbf{y}_i \rangle \rangle$$

where $\mathbf{x}$ and the $\mathbf{y}_i$ are random vectors.

For the analytic derivations I only consider single angles rather than a vector of angles. It is clear that the variance of a dot-product of circular vectors is proportional to $1/n$, because it is a sum of n independent random variables, multiplied by $1/n$. For the same reason, the expected value of the dot-product does not vary with n.

First, consider the dot-product of dissimilar angles: θ and ϕ independently distributed as $U(-\pi, \pi)$. We can substitute $\psi \stackrel{d}{=} U(-\pi, \pi)$ for $(\theta - \phi \bmod 2\pi)$ because the latter is distributed uniformly in $(-\pi, \pi]$.

$$
\begin{aligned}
E[\theta \cdot \phi] &= E[\cos(\theta - \phi)] \\
&= E[\cos(\psi)] \qquad \text{for } \psi \stackrel{d}{=} U(-\pi, \pi)
\end{aligned}
$$

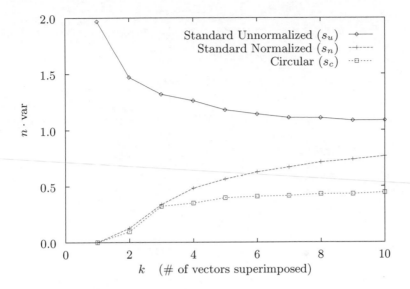

FIGURE 70 Variances of the dot-product of a random vector with superpositions of it and $(k-1)$ other vectors. The data are for $n = 512$ and $10,000$ runs.

$$
\begin{aligned}
&= \int_{-\pi}^{\pi} \frac{2}{\pi} \cos(\psi)d\psi \\
&= 0 \\
\mathrm{var}[\theta \cdot \phi] &= \mathrm{E}[\cos^2(\theta - \phi)] \\
&= \mathrm{E}[\cos^2(\psi)] \qquad \text{for } \psi \overset{d}{=} \mathrm{U}(-\pi, \pi) \\
&= \int_{-\pi}^{\pi} \frac{2}{\pi} \cos^2(\psi)d\psi \\
&= \frac{1}{2}
\end{aligned}
$$

Next consider the dot-product of an angle with itself (i.e., $k = 0$ in the graphs). Since $\cos(0) = 1$, we have

$$
\begin{aligned}
\mathrm{E}[\theta \odot \theta] &= 1 \\
\mathrm{var}[\theta \odot \theta] &= 0
\end{aligned}
$$

Finally consider the dot-product of θ with $\theta \oplus \phi$ (i.e., $k = 1$ in the graphs). The experimentally observed means and variances are shown in parentheses.

$$
\begin{aligned}
\mathrm{E}[\theta \cdot (\theta \oplus \phi)] &= \mathrm{E}[\cos(\theta - (\theta \oplus \phi))] \\
&= \mathrm{E}[\cos(\phi/2)] \\
&= \int_{-\pi}^{\pi} \frac{2}{\pi} \cos(\phi/2) d\phi \\
&= \frac{2}{\pi} \quad = \quad 0.63662\ldots \quad (0.6365) \\
\mathrm{var}[\theta \cdot (\theta \oplus \phi)] &= \mathrm{E}[(\frac{2}{\pi} - \cos(\theta - (\theta \oplus \phi)))^2] \\
&= \mathrm{E}[(\frac{2}{\pi} - \cos(\phi/2))^2] \\
&= \int_{-\pi}^{\pi} \frac{2}{\pi} (\frac{2}{\pi} - \cos(\phi/2))^2 d\phi \\
&= \frac{-8 + \pi^2}{2\pi^2} \quad = \quad 0.094715\ldots \quad (0.09552)
\end{aligned}
$$

H.2 Means and variances of dot-products for similarity and decoding

The means and variances of dot-products for similarity and decoding are easy to calculate, especially in cases where no superposition is involved. Consider the various dot-products of convolution expressions from Table 3. For *hits* in decoding (or comparison), the dot-product is 1 and the variance is 0, because the decoding is exact. For *misses*, the expected dot-product is 0, and the variance is 1/2, as with $\theta \cdot \phi$ in the previous section. The means and variances of dot-products involving higher-order bindings follow the same simple pattern. Results from simulations, shown in Table 33, agree with these calculations.

There is no need to consider decoding and similarity separately, as there was with normalized standard vectors, since the decoding/similarity identity

$$(\mathbf{a} \circledast \mathbf{b}) \circledast \mathbf{c}^* \cdot \mathbf{d} = (\mathbf{a} \circledast \mathbf{b}) \cdot (\mathbf{c} \circledast \mathbf{d})$$

holds for circular vectors:

$$
\begin{aligned}
(\theta \odot \phi) \odot (-\psi) \cdot \gamma &= \cos((\theta + \phi) - \psi - \gamma) \\
&= \cos((\theta + \phi) - (\psi + \gamma)) \\
&= (\theta \odot \phi) \cdot (\psi \odot \gamma)
\end{aligned}
$$

	Circular Decoding and Similarity				Normalized Decoding Experimental		Normalized Similarity Experimental	
	Analytic		Experimental					
Expression	mean	$n \cdot$ var	mean	$n \cdot$ var	mean	$n \cdot$ var	mean	$n \cdot$ var
(1) $a \cdot a$	1	0	1.0000	0.0000	1.0000	0.0000	1.0000	0.0000
(2) $a \cdot b$	0	1/2	0.0000	0.5003	0.0002	0.9952	0.0000	0.9842
(3) $a \cdot a \odot b$	0	1/2	0.0006	0.5028	−0.0001	1.9897	−0.0002	2.0480
(4) $a \cdot b \odot c$	0	1/2	−0.0004	0.4989	−0.0004	0.9995	−0.0001	0.9926
(5) $a \odot a \odot a^* \cdot a$	1	0	1.0000	0.0000	1.0000	0.0000	0.8201	0.5014
(6) $a \odot b \odot a^* \cdot b$	1	0	1.0000	0.0000	1.0000	0.0000	0.7088	0.4524
(7) $a \odot b \odot a^* \cdot a$	0	1/2	0.0000	0.5003	0.0003	2.9795	0.0002	2.9631
(8) $a \odot b \odot a^* \cdot c$	0	1/2	0.0005	0.4903	−0.0001	1.9378	−0.0001	0.9974
(9) $a \odot b \odot c^* \cdot c$	0	1/2	0.0001	0.4998	0.0000	1.0049	0.0006	1.9434
(10) $a \odot b \odot c^* \cdot d$	0	1/2	−0.0006	0.4954	−0.0001	1.0135	0.0003	1.0149

TABLE 33 Means and variances of dot-products for decoding and comparing bindings. The experimental results for the circular system are for $n = 512$ and 10,000 runs. The last four columns of data for the corresponding operations in the normalized standard system are from Table 32, repeated here for easy comparison. There is only one set of statistics for circular vectors because the decoding/similarity identity holds.

H.3 Results on analogical similarity estimation

Circular vectors can be used for estimation of analogical similarity. I ran Experiment 2 (contextualized HRRs) from Chapter 6 with circular vectors (with 2048 angles). The results are very similar to what is achieved with the standard representation. The means come in the same rank order, but there are more individual violations of the ordering

$$\text{LS} > \text{CM} > \text{AN} > (\text{SS}^{\times \text{I}}, \text{SS}^{\times \text{H}}, \text{SS}^{-\text{H}})$$
$$> (\text{FA}^{\times \text{I}}, \text{FA}^{\times \text{H}}) > \text{OO}^{\times \text{H}} > \text{OO}^{-\text{H}}$$

(11 violations for circular vectors compared to 0 for standard vectors). However, these violations are all with the order of SS and FA, which are less important. Overall, the means are somewhat lower, which is not good, but the variances are lower and more uniform, which is good.

Table 34 shows the means and variances for each of the comparisons, for Experiment 2 and vectors with dimension 2048. The means for standard vectors are the same as in Table 23.

Probe: Spot bit Jane, causing Jane to flee from Spot.

		Dot-products			
		Standard		Circular	
Episodes in long-term memory:	Type	Avg	Sd	Avg	Sd
E1: Fido bit John, causing John to flee from Fido.	LS	0.81	0.011	0.63	0.010
E2: Fred bit Rover, causing Rover to flee from Fred.	CM	0.69	0.016	0.54	0.012
E3: Felix bit Mort, causing Mort to flee from Felix.	AN	0.61	0.018	0.48	0.013
E4: Mort bit Felix, causing Felix to flee from Mort.	AN	0.61	0.018	0.48	0.014
E5: Rover bit Fred, causing Rover to flee from Fred.	SS$^{\times I}$	0.53	0.025	0.40	0.013
E6: John fled from Fido, causing Fido to bite John.	SS$^{\times H}$	0.53	0.023	0.35	0.015
E7: Mort bit Felix, causing Mort to flee from Felix.	FA$^{\times I}$	0.39	0.022	0.31	0.016
E8: Mort fled from Felix, causing Felix to bite Mort.	FA$^{\times H}$	0.39	0.026	0.27	0.015
E9: Fido bit John, John fled from Fido.	SS^{-H}	0.51	0.020	0.35	0.012
E10: Fred stroked Rover, causing Rover to lick Fred.	OO$^{\times H}$	0.25	0.024	0.19	0.017
E11: Fred stroked Rover, Rover licked Fred.	OO^{-H}	0.12	0.022	0.06	0.017

TABLE 34 Results from Analogy Experiment 2 for normalized standard vectors and circular vectors.

Appendix I

Arithmetic tables: an example of HRRs with many items in memory

Distributed representations are generally more efficient with respect to representational resources than localist representations, because they allow many more than n objects to be represented over n units. The analysis of capacity given in Appendix D indicates that HRRs should share this property. In this Appendix I describe a simulation that demonstrates this. I store approximately 5000 different HRRs in a clean-up memory, using 512 dimensional vectors.

Also, this simulation provides a counterexample to Halford et al.'s (1994) claim that role-filler representations do not permit one component of a relation to be retrieved given the others.

In Section 3.7 I suggested that a fast estimate of the dot-product (computed using bitwise comparison) could be used to speed up the comparison process. I used this technique in the simulations reported here, and found that it worked well.

I.1 The objects and relations

The base vectors, which have elements distributed as $N(0, 1/n)$ ($n = 512$) are:

$$\text{optimes} \qquad \text{opplus}$$
$$\text{operand} \qquad \text{result}$$
$$\text{number}_x \quad \text{for} \quad x = 0..2500$$

The relations concern multiplication and addition. They are statements like "two times eight equals sixteen". In general, the relations are:

$$\text{times}_{x,y} \; = \; \langle \text{optimes} + \text{operand} * (\text{number}_x + \text{number}_y)$$
$$+ \, \text{result} \circledast \text{number}_{x*y} \rangle$$

273

$$\text{plus}_{x,y} \;=\; \langle \text{opplus} + \text{operand} * (\text{number}_x + \text{number}_y)$$
$$+ \text{result} \circledast \text{number}_{x+y} \rangle$$

where x and y range from 0 to 50 with $y \leq x$. I use the same role for each operand, since they have equivalent status ($x \times y = y \times x$).

There are 1326 instances of each relation. Examples are:

$$\text{times}_{21,12} \;=\; \langle \text{optimes} + \text{operand} * (\text{number}_{21} + \text{number}_{12})$$
$$+ \text{result} \circledast \text{number}_{252} \rangle$$
$$\text{plus}_{42,25} \;=\; \langle \text{opplus} + \text{operand} * (\text{number}_4 2 + \text{number}_2 5)$$
$$+ \text{result} \circledast \text{number}_{67} \rangle$$

The 2501 number vectors, along with the 2652 relation vectors, are stored in the same clean-up memory.

I.2 Queries to the memory

We can "look up" a relation by supplying sufficient information to distinguish it from other relations. For example, we can look up "21 times 12 equals 252" by finding the most similar relation to any of the following:

$\langle \text{optimes} + \text{operand} * (\text{number}_{21} + \text{number}_{12}) \rangle$
$\langle \text{optimes} + \text{operand} * \text{number}_{12} + \text{result} \circledast \text{number}_{252} \rangle$
$\langle \text{optimes} + \text{operand} * \text{number}_{21} + \text{result} \circledast \text{number}_{252} \rangle$
$\langle \text{operand} * (\text{number}_{21} + \text{number}_{12}) + \text{result} \circledast \text{number}_{252} \rangle$

In the first three cases, the remaining component can be found by decoding the retrieved relation with the role vector for the missing component, e.g.,

$$\text{times}_{21,12} \circledast \text{result}^*,$$

and retrieving the most similar vector in the clean-up memory, which will be number_{252} for this example. To discover a missing relation name, we need to have a separate clean-up memory containing only relation names (or use an alternative encoding in which there is a role for relation names).

One run of the system was tried, with $n = 512$, making four queries for each relation – each query had 3 of the 4 components present (i.e., relation name missing, one operand missing, or result missing). This amounted to 10,608 queries – in all cases the most-similar vector returned by the clean-up memory was the HRR for the correct full relation. After retrieving the relation, the missing component was decoded, except for the relation name. E.g., after retrieving the HRR representing the relation $\text{times}_{21,12}$ by finding the most similar vector to $\langle \text{optimes} + \text{operand} * (\text{number}_{21} + \text{number}_{12}) \rangle$ in clean-up memory (the query vector is missing the result component), the filler of the result role was decoded by computing $\mathbf{times}_{21,12} \circledast \mathbf{result}^*$ and passing this vector through the clean-up memory, which should produce the vector for $\mathbf{number}_{252}$. This comprised a further 7,956 queries. Again, in all cases the clean-up memory returned the vector that represented the correct missing filler.

Relations can be retrieved using fewer components. For example, the most similar relation to $\langle \mathbf{result} \circledast \mathbf{number}_{221} \rangle$ is $\mathbf{times}_{17,13}$.

The above retrieval process requires that we know the roles of each component. If we wish to be able to retrieve relations given some components whose roles we do not know, then we must store the fillers in plain form in the relation, e.g.,

$$\mathbf{times}_{x,y} \;=\; \langle \mathbf{optimes} + \langle \mathbf{number}_x + \mathbf{number}_y + \mathbf{number}_{x*y} \rangle$$
$$+\, \mathbf{operand} * (\mathbf{number}_x + \mathbf{number}_y)$$
$$+\, \mathbf{result} \circledast \mathbf{number}_{x*y} \rangle$$

This is the type of representation I used for the analogy experiments (Chapter 6).

I.3 Using fast estimates of the dot-product

Comparing a 512-dimensional vector against 5,153 vectors in clean-up memory takes considerable time. The technique described in Section 3.7 reduces the computation by using a fast bitwise estimate of the dot-product to judge when it is necessary to compute the floating-point dot-product. Table 35 shows the CPU times[74] for 10,608 accesses to clean-up memory, with each access involving comparisons against 5,153 vectors.

The first column is half the width of the interval s (see Section 3.7 for a definition), in approximate standard deviations. A spread of four standard deviations on each side should be very safe. The second column shows the number of times that the use of the fast estimate resulted in the wrong vector being selected by the clean-up memory. The third column shows the total execution time for the entire program, including the construction of the base and relations vectors and the loading of clean-up memory. This startup time was negligible – around 80 seconds. The last column shows the percentage of vectors for which the floating-point dot-product was calculated. The first row is from a run that did not use the fast estimates at all.

---

[74]On an 1993 SGI machine with a MIPS R4400 CPU and a MIPS R4010 FPU, and a 150MHz clock.

Spread	Errors	Total Time (seconds)	Percent of F.P. dot-products
N/A	0	6824	100
4	0	4287	46
3	0	3512	33
2	0	2876	23
1	0	2002	9.1
0.5	0	1623	3.1
0.1	1	1438	0.60
0	1	1460	0.49

TABLE 35 CPU times from runs using fast bitwise comparisons. The times are for 10,608 accesses to a clean-up memory containing 5,153 vectors of dimension 512.

The number of errors is surprisingly low, even for very low spreads. This is probably due to the fact that in this task the best match is nearly always significantly better than the next best match. This makes it very likely that the fast estimate of the dot-product for the true best match is greater than the fast estimate for any other vector. In general, it is probably not safe to use low spreads.

The speedup achieved ($\approx$ 1.4 to 4 times) is reasonable, but not exceptionally good. The speedup will be greater for higher n and for more vectors in the clean-up memory. Further speedup could probably be gained by optimizing the code and the memory organization for the fast comparisons, and by improving the algorithm using ideas such as those presented in Seidl and Kriegel (1998).

References

Abramowitz, M. and I. A. Stegun, eds. 1965. *Handbook of mathematical functions with formulas, graphs, and mathematical tables*. New York: Dover.

Ackley, D. H., G. E. Hinton, and T. J. Sejnowski. 1985. A learning algorithm for Boltzmann machines. *Cognitive Science* 9:147–169.

Ajjanagadde, V. and L. Shastri. 1991. Rules and variables in neural nets. *Neural Computation* 3:121–134.

Anderson, J., J. W. Silverstein, S. A. Ritz, and R. S. Jones. 1977. Distinctive features, categorical perception, and probability learning: Some applications of a neural model. *Psychological Review* 84:413–451.

Anderson, J. A. 1973. A theory for the recognition of items from short memorized lists. *Psychological Review* 80(6):417–438.

Anderson, J. A., K. T. Spoehr, and D. J. Bennett. 1991. A study in numerical perversity: Teaching arithmetic to a neural network. Tech. Rep. 91-3, Department of Cognitive and Linguistic Science, Brown University, Providence, RI.

Baldi, P. and K. Hornik. 1989. Neural networks and principal components analysis: Learning from examples without local minima. *Neural Networks* 2:53–58.

Baum, E. B., J. Moody, and F. Wilczek. 1988. Internal representations for associative memory. *Biological Cybernetics* 59:217–228.

Blair, A. D. 1997. Scaling up raams. Tech. Rep. CS-97-192, Brandeis University Computer Science. http://www.cse.unsw.edu.au/ blair/tr_sur.pdf.

Bod, R. 1998. *Beyond Grammar: An Experience-Based Theory of Language*. No. 88 in Lecture notes. Stanford, CA: CSLI Publications, distributed by Cambridge University Press.

Borsellino, A. and T. Poggio. 1973. Convolution and correlation algebras. *Kybernetik* 13:113–122.

Bourlard, H. and Y. Kamp. 1988. Auto-association by multilayer perceptrons and singular value decomposition. *Biological Cybernetics* 59:291–294.

Brachman, R. J. 1985a. On the epistemological status of semantic networks. In R. J. Brachman and H. Levesque, eds., *Readings in Knowledge Representation*, pages 191–216. San Mateo, CA: Morgan Kaufmann.

Brachman, R. J. 1985b. Prologue to reflection and semantics in a procedural language. In R. J. Brachman and H. Levesque, eds., *Readings in Knowledge Representation*, pages 31–40. San Mateo, CA: Morgan Kaufmann.

Brigham, E. O. 1974. *The Fast Fourier Transform*. Englewood Cliffs, NJ: Prentice Hall.

Casey, M. 1996. The dynamics of discrete-time computation, with application to recurrent neural networks and finite state machine extraction. *Neural Computation* 8(6):1135–1178.

Catrambone, R. and K. J. Holyoak. 1989. Overcoming contextual limitations on problem-solving transfer. *Journal of Experimental Psychology: Learning, Memory, and Cognition* 15:1147–1156.

Chalmers, D. J. 1990. Syntactic transformations on distributed representations. *Connection Science* 2(1&2):53–62.

Charniak, E. and E. Santos. 1987. A connectionist context-free parser which is not context-free but then it is not really connectionist either. In *Proceedings of 9th Annual Conference of the Cognitive Science Society*, pages 70–77. Hillsdale, NJ: Erlbaum.

Collins, M. and N. Duffy. 2002. New ranking algorithms for parsing and tagging: Kernels over discrete structures, and the voted perceptron. In *Proceedings of the 40th Annual Meeting of the Association for Computational Linguistics (ACL)*, pages 263–270.

Cottrell, G. W. and S. L. Small. 1983. A connectionist scheme for modeling word-sense disambiguation. *Cognition and Brain Theory* 6:89–120.

Das, S., C. L. Giles, and G.-Z. Sun. 1992. Learning context-free grammars: Capabilities and limitations of a recurrent neural network with an external stack memory. In *Proceedings of the 14th Annual Conference of the Cognitive Science Society*. Hillsdale, NJ: Erlbaum.

Das, S. and M. C. Mozer. 1994. A hybrid gradient-descent/clustering technique for finite state machine induction. In J. D. Cowan, G. Tesauro, and J. Alspector, eds., *Advances in Neural Information Processing Systems 6 (NIPS*93)*, pages 19–26. San Mateo, CA: Morgan Kaufmann.

Davis, P. J. 1979. *Circulant matrices*. New York, NY: John Wiley & Sons.

Deerwester, S., S. T. Dumais, T. K. Landauer, G. W. Furnas, and R. A. Harshman. 1990. Indexing by latent semantic analysis. *Journal of the Society for Information Science* 41(6):391–407.

DePiero, F. W. and D. K. Krout. 2003. An algorithm using length-r paths to approximate subgraph isomorphism. *Pattern Recognition Journal* 24:33–46.

Derthick, M. 1990. Mundane reasoning by settling on a plausible model. *Artificial Intelligence* 46(1-2):107–158.

Dolan, C. P. 1989. Tensor manipulation networks: Connectionist and symbolic approaches to comprehension, learning, and planning. Computer Science Department, AI Lab. Technical Report UCLA-AI-89-06, UCLA, Los Angeles, CA.

Dolan, C. P. and P. Smolensky. 1989. Tensor product production system: a modular architecture and representation. *Connection Science* 1(1):53–68.

Eliasmith, C. and P. Thagard. 2001. Integrating structure and meaning: a distributed model of analogical mapping. *Cognitive Science* 25:245–286.

Elliot, D. F. 1986. *Handbook of Digital Signal Processing Engineering Applications*. San Diego, CA: Academic Press, Inc.

Elman, J. 1991. Distributed representations, simple recurrent networks and grammatical structure. *Machine Learning* 7(2&3):195–226.

Elman, J. L. 1988. Finding structure in time. Tech. Rep. CRL-8801, Center for Research in Language, UCSD, San Diego, CA.

Elman, J. L. 1990. Finding structure in time. *Cognitive Science* 14:179–211.

Etherington, D. W. and R. Reiter. 1983. On inheritance hierarchies with exceptions. In *Proceedings of the AAAI-83*, pages 104–108. Washington, DC.

Falkenhainer, B., K. D. Forbus, and D. Gentner. 1989. The Structure-Mapping Engine: Algorithm and examples. *Artificial Intelligence* 41:1–63.

Feldman, J. A. and D. H. Ballard. 1982. Connectionist models and their properties. *Cognitive Science* 6:205–254.

Fisher, A. D., W. L. Lippincott, and J. N. Lee. 1987. Optical implementations of associative networks with versatile adaptive learning capabilities. *Applied Optics* 26(23):5039–5054.

Fodor, J. A. and Z. W. Pylyshyn. 1988. Connectionism and cognitive architecture: A critical analysis. *Cognition* 28:3–71.

Földiák, P. 2002. Sparse coding in the primate cortex. In M. Arbib, ed., *The Handbook of Brain Theory and Neural Networks*, pages 895–899. Cambridge, MA: MIT Press, 2nd edn.

Forbus, K. D., D. Gentner, and K. Law. 1994. MAC/FAC: A model of similarity-based retrieval. *Cognitive Science* 19:141–205.

Gabel, R. A. and R. A. Roberts. 1973. *Signals and linear systems*. New York, NY: John Wiley & Sons.

Gabor, D. 1968. Holographic model for temporal recall. *Nature* 217:1288–1289.

Gayler, R. W. 1998. Multiplicative binding, representation operators and analogy. In K. Holyoak, D. Gentner, and B. Kokinov, eds., *Advances in analogy research: Integration of theory and data from the cognitive, computational, and neural sciences.*. Sofia, Bulgaria: New Bulgarian University. Only the abstract appears in the proceedings. Full text available at http://cogprints.soton.ac.uk.

Geman, S. and D. Geman. 1984. Stochastic relaxation, Gibbs distributions, and the Bayesian restoration of images. *IEEE Transactions on Pattern Analysis and Machine Intelligence* 6:721–741.

Gentner, D. 1983. Structure-mapping: A theoretical framework for analogy. *Cognitive Science* 7:155–170.

Gentner, D. and K. D. Forbus. 1991. MAC/FAC: A model of similarity-based retrieval. In *Proceedings of the 13th Annual Cognitive Science Society Conference*, pages 504–509. Hillsdale, NJ: Erlbaum.

Gentner, D. and A. B. Markman. 1993. Analogy – watershed or Waterloo? Structural alignment and the development of connectionist models of analogy. In C. L. Giles, S. J. Hanson, and J. D. Cowan, eds., *Advances in Neural Information Processing Systems 5*, pages 855–862. San Mateo, CA: Morgan Kaufmann.

Gentner, D., M. J. Rattermann, and K. D. Forbus. 1993. The roles of similarity in transfer: Separating retrievability from inferential soundness. *Cognitive Psychology* 25(4):524–575.

Gick, M. L. and K. J. Holyoak. 1983. Schema induction and analogical transfer. *Cognitive Psychology* 15:1–38.

Giles, C. L., G. Z. Sun, H. H. Chen, Y. C. Lee, and D. Chen. 1990. Higher order recurrent networks and grammatical inference. In D. S. Touretzky, ed., *Advances in Neural Information Processing Systems 2*, pages 380–387. San Mateo, CA: Morgan Kaufmann.

Giles, L., C. Miller, D. Chen, H. Chen, G. Sun, and Y. Lee. 1992. Learning and extracting finite-state automata with second-order recurrent neural networks. *Neural Computation* 4(3):393–405.

Goldstone, R. L., D. L. Medin, and D. Gentner. 1991. Relational similarity and the nonindependence of features in similarity judgements. *Cognitive Psychology* 23:222–262.

Green, D. M. and J. A. Swets. 1966. *Signal Detection Theory and Psychophysics*. New York, NY: Wiley.

Hadley, J. A., A. F. Healy, and B. B. Murdock. 1992. Output and retrieval interference in the missing-number task. *Memory and Cognition* 20:69–82.

Halford, G. S., W. H. Wilson, J. Guo, R. W. Gayler, J. Wiles, and J. E. M. Stewart. 1994. Connectionist implications for processing capacity limitations in analogies. In K. J. Holyoak and J. Barnden, eds., *Analogical Connections*, vol. 2 of *Advances in Connectionist and Neural Computation Theory*. Norwood, NJ: Ablex.

Harris, C. 1989. Connectionist explorations in cognitive linguistics. Unpublished.

Haussler, D. 1999. Convolution kernels on discrete structures. Tech. Rep. UCS-CRL-99-10, UC Santa Cruz, Santa Cruz, CA. http://www.cse.ucsc.edu/haussler.

Hinton, G. E. 1981. Implementing semantic networks in parallel hardware. In G. E. Hinton and J. A. Anderson, eds., *Parallel Models of Associative Memory*. Hillsdale, NJ: Erlbaum.

Hinton, G. E. 1987. Representing part-whole hierarchies in connectionist networks. Unpublished manuscript.

Hinton, G. E. 1989. Learning distributed representations of concepts. In R. G. M. Morris, ed., *Parallel Distributed Processing: Implications for Psychology and Neurobiology*, pages 46–61. Oxford, UK: Oxford University Press. Reprint of a paper of the same title in Proceedings of the Eighth Annual Conference of the Cognitive Science, Hillsdale, NJ: Erlbaum.

Hinton, G. E. 1990. Mapping part-whole hierarchies into connectionist networks. *Artificial Intelligence* 46(1-2):47–76.

Hinton, G. E. and Z. Ghahramani. 1997. Generative models for discovering sparse distributed representations. *Philosophical Transactions of the Royal Society of London, B* 352:1177–1190.

Hinton, G. E., J. L. McClelland, and D. E. Rumelhart. 1986. Distributed representations. In D. E. Rumelhart, J. L. McClelland, and the PDP research group, eds., *Parallel Distributed Processing: Explorations in the Microstructure of Cognition.*, vol. 1, pages 77–109. Cambridge, MA: MIT Press.

Holyoak, K. J. and K. Koh. 1987. Surface and structural similarity in analogical transfer. *Memory and Cognition* 15:332–340.

Holyoak, K. J. and P. Thagard. 1989. Analogical mapping by constraint satisfaction. *Cognitive Science* 13:295–355.

Hopfield, J. J. 1982. Neural networks and physical systems with emergent collective computational abilities. *Proceedings of the National Academy of Sciences U.S.A.* 79:2554–2558.

Hummel, J. E. and K. J. Holyoak. 1992. Indirect analogical mapping. In *Proceedings of the 14th Annual Cognitive Science Society Conference*, pages 516–521. Hillsdale, NJ: Erlbaum.

Hummel, J. E. and K. J. Holyoak. 1997. Distributed representations of structure: A theory of analogical access and mapping. *Psychological Review* 104(3):427–466.

Humphreys, M. S., J. D. Bain, and R. Pike. 1989. Different ways to cue a coherent memory system: A theory for episodic, semantic, and procedural tasks. *Psychological Review* 96(2):208–233.

Hyvärinen, A. and E. Oja. 2000. Independent component analysis: Algorithms and applications. *Neural Networks* 13(4-5):411–430.

Johnson, H. M. and C. M. Seifert. 1992. The role of predictive features in retrieving analogical cases. *Journal of Memory and Language* 31(5):648–667.

Johnson, N. F. 1972. Organization and the concept of a memory code. In A. W. Melton and E. Martin, eds., *Coding processes in human memory*, pages 125–159. Washington DC: Winston.

Jordan, M. I. 1986. Attractor dynamics and parallelism in a connectionist sequential machine. In *Proceedings of the 8th Annual Conference of the Cognitive Science Society*, pages 531–546. Hillsdale, NJ: Erlbaum.

Kanerva, P. 1988. *Sparse Distributed Memory*. Cambridge, MA: MIT Press.

Kanerva, P. 1996. Binary spatter-coding of ordered k-tuples. In C. von der Malsburg, W. von Seelen, J. C. Vorbruggen, and B. Sendhoff, eds., *Artificial Neural Networks–ICANN Proceedings*, vol. 1112 of *Lecture Notes in Computer Science*, pages 869–873. Berlin: Springer.

Kanerva, P. 2001. Analogy as a basis of computation. In Y. Uesaka, P. Kanerva, and H. Asoh, eds., *Foundations of real-world intelligence*, no. 125 in CSLI lecture notes, pages 254–272. CSLI Publications, Center for the Study of Language and Information, Leland Stanford Junior University.

Kempen, G. and T. Vosse. 1989. Incremental syntactic tree formation in human sentence processing: a cognitive architecture based on activation decay and simulated annealing. *Connection Science* 1(3):273–290.

Le Cun, Y., B. Boser, J. S. Denker, D. Henderson, R. E. Howard, W. Hubbard, and L. D. Jackel. 1989. Back-propagation applied to handwritten zipcode recognition. *Neural Computation* 1(4):541–551.

Le Cun, Y., B. Boser, J. S. Denker, D. Henderson, R. E. Howard, W. Hubbard, and L. D. Jackel. 1990. Handwritten digit recognition with a back-propagation network. In D. S. Touretzky, ed., *Advances in Neural Information Processing Systems 2*, pages 396–404. San Mateo, CA: Morgan Kaufmann.

Legendre, G., Y. Miyata, and P. Smolensky. 1991. Distributed recursive structure processing. In D. S. Touretzky and R. Lippman, eds., *Advances in Neural Information Processing Systems 3*, pages 591–597. San Mateo, CA: Morgan Kaufmann.

Levesque, H. J. and R. J. Brachman. 1985. A fundamental tradeoff in knowledge representation and reasoning (revised version). In R. J. Brachman and H. J. Levesque, eds., *Readings in Knowledge Representation*, pages 41–70. San Mateo, CA: Morgan Kaufmann.

Lewandowsky, S. and B. B. Murdock. 1989. Memory for serial order. *Psychological Review* 96(1):25–57.

Liepa, P. 1977. Models of content addressable distributed associative memory. Unpublished manuscript.

Lodhi, H., J. Shawe-Taylor, N. Cristianini, and C. J. C. H. Watkins. 2000. Text classification using string kernels. In *NIPS*, pages 563–569.

Longuet-Higgins, H. C. 1968. Holographic model of temporal recall. *Nature* 217:104.

MacLennan, B. 1991. Characteristics of connectionist knowledge representation. Tech. Rep. CS-91-147, Computer Science Department, University of Tennessee, Knoxville.

Markman, A. B., D. Gentner, and E. J. Wisniewski. 1993. Comparison and cognition: Implications of structure-sensitive processing for connectionist models. Unpublished manuscript.

Marr, D. 1982. *Vision*. San Francisco: W. H. Freeman.

Maskara, A. and A. Noetzel. 1992. Forcing simple recurrent neural networks to encode context. In *Proceedings of the 1992 Long Island Conference on Artificial Intelligence and Computer Graphics*.

McClelland, J. L. and A. H. Kawamoto. 1986. Mechanisms of sentence processing: Assigning roles to constituents. In J. L. McClelland, D. E. Rumelhart, and the PDP Research Group, eds., *Parallel Distributed Processing: Explorations in the Microstructure of Cognition*, vol. 2, pages 272–326. Cambridge, MA: MIT Press.

Metcalfe, J. 1991. Recognition failure and CHARM. *Psychological Review* 98(4):529–553.

Metcalfe Eich, J. 1982. A composite holographic associative recall model. *Psychological Review* 89:627–661.

Metcalfe Eich, J. 1985. Levels of processing, encoding specificity, elaboration, and charm. *Psychological Review* 92:1–38.

Miikkulainen, R. 1993. *Subsymbolic Natural Language Processing*. Cambridge, MA: The MIT Press.

Miikkulainen, R. and M. G. Dyer. 1989. Encoding input/output representations in connectionist cognitive systems. In D. S. Touretzky, G. E. Hinton, and T. J. Sejnowski, eds., *Proceedings of the 1988 Connectionist Models Summer School*. San Mateo, CA: Morgan Kaufmann.

Miller, G. A. 1956. The magical number seven plus or minus two: Some limits on our capacity for processing information. *Psychological Review* 63:81–97.

Murdock, B. B. 1982. A theory for the storage and retrieval of item and associative information. *Psychological Review* 89(6):316–338.

Murdock, B. B. 1983. A distributed memory model for serial-order information. *Psychological Review* 90(4):316–338.

Murdock, B. B. 1985. Convolution and matrix systems: A reply to Pike. *Psychological Review* 92(1):130–132.

Murdock, B. B. 1987. Serial-order effects in a distributed-memory model. In D. S. Gorfein and R. R. Hoffman, eds., *Memory and Learning: The Ebbinghaus Centennial Conference*, pages 277–310. Hillsdale, NJ: Erlbaum.

Murdock, B. B. 1992. Serial organization in a distributed memory model. In A. Healy, S. Kosslyn, and R. Shiffrin, eds., *From learning theory to connectionist theory: Essays in honor of William K. Estes*, vol. 1, pages 201–225. Hillsdale, NJ: Erlbaum.

Murdock, B. B. 1993. TODAM2: A model for the storage and retrieval of item, associative, and serial-order information. *Psychological Review* 100(2):183–203.

Neal, R. M. 1992. Connectionist learning of belief networks. *Artificial Intelligence* 56:71–113.

Neumann, J. 2001. *Holistic Processing of Hierarchical Structures in Connectionist Networks*. Ph.D. thesis, University of Edinburgh. http://www.cogsci.ed.ac.uk/jne/holistic_trafo/thesis.pdf.

Neumann, J. 2002. Learning the systematic transformation of holographic reduced representations. *Cognitive Systems Research* 3(2):227–235.

Niklasson, L. and T. van Gelder. 1994. Can connectionist models exhibit non-classical structure sensitivity? In *Proceedings of the 16th Annual Conference of The Cognitive Science Society*, pages 664–669. Hillsdale, NJ: Erlbaum.

Novick, L. R. 1988. Analogical transfer, problem similarity, and expertise. *Journal of Experimental Psychology: Learning, Memory, and Cognition* 14:510–520.

Olshausen, B. A. and D. J. Field. 1996. Emergence of simple-cell receptive field properties by learning a sparse code for natural images. *Nature* 381:607–609.

Page, M. 2000. Connectionist modelling in psychology: A localist manifesto. *Behavioral and Brain Sciences* 23(4):443–512.

Pearl, J. 1988. *Probabilistic Reasoning in Intelligent Systems: Networks of Plausible Inference*. San Mateo, CA: Morgan Kaufman.

Pearlmutter, B. A. 1995. Gradient calculations for dynamic recurrent neural networks: A survey. *IEEE Transactions on Neural Networks* 6(5):1212–1228.

Pike, R. 1984. Comparison of convolution and matrix distributed memory systems for associative recall and recognition. *Psychological Review* 91(3):281–294.

Pinker, S. and A. Prince. 1988. On language and connectionism: Analysis of a parallel distributed processing model of language acquisition. *Cognition* 28(1-2).

Plate, T. 2000. Randomly connected sigma-pi neurons can form associator networks. *Network: Computation in Neural Systems* 11(4):321–332.

Plate, T. A. 1995. Holographic reduced representations. *IEEE Transactions on Neural Networks* 6(3):623–641.

Plate, T. A. 1997. A common framework for distributed representation schemes for compositional structure. In F. Maire, R. Hayward, and J. Diederich, eds., *Connectionist Systems for Knowledge Representation and Deduction*, pages 15–34. Queensland University of Technology.

Pollack, J. B. 1990. Recursive distributed representations. *Artificial Intelligence* 46(1-2):77–105.

Rachkovskij, D. 2001. Representation and processing of structures with binary sparse distributed codes. *IEEE Transactions on Knowledge and Data Engineering* 13(2):261–276.

Rachkovskij, D. A. and E. M. Kussul. 2001. Binding and normalization of binary sparse distributed representations by context-dependent thinning. *Neural Computation* 13(2):411–452.

Rattermann, M. J. and D. Gentner. 1987. Analogy and similarity: Determinants of accessibility and inferential soundness. In *Proceedings of the Ninth Annual Meeting of the Cognitive Science Society*, pages 23–34. Hillsdale, NJ: Erlbaum.

Reichardt, W. 1957. Autokorrelations-auswertung als funktionsprinzip des zentralnewvensystems (Auto-correlations as a functional principle of the central nervous system). *Z. Naturforsch* 12b:448–457. Cited in Borsellino and Poggio [1973] and Schönemann [1987].

Rodriguez, P. 2001. Simple recurrents networks learn context-free and context-sensitive languages by counting. *Neural Computation* 13(9):2093–2118.

Rodriguez, P., J. Wiles, and J. Elman. 1999. A recurrent neural network that learns to count. *Connection Science* 11(1):5–40.

Rosenfeld, R. and D. S. Touretzky. 1987. Four capacity models for coarse-coded symbol memories. Tech. Rep. CMU-CS-87-182, Carnegie-Mellon University, Pittsburgh, PA.

Rosenfeld, R. and D. S. Touretzky. 1988. Coarse-coded symbol memories and their properties. *Complex Systems* 2(4):463–484.

Ross, B. 1989. Distinguishing types of superficial similarities: Different effects on the access and use of earlier problems. *Journal of Experimental Psychology : Learning, Memory, and Cognition* 15(2):456–468.

Rumelhart, D. E., G. E. Hinton, and R. J. Williams. 1986a. Learning internal representations by error propagation. In *Parallel Distributed Processing: Explorations in the Microstructure of Cognition*, vol. 1, pages 318–362. Cambridge, MA: MIT Press.

Rumelhart, D. E. and J. L. McClelland. 1986a. On learning the past tenses of English verbs. In J. L. McClelland, D. E. Rumelhart, and the PDP Research Group, eds., *Parallel Distributed Processing: Explorations in the Microstructure of Cognition*, vol. 2, pages 216–271. Cambridge, MA: MIT Press.

Rumelhart, D. E. and J. L. McClelland. 1986b. PDP models and general issues in cognitive science. In D. E. Rumelhart, J. L. McClelland, and the PDP research group, eds., *Parallel Distributed Processing: Explorations in the Microstructure of Cognition*, vol. 1, pages 110–146. Cambridge, MA: MIT Press.

Rumelhart, D. E., J. L. McClelland, and the PDP Research Group, eds. 1986b. *Parallel Distributed Processing: Explorations in the Microstructure of Cognition*, vol. 1. Cambridge, MA: MIT Press.

Sampson, G., R. Haigh, and E. Atwell. 1989. Natural language analysis by stochastic optimization: a progress report on project april. *Journal of Experimental and Theoretical Artificial Intelligence* pages 271–287.

Schönemann, P. H. 1987. Some algebraic relations between involutions, convolutions, and correlations, with applications to holographic memories. *Biological Cybernetics* 56:367–374.

Seidl, T. and H.-P. Kriegel. 1998. Optimal multi-step k-nearest neighbor search. In *SIGMOD Conference*, pages 154–165.

Seifert, C. M., G. McKoon, R. P. Abelson, and R. Ratcliff. 1986. Memory connections between thematically similar episodes. *Journal of Experimental Psychology : Learning, Memory, and Cognition* 12:220–231.

Sejnowski, T. J. and C. R. Rosenberg. 1986. *NETtalk: A parallel network that learns to read aloud.* Technical report 86-01, Department of Electrical Engineering and Computer Science, Johns Hopkins University, Baltimore, MD.

Selman, B. and G. Hirst. 1985. A rule-based connectionist parsing system. In *Proceedings of the 7th Annual Conference of the Cognitive Science Society*, pages 212–221. Hillsdale, NJ: Erlbaum.

Servan-Schreiber, D., A. Cleeremans, and J. L. McClelland. 1991. Graded state machines: The representation of temporal contingencies in simple recurrent networks. *Machine Learning* 7(2/3):161–194.

Shastri, L. 1988. *Semantic networks: an evidential formalization and its connectionist realization.* London: Pitman.

Simard, P. and Y. LeCun. 1992. Reverse TDNN: an architecture for trajectory generation. In J. M. Moody, S. J. Hanson, and R. P. Lippman, eds., *Advances in Neural Information Processing Systems 4 (NIPS*91)*. San Mateo, CA: Morgan Kaufmann.

Slack, J. N. 1984a. A parsing architecture based on distributed memory machines. In *Proceedings of the Association for Computational Linguistics (COLING-84)*, pages 92–95. Association for Computational Linguistics, Stanford, CA.

Slack, J. N. 1984b. The role of distributed memory in natural language processing. In T. O'Shea, ed., *Advances in Artificial Intelligence: Proceedings of the Sixth European Conference on Artificial Intelligence, ECAI-84.* Netherlands: Elsevier Science Publishers.

Slack, J. N. 1986. A parsing architecture based on distributed memory machines. In *Proceedings of the Association for Computational Linguistics (COLING-86)*, pages 476–481. Association for Computational Linguistics.

Smolensky, P. 1986. Neural and conceptual interpretation of PDP models. In J. L. McClelland, D. E. Rumelhart, and the PDP Research Group, eds., *Parallel Distributed Processing: Explorations in the Microstructure of Cognition*, vol. 2, pages 390–431. Cambridge, MA: MIT Press.

Smolensky, P. 1990. Tensor product variable binding and the representation of symbolic structures in connectionist systems. *Artificial Intelligence* 46(1-2):159–216.

Smolensky, P., G. Legendre, and Y. Miyata. 1992. Principles for an integrated connectionist/symbolic theory of higher cognition. Technical Report CU-CS-600-92, University of Colorado at Boulder, Boulder, CO.

Sopena, J. M. 1991. ESRP: A distributed connectionist parser that uses embedded sequences to represent structure. Tech. rep., Dept. Psicologia Bàsica, Universitat de Barcelona. Distributed on the *connectionists* electronic mailing list.

St. John, M. F. and J. L. McClelland. 1990. Learning and applying contextual constraints in sentence comprehension. *Artificial Intelligence* 46:217–257.

Tabor, W. 2000. Fractal encoding of context-free grammars in connectionist networks. *Expert Systems: The International Journal of Knowledge Engineering and Neural Networks* 17(1):41–56.

Tabor, W. 2002. The value of symbolic computation. *Ecological Psychology* 14(1/2):21–51.

Tabor, W., C. Juliano, and M. K. Tanenhaus. 1997. Parsing in a dynamical system: An attractor-based account of the interaction of lexical and structural constraints in sentence processing. *Language and Cognitive Processes* 12(2/3):211–271.

Thagard, P., K. J. Holyoak, G. Nelson, and D. Gochfeld. 1990. Analog Retrieval by Constraint Satisfaction. *Artificial Intelligence* 46:259–310.

Touretzky, D. S. 1986a. Boltzcons: Reconciling connectionism with the recursive nature of stacks and trees. In *Proceedings of the 8th Annual conference of the Cognitive Science Society*. Hillsdale, NJ: Erlbaum.

Touretzky, D. S. 1986b. *The Mathematics of Inheritance Systems*. London: Pitman.

Touretzky, D. S. 1986c. Representing and transforming recursive objects in a neural network, or "Trees *do* grow on Boltzmann machines". In *Proceedings of the 1986 IEEE International Conference on Systems, Man, and Cybernetics*. IEEE Press.

Touretzky, D. S. 1990. BoltzCONS: Dynamic symbol structures in a connectionist network. *Artificial Intelligence* 42(1-2):5–46.

Touretzky, D. S. and S. Geva. 1987. A distributed connectionist representation for concept structures. In *Proceedings of the 9th Annual Conference of the Cognitive Science Society*. Hillsdale, NJ: Erlbaum.

Touretzky, D. S. and G. E. Hinton. 1985. Symbols among the neurons: Details of a connectionist inference architecture. In *Proceedings of the 9th International Joint Conference on Artificial Intelligence*, pages 238–243. San Mateo, CA: Morgan Kaufmann.

Touretzky, D. S. and G. E. Hinton. 1988. A distributed connectionist production system. *Cognitive Science* 12(3):423–466.

Tversky, A. 1977. Features of similarity. *Psychological Review* 84(4):327–352.

van Gelder, T. 1990. What is the "D" in "PDP"? An overview of the concept of distribution. In S. Stich, D. E. Rumelhart, and W. Ramsey, eds., *Philosophy and Connectionist Theory*. Hillsdale, NJ: Erlbaum.

Vishwanathan, S. V. N. and A. J. Smola. 2003. Fast kernels for string and tree matching. In S. Becker, S. Thrun, and K. Obermayer, eds., *Advances in Neural Information Processing Systems (15)*. Cambridge, MA: MIT Press.

Waltz, D. L. and J. B. Pollack. 1985. Massively parallel parsing: A strongly interactive model of natural language interpretation. *Cognitive Science* 9:51–74.

Watrous, R. and G. Kuhn. 1992. Induction of finite state languages using second-order recurrent networks. *Neural Computation* 4(3):406–414.

Weber, E. U. 1988. Expectation and variance of item resemblance distributions in a convolution-correlation model of distributed memory. *Journal of Mathematical Psychology* 32:1–43.

Wharton, C. M., K. J. Holyoak, P. E. Downing, T. E. Lange, T. D. Wickens, and E. R. Melz. 1994. Below the surface: Analogical similarity and retrieval competition in reminding. *Cognitive Psychology* 26:64–101.

Williams, R. J. and D. Zipser. 1989. A learning algorithm for continually running fully recurrent neural networks. *Neural Computation* 1(2):270–280.

Willshaw, D. 1989a. Comments on chapter 3 (Holography, associative memory, and inductive generalization). In G. E. Hinton and J. A. Anderson, eds., *Parallel Models of Associative Memory (updated edition)*, pages 99–101. Hillsdale, NJ: Erlbaum.

Willshaw, D. 1989b. Holography, associative memory, and inductive generalization. In G. E. Hinton and J. A. Anderson, eds., *Parallel Models of Associative Memory (updated edition)*, pages 103–124. Hillsdale, NJ: Erlbaum.

Willshaw, D. J., O. P. Buneman, and H. C. Longuet-Higgins. 1969. Non-holographic associative memory. *Nature* 222:960–962.

Zemel, R. S. and G. Hinton. 1994. Developing population codes by minimizing description length. In J. D. Cowan, G. Tesauro, and J. Alspector, eds., *Advances in Neural Information Processing Systems 6 (NIPS*93)*, pages 11–18. San Mateo, CA: Morgan Kaufmann.

Zemel, R. S. and G. Hinton. 1995. Learning population codes by minimizing description length. *Neural Computation* 7(3):549–564.

Subject Index

Author Index